W9-CAH-364

®

References for the Rest of Us! ®

COMPUTER BOOK SERIES FROM IDG

Are you baffled and bewildered by programming? Does it seem like an impenetrable puzzle? Do you find that traditional manuals are overloaded with technical terms you don't understand? Do you want to know how to get your PC to do what you want? Then the *...For Dummies* ® programming book series from IDG is for you.

...For Dummies programming books are written for frustrated computer users who know they really aren't dumb but find that programming, with its unique vocabulary and logic, makes them feel helpless. *...For Dummies* programming books use a humorous approach and a down-to-earth style to diffuse fears and build confidence. Lighthearted but not lightweight, these books are a perfect survival guide for first-time programmers or anyone learning a new environment.

> **"Simple, clear, and concise.
> Just what I needed."**
> **— Steve P., Greenville, SC**

> **"Finally, someone made
> learning to program easy and
> entertaining. Thanks!"**
> **— Diane W., Chicago, IL**

> **"When I saw this book I decided
> to give programming one last try.
> And I'm glad I did!"**
> **— Paul G., St. Louis, MO**

Millions of satisfied readers have made *...For Dummies* books the #1 introductory-level computer book series and have written asking for more. So, if you're looking for a fun and easy way to learn about computers, look to *...For Dummies* books to give you a helping hand.

IDG BOOKS
WORLDWIDE ™

2/96

CLIENT/SERVER COMPUTING FOR DUMMIES®

CLIENT/SERVER COMPUTING FOR DUMMIES®

Doug Lowe

IDG Books Worldwide, Inc.
An International Data Group Company

Foster City, CA ♦ Chicago, IL ♦ Indianapolis, IN ♦ Southlake, TX

Client/Server Computing For Dummies®

Published by
IDG Books Worldwide, Inc.
An International Data Group Company
919 E. Hillsdale Blvd.
Suite 400
Foster City, CA 94404

Copyright © 1995 by IDG Books Worldwide, Inc. All rights reserved. No part of this book (including interior design, cover design, and illustrations) may be reproduced or transmitted in any form, by any means, (electronic, photocopying, recording, or otherwise) without the prior written permission of the publisher.

Library of Congress Catalog Card No.: 95-79569

ISBN: 1-56884-329-1

Printed in the United States of America

First Printing, June 1995

10 9 8 7 6 5 4 3 2

1A/SZ/QT/ZW/BR/IN

Distributed in the United States by IDG Books Worldwide, Inc.

Distributed by Macmillan Canada for Canada; by Computer and Technical Books for the Caribbean Basin; by Contemporanea de Ediciones for Venezuela; by Distribuidora Cuspide for Argentina; by CITEC for Brazil; by Ediciones ZETA S.C.R. Ltda. for Peru; by Editorial Limusa SA for Mexico; by Transworld Publishers Limited in the United Kingdom and Europe; by Al-Maiman Publishers & Distributors for Saudi Arabia; by Simron Pty. Ltd. for South Africa; by IDG Communications (HK) Ltd. for Hong Kong; by Toppan Company Ltd. for Japan; by Addison Wesley Publishing Company for Korea; by Longman Singapore Publishers Ltd. for Singapore, Malaysia, Thailand, and Indonesia; by Unalis Corporation for Taiwan; by WS Computer Publishing Company, Inc. for the Philippines; by WoodsLane Pty. Ltd. for Australia; by WoodsLane Enterprises Ltd. for New Zealand.

For general information on IDG Books Worldwide's books in th U.S, please call our Consumer Customer Service department at 800-762-2974. For reseller information, including discounts and premium sales, please call our Reseller Customer Service department at 800-434-3422.

For information on where to purchase IDG Books Worldwide's books outside the U.S., contact IDG Books Worldwide at 415-655-3021 or fax 415-655-3295.

For information on translations, contact Marc Jeffrey Mikulich, Director, Foreign & Subsidiary Rights, at IDG Books Worldwide, 415-655-3018 or fax 415-655-3295.

For sales inquiries and special prices for bulk quantities, write to address above or call IDG Books Worldwide at 415-655-3200.

For information on using IDG Books Worldwide's books in the classroom, or ordering examination copies, contact the Education Office at 800-434-2086 or fax 817-251-8174.

For authorization to photocopy items for corporate, personal, or educational use, please contact Copyright Clearance Center, 222 Rosewood Drive, Danvers, MA 01923, or fax 508-750-4470.

Limit of Liability/Disclaimer of Warranty: Author and Publisher have used their best efforts in preparing this book. IDG Books Worldwide, Inc., and Author make no representation or warranties with respect to the accuracy or completeness of the contents of this book and specifically disclaim any implied warranties of merchantability or fitness for any particular purpose and shall in no event be liable for any loss of profit or any other commercial damage, including but not limited to special, incidental, consequential, or other damages.

Trademarks: All brand names and product names used in this book are trademarks, registered trademarks, or trade names of their respective holders. IDG Books Worldwide, Inc., is not associated with any product or vendor mentioned in this book.

is a trademark under exclusive license to IDG Books Worldwide, Inc., from International Data Group, Inc.

About the Author

Doug Lowe has written something like 25 computer books, including IDG's *Networking For Dummies,* five other *...For Dummies* books, and more books on programming IBM mainframe computers than anyone would like to remember. He has seen many computing fads come and go over the years, but believes that client/server computing is not one of them.

ABOUT IDG BOOKS WORLDWIDE

Welcome to the world of IDG Books Worldwide.

IDG Books Worldwide, Inc., is a subsidiary of International Data Group, the world's largest publisher of computer-related information and the leading global provider of information services on information technology. IDG was founded more than 25 years ago and now employs more than 7,700 people worldwide. IDG publishes more than 250 computer publications in 67 countries (see listing below). More than 70 million people read one or more IDG publications each month.

Launched in 1990, IDG Books Worldwide is today the #1 publisher of best-selling computer books in the United States. We are proud to have received 8 awards from the Computer Press Association in recognition of editorial excellence and three from Computer Currents' First Annual Readers' Choice Awards, and our best-selling ...*For Dummies*® series has more than 19 million copies in print with translations in 28 languages. IDG Books Worldwide, through a joint venture with IDG's Hi-Tech Beijing, became the first U.S. publisher to publish a computer book in the People's Republic of China. In record time, IDG Books Worldwide has become the first choice for millions of readers around the world who want to learn how to better manage their businesses.

Our mission is simple: Every one of our books is designed to bring extra value and skill-building instructions to the reader. Our books are written by experts who understand and care about our readers. The knowledge base of our editorial staff comes from years of experience in publishing, education, and journalism — experience which we use to produce books for the '90s. In short, we care about books, so we attract the best people. We devote special attention to details such as audience, interior design, use of icons, and illustrations. And because we use an efficient process of authoring, editing, and desktop publishing our books electronically, we can spend more time ensuring superior content and spend less time on the technicalities of making books.

You can count on our commitment to deliver high-quality books at competitive prices on topics you want to read about. At IDG Books Worldwide, we continue in the IDG tradition of delivering quality for more than 25 years. You'll find no better book on a subject than one from IDG Books Worldwide.

John J. Kilcullen

John Kilcullen
President and CEO
IDG Books Worldwide, Inc.

IDG Books Worldwide, Inc., is a subsidiary of International Data Group, the world's largest publisher of computer-related information and the leading global provider of information services on information technology. International Data Group publishes over 250 computer publications in 67 countries. Seventy million people read one or more International Data Group publications each month. International Data Group's publications include: **ARGENTINA:** Computerworld Argentina, GamePro, Infoworld, PC World Argentina; **AUSTRALIA:** Australian Macworld, Client/Server Journal, Computer Living, Computerworld, Digital News, Network World, PC World, Publishing Essentials, Reseller; **AUSTRIA:** Computerwelt, PC TEST; **BELARUS:** PC World Belarus; **BELGIUM:** Data News; **BRAZIL:** Annuário de Informática, Computerworld Brazil, Connections, Super Game Power, Macworld, PC World Brazil, Publish Brazil, SUPERGAME; **BULGARIA:** Computerworld Bulgaria, Networkworld/Bulgaria, PC & MacWorld Bulgaria; **CANADA:** CIO Canada, ComputerWorld Canada, InfoCanada, Network World Canada, Reseller World; **CHILE:** Computerworld Chile, GamePro, PC World Chile; **COLUMBIA:** Computerworld Colombia, GamePro, PC World Colombia; **COSTA RICA:** PC World Costa Rica/Nicaragua; **THE CZECH AND SLOVAK REPUBLICS:** Computerworld Czechoslovakia, Elektronika Czechoslovakia, PC World Czechoslovakia; **DENMARK:** Communications World, Computerworld Danmark, Macworld Danmark, PC World Danmark, PC World Danmark Supplements, TECH World; **DOMINICAN REPUBLIC:** PC World Republica Dominicana; **ECUADOR:** PC World Ecuador, GamePro; **EGYPT:** Computerworld Middle East, PC World Middle East; **EL SALVADOR:** PC World Centro America; **FINLAND:** MikroPC, Tietoverkko, Tietoviikko; **FRANCE:** Distributique, Golden, Info PC, Le Guide du Monde Informatique, Le Monde Informatique, Reseaux & Telecoms; **GERMANY:** Computer Business, Computerwoche, Computerwoche Extra, Computerwoche Focus, Electronic Entertainment, GamePro, I/M Information Management, Macwelt, PC Welt; **GREECE:** GamePro, Macworld & Publish; **GUATEMALA:** PC World Centro America; **HONDURAS:** PC World Centro America; **HONG KONG:** Computerworld Hong Kong, PCWorld Hong Kong, Publish in Asia; **HUNGARY:** ABCD CD-ROM, Computerworld Szamitastechnika, PC & Mac World Hungary, PC-X Magazine; **INDIA:** Computerworld India, PC World India, Publish in Asia; **INDONESIA:** InfoKomputer PC World, Komputek Computerworld, Publish in Asia; **IRELAND:** ComputerScope, PC Live!; **ISRAEL:** PC World 32 BIT, People & Computers; **ITALY:** Computerworld Italia, Computerworld Italia Special Editions, Lotus Italia, Macworld Italia, Networking Italia, PC Shopping, PC World Italia, PC World/Walt Disney; **JAPAN:** Macworld Japan, Nikkei Personal Computing, SunWorld Japan, Windows World Japan; **KENYA:** East African Computer News; **KOREA:** Hi-Tech Information/Computerworld, Macworld Korea, PC World Korea; **MACEDONIA:** PC World Macedonia; **MALAYSIA:** Computerworld Malaysia, PC World Malaysia, Publish in Asia; **MEXICO:** Computerworld Mexico, GamePro, Macworld, PC World Mexico; **MYANMAR:** PC World Myanmar; **NETHERLANDS:** Computable, Computer! Totaal, LAN Magazine, Macworld, Net Magazine; **NEW ZEALAND:** Computer Buyer, Computerworld New Zealand, MTB, Network World, PC World New Zealand; **NICARAGUA:** PC World Costa Rica/Nicaragua; **NIGERIA:** PC World Africa; **NORWAY:** Computerworld Norge, Computerworld Privat, CW Rapport Klient/Tjener, CW Rapport Nettverk & Telecom, CW Rapport Offentlig Sektor, IDG's KURSGUIDE, Macworld Norge, Multimedia World, PC World Ekspress, PC World Nettverk, PC World Norge, PC World's Produktguide, Windows Spesial; **PAKISTAN:** Computerworld Pakistan, PC World Pakistan; **PANAMA:** GamePro, PC World Panama; **PARAGUAY:** PC World Paraguay; **P. R. OF CHINA:** China Computerworld, China Infoworld, Computer & Communication, Electronic Product World, Electronics Today, Game Camp, PC World China, Popular Computer Week, Software World, Telecom Product World; **PERU:** Computerworld Peru, GamePro, PC World Profesional Peru, PC World Peru; **POLAND:** Computerworld Poland, Computerworld Special Report, Macworld, Networld, PC World Komputer; **PHILIPPINES:** Computerworld Philippines, PC Digest, Publish in Asia; **PORTUGAL:** Cerebro/PC World, Correio Informático/Computerworld, Mac•In/PC•In Portugal; **PUERTO RICO:** PC World Puerto Rico; **ROMANIA:** Computerworld Romania, PC World Romania, Telecom Romania; **RUSSIA:** Computerworld Rossiya, Network World Russia, PC World Russia; **SINGAPORE:** Computerworld Singapore, PC World Singapore, Publish in Asia; **SLOVENIA:** MONITOR; **SOUTH AFRICA:** Computing S.A., Network World S.A., Software World; **SPAIN:** Computerworld España, COMUNICACIONES WORLD, Dealer World, Macworld España, PC World España; **SWEDEN:** CAP&Design, Computer Sweden, Corporate Computing, MacWorld, Maxi Data, MikroDatorn, Nätverk & Kommunikation, PC/Aktiv, PC World, Windows World; **SWITZERLAND:** Computerworld Schweiz, Macworld Schweiz, PCtip; **TAIWAN:** Computerworld Taiwan, Macworld Taiwan, PC World Taiwan, Publish Taiwan, Windows World; **THAILAND:** Thai Computerworld, Publish in Asia; **TURKEY:** Computerworld Monitör, MACWORLD Turkiye, PC WORLD Turkiye; **UKRAINE:** Computerworld Kiev, Computers & Software Magazine, PC World Ukraine; **UNITED KINGDOM:** Acorn User, Amiga Action, Amiga Computing, Amiga, Appletalk, CD Powerplay, CD-ROM Now, Computing, Connexion, GamePro, Lotus Magazine, Macaction, Macworld, Open Computing, Parents and Computers, PC Home, PC Works, The WEB; **UNITED STATES:** Cable in the Classroom, CD Review, CIO Magazine, Computerworld, Computerworld Client/Server Journal, Digital Video Magazine, DOS World, Electronic, InfoWorld, I-Way, Macworld, Maximize, MULTIMEDIA WORLD, Network World, PC World, PUBLISH, SWATPro Magazine, Video Event, WebMaster; **URUGUAY:** PC World Uruguay; **VENEZUELA:** Computerworld Venezuela, GamePro, PC World Venezuela; and **VIETNAM:** PC World Vietnam   10/17/95

Acknowledgments

The most enjoyable aspect of writing a book is taking the opportunity to thank everyone who helped along the way, not only because it finally sinks in that the book is actually *finished*, but also because a lot of people have helped bring this book together and I am indebted to them all.

I thought John Kilcullen was joking when he suggested that we do a ...*For Dummies* book on client/server, until I saw an article on client/server computing in *Newsweek,* of all places. Once again, John was right on the mark. Thanks also to Chris Williams and Amy Pedersen at IDG Books for working through the details and getting this project off the ground.

Thanks to project editors Anne Marie Walker and Jim Markham. Both did an excellent job whipping this book into shape and not jumping on me too hard as deadlines came and went. Deb Kaufmann did a great job editing the manuscript, and made some key suggestions for improvements. Thanks also to all the behind-the-scenes folks at IDG, whom I don't even know, for all the detailed proofreading and the careful production work.

Thanks a million to Joe Salmeri, who gave this book an extremely thorough and detailed technical review. Outstanding job! See you 'round in the betasphere.

Thanks also to all the good folks in the client/server industry who supplied valuable information for this book, especially the vendor information found in the Bonus section. There's not room to list everyone, but I would like to especially thank Paula Smail of IBM. Paula was able to pull together information about all of IBM's client/server offerings, and for a company as outrageously large as IBM, this is no small feat. I appreciate the help!

The publisher would like to give special thanks to Patrick McGovern, without whom this book would not have been possible.

Credits

**Senior Vice President
and Publisher**
Milissa L. Koloski

Associate Publisher
Diane Graves Steele

Brand Manager
Judith A. Taylor

Editorial Managers
Kristin A. Cocks
Mary Corder

Product Development Manager
Mary Bednarek

Editorial Executive Assistant
Richard Graves

Editorial Assistants
Constance Carlisle
Chris Collins
Kevin Spencer

Production Director
Beth Jenkins

Production Assistant
Jacalyn L. Pennywell

**Supervisor of
Project Coordination**
Cindy L. Phipps

Supervisor of Page Layout
Kathie S. Schnorr

Supervisor of Graphics and Design
Shelley Lea

Reprint/Blueline Coordination
Tony Augsburger
Patricia R. Reynolds
Todd Klemme
Theresa Sánchez-Baker

Media/Archive Coordination
Leslie Popplewell
Melissa Stauffer
Jason Marcuson

Project Editor
Jim Markham

Editor
Deb Kaufmann

Technical Editor
Joseph M. Salmeri

Production Page Layout
Publishers' Design and Production
Services, Inc.

Indexer
Liz Cunningham

Book Design
University Graphics

Cover Design
Kavish + Kavish

Contents at a Glance

Table of Contents

Introduction

● ●

*W*elcome to *Client/Server Computing For Dummies*, the book written especially for those of you who are forced to learn about client/server at gunpoint and want to learn just enough to save your neck.

Did you just come out of a meeting at which you were informed that your entire department's computer system would be replaced with a new client/server system, and you are being put in charge?

Did the delivery person just dump a 37.5-pound box labeled "Client/server development tools" on your desk, along with a note from your manager that reads, "Learn it or else?"

Did your boss just get back from a technology seminar and won't stop talking about how wonderful client/server computing is and muttering on about how things are going to have to change around here, and soon?

Good news! You've found the right book. Help is here, within these humble pages.

This book talks about client/server computing in everyday terms. No lofty prose here. The language is friendly. You don't need a graduate degree in computer science to get through it. I have no Pulitzer ambitions for this book.

Occasionally, I'll even take a carefully aimed potshot at the hallowed and sacred traditions of computerdom, just to bring a bit of fun to an otherwise dry subject. If that doesn't work, I may even throw in an occasional lawyer joke.

The goal is to bring the lofty precepts of client/server computing down to earth where you can touch them and squeeze them and say, "What's the big deal? I get it now."

About This Book

This isn't the kind of book you pick up and read from start to finish, as if it were a cheap novel. If I ever see you reading it at the beach, I'll kick sand in your face. This book is more like a reference, the kind of book you can pick up, turn to just about any page, and start reading whenever you get the urge to learn something new about client/server.

There are 26 chapters, each one covering a specific aspect of client/server computing. Just turn to the chapter you're interested in and start reading.

If you get lost, turn to the index and look up whatever is confusing you. Or check the glossary: I included a huge glossary because any discussion of client/server computing is bound to be rife with jargon and terminology that most people are afraid to admit they don't know.

How This Book Is Organized

Inside this book, the chapters are arranged into several parts. The chapters are in logical sequence, so it makes sense to read them in order, if you want to read the book that way. You don't have to, though. Be an individual if you want! Read the book from back to front, or cast lots to determine what order you read the chapters in.

Here's the low-down on what's in each of the parts:

Part I: Welcome to Client/Server Computing!

In this part, you learn the basics of client/server computing: what it is , why everyone is so interested in it, when it is appropriate and when it isn't, and so on. This is a good place to start it you're clueless about what client/server is.

Part II: Of Clients, Servers, and Networks

The chapters in this part describe the basic components that are required to snap together a working client/server system. You'll learn about client computers, graphical user interfaces, operating systems, server computers, and local and wide area networks. Oh boy!

Part III: A Database Primer

The lion's share of client/server systems revolve around relational databases and SQL. In case you don't know what a relational database is and how SQL works (and why should you?), the chapters in this part will fill you in. It starts with basics like what a database is, progresses to an explanation of SQL and how it works, and winds up with an explanation of distributed databases.

Part IV: Building Client/Server Systems

The chapters in this part explain what programmers have to know to develop client/server systems. If you're not a programmer, this part will help you understand what the heck the programmers are talking about when they speak of ERDs, OOP, and OLE! If you are a programmer, this part will bring you up to speed on what kinds of tools are available for client/server programming.

Part V: Client/Server Hot Topics

This part tackles several subjects that are, shall we say, hot potatoes.

Part VI: The Part of Tens

It turns out that all *...For Dummies* books (well, most of them anyway) include a collection of chapters that include lists of interesting snippets: Ten Client/Server Commandments, Ten Client/Server Acronyms decoded, things of that sort. This is also the part you can turn to if you're too lazy (or too busy) to read the whole book, because it includes a summary of the most important points of client/server computing.

The Bonus Section

At no added charge, I threw in a bonus Client/Server Trade Show for Dummies. The Trade Show is a description of 16 client/server vendors and their products. The list isn't exhaustive, but it does include the most popular client/server products. Following that, also at no extra charge, I've included an extensive Glossary. What a deal!

What You Don't Need to Read

Much of this book is skippable. I've carefully placed extra-technical information in self-contained sidebars and clearly marked them so you can give them a wide berth. Don't read this stuff unless you just gots to know, and you feel really lucky. Don't worry; I won't be offended if you don't read every word.

Icons Used in This Book

As you are reading all this wonderful prose, you'll occasionally see the following icons. They appear in the margins to draw your attention to important information. They are defined as follows:

Look out! Some technical drivel is around the corner. Read only if you have your pocket protector firmly attached.

Watch out! This icon highlights information that can help you avert disaster.

When you see this icon, you can say, "I knew that!" You learned this information earlier, and I'm just reminding you.

Pay special attention to this icon — it introduces or summarizes a key concept, one that you should make sure you remember in case it shows up on *Jeopardy*.

This icon informs you that I'm about to stick my neck out and spout off an opinion. Feel free to disagree. Call me names if you want. Report me to the proper authorities if I offend.

And a little gray square, like the one after this sentence, indicates the end of the iconized material. ■

The Bonus Section also includes some icons of its own; you'll be introduced to those at the beginning of that section.

Where to Go from Here

Yes, you can get there from here. With this book in hand, you're ready to charge full speed ahead into the strange and wonderful world of client/server computing. Browse through the table of contents and decide where you want to start. Be bold! Be courageous! Be adventurous! Above all else, have fun!

Part I

Welcome to Client/Server Computing!

The 5th Wave   By Rich Tennant

In This Part...

*I*f you tend to nod your head a lot when the term "client/server" comes up, but aren't exactly sure what it means, join the club. It seems that everyone is talking about client/server these days. Client/server has moved beyond the strange realm of computerdom inhabited by techy computer nerds: Articles about client/server computing are showing up in magazines like *Time* and *Forbes*.

Fear not: the chapters in this Part are just what you need. Here, you'll find a gentle introduction to what client/server computing is all about and why everyone seems so excited about it. You'll learn what client/server is and what it isn't, things to consider when you're thinking about changing to client/server, and how it relates to the overall movement of business reengineering. Plus, I'll dispell some of the more common myths about client/server, and describe some of the many faces this new form of computing can wear.

Have fun!

Chapter 1

What the Heck Is Client/Server Computing?

*W*elcome to the world of client/server computing, an exciting new kind of computing which is recommended by four out of five dentists surveyed, tastes great, and is less filling. Client/server computing helps you get the weight off fast and keep it off (I lost 30 pounds), plus it fosters a return to family values, promises to help balance the federal budget deficit, and reduce the national debt.[1]

It's sadly true that all of the hype and hysteria surrounding client/server computing sounds a lot like a late night infomercial. The computer industry flips from one computing fad to the next, remote control in hand, the way my brother-in-law flips through TV channels on a Sunday afternoon. "Structured Programming will save the day!" *Flip.* "Relational Database will deliver us from evil!" *Flip.* "Fourth-generation languages are the solution!" *Flip.* "Downsizing! That's the future!" *Flip.* "Object-Oriented Programming...that's the ticket. Oops!" *Flip. Flip. Flip*

The computer industry is such a faddish business. It seems to always be searching for the Lone Ranger's Silver Bullet, the one that will travel straight and true, never miss its mark, and solve every computing problem. Unfortunately, most of the industry's Silver Bullets have turned out to be like Deputy

[1]Your results may vary. See manufacturer's warranty for further details. Void where prohibited.

Fife's bullet — you know, the one Sheriff Andy lets him carry in his pocket: looks good, but in the end not so useful.

Is client/server computing just another fad? I don't think so. All indications are that it is here to stay. More and more, we're hearing that client/server is playing a key role in the computing plans of just about every major corporation, and even smaller companies are now starting to get into the game.

There's good reason for the computing world to be excited about client/server computing, as it does indeed promise many substantial benefits to those who learn to see beyond the hype and hysteria and harness this new technology.

There's only one real problem: most of us still don't know exactly what client/server computing is. Does it mean throwing away the mainframe and replacing it with networked PCs? Or is it just setting up a network system that uses a centralized database? Or is it creating an attractive Windows-type interface to replace all those clunky old mainframe systems that no one could ever figure out how to use?

This chapter will answer all these questions and more. It's a gentle introduction to the strange new world of client/server computing. Hope you enjoy the ride.

Client/Server Computing Defined

So what *is* behind all the hype and hysteria? It's time to spell out exactly what client/server computing is. This is easier said than done. Client/server is one of the most used and abused computer terms around, and it's hard to get even two experts to agree on its meaning. But let's not let that stop us. Here are some definitions of client/server computing from various viewpoints:

- A type of technological varnish or veneer that can be applied to an aging computer product (hardware or software) in an effort to increase sales (*opportunistic* view)

- The latest in a series of technological religions whose adherents believe that their approach to computing — and their approach only — will save the world from the current computer crisis (*escatalogical* view)

- A buzzword that must be applied to any new computer project in order to obtain management approval (*real-world* view)

- Using three basic components to share the computing workload: a client computer, a server computer, and a network that connects them

Any guesses which definition we'll be using here? I'll elaborate on that last one a bit:

Client/server computing divides a computer application into three basic components — a client, a server, and a network that connects the client to the server (you can think of the network as the slash in client/server computing). The client and the server are both computers with varying degrees of processing power, and both the client and the server computers share the computing workload necessary to get the job done. ▪

In most cases, the client computer is a personal computer sitting on the user's desk. The server computer is a network server, which may be an advanced PC, a minicomputer (called a *midrange* computer these days) or a mainframe. The network is whatever is necessary to connect the client to the server.

So what's all the fuss about? This definition seems fairly simple. The fuss, of course, is about what you can or might be able to *do* with client/server computing. Here are some examples:

- ✔ Create customized business applications that access data on mainframe computers, but are as easy to use as off-the-shelf PC applications like word processing and spreadsheet programs.

- ✔ Develop applications that tie together data that is stored in otherwise incompatible computer systems — for example, a marketing system might access data stored in the corporate mainframe in Chicago, a departmental minicomputer in Cleveland, and the PC down the hall.

- ✔ Build a so-called Executive Information System that summarizes the mass quantity of information that is typically stored in mainframe computers and present it in a form that even the CEO can understand.

We'll look at each component of a client/server system and explore client/server applications in depth in later chapters. But before we do, a bit of background is in order.

History of the Computing World, Part 1

A good place to begin exploring the world of client/server computing is with a brief history of the computing industry. Figure 1-1 shows a helpful timeline that correlates the great periods of computing history with other contemporary events of incidental importance.

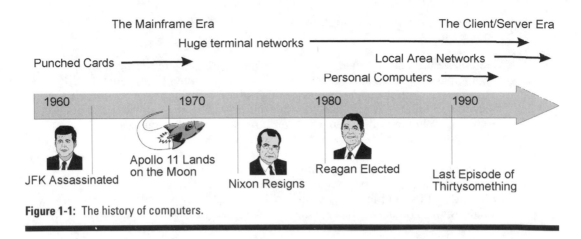

Figure 1-1: The history of computers.

Back in the Dark Ages

A long time ago, sometime between the time The Fonz was learning to ride his motorcycle and Ronald Reagan was still in show business, the first computer companies began selling computers that were made out of spare vacuum tubes left over from radios that couldn't be fixed. These early computers filled entire rooms, and although they weren't nearly as fast as modern Pentium computers, they could divide accurately and so they became very popular with businesses that could afford them.

Computer manufacturers soon learned how to shrink computer components, first by replacing bulky vacuum tubes with tinier transistors, then by replacing transistors with even tinier integrated circuits. The computers themselves didn't really get any smaller, of course: computer companies just stuffed more shrunken components into the same room-sized boxes to make the computers more powerful.

In the sixties and seventies, mainframe computers became an important part of many American businesses. Important enough that an entire department was formed to keep the odd people who ran the computers away from everyone else in the company. Every few years the people in the computer department would begin to feel neglected, so they'd change the name of the department to make themselves feel more important. They started out as the *Data Processing (DP) department*, then changed to *Information Systems (IS) division* and finally became the *Information Technology (IT) group*. The important thing is that the name had to be conducive to a two- or three-letter acronym (TLA) because that's the kind of language these odd computer people spoke. (Okay, you're right: Computer people are still trying to learn how to speak plain English.)

The most important thing to know about these days of mainframe computers is that the computer department (whatever it was called) had absolute, total control over the computer. If a poor end user realized that a simple two-page computer report would save the company millions of dollars, he or she would have to submit an Information Systems Programming Request Form in triplicate, wait for the computer department to conduct a feasibility study, prepare an environmental impact report, and put up with an obnoxious programmer/analyst who said things like "We're going to have to run I-E-B-somesuch to reindex the ISAM dataset to extract the deactivated history record segments to a spool file before we do a merge-purge, a sort, and a double backflip. You'd better pray we don't run out of extents." And maybe, when the system was finally delivered two years later, the report would still be useful.

Then along came this upstart called the *personal computer* (PC) that upset the whole Apple cart in 1981. Those who were gutsy enough to try the new PC discovered that they could often solve their problems using off-the-shelf programs such as Lotus 1-2-3 and dBase faster than the computer department could even acknowledge a request for help. And the price of a new PC was just under the limit that many department managers could spend without getting corporate approval. PCs began to appear everywhere.

Soon the users of these computers realized that they needed to share information with one another, so small local area networks (LANs) were developed to allow the PCs to talk to each other. With networks in place, PC users decided that the LAN could do the job of the mainframe better, faster, and cheaper, so they ignored the IS department's pleas for restraint. Networks popped up everywhere. Which brings us to the current state of computer affairs...

The mess we're in today

Most large organizations now have lots of PCs haphazardly connected to one another via local area networks and one or more mainframe computers that run the business. This arrangement has some unpleasant side effects:

> ✔ The computing world is split into two camps: the PC camp and the mainframe camp. These two groups don't particularly like each other. Each thinks the other has poor table manners and is prone to belch at inappropriate moments. They have a chip on the shoulder attitude, and they're so by-God stubborn they can stand touching noses for a week at a time and never see eye to eye. But they're beginning to realize that they have to learn how to get along. Client/server computing (the subject of this book) simply won't work unless they do.

✔ Vital corporate data that used to be collected in a central location (the mainframe computer) is now spread all over the place. The typical company's data store looks something like my youngest daughter's bedroom: Some data is on the mainframe, some is on the various PC networks, some is on individual desktop computers, some is stuffed under the bed, and some of it is just piled up on the floor in plain view. Client/server computing is often viewed as a way to bring all of this disparate data together. ■

Don't you love that phrase, "disparate data"? It has such a nice alliteration to it, plus it sounds so much like "desperate data."

✔ Data on mainframe computers is backed up systematically. Data on networks may or may not be. Data on individual PCs probably hasn't been backed up in months. (When was the last time you backed up your computer?)

Actually, the last point about backup is just the tip of the iceberg when it comes to system management issues. Mainframers have been managing computer systems for 30 years. They're pretty good at it, too. PC users usually aren't. ■

✔ Computer users have been spoiled by how easy the PC is to use. Now they expect the mainframe to be as easy to use as the PC. This means that mainframe programmers must work into the wee hours of the morning transforming old, unfriendly mainframe computer programs into friendly, easy-to-use programs that look like their PC counterparts. Client/server computing is one of the chief ways computer programmers hope to pull off this miracle off.

Most large companies have a large stash of computer software that is outdated in appearance (that is, it doesn't *look* as good as a modern Windows program) but still gets the job done. Many of these systems are so complex that rewriting them to work on PCs instead of mainframes would be so expensive only Ross Perot could pull it off. These *legacy systems* are the bread-and-butter of most businesses today, providing essential business functions such as order processing, billing, payroll, accounts receivable, and accounts payable systems. (Because the term *legacy* has negative connotations, some mainframers are now trying to get us to say *heritage systems* instead of *legacy systems*. But a rose by any other name...) ■

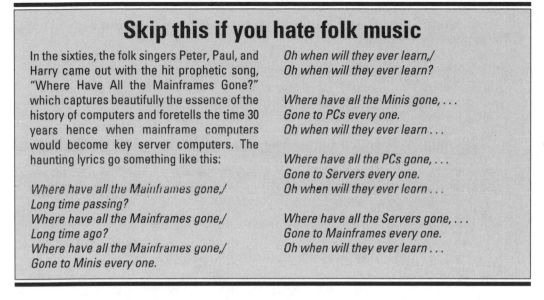

Skip this if you hate folk music

In the sixties, the folk singers Peter, Paul, and Harry came out with the hit prophetic song, "Where Have All the Mainframes Gone?" which captures beautifully the essence of the history of computers and foretells the time 30 years hence when mainframe computers would become key server computers. The haunting lyrics go something like this:

Where have all the Mainframes gone,/
Long time passing?
Where have all the Mainframes gone,/
Long time ago?
Where have all the Mainframes gone,/
Gone to Minis every one.

Oh when will they ever learn,/
Oh when will they ever learn?

Where have all the Minis gone, . . .
Gone to PCs every one.
Oh when will they ever learn . . .

Where have all the PCs gone, . . .
Gone to Servers every one.
Oh when will they ever learn . . .

Where have all the Servers gone, . . .
Gone to Mainframes every one.
Oh when will they ever learn . . .

Two Unavoidable Questions

You could probably avoid the two questions that follow if you try hard enough, but they're bound to come up sooner or later. The first one has been on the tip of everyone's tongue for a few years now. The second is just starting to gain momentum.

Is the mainframe dead?

Is the age of mainframe computing finally dead? Are those huge conglomerations of silicon and metal worth more as scrap metal than as computers?

The death of the mainframe has been suggested many times during the past 15 years, but it hasn't yet come to pass and client/server computing assures that it never will. As you'll discover in this book, the mainframe computer is the ultimate server. (Peek ahead to Chapter 19 for more on this hot topic.)

I chuckle when mainframe computers are referred to as dinosaurs. Invariably this is meant to malign the mainframe as an obsolete, slow, dim-witted beast on the verge of extinction. Keep in mind the most current theories on dinosaurs: They weren't slow or dim-witted; in fact, some of them were quite agile and intelligent. They did not really become extinct, they just downsized: They've evolved into the nimble little creatures we now know as birds. A downsized dinosaur is probably plucking worms out of the lawn in your back yard or dive bombing your cat this very moment.

I don't really like cats. I think they deserve whatever treatment they get from downsized dinosaurs. ■

A similar evolution is likely to occur with mainframe computers, and it may well look like extinction to casual observers. Here are some reasons why mainframes won't be fading out any time soon, even though they don't have good games:

- Mainframe computer professionals have a decades-long head start on dealing with the everyday problems of managing computer systems: managing software changes, predicting performance, providing for disaster recovery, and so on. There is much to be learned from those who have gone before.

- Desktop computers today have the raw computer processing power of mainframes just a decade ago. But they still have a long way to go to catch up in operating system software.

- Mainframe computers make the ultimate servers in client/server systems. In many cases, they are ideally suited for the task.

Is the PC dead?

Is the PC dead? This question has been looming in the background ever since the first PC users hooked their computers up together to create a simple network. After all, once a personal computer becomes a part of a network, it isn't really a *personal* computer anymore.

Putting your personal computer on a network changes everything. It forces you back into a mainframe-computer bureaucracy mode of thinking. If you mess up an isolated computer, that's your problem. But if you mess up with a networked computer, it could become everyone's problem. Like a mainframe computer, a network of personal computers must be carefully managed.

So yes, the personal computer is dead, or at least dying. This isn't to say fewer users are purchasing desktop computers based on Windows and MS-DOS, it merely means that these computers aren't really *personal* computers anymore. Personal computers and their users are rapidly becoming citizens in a networked computing world and the *clients* in the client/server equation.

With a networked computer, you are not the master of your domain. You must learn to get along with other members of the network: don't delete files if you're not sure they're yours; don't send a 700-page report to the printer when you know everyone else is scrambling to get their documents printed, too; and don't copy 200MB of old files to the network disk unless you're sure there is enough disk space.

One of the most challenging aspects of client/server computing (from a technical standpoint, at least) is setting up a network that enables desktop computers to not only communicate with one another but also to communicate with whatever mainframe and minicomputers are in place. It's like getting people from New Jersey, New Orleans, and London together for a talk. They all speak English, but no one can understand what anyone else is saying.

Remember, when I say that the personal computer is dead, I don't mean that people are going to start buying mainframe computers instead of PCs. I simply mean that you can no longer afford to think about your desktop computer as some sort of computational island. ■

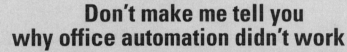

Don't make me tell you why office automation didn't work

One reason the personal computer is dead is because of its use as an Office Automation tool. The whole idea of Office Automation began in the early 1970s when Wang Laboratories introduced the first low-cost word processing systems. Businesses felt that if they could automate the tasks performed by office workers, they could increase worker productivity and cut the bottom line.

When the PC came out a decade later, businesses thought the goal of Office Automation — the so-called "paperless office" — would finally be realized. By replacing all of the typewriters, 10-key calculators, and file cabinets with computers, businesses expected major productivity gains.

Unfortunately, it didn't work out that way. Most office workers who use PCs, even the ones who use them proficiently, are no more productive than they were before they had PCs. Study after study has shown that offices today are no more productive than they were 10 or 15 years ago.

Why not? Partly because PCs encourage us to waste time on unimportant aspects of our work. We toil over every word of every letter or memo as if it we were going after the Pulitzer Prize. Then we waste time dressing up the letter or memo with just the right typeface and clip art as if our jobs depend on how good our memos look. As a result, most office workers don't get their work done any faster with a computer.

In truth, Office Automation is an empty promise. There really isn't any bottom-line profit to be gained by replacing typewriters with computers. Businesses do not become more profitable by making their internal memos look better (though workers are probably having more fun — would you want to go back to a typewriter?).

The real gains come through reengineering business processes, not automating routine office chores. Personal computers and client/server computing can play a major role in reengineering, as outlined in Chapter 2.

Dumb and Dumber Computing

The best way to understand what client/server computing is all about is to look at the extremes of what could be called *dumb computing* — computer applications in which either the client or the server plays dumb, refusing to do their share of the work.

Dumb clients

In an old-fashioned mainframe computer system, the client is a "dumb" terminal that has minimal processing power, and the server is the mainframe computer itself. As Figure 1-2 illustrates, the server computer does nearly all of the work in this type of arrangement. That's why mainframe computers are so grumpy.

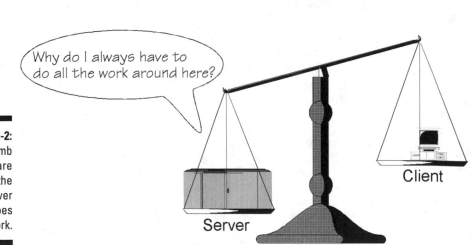

Dumb Client

Figure 1-2:
When dumb terminals are used, the server computer does all the work.

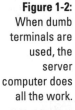

This type of computer processing is sometimes called *host processing* because the host computer — that is, the mainframe — does all of the processing work. The client — that is, the terminal — is just along for the ride. ■

Keep the following points about host processing in mind:

- ✔ More than one client terminal can access a single host computer. For host processing to work satisfactorily, the host computer itself must be powerful enough to service as many client terminals as the application calls for. In a nationwide airline reservation system, that might mean tens of thousands of client terminals. That's why mainframe computers are so powerful and expensive.

- ✔ The dumb terminal doesn't have to be an old-fashioned mainframe computer terminal. It may well be a high-powered PC that's *pretending* to be a dumb terminal. This has become very common as companies have replaced old IBM 3270-type terminals with PCs. Workers can use their PCs for PC chores such as word processing and spreadsheets, or they can flip the PC into dumb terminal mode to access their mainframe applications. Once flipped into dumb terminal mode, the PC takes a nap while the host computer does all the work.

- ✔ The only thing worse than smart computers playing dumb is smart people playing dumb.

Dumb servers

The alternative to a dumb terminal is a dumb server. This is how most applications that run on local area networks are set up. The entire work of the application is performed on a client computer — a PC — at the user's desk. The server computer is called upon whenever a file is needed or something needs to be printed, but it doesn't do any real work. Figure 1-3 shows the balance of power in this type of arrangement.

A dumb server can have one or both of two functions. It can be:

- ✔ a *file server*, which means that its disk drive houses the files used by the application, or

- ✔ a *print server*, which means that it has a printer attached to it.

In a small network, the same computer may be both the file server and the print server. In a larger network, the file and print servers are likely to be separate computers.

Dumb server systems quickly become inefficient as more users are added to the system. To see why, suppose five users access a large customer database file that lives on a file server. If one of the users decides to display a list of all customers whose year-to-date sales exceed $1,000, the entire customer file must be sent over the network from the server computer to the user's client computer. That can tie up the network, slowing down the other four users. However, the situation is probably tolerable. But suppose there are 500 users

Dumb Server

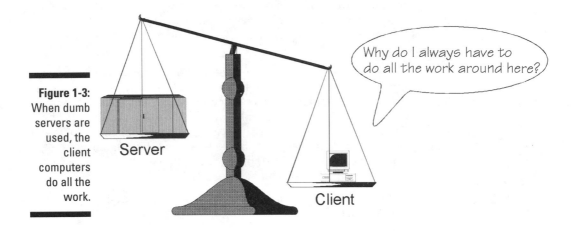

Figure 1-3:
When dumb
servers are
used, the
client
computers
do all the
work.

instead of five, and 100 of the users want the list of customers whose sales are over $1,000. Now the entire file must be sent over the network simultaneously to 100 different client computers. The entire network will slow to a crawl.

The solution to this problem is client/server computing.

Definition of Client/Server Computing: Take Two

The best definition for client/server computing I can come up with is inspired by Mr. Miyagi, the Karate master in the *Karate Kid* movies. At one point in one of the movies (I don't remember which), he tells his student Daniel that he must "find balance."

Client/server computing is an effort to find balance between the extremes of the dumb client and dumb server forms of computing. Figure 1-4 shows the balance of processing power when both the client and the server share the workload.

Client/server computing recognizes that there are fully capable computers at both ends of the network cable and attempts to spread the work out equitably to take advantage of both.

Client/Server Balance

Figure 1-4:
In a
client/server
arrange-
ment, the
server and
the client
computers
share the
workload.

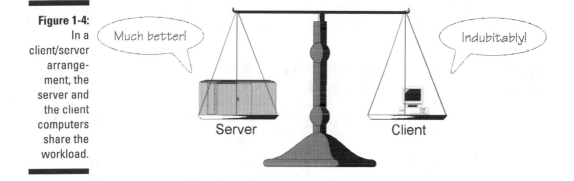

The exact distribution of work between the client and server computer varies depending on the type of application. Typically, though, the client computer is responsible for all of the work required to present a fancy, easy-to-use Windows-based interface to the user, complete with dialog boxes, buttons, scroll bars, pull-down menus, icons, help, and any other goodies necessary to make the program easy to use (or at least make users *think* the program is easy to use). The server computer is responsible for managing database access: not just retrieving records, but sorting them, selecting just the ones the client is interested in, possibly making sure that other clients don't try to change the records you're looking at while you're looking at them, and a whole bunch of other stuff that we're not ready to even talk about yet.

The main benefit of client/server computing over dumb client computing is that with client/server computing, it becomes realistic to add whatever bells and whistles are necessary to make the program easy to use. If the server computer had to do all of the processing, there wouldn't be time to handle all the dialog boxes and other fancy interface stuff that Windows users have come to know and love on behalf of all the clients connected to the server. Plus, the burden on the network would be overwhelming as the server would have to send an outrageous amount of information to the terminal just to display a simple dialog box.

The advantages of client/server computing over dumb server computing can be illustrated by an example. Suppose a user wants to display all customers whose year-to-date sales exceed $1,000. Instead of sending the entire customer file over the network to the client computer, the client computer asks the server computer to just send the over-$1,000 customers. The server computer then does the work of searching through the entire customer file to extract the ones requested. Then, only those records requested by the client are actually sent over the network. By working together, the client and the server have spared the network the unnecessary burden of sending every record in the file when only a few records are actually needed.

Database access as described in this example is only one use of client/server computing. You'll find other common uses outlined in Chapter 4.

What Client/Server Isn't

Now that I've given a basic idea of what client/server computing is, I want to spell out a few things that client/server is *not*.

- ✔ **Client/server isn't networking.** Client/server computing depends on networking for its very existence, but the mere presence of a network does not imply that client/server computing is being used. This is a confusing point because local area networks use the term *client* to refer to computers connected to the network and server to refer to computers that are dedicated to sharing disk space and printers. For an application to be a true client/server application, the server must do more than simply share files and printers: it must share the application's workload with the client computers.

- ✔ **Client/server isn't database access.** Database access is one of the most common divisions of labor in client/server systems, but not all database applications are client/server, and not all client/server applications utilize databases. For example, if you use a database program such as Paradox or dBase to create a database application, then move the database files to a network file server, you have not created a client/server application because the server computer does nothing more than house the database files.

- ✔ **Client/server isn't GUI.** Another common division of labor in client/server applications is to have the client computer provide the fancy *graphical user interface*, or GUI. However, not all applications that use a Windows-like GUI are client/server applications, and client/server applications do not *have* to use a GUI.

- ✔ **Client/server isn't business reengineering.** Client/server computing by itself will not improve the way your company does business. Client/server computing is often associated with reengineering because it is a new technology that, when properly used, can implement the kind of nontraditional applications that reengineering efforts frequently call for. However, client/server computing and reengineering are not one and the same. Chapter 2 spells out the role of client/server computing in reengineering.

✔ **Client/server isn't downsizing.** Client/server is often thought of as an excuse for getting rid of the mainframe. Sometimes it works out that way, but sometimes it doesn't. A client/server project may call for replacing dumb terminals with desktop computers to use as clients, leaving the mainframe in place to act as the server. In this case, client/server actually *upsizes* the application.

✔ **Client/server isn't synonymous with open systems.** *Open systems* refers to the techniques of making inherently incompatible computer systems compatible. Client/server projects often depend on open systems for their success because they require that PC-based networks and mainframe-based networks be able to communicate with one another. Open systems is just one of many issues that must be dealt with in a client/server project.

✔ **Client/server isn't a conspiracy.** Client/server computing is not a conspiracy by PC advocates to get rid of mainframes. Nor is it a conspiracy by mainframe old-timers to ensure their job security. It is, for the most part, a recognition of the best of both worlds. It is a way to develop computer applications that are as easy to use as PC applications and as dependable as mainframe applications.

✔ **Client/server isn't a Silver Bullet.** Client/server computing is not like the Lone Ranger's bullet, which flew true and always found its target. Applying the client/server label to a project will not guarantee its success. As this book will point out, there are many pits to fall into along the client/server path.

That doesn't mean that the client/server way is to be avoided or approached with fear and trepidation. I'm reminded of the scene in *The Wizard of Oz* when the Scarecrow, Tin Man, and the Cowardly Lion come across a sign on the way to the Witch's castle that reads, "I'd turn back if I were you." Client/server may not be a Silver Bullet, but neither is it a Witch's castle. I hope this book will give you the brains, the heart, and the nerve to plow full speed ahead into the client/server world. Onward!

Chapter 2

Client/Server and Your Business

*B*efore we go charging ahead with the rest of this book on client/server, it might be a good idea to think about whether client/server is the best way to go for your particular business or situation. I'll outline some things you might want to consider, and some alternatives to client/server. Then, assuming you haven't put down this book and gone in search of ...*For Dummies* books on other solutions, you can read on and learn about how client/server can facilitate business reengineering, one of the hot topics in business today.

Should You or Shouldn't You? (Making the Client/Server Decision)

With all the hoopla surrounding client/server computing, is it a given that all new computer systems should be developed using the client/server model? Not at all. That's a decision that must be made on a case-by-case basis, according to the particulars of the situation rather than a blind client/server-is-all ideology.

A decision on whether to go with client/server should consider at least the following questions:

- How much will a graphical front-end interface (a GUI) improve the users' effectiveness? In some cases, a GUI may actually slow down users. (Client/server GUIs are covered in Part II.)
- Do you have the technical expertise necessary to switch to client/server development?
- Will the cost of retraining IS staff and acquiring new client/server technology outweigh the benefits of the new system?
- Are any of the major building blocks for a client/server system already in place?
- Do you have the political clout to bring end-user groups and IS staff together for a client/server project?
- Will the "pilot system" — your first client/server development effort — demonstrate the potential payback of client/server technology?
- Will the client/server system have demanding response time requirements?
- Are the expectations of end users and management realistic?
- Is the budget realistic? Client/server systems are rarely less expensive than their mainframe counterparts. The reason for going to client/server is not to save money, but to provide new capabilities that could not be achieved before.

Picking a Client/Server Pilot Project

The *pilot project* is your first venture into client/server computing. It is the "proof-of-concept" project that will determine whether your company will commit itself to client/server.

More accurately, the pilot project determines which client/server technology your company will commit to, not whether or not it will commit to client/server in general. Few companies are going to revert to traditional mainframe computer development because their first client/server project fails. Instead, they will look at the reasons for the failure and try again.

There are two schools of thought regarding what type of computer system should be chosen for a client/server pilot project. One school of thought says to pick a low-risk project for your client/server pilot. That way, if the project fails, not much is lost. You can easily tuck your tail between your legs, retreat into your office, and sulk for a few days. When you come out, no one will remember the failed project, and you can get on with your life. Of course, a low-risk project is usually also a low-return project. Even if it succeeds, no one may notice.

The other school of thought says to pick the most visible and risky project you can find for your first experiment with client/server. Enlist the support of upper management, get the budget you need, and charge into it full-steam. If the project fails, your next office will probably be under a freeway overpass or on a park bench. But if it succeeds, it will succeed big. The benefits of client/server will be impossible to ignore.

In some ways, a high-risk client/server pilot project probably has a better chance of succeeding than a low-risk project. After all, the more critical the application, the more likely management is to throw the best talent at it, to give it some budget flexibility, and to remain committed to the project through thick and thin. Once a low-risk, low-return project starts to fall behind, it's all too easy to sweep it under the rug.

The choice of application for a client/server pilot project is critical, and the best choice is one that balances the benefits of a low-risk, low-return project against the benefits of a high-risk, high-return project.

No matter which project you settle on for your first venture into client/server, count on the following:

- ✔ Your budget won't be adequate. You're venturing into unknown territory, and you don't know what to expect. Plan on budget trouble.

- ✔ Your schedule won't be adequate. You'll underestimate the time it requires for the IS staff to become familiar with all the new tools that go hand-in-hand with client/server development.

- ✔ Open systems is a myth (more about that in the next chapter). The hardest part of client/server is getting the pieces to fit together.

- ✔ The users will want more than you can deliver.

- ✔ The IS staff may revolt.

Count on hurdles at every turn, and you'll be prepared. Keep in mind that just as the client/server system may be reengineering the business, the client/server project is reengineering the IS staff. (I put that in so you'd have to keep on reading to find out what business reengineering is.)

Alternatives to Client/Server

There are alternatives to client/server that should be considered before you commit a project to client/server. These alternatives include:

✔ Moving an existing mainframe application to a smaller hardware platform. If the mainframe system is based on IBM's CICS transaction processing system, for example, you can move it to an AS/400 minicomputer, Unix, or an OS/2 LAN server.

✔ Replacing mainframe computer terminals with PCs that are able to emulate the terminals. That way, users can access PC applications such as word processors and spreadsheets, and still run mainframe programs in a window.

✔ Replacing an existing mainframe system with a packaged system that does the job better. The packaged system may or may not use the client/server model, but even if it does, you are spared many of the harsh details of switching to client/server. (Yes, I'll tell you about those later.)

✔ Beautifying an existing mainframe application by adding a GUI front end to existing CICS applications. There are programs designed specifically to do this. Usually, however, this is only a temporary fix. It is like putting a Band-Aid on a gushing wound.

If any of these alternatives sounds like it will do the job, you may not need to invest in client/server at all. However, each has severe limitations and is best used as a temporary fix rather than a long-term solution (with the possible exception of purchasing a packaged client/server system, which may be an ideal solution for the short and long term).

What Is Business Reengineering?

Reengineering refers to the process of rethinking the way a business operates in the hope of improving its efficiency not just a little bit, but by orders of magnitude. In essence, it means reinventing the business, discarding the preconceived notions that subtly limit the effectiveness of the business.

Client/server computing is often tied up with reengineering projects because client/server technology is often required to implement the new systems that this type of effort call for. I'm not going to get into all the details of what reengineering is all about; I just want to give you a general idea of what it is, drop a little jargon so you'll be able to speak its language, and explain why client/server is often used in reengineering projects.

Reengineering does not mean studying the way work is done and fine-tuning it for peak efficiency. It is not a management technique such as Management by Objectives (MBO), Management by Walking Around (MBWA), or my personal favorite, Management by Taking Long Afternoon Naps (MBTLAN). Nor is reengineering a quality program such as Total Quality Management (TQM).

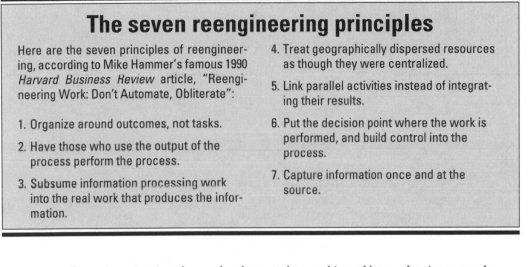

The seven reengineering principles

Here are the seven principles of reengineering, according to Mike Hammer's famous 1990 *Harvard Business Review* article, "Reengineering Work: Don't Automate, Obliterate":

1. Organize around outcomes, not tasks.

2. Have those who use the output of the process perform the process.

3. Subsume information processing work into the real work that produces the information.

4. Treat geographically dispersed resources as though they were centralized.

5. Link parallel activities instead of integrating their results.

6. Put the decision point where the work is performed, and build control into the process.

7. Capture information once and at the source.

Reengineering involves a fundamental reworking of how a business works, not just in baby steps but in great-big risk-taking steps. It could be defined as reinventing business processes from the ground up to obtain quantum leaps, not incremental gains, in performance.

For example, reengineering of the Accounts Payable department wouldn't start by focusing on the paper flow or the proper payment of invoices to make sure the maximum discount is taken; it would instead start by asking why we have an Accounts Payable department in the first place. It could be that the entire function could be done away with and incorporated into a larger process.

Process orientation

Reengineering focuses on *processes*. In fact, reengineering is sometimes referred to as *BPR*, which stands for *business process reengineering*. BPR is closely related to CPR (cardiopulmonary resuscitation), which is what some companies actually need before BPR can begin. (Or, maybe they need BPR before CPR will make any difference.)

A *process* is a what a business does to produce something of value to customers. A process involves inputs, an output that is of value, and a set of activities that transforms the input into the output.

For example, a manufacturing company might identify processes such as the following:

- ✔ Developing new products
- ✔ Acquiring new customers
- ✔ Determining what customers need or want
- ✔ Manufacturing products
- ✔ Fulfilling orders
- ✔ Servicing customer problems

There is no "correct" list of processes that apply to all companies, even competing companies in the same industry. Each company must identify its own view of its fundamental processes.

When a process has been identified and selected for reengineering, the activities required to carry out to complete the process are detailed. Then, the process can be redesigned. Entire steps can sometimes be left out of the process with no ill effect. Sometimes several jobs can be combined into one job with greater responsibility and more focus on the actual process being performed. And multiple versions of the process might be designed so that simple and complex situations can be handled separately.

Customer focus

One of the hallmarks of reengineering is a renewed focus on the customer as the ultimate reason that business exists. Reengineering projects often involve identifying the customer-based reason for every aspect of how a business operates.

Businesses engaged in reengineering often discover that much of what they do has nothing to do with satisfying actual customer needs. Customers really do not care about warehouse operations, logistics, human resources, or many of the other functions that frequently dominate the organizational structure of the business. These activities can often be redesigned in a way that produces actual customer value.

Case workers

A common technique of reengineering is assigning case workers to take complete charge of a business process. For example, IBM did this in the early 1980s with its credit-approval process, which was handled by the IBM Credit Corp. Before reengineering, IBM Credit Corp. had split the credit-approval process into a series of discrete steps which were handled assembly-line fashion by specialists. The entire process took 6–10 days, which was ample opportunity for customers to have second thoughts and cancel the order.

IBM replaced the specialists with case workers — individuals who would personally handle all aspects of a credit application. The result was that the entire process was trimmed from 6–10 days to 4 hours.

In the reengineering way, the old management/clerical structure is replaced by a case worker structure, where front-line workers *are* trusted with decisions, and specialists are available to handle those situations in which the case worker needs expert help.

What Does Reengineering Have to Do with Client/Server Computing?

Were you wondering when I was going to get around to this? Traditionally, computers have been used to automate existing business functions. That means that businesses are able to perform those functions faster using computers, but the business functions *themselves* remain essentially unchanged from the way they operated before the use of computers.

The problem with this approach is that it doesn't take advantage of what computers can really do. In fact, it doesn't even begin to scratch the surface. Most companies use computers like super-fast typewriters, 10-key calculators, and filing cabinets.

One of the key ideas behind reengineering is to look for ways to take advantage of the true capabilities of computers by radically reorganizing the way business works. ▪

For example, instead of using computers to automate the Accounts Payable department by computerizing payment of vendor invoices, why not put computers in the warehouse and initiate vendor payments the moment goods are received, and tell the vendors to stop sending invoices? Then, you can eliminate the Accounts Payable department altogether, or at least scale it back dramatically by handling *most* vendor payments in this way.

Reengineering efforts often center around processes that are currently handled by several different departments, such as Sales, Product Development, and Manufacturing. In all likelihood, these departments have separate computer systems with their own databases and applications. These systems may be compatible with one another, or they might be totally incompatible: one might be based on a DEC minicomputer, another on an IBM mainframe, and the third on a PC LAN. Client/server computing provides the technology necessary to build an integrated computer application that accesses information stored in all of these systems.

Reengineering also often emphasizes case workers and putting decision-making in the hands of front-line workers, and so may depend on computer systems that are easier to use than ever before. Client/server provides the tools needed to build complicated computer systems that access data from databases all over the enterprise, but provide a single interface that can be used without a lot of specialized training.

Some reengineering projects call for portions of the actual work to be done by the customer. Automated teller machines (ATMs) are a classic example of this: the customer gladly does the work once done by a teller. Client/server computing is perfect for this type of application, because it provides an easy-to-use front-end interface to corporate data stored on the mainframe.

The big turnaround at Sears

Everyone knows about the trouble Sears was in a few years ago. In 1992, Sears had a net loss of $2.5 billion. The following year, Sears posted a profit of $2.4 billion, almost a $5 billion turnaround from one year to the next.

Sears did it through a major reengineering effort that examined everything that went on in the store and converted back-office stuff that didn't serve customers into customer-oriented activities.

Client/server computing has played and continues to play a major role in this reengineering effort. As an example, go to your local Sears store tonight and buy a refrigerator.

You'll discover that the salesperson can schedule home delivery of the refrigerator using a computer on the showroom floor. In the old days, scheduling delivery was handled by the delivery department. Now the customer gets immediate satisfaction that the refrigerator will be delivered at a convenient time.

The client/server architecture at Sears consists of a huge mainframe-based facility at the famous Sears tower in Chicago, OS/2-based server computers in each store, and DOS-based client computers scattered throughout the stores.

The Size Thing

Downsizing, upsizing, and rightsizing are popular buzzwords that are often mentioned in both a business context and a computer context. The business and computer meanings of these words are related, but different.

Downsizing

Downsizing refers to the process of making something smaller, such as when Mike TeeVee went through the Wonkavision machine in *Willy Wonka and the Chocolate Factory*.

When applied to entire corporations, "downsizing" is usually a euphemism for "massive layoffs." Downsizing is what IBM does when nobody wants mainframe computers anymore.

Because so many people know that "downsizing" means "layoffs," corporate chieftains usually refer to it by another name. "Reorganization" and "restructuring" are their favorites. "Rightsizing," which is covered in an upcoming section, is another.

Downsizing is not the same as reengineering, although a reengineering effort may lead to downsizing. For example, downsizing a sales force might mean firing 20% of all the sales representatives and asking those who made the cut to cover 20% more territory each. In contrast, an effort to reengineer a sales force might discover that the sales force is actually unnecessary, so they should all be fired. Or it might discover that telemarketing is the better way to sell the product, so the sales force should be replaced with telemarketers. Or, it might actually reveal that the sales force is spread way too thin and sales would quadruple if the sales force were merely doubled.

The point is that sometimes reengineering results in a smaller work force, sometimes it doesn't. But even if it does, there's an important difference: Downsizing means to scale the existing organization downward; reengineering means to discard the existing organization and start over. ■

In terms of computers, downsizing means replacing big computers with small ones. For example, a mainframe-based customer service system is replaced with a PC-based LAN system. Client/server computing is often used when downsizing, but client/server computing (like reengineering) doesn't necessarily imply downsizing.

Computer downsizing is sometimes viewed as a cost-cutting measure, but studies have shown that this doesn't work. Desktop computers, it turns out, usually cost just as much to operate as mainframes, and sometimes more. ■

Sometimes downsizing involves replacing a custom-developed mainframe system with an off-the-shelf package that runs on a LAN. This can reduce the costs of maintaining the custom software, but usually at the cost of flexibility: you'll have to adapt the way you do business to the software, rather than the other way around.

Downsizing sometimes involves "rehosting" existing mainframe applications. For example, a mainframe application that runs under CICS can be moved to an IBM AS/400 midrange system or even to a PC LAN.

Upsizing

Upsizing means making something bigger, like what the Oompa-Loompas tried to do to Mike TeeVee when they took him to the Taffy-Pulling Room (TPR).

Upsizing is the opposite of downsizing: It means hiring people to meet increased demand. Upsizing is growth. It is scaling the organization upward to support an increase in business.

✔ Upsizing is what Microsoft might get to do if a bazillion people buy Windows 95.

✔ You don't hear much about upsizing computers, but it does happen. For example, a company might outgrow a PC LAN and decide to install an AS/400 server. Or it may even decide to move the database to the mainframe.

Client/server computing makes upsizing possible because it separates the client from the server. Without client/server computing, moving an application to a larger platform — for example, from a PC LAN to a DEC minicomputer — would involve replacing the entire application. With client/server, all you have to replace is the server: The client side of the application can run with only minimal changes. ■

Upsizing is what the computer business was all about until IBM introduced the Personal Computer in 1981. Until then, the only real way to provide more computing services for growing companies was to replace existing mainframes with bigger mainframes.

Rightsizing

Rightsizing means growing or shrinking until you are just the right size. It's what Alice did in *Alice in Wonderland.* First she was too big, then she was tiny, then big, then tiny, then back to her correct size.

Rightsizing is often used as a euphemism for downsizing. Most companies, when they are growing, say they are growing. This impresses their stockholders, their bankers, and their customers. When business is on the decline, they downsize. Downsizing does not impress stockholders, bankers, or customers, so they say they are "rightsizing."

When applied to computers, the term *rightsizing* means moving computer applications to appropriate computer platforms. In other words, if an application belongs on a mainframe, put it on a mainframe. If it belongs on a minicomputer, put it on a minicomputer. And if it belongs on a PC, put it on a PC.

Client/server computing is perfect for rightsizing. It allows you to move the server side of the equation to whatever platform is appropriate — mainframe, minicomputer, or PC — without overly disturbing the clients.

It's amazing how often Alice is used to make a point in computer books. If you've read a lot of computer books, you know what I mean. If you haven't, take my word for it: Lewis Carrol is a computer-nerd cult hero.

Leftsizing and capsizing

Leftsizing, according to Republicans, is what the Democrats have been doing to us for the past 40 years.

Capsizing is what happens when the whole downsizing, upsizing, and rightsizing thing gets out of hand.

Chapter 3

Client/Server Myths Dispelled

- -

In This Chapter

▶ Myth #1: Client/server is cheaper

▶ Myth #2: GUI is always good

▶ Myth #3: Client/server programs are easy to develop

▶ Myth #4: The mainframe legacy is a burden

▶ Myth #5: Client/server is new

▶ Myth #6: Client/server requires multiple vendors and open systems

▶ Myth #7: PC programmers are more cool than mainframe programmers

▶ Myth #8: Client/server will save the planet

- -

*I*n all the excitement about client/server computing over the past few years, many myths have developed about what it is and what it can do. Some of these myths are grounded in truth; others are way off the mark. This chapter shines the light of truth on some of the more common client/server myths.

Myth #1: Client/Server Is Cheaper

Don't get caught thinking that the reason to go client/server is because it's cheaper, because it isn't true. Sure, you can buy a decent desktop computer for as little as $1,500 these days, and mainframes cost hundreds of thousands or even millions of dollars. But that doesn't make them more expensive. It's the total cost *per user* that matters. The mainframe cost may seem outrageous, but it may be able to support 5000 users instead of just one.

If you compare the total cost of operating mainframe computers with dumb terminals with the total cost of operating a client/server network with desktop PC clients and high-powered servers, mainframes will probably be cheaper on a per-user basis. Maybe *significantly* cheaper — the PC-based networked computers may be two or three times as expensive to operate per user than a comparable mainframe system.

Don't forget that there are other costs involved in computer systems beyond the cost of purchasing the hardware, such as:

✔ The cost of developing or purchasing and installing the software for the new system. If you have to hire programmers, the costs can really add up. (Don't forget to factor in the total cost of having your own programmers: salary, benefits, the cost of space and office support, pizza and beer, and other costs that may arise.)

✔ The cost of supporting the network. Computer networks don't take care of themselves — least they require an administrator to keep them running smoothly.

✔ The cost of training users on the new system.

Of course, you'll want to buy each user a copy of this book. I'm sure the good people at IDG Books Worldwide will be more than happy to cut you a deal if you order several thousand copies.

I've mentioned only the obvious costs of setting up and running a computer system here. None of these costs really reflect the true cost of the new system, which is the cost of *using* the system (or in a more positive light, the *savings* or *income* gained by using the system).

Myth #2: GUI Is Always Good

Client/server is often used as a technique to provide a graphical user interface (GUI) for applications that previously ran on a mainframe. This is sometimes a good idea, but not always.

Take the familiar Automated Teller Machine (ATM) as an example. You walk up to it and see a message similar to the following displayed on the screen:

```
Please insert your card.
```

So you dutifuly insert your card in the machine. Now you see a message that says:

```
Please type your secret code.
```

You type your secret code. Next, you see a menu of choices:

```
Deposit
Cash Withdrawal
Account Balance Inquiry
Fast Cash
```

You press the button next to the menu choice you want. The ATM then asks whether you want to withdraw from your checking account or your savings account, and so on until you have completed your transaction.

Would the ATM be easier to use if it were Windows-based? Just think of all the options the user would have: Instead of being forced to press the Cash Withdrawal button, the user could select the Transaction | Cash Withdrawal command from the menu by using the Ctrl+Shift+W keyboard shortcut, by clicking on the Withdrawal button in the Toolbar, or by dragging the Money icon and dropping it on the Wallet icon. And the user would be able to play Solitaire while waiting for the receipt to print. Figure 3-1 shows what a Windows ATM might look like.

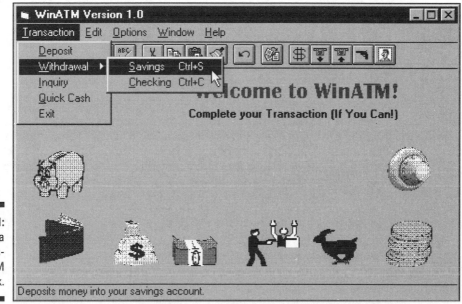

Figure 3-1:
How a Windows-based ATM might look.

Even with all of these enhancements, you still wouldn't be able to get your money out of the machine any faster than you can now. Not all applications require or benefit from a Windows-style graphical user interface.

Another type of application that is a poor candidate for conversion to client/server is raw data entry. IRS data entry operators sit at the computer all day, entering the same type of data over and over. These applications have to provide a data-entry procedure that is as efficient as possible. Forcing these users to use a GUI interface would probably slow them down rather than speed them up.

Even if an application would be easier to use if it had a Windows-like interface, would it justify the cost of conversion? That depends on how much the new interface will improve the bottom line. The point is that a fancy graphical interface is not always necessary or appropriate.

There are, of course, many good uses for graphical user interfaces, even for raw data entry. For example, a company that uses a field sales force might enable its sales reps to enter orders directly using laptop computers attached to a server computer via modems, provided the laptop order-entry program is easy enough for the sales reps to use. Or, a catalog showroom company may discover that it can eliminate its order processing department altogether by having customers enter their orders at computer kiosks located throughout the store (the program would have to be *really* easy to use).

Myth #3: Client/Server Programs Are Easy to Develop

Client/server applications can be built using any number of different development tools. At the one extreme, skilled computer programmers can use traditional programming languages such as COBOL, C, or C++ to create both the client and server portions of the client/server application. More likely, though, a more visual programming tool such as Visual Basic or Power-Builder will be used and a database management system will be used for the server. (You'll learn about developing client/server systems in Part IV.)

It certainly is a lot easier to create a Windows program using Visual Basic than C, and programming tools such as PowerBuilder make the development process even easier. So it's natural to assume that a client/server application should be easier to develop than a traditional mainframe application.

Not!

The client/server computing model introduces all sorts of complexities into the design of even simple applications:

✔ Client/server systems usually require that hardware and software from different vendors work together.

For example, you might have an IBM mainframe running the MVS operating system and PCs running NetWare and Unix as server computers, whereas generic PCs running Windows operate as the client computers. Getting these systems connected on the same network and all talking to each other can be a nightmare.

✔ The programming development environment for client/server applications is much more complex than the development environment for mainframe applications.

In addition, your company's programmers are probably not as experienced with client/server development tools as with the mainframe tools. When it comes to client/server software development, there is a *lot* to learn. Windows programming, even with an easy-to-use tool such as Visual Basic, is a major undertaking.

Myth #4: The Mainframe Legacy Is Bad

In some circles, existing mainframe computer applications are beginning to look more like a burden than a benefit. It may well be that computer systems that were developed 10, 15, 20, or even 25 years ago seem crude when compared with the fancy applications being developed today. The modern PC is capable of supporting programs that are much easier to use than the IBM 3270 terminal-based programs of a decade ago.

But keep in mind that many of those so-called "legacy" applications are the ones that keep the business running, and for the most part they work pretty well. There's no cause to write these applications off because they don't look as flashy as newer Windows-based programs.

Myth #5: Client/Server Is New

Client/server computing is touted as the new computing model that will take us through the end of this century and into the next, as a totally new technology that the old breed of mainframe programmer can't possibly understand.

Wrong.

Although most mainframe application programmers have not been exposed to client/server computing until recently, client/server is actually an old concept that has resurfaced recently with renewed vigor.

For example, database researchers have long studied the possibility of using separate *database machines* to handle database processing on mainframes. With a database machine in place, all of the work of querying and updating the database would be handled by the database machine rather than the mainframe, in client/server style. The database machine could be a regular computer running a regular database program, or it could be a specialized computer designed especially for database access.

Bell Laboratories built a prototype of such a machine in the early 1970s. In other words, Bell Labs was doing client/server computing a decade before PCs were even invented.

As another example, consider that the IBM 3270 terminal — the standard mainframe computer terminal for nearly 30 years now — was actually considered to be a *smart* terminal when it first came out. Prior to the 3270, the host computer (that is, the mainframe) had to handle every detail of presenting information on the terminal screen and collecting information from the terminal keyboard, byte by byte.

The 3270 added a degree of intelligence, albeit crude by today's standards, to the terminal. With the 3270, the terminal itself handled such functions as moving the cursor one character to the right when the user pressed the right-arrow key, deleting the character to the left of the cursor when the user pressed the Backspace key, storing the edited information entered by the user in an internal buffer, and sending the contents of the buffer to the host computer when the Enter key was pressed. In short, the terminal controller handled many aspects of the user interface.

This wasn't client/server computing, of course, because the 3270 terminal wasn't programmable. However, it did at least begin to address one of the main motivations for client/server computing: The user interface should be provided by the client, not the server. This freed up the host computer for other work and reduced the amount of traffic on the network. The goal of placing computing power where it belongs is nothing new.

Myth #6: Client/Server Requires Multiple Vendors and Open Systems

Client/server computing is often thought of as including computers from several different vendors, such as IBM mainframe computers, DEC minicomputers, and PC networks running NetWare or Unix. The ability to integrate computers from different manufacturers is one of the strengths of the client/server model, but it's not a requirement.

In fact, it's quite possible to set up a company-wide client/server system using mainfames, minicomputers, and PC networks, all using equipment and software from a single vendor. IBM's catalog of client/server products is about the size of the Manhattan phone book.

CICS, the transaction processor that once ran only on IBM mainframes, now runs on AS/400 minicomputers, personal computers that run OS/2, and IBM's RISC 6000 computers running AIX, plus a few other platforms. Likewise, there's a version of the DB2 database management system to run on just about any computer IBM sells.

In short, you can fully implement client/server computing and remain a true-blue IBM shop.

That doesn't mean you'd want to, of course. As I said, the ability to work with products from different vendors is one of the best things about client/server. If there's something about DB2 you don't like, shop around for a database program you do like. There are plenty to choose from.

Myth #7: PC Programmers Are More Cool Than Mainframe Programmers

This one simply isn't true. Many old mainframers programmers are really cool. Some of them still have their bell-bottoms and at least one set of really cool shades, and a great 8-track collection. So give us a break. (Oops...I mean give *them* a break.)

Myth #8: Client/Server Will Save the Planet

The zealots of client/server computing, like other fanatics, are certain that their way and only their way will pave the way to a new world order.

Yawn.

For as long as I've been involved in computers (don't ask), a new messiah comes along every three or four years promising deliverance. They have all had their merits, but none of them actually saved the planet. We still have polution and world hunger and wild despots in every corner of the globe. And computers are still too hard to use, they still aren't delivering on their promise to improve business productivity, and it still takes way too long to create new computer applications from scratch.

Client/server is just the latest one on the list. It *is* an important technology, and it is likely to be around for a while because it is based on sound technical grounds and it is an ideal way to get the hodgepodge of otherwise incompatible computer networks that have been built over the last 10 years to work together.

But it's no Silver Bullet. This chapter has pointed out the shaky ground many of the current promises of client/server computing are standing on. No matter how you slice it, client/server is a hard technology to master.

Now that your illusions about client/server are shattered, let's get on to more solid ground and look at the real-world applications that client/server computing is being used for.

Chapter 4

A Smorgasbord of Client/Server Applications

*N*ow that you've got a few definitions of client/server under your belt, and have had a peek at some of its promises and illusions, it's time for a quick look at the popular types of client/server applications. With luck, the client/server application you are considering will fall into one of these neat little boxes.

Database Applications

The client/server applications that come to mind first for most people are database applications.

In a client/server database application, database software runs on the server computer and a program that can access the database runs on the client computers. The client program, called the *front end*, allows users to access information stored in the database using an easy Windows-style interface. The server program, called the *back end*, handles the database side of the application. The front-end program requests services of the back end by querying the server. These queries from the front end are in the form of SQL statements (for Structured Query Language). The back end processes the SQL statements and returns the results to the front-end program. ■

Client/Server Database Processing

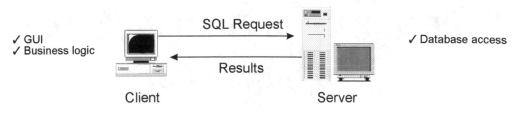

✓ GUI
✓ Business logic

SQL Request

Results

Client

Server

✓ Database access

Figure 4-1: In client/server database processing, the client is the front end and the server is the back end.

Figure 4-1 shows the client/server version of database processing. The client is responsible for the user interface (GUI) and business logic (the part of the program that implements business policies, such as whether or not credit should be approved or a discount applied to an order), and the server provides database access.

For more about SQL and SQL back-end servers, see Chapters 11 and 12.

The server computer in this type of arrangement can be just about anything: an Intel-based PC running a network operating system such as Windows NT, OS/2, Unix, or NetWare; a minicomputer such as an IBM AS/400 or a DEC VAX; or a mainframe computer such as an IBM 3090 running MVS.

The database back-end software will probably be one of the following, all of which are available on a variety of platforms including mainframes, minicomputers, and PCs:

- ✔ *Oracle Server* from Oracle Corp. Oracle is the most popular database back end these days.

- ✔ *Sybase SQL Server*, the number-two SQL database back end, made by Sybase, Inc.

- ✔ *Informix Online*, yet another SQL database server, this one from (you guessed it) Informix, Inc.

- ✔ *Microsoft SQL Server*, a SQL database back end that is based on SYBASE and runs only on Windows NT. (Older versions of SQL Server ran on OS/2.)

- ✔ *DB2*, IBM's relational database for mainframes running MVS, which has recently been adapted to run on AS/400, OS/2, Unix, and IBM's RISC/6000 computers.

As for the client computer, it can run just about any software that can access SQL databases over a network. For example:

- ✔ PC-based database programs, including Paradox, Microsoft Access, and Lotus Approach
- ✔ Windows database programs written in the C or C++ programming languages
- ✔ Programs developed using Visual Basic, PowerBuilder, SQLWindows, or any of the other so-called "visual" programming tools

Transaction Processing

A *transaction* is a set of two or more database updates that must be completed in an all-or-nothing fashion. For example, a single customer order may require updates to the customer file, the inventory file, the orders file, the accounts receivable file, and who knows what other files that might be involved. Transaction processing takes care of all the database updates for one or many transactions. All of these database updates must be completed, or they must all be ignored. ■

You can imagine the problems that could result if the program updated the accounts receivable file but not the orders file: The customer would receive a bill but no product! (For some companies, this might be considered a feature rather than a bug.)

Another term for transaction processing is *OLTP* (On Line Transaction Processing). OLTP applications are sometimes also referred to as *mission-critical applications*, because they are the applications the company depends on for its livelihood: Take away the OLTP application and the company goes out of business.

Transaction processing has been the bread and butter of mainframe computers for decades. Until recently, PC LANs and client/server computing were useful for simple database access, but not for high-powered transaction processing. These applications need more speed, power, and reliability than most client/server systems were able to provide until very recently.

All that is changing, however, as client/server technology grows up. The client/server model can now be used for sophisticated transaction processing that once called for a mainframe-only design.

Figure 4-2 shows the balance of work between client and server in a client/server transaction processing application. You can see that the client is still responsible for handling the GUI and at least portions of the business

Client/Server Transaction Processing

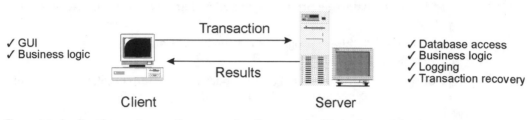

Figure 4-2: In client/server transaction processing, the server has duties beyond database access.

logic. However, the server has additional functions beyond simple database access: It too may carry out some of the business logic required by the application (for example, what to do if the item ordered by the customer isn't available at the main warehouse). Plus, it has the additional duties of logging the transaction and recovering in case the transaction fails midway, making sure that the transaction's database updates are properly undone.

Simple transaction processing can be handled by most SQL back ends using a feature called *stored procedures*. The stored procedure is a sequence of SQL statements that perform the necessary database updates. (A related feature called *triggers* is also sometimes used. A trigger is similar to a stored procedure, but is invoked automatically when some event, such as an update to a particular database field, occurs.)

The transaction-processing plot thickens when more than one server is involved with a single transaction, which is often the case. For example, the inventory database and the customer database may be stored on separate servers. In this case, the transaction still must make sure that all database updates are synchronized.

Electronic Mail

One of the most common forms of client/server computing is electronic mail. E-mail is the electronic equivalent of Mr. McFeeley the mailman, one of your neighbors and mine from *Mr. Rogers' Neighborhood*. With e-mail, you can send messages to and receive messages from other network users, instead of writing a message on the back of a napkin, sealing it in an envelope, and giving it to Mr. McFeeley to deliver. E-mail stores messages on disk and delivers them electronically to the appropriate network neighbors.

E-mail is a straightforward proposition when only a single local area network is involved. Most LAN packages come bundled with an adequate e-mail program, and you can purchase fancy e-mail programs such as Lotus cc:Mail or Microsoft Mail if the bare-bones LAN programs don't suit your needs.

E-mail is a bit more complicated when more than a single LAN is involved, though. A company with multiple offices and a hodge-podge of computer platforms needs some sort of e-mail backbone so that any member of the company can send messages to and receive messages from any other member of the company, without worrying about whether they are on the local NetWare network, the AS/400 system in Detroit, or the mainframe in Seattle.

A good e-mail system should also integrate e-mail within the company with e-mail to or from the outside world. In other words, the e-mail system should provide access to the famous Information Superhighway. It should allow you to send a message to an old college buddy just as easily as you send a message to Bob in Accounting. That's where client/server comes in.

In a large network, a server computer can be set up to operate as a dedicated mail server. All this server does, all day long, is sort and deliver mail. The server component of the e-mail package runs on the mail server computer.

At present, Microsoft Mail is the major offering in client/server e-mail software. Although the current incarnation of Lotus cc:Mail isn't based on a client/server model, Lotus is readying a new version that is.

Microsoft Office comes with the client software for Microsoft Mail. If all the users on a network already have Microsoft Office, you can set up a client/server e-mail system by purchasing the Microsoft Mail Server software from Microsoft.

E-mail is a useful but primitive form of electronic communication. Groupware, discussed next, is where the *real* communication action is.

Groupware

Yet another kind of client/server application is called *groupware*. This does not mean that everybody in your office wears the same T-shirt with the company logo on it. Groupware is a fuzzy new type of application that is designed to let people work together efficiently on collaborative projects. Groupware includes but is not limited to:

- Electronic mail
- Document routing and workflow

- Compound document managment (multimedia)
- Scheduling and calendar management
- Imaging
- Forms management

Groupware is ideal for applications that center around various types of documents that are created, reviewed, updated, and used by several users. ▪

For example, customer service in most companies revolves around a call form created when the service call is first received. Several people may be involved in adding information to the call form, reviewing it, passing it on to the individuals who can best handle the situation, tracking the call so it doesn't fall through the proverbial cracks, referring the call to higher powers if necessary, and so on until the customer is satisfied and the call form is stamped "closed." Every time the customer is contacted, the call form must be updated. With groupware, all of the people involved in processing the form can access it electronically and pass it back and forth.

The best-known groupware is Lotus Notes. In fact, at this writing, Notes is really the *only* player in the client/server groupware game, though that will change as other players including Microsoft enter the field. For now, if you want to do groupware, do it with Notes.

Lotus Notes includes a powerful scripting language that lets you create completely customized applications. It's more than just a fancy e-mail system; what it *is* can be difficult to say.

Notes wins the award for "Most Popular Software That Nobody Can Explain." I remember sitting in on a Lotus demonstration of Notes at a trade show, in which the presenter spent about 20 minutes answering the question, "What is Notes?" Everyone was still confused. Ask a Notes user to explain what Notes is and he or she will probably cough a few times, shrug, and say something like, "Well, it's kind of hard to describe." But ask if he or she *likes* Notes and you'll get cartwheels and backflips.

Facelifts for Legacy Applications

One final type of client/server application you may encounter is improved legacy applications. These client/server systems are built when users complain that they're sick of using boring 3270 terminals, and they want the payroll system converted to Windows right now or they're going on strike. With payday looming, a team of programmers goes to work converting the payroll system to Windows.

How do they do it? Do they rewrite all of the COBOL payroll programs in C? Not a chance. None of the programmers know diddly about C, and they probably can't even find the original source code for the COBOL payroll programs, so they wouldn't know where to start.

Instead, they use a program that is colorfully known as a *screen scraper*. The screen scraper studies the 3270 displays used by the payroll program, then converts them to the Windows interface, adding dialog boxes, menus, and all the accompanying bells and whistles. Then, it fools the mainframe into thinking that the PC running Windows is actually a 3270 terminal. The payroll system running on the mainframe doesn't realize that anything has been changed. It sends data intended for a 3270 display, but the screen scraper program receives the data, folds, spindles, and mutilates it, and voilà! a Windows dialog box.

Believe it or not, this sometimes actually works.

The problem with screen scrapers is that they don't go far enough in improving the existing applications. All they really do is put a smiley face on the same old programs. This may make the programs a bit easier to use and get disgruntled users off the programmers' backs (at least for a while), but it won't make a dramatic improvement in the bottom line. ∎

Screen scrapers *can* be useful if the original source code for the mainframe application has been lost (don't laugh — it happens), or if the application is complicated enough that recoding it could turn into a nightmare.

The best-known client/server product in this category is EASEL, by Easel Corp.

Now that your appetite has been whetted by looking over this smorgasbord of client/server applications, you're ready to dig in to the basic building-blocks of client/server computing in Part II: clients, servers, and networks.

Part II
Of Clients, Servers, and Networks

The 5th Wave   By Rich Tennant

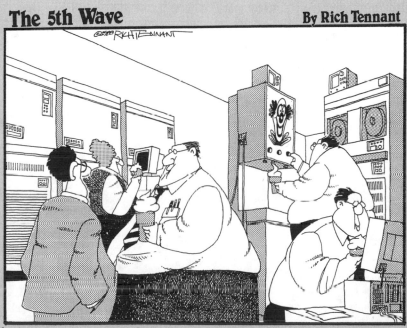

"WE'RE USING A 4-TIERED SYSTEM – PC, TO MINI, TO MR. SMOOTHY, TO MAINFRAME."

In This Part...

The basic building blocks of any client/server system are client computers, server computers, and networks (you could look at the network as the slash in "client/server" that ties the clients and the servers together).

The chapters in this part introduce you to these building blocks. You'll learn what types of computers are suitable for clients and servers, why the graphical user interface (GUI) is so important in client/server, and how local and wide area networks link computers together.

Chapter 5

The Right Kind of Client

● ●

In This Chapter

▶ What client computers do

▶ Choices in client computer hardware

▶ Operating systems for client computers

● ●

*A*mong the most critical choices a client/server developer must make is what kind of client computer to put on the user's desk. IBM-compatible PCs? 486 or Pentium? How much memory? How much disk? Would Macintosh computers be better? Windows 3.1, Windows 95, or OS/2 Warp?

These decisions can influence the outcome of a client/server project. Unfortunately, the developer rarely has the opportunity to make these decisions unencumbered. Usually, the client computers are already in place — the users already have four-year-old PCs that can barely run Windows — and you're expected to use them to deploy a state-of-the-art client/server system with bells and whistles that would tax even the most advanced workstations. Upgrading is out of the question: There's no budget for it.

Such is life. Skip this chapter if you find the whole subject depressing.

Client computers are most often desktop computers running Microsoft Windows. Sometimes they run OS/2, sometimes they're Macintoshes, and in rare cases they're Unix workstations. We'll deal with all these choices, but first let's review what client computers are supposed to do and general features to look for.

What the Client Computer Does

The client/server equation can be divided into three parts, the client computer, the network infrastructure (denoted by the slash), and the server computer.

A client computer is a front-line computer, one that actually interacts with a user. In most client/server systems, the client computer has two responsibilities: presentation management and application logic. In addition to its client responsibilities, the client computer can also have its own desktop applications such as a word processor or spreadsheet.

Presentation management

In most client/server systems, the client handles the user-interaction part of the application. The computer nerd term for this is *presentation management*.

Presentation management includes handling the details of displaying information on the computer screen. This means displaying windows, dialog boxes, text, graphs, and anything else that appears on the screen.

Presentation management also includes dealing with input from the user. User input normally comes from the keyboard, but it can also come from a mouse or other pointing device such as a trackball, stylus, or a light pen. In some cases the input comes from a touch screen or from a bar-code scanner.

✔ Presentation management usually implies a graphical user interface (GUI) such as Windows or OS/2 Warp, but that's not necessarily the case. (GUI is discussed ad nauseum in the next chapter.) The client portion of a client/server program may well be a text-based DOS program.

✔ Client/server makes it possible to implement several different user interfaces for the same application. For example, a text-based client program could be used for text-only client computers, while a Windows-based client program could be used for more powerful client computers capable of running Windows. The same server program would service both client programs.

While we're talking about presentation, do you know why there are 80 characters per row in a text terminal, and on a PC screen when operated in text mode? Because IBM punched cards, developed in the 1940s, had 80 characters punched into each card.

Application logic

Depending on the capabilities of the software used to implement the client/server system and the whims of the programmers, the client computer may also be responsibile for some or all of the *application logic* — that part of the program that decides what to do in various situations.

TECHNICAL STUFF

Why graphics take so much computing horsepower (as if you cared)

In the days of simple monochrome text-only terminals, displaying information on the screen was an efficient operation. All the terminal had to do was display rows of text characters, usually 24 rows each consisting of 80 characters. The terminal included a small amount of memory called a *buffer*, which was just large enough to hold 1 byte of data for each character that could be displayed. With 24 lines of 80 characters each, the buffer had to be 1920 bytes. Thus, an entire screenful of information would fit in under 2K of memory.

More advanced text-only displays can show text in various colors and with special attributes such as bright, underlined, or blinking. To accomplish this, the size of the buffer must be doubled, so that 2 bytes are used for each character position on the display: 1 byte for the character to be displayed, the other to store the character's *attributes*. This arrangement requires just under 4K to hold an entire screenful of data along with the attributes.

To provide a modern graphical display of information as is found in Windows, OS/2, Macintosh, or Unix computers, accessing each character displayed on the screen isn't enough. Instead, programs must be able to individually control every dot on the screen. (The computer nerd term for these dots is *pixel*.)

On a monochrome screen, each pixel can be either on or off, so only one bit of buffer memory is required to represent each pixel. On a color screen, each pixel requires enough bits to represent all of the colors than can be displayed. The more colors that are displayed, the more bits required. For example, a 16-color display requires 4 bits per pixel, but 8 bits per pixel are required for 256 colors.

The standard VGA screen found on most IBM-compatible client computers is 640×480, which means the display is 640 pixels across and 480 pixels down. That means the entire display consists of more than 300,000 pixels. Super VGA displays can display 1024×768, more than three quarters of a million pixels.

Simple arithmetic tells you that a lot of memory is required for these displays. For example, to display 256 different colors on a 1024×768 screen, multiply 1024 by 768 to get the number of pixels on the screen, then multiply by 8 to get the number of bits per pixel. This gives you the number of bits needed to store the image. Now, divide by 8 to convert bits to bytes. The result: 786,432. To display True-Color, which uses 24 bits per pixel, nearly 2.5MB of memory are required.

It takes a lot of computing horsepower to throw that much data around.

For example, what happens in an order-entry application if a customer wants to order some noggins, piggins, and firkins on credit, when the company policy is *cash*? In that case, the program must inform the user that cash is required.

✔ Sometimes this application logic is referred to as the *business logic*, because it is the portion of the program that implements business policies.

✔ It's possible to place the application logic on the server computer. Or, the application logic can be split — some of it can live on the client, some on the server.

✔ A *noggin* is small mug. A *piggin* is a wooden milk pail. And a *firkin* is a small cask that was sometimes used to hold beer or butter.

Desktop applications

In most systems these days, the client computer needs to do more than serve as the client for the client/server system in question: It needs to provide access to other applications as well. For example, the client computer for an accounting application may also need access to a spreadsheet program such as Lotus 1-2-3 or Excel and a word processing program such as WordPerfect or Microsoft Word.

Feature This: What to Look for in a Client Computer

For a computer to run both the client portion of a client/server application and other desktop applications, it should have the following capabilities or features:

✔ **Multitasking.** The computer must be able to run the client software and other desktop applications at the same time. It's no good if the user has to exit the client/server accounting package to access the spreadsheet program.

✔ **Lots of memory.** A typical 486 computer sold today with 4MB of RAM may be enough to run Windows 3.x and one application program, but that's not enough memory to run several programs at once. Ideally, the client computers should have 8MB or more RAM.

✔ **Local disk storage.** If possible, the client computer should have its own disk drive if it is to be used for desktop applications such as word processing or spreadsheet analysis. (A shared network drive will work too, but local disk storage is more efficient.)

Client Computer Choices

With so many computer platforms available today, how do you pick which to use for the clients in a client/server application? In most cases, the choice has already been made: The client computers are the ones that are already on the users' desks.

If you're lucky, someone made a rule years ago that all desktop computers would be compatible, that all computers would be equipped with two or three times as much memory and disk space as is currently needed, and that all computers would be replaced every two years with new models.

Welcome back. In the real world, there is a hodge-podge of computers on the desktops. The lucky and influential users have the most modern computers, but their hand-me-downs are still floating around. A typical office these days has representatives from just about every period of PC development: Pentium, 486, 386, 286, and maybe even 8088-based PCs, with a handful of Macintoshes thrown in just for fun.

One of the challenges of client/server computing is making the hodge-podge of desktop computers that are already in place work together.

IBM-compatible PCs

The most popular type of desktop computer — and therefore the most popular kind of client in client/server systems — is the IBM-compatible PC. These computers are based on Intel's line of processor chips, beginning in 1981 with the 8088 chip, then the 80286, 386, 486, and currently the Pentium.

So many companies manufacture IBM-compatible computers that PCs have become a commodity. Prices fluctuate faster than the price of pork bellies or cattle futures.

When evaluating IBM-compatible computers for use as clients, there are several factors to consider: the processor and memory, the display, and disk storage.

Processors and memory

Do not bother trying to create a client/server system using an ancient 8088 or 80286-based computer. These computers are not capable of running Windows satisfactorily (if at all), and most client/server systems use Windows on the client computer. That is reminiscent of the Star Trek episode where Kirk and Spock are zapped back into the 1920s, and Spock tries to build a mnemonic memory circuit using "stone knives and bearskins." Although Spock got his mnemonic memory circuit (whatever that is) working, your client/server project will be doomed to failure if you try to use ancient client computers.

Think twice before using an older 80386 system, as well. For a client/server system to have adequate performance, the client computers should ideally have 486 processors, or Pentium processors if you can afford them.

And don't take shortcuts with the memory, either. Client/server computing raises the bar on memory requirements. You might be able to get by with 4MB of memory on each client, but 8MB or more is better.

If you're stuck with a bunch of older computers, you may want to start looking at non-Windows alternatives for the client software. Unfortunately, that severely limits the types of applications you can create.

A stroll down memory lane

Here are quick definitions of the most common types of PC memory you're likely to hear about as the client/server gurus argue about what kind of PCs are suitable as client computers:

Conventional memory. This refers to the first 640K of memory on a PC. Programs that run under the MS-DOS operating system must be able to squeeze themselves into this puny (by today's standards) amount of memory.

Upper memory. Upper memory is the 384K block of memory that follows immediately after conventional memory. It is reserved for hardware devices that require access to memory, such as disk drives and video monitors. With a bit of black magic, MS-DOS can utilize some of this memory too.

Note: Between them, conventional memory and upper memory fill up the first 1MB of RAM (640K + 384K = 1024K, which is the same as 1MB).

Expanded memory. To access more than 1MB of memory on an 8088 computer, memory expansion cards were used. The memory accessed via these cards was called *expanded memory.* Even though expanded memory isn't necessary in computers that use 80286 or later processors, many programs (mostly older programs) still insist on using it.

Extended memory. Any memory installed beyond the first 1MB of conventional and upper memory is called *extended memory.* For example, if you use a 486 computer with 8MB of RAM, you have 1MB of conventional plus upper memory and 7MB of extended memory.

Because some programs still insist on using old-fashioned expanded memory, 80386 or better computers can use extended memory to simulate expanded memory. I won't go into details here, because this box has already gotten way out of hand and I can see you're drifting off.

Video displays

The video display for IBM-compatible computers has evolved from simple text-only monochrome displays to the advanced high-resolution color displays that are commonplace today. For client/server systems, make sure you have VGA or better.

Table 5-1 shows the three letter acronyms (TLAs) that stand for the various types of display adapters, plus the standard resolution for each adapter.

Table 5-1: Video adapters used on IBM-compatible computers

Adapter Type	TLA	Standard Resolution
Monochrome Display Adapter	MDA	Text only (80 characters by 25 lines)
Color Graphics Adapter	CGA	640×200
Enhanced Graphics Adapter	EGA	640×350
Video Graphics Array	VGA	640×480
Super VGA	SVGA	800×600 or 1024×768

- *Resolution* refers to the number of tiny dots that the monitor can display across and down the screen, not the monitor's good intentions to lose ten pounds in January.

- Nearly all IBM-compatible computers sold today come with SVGA monitors capable of displaying 1024×768 resolution.

- EGA monitors are acceptible for text-mode displays, but Windows looks pretty crude with EGA. Any CGA monitors remaining in your organization should be immediately thrown out the third-story window, after first checking for pedestrians below.

- CGA actually stands for Crayon Graphics Adapter.

- Standard VGA display adapters can display 256 different colors on the screen at once, but most SVGA adapters offer more colors. *True Color* mode uses 24 bits per pixel to store color information. This allows up to 16.7 million different colors to be displayed.

Disk drives

The disk drives in client computers are a less significant issue in deploying client/server applications, except that each client computer must obviously have enough disk space available to store the client portion of the software and any data files that might need to be stored locally.

In most cases, it's best to provide a local disk drive for each client computer. However, client/server applications can utilize so-called "diskless work-stations" for which the only disk access is to disk storage located on a network file server.

Consider yourself fortunate. In discussing client hardware, I've spared you the alphabet soup of terms and acronyms that deal with disk drives (IDE, EIDE, SCSI, RAID, to name a few). I won't throw you into the soup until we talk about server computers in Chapter 7.

Other goodies

The following equipment may or may not be needed on the client computers, depending on the particulars of the application:

- **Mouse.** If the client software is to run under Windows, OS/2, or another graphical environment, a mouse or other similar pointing device is a must.
- **Printer.** A shared printer available through the network is okay, but some client/server applications may work better with printers attached directly to the client computers.
- **Sound card.** More and more computers are being sold with sound cards so that the computer can talk, sing, and belch realistically. If your client/server application needs to talk, sing, or belch, you'll need to make sure the client computers have sound cards.
- **Other goodies** such as a CD-ROM drive, scanner, bar-code reader, slicer/dicer, pencil sharpener, and Ginsu knife set are probably not required by the client/server application but might serve as bribes to entice otherwise disgruntled users to at least try to tolerate the new system.

The Macintosh

Apple's Macintosh computers are rarely used as the primary client computers in client/server applications. So if you want, you can skip right over this section. You might offend some Macintosh fanatics, but they're probably not looking. Besides, they're used to being ignored.

Many companies have pockets of Macintosh computers in place, mostly in the advertising department because of the Mac's legendary graphics abilities. These Macs may already be networked together, since Apple's AppleTalk local area network is built into every Mac sold.

Networking Macs with other computers is another story, which I won't get into here but will touch upon in Part IV if I have to. It's enough to say at this point that it is possible for Macintosh computers to join the network, so Macs can be used as the client computers in a client/server environment.

- ✔ Macintosh computers come with their own operating system, so you don't have to worry about deciding between DOS, Windows 3.1, Windows for Workgroups, Windows 95, OS/2, or who knows what else.

- ✔ All Macintosh computers have graphics displays, since the Mac and its operating system are inherently graphics-oriented. Of course, some Macs have more powerful graphics abilities, but they are all capable of handling the presentation management aspects of a client/server application.

- ✔ The Macintosh world doesn't suffer from the memory ailments that the PC world does, trying to juggle conventional, upper, extended, and expanded memory. In a Mac, memory is memory. As on a PC, however, more is better.

The main thing to consider if you're considering using Macintosh as your client computer system is this: Is there a Mac version of the client software you want to use? For example, Lotus offers a Macintosh version of Notes and Powersoft is working on a Mac version of PowerBuilder. Find out for sure before you commit yourself to using Macs as clients. ■

Unix workstations

PCs and Macs aren't the entire desktop computing universe. One other type of computer that sometimes pops up is the so-called *workstation* computer that runs the Unix operating system.

Workstation computers tend to be based on high-powered RISC processors, which are generally considered to be faster than ordinary processors, although this is a subject of heated debate among reclusive computer nerds who don't have anything else to think about.

What this means is that high-powered workstation computers (and their users) usually don't want to be bothered with the petty little applications that are the targets of most client/server developments.

Unix comes in several versions from different vendors. Table 5-2 lists the most popular workstation computers and the flavors of Unix they use.

The one type of client/server application that high-brow Unix workstation users *are* likely to be interested in is groupware. Fortunately, Lotus Notes is available in Unix versions that fit the most popular of these workstations.

RISC stands for *Reduced Instruction Set Computer*, but that's not important. Even less important is that CISC stands for *Complex Instruction Set Computer*.

Unix workstations can also be built around Intel 486 and Pentium processors, which are considered to be CISC processors. ■

Table 5-2: Workstation computers and their Unix preferences

Workstation	Vendor	Unix Preference
SPARC	Sun Microsystems	Solaris
RS 6000	IBM	AIX
HP 9000	Hewlett-Packard	HP-UX

We Have to Operate

Here is the lowdown on the various operating systems that can be used for client computers.

DOS

DOS is far and away the most commonly used operating system. DOS's familiar C:\ prompt graces (or curses, depending on your point of view) millions — yea, tens of millions — of PCs throughout the world.

DOS stands for *Disk Operating System*, but that won't be on the test.

✔ There are three major flavors of DOS, sold by three companies: Microsoft, IBM, and Novell. It doesn't matter which you use; all three will work in client/server systems.

DOS is hamstrung by its need to remain compatible with even the oldest 8088-based computers. Hence the famous "640KB memory limit."

By itself, DOS does not provide the all-important GUI necessary for most client/server applications. Windows must be used alongside DOS to provide the GUI. ■

Windows 3.1

Windows 3.1 (and its predecessor Windows 3.0) are the most commonly used GUI. Figure 5-1 shows what Windows looks like.

When Windows takes over the computer, many of the memory limitations of DOS are overcome: Programs are no longer limited to 640KB of conventional memory. Windows has its own memory problems to contend with — see the sidebar, "Windows and its (not!) unlimited resources" — but they're not as crippling as DOS's memory limitations.

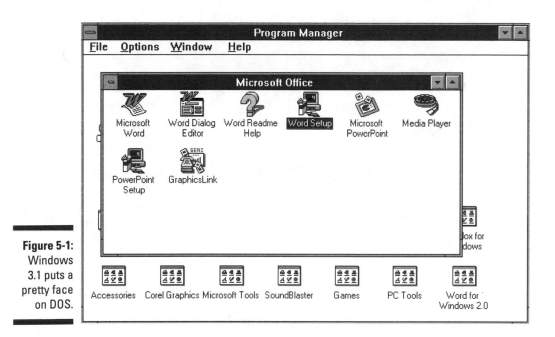

Figure 5-1:
Windows
3.1 puts a
pretty face
on DOS.

Windows and its (not!) unlimited resources

Although Windows circumvents the tyranny of the infamous DOS 640K memory limit, it introduces a form of memory oppression of its own: the system resources limit. System resources are the details that Windows must keep track of to provide its fancy graphical user interface: Details such as windows, menus, dialog boxes, icons, scroll bars, check boxes, buttons, and other fancy gizmos. Windows keeps track of these resources using several special areas of memory called *resource heaps*. Believe it or not, these resource heaps are limited to 64K of memory each.

In its early days, the 64K heap limit wasn't a problem. But with today's programs that have

gorged themselves on a gluttonous diet of bells and whistles, the heaps can fill up quickly. Windows can run out of resource space when several resource-hungry programs are run simultaneously. Windows deceptively displays "out of memory" messages when resource heaps fill up, so even computers with 16MB or more of RAM can bump into memory walls with Windows 3.1.

Oh, and guess what: Client/server programs tend to be (you guessed it) in the resource-hungry category. Windows 95 promises to alleviate the system resource crunch, so it's bound to be a popular choice for client/server computing.

Mom, when do I get a turn? (or, the great multitasking debate)

There are basically two approaches to multi-tasking: non-preemptive and preemptive.

In *non-preemptive multitasking*, once a program gets control of the computer, it gets to keep it until it decides to voluntarily let go so that another program can have a turn. Non-preemptive multitasking, which is used in Windows 3.1, works so long as all of the programs obey common rules of courtesy and relinquish control on a timely basis.

Unfortunately, some programs are less likely to give up control of the computer than kids are to give up control of the Nintendo. Once they get in control, they stay there until they're good and ready to move on. Such programs should read, "Everything I Need To Know About Non-Preemptive Multitasking I Learned In Kindergarten."

Preemptive multitasking, or "true multitasking" as computer nerds are likely to call it, is when the operating system doles out little pieces of CPU time and interrupts each program when that program's turn is up. It's a much more complicated proposition, but it doesn't require that programs politely step aside on their own.

By the way, like so many things in the PC world, the multitasking debate has been raging for years. IBM's popular mainframe transaction processing system, CICS, uses non-preemptive multitasking, and it is able to support thousands of terminal users all simultaneously accessing and updating centralized databases. Purists may snub their noses, but it works.

Windows also provides multitasking of the non-preemptive variety. Technically (that's your clue to skip the rest of this paragraph), *non-preemptive multitasking* means that programs must voluntarily give up control of the computer so that other programs can have a turn. Computer nerds often look down their collective noses at Windows and its non-preemptive multitasking, preferring the more chic preemptive multitasking found in "real" operating systems like OS/2 and Windows NT. But Windows 3.1 somehow manages to get the job done in spite of its inferior multitasking techniques, allowing users to run several programs at once without noticeable discomfort. (If you're interested in learning more about how this works, consult a therapist before reading the sidebar, "Mom, when do I get a turn?") ■

> ✔ There are still many computers running Windows 3.0. Upgrade them as quickly as you can: Windows 3.1 is a big improvement. If Windows 95 (or Windows 96, or whatever) is available when you read this, skip Windows 3.1 and go straight to Windows 95.

✔ Actually, Windows 3.1 was recently surpassed by Windows 3.11. The difference between 3.11 and 3.1 is trivial, though, so you can treat them interchangeably. (And, of course, if Microsoft manages to finish Windows 95 by the time you read this, you can forget what I said about Windows 3.11.)

Windows for Workgroups, however, is a separate animal entirely. Windows for Workgroups can be thought of as the networking version of Windows, but Microsoft earned the coveted "Dumbest Version Number of the Year" award when it decided to introduce a major update to Windows for Workgroups under the version number 3.11. Windows for Workgroups 3.11 includes a new superfast 32-bit file access system that Windows 3.11 does not include.

Both Windows and Windows for Workgroups are likely to fade away after Windows 95 takes hold.

Windows 95

Windows 95, aka "Chicago," aka Windows 4.0, and possibly aka Windows 96, is Microsoft's long-awaited, much-anticipated replacement for the aging Windows 3.1. Figure 5-2 shows what the desktop looks like in Windows 95.

Figure 5-2:
The new
look of
Windows
95.

Windows 95 will improve on Windows 3.1 in many ways, the most important of which are as follows (in no particular order):

- It has a new and improved graphical user interface that is "document-centric" rather than "program-centric." This means that users are to think in terms of documents rather than in terms of application programs. Check out Chapter 6 if you're interested in the details of how this new user interface works.

- Lots of new gizmos have been added to Windows 95 in an effort to make the system easier to use. Examples of this include a taskbar that provides an easy way for users to flip from program to program, a start menu for launching programs (so much for "document-centricity"), and the ability to right-click almost anything to access a quick menu of things you can do.

- No need to think of DOS and Windows as separate products. They've been merged into a single product.

- Letting Windows know what kind of printer, modem, mouse, or other hardware you're using (hardware configuration) should be easier. The "Plug and Play" feature automates the configuration process. This feature may end up being known as "Plug and Pray."

- Full compatibility with existing Windows and DOS programs. No need to upgrade all your software, unless you want...

- Preemptive multitasking! Of course, you have to upgrade all of your existing Windows programs to Windows 95 versions of the programs to take advantage of this feature.

- Free Microsoft Exchange client software, in case you just happen to settle on Exchange as your platform for developing groupware client/server applications.

- Better system resource management, so that you're not always running out of resource heap space. (Refer back to the sidebar "Windows and its (not!) unlimited resources" earlier in this chapter if you don't know what I'm talking about.)

- My, isn't there a lot of new stuff in Windows 95?

- No more Program Manager and File Manager! They've been replaced with a new program called Explorer, which does the same things except in new and different ways, just to confuse all those loyal users who finally figured out how to use Program Manager and File Manager. Bother.

- Configuration files like SYSTEM.INI have been replaced with a centralized configuration storehouse called the *registry*. Well, not actually: Now you have to worry about SYSTEM.INI *and* the registry. Double bother.

The warped world of OS/2

IBM's OS/2 is the main challenger to Windows as the GUI provider for client computers. With its latest version, OS/2 3.0 "Warp," IBM has finally positioned OS/2 as a desktop operating system that can compete with Windows for the hearts and minds of everyday computer users.

OS/2 Warp and its predecessor OS/2 2.x has a user interface similar to Windows 95. OS/2 1.x had an interface that more closely resembled Windows 3.1.

Although OS/2 has many technical advantages over Windows 3.1, Windows 95 narrows the technical gap to a hair's width. The real issues that come into play when chosing between OS/2 and Windows are economic and political, not technical.

- The main concern with OS/2 is that IBM has pushed it forward as a desktop operating system to compete with Microsoft Windows. The problem is that it isn't winning, and it's not likely to win anytime soon. Some are worried that IBM may face the music and pull the plug on OS/2, leaving those unfortunate souls who have committed to OS/2 as their client operating system up the proverbial creek. I don't think this is likely, but on the other hand, even IBM can't keep spending money on unprofitable products forever. (Maybe IBM should sell OS/2 to the government.)

- OS/2 is usually the second (or sometimes the third) platform for which software companies develop their products; the first platform is inevitably Windows. That means that OS/2 versions of software will forever lag behind their Windows counterparts.

- For OS/2 to survive in the marketplace, IBM has given it the ability to run Windows 3.1 programs. This nails the coffin shut as far as OS/2 software development is concerned. Why would software developers spend a fortune to develop specific OS/2 versions of their programs, knowing that the OS/2 market is small and the Windows versions of their programs will run under OS/2?

- OS/2 on the server computer is a different story altogether. See Chapter 7 for the vivid details.

Unix

This chapter wouldn't be complete without a brief mention of Unix as a client operating system. So, here it is, briefly:

Unix can be used as the operating system on client computers.

It usually isn't, however. Unix *is* the operating system of choice for SQL database server computers, as you'll see when you get to Chapter 11. But it's not usually used on desktop computers.

Why not? Simply because Unix is a bit much for client computers. It's just too high-powered and complex for users to fuss with. Unix is a multiuser operating system that just begs to be used on a server. Unix finds itself unfulfilled when used on a single user's desktop computer.

Now that we've looked at the hardware and software that makes up the client computer, the next chapter jumps headfirst into the details of the graphical user interface — the GUI — that makes client software so easy to use, at least in theory.

Chapter 6

GUI, Schmooey!

· ·

In This Chapter

▶ What is a GUI?

▶ Windows, menus, dialog boxes, and other GUI stuff

▶ Compound documents and OLE

▶ Properties and object-oriented user interfaces

▶ How to win a GUI argument

· ·

*O*ne of the main reasons for using client/server computing is to create computer applications that are easier to use than old-fashioned terminal-based mainframe applications. What makes client/server applications easier to use is the *graphical user interface*, or *GUI* (pronounced *gooey*, like butterscotch syrup or melted marshmallows).

This chapter explains what a GUI is and describes the most important elements of the most popular GUI, Microsoft Windows. The examples shown here use the forthcoming Windows 95 release of Windows, but the elements of Windows 3.1, OS/2, and the Macintosh GUI are similar.

If you're already a GUI wizard and know all about radio buttons and combo boxes, feel free to skim over most of this chapter, or even skip it altogether.

What Is a GUI?

All computer programs have a *user interface*. The user interface is how the person using the program interacts with the program: how information is displayed on the computer screen, how the user gets information into the program and invokes program functions, and so on.

Before graphical user interfaces such as the Macintosh and Windows, each program had its own unique user interface style with different approaches to issuing commands from the keyboard.

The two most famous pre-GUI user interfaces were: (1) DOS-based Lotus 1-2-3, the spreadsheet program, which used a menu of commands accessed when the user pressed the slash key; and (2) WordPerfect, a DOS-based word processing program that used the function keys alone or in combination with the Shift, Ctrl, or Alt keys to invoke commands.

While some programs copied the user interface of either Lotus 1-2-3 or WordPerfect, others created their own unique user interfaces. This meant the poor user had to learn an entirely new user interface with practically every new program. I can feel the vigorous nodding of many heads here.

Then along came the Macintosh and, a bit later, Windows, with the novel idea of providing a consistent, graphically based user interface that all programs would utilize. Once the user learned how to use one program, he or she would already be halfway to second base on any other program.

A graphical user interface is based on the following concepts:

- ✔ All programs should interact with the user in a consistent fashion. For example, there should only be one way to call up a menu, and the menu commands to perform similar functions like printing a file or exiting the program should be the same in every program.

- ✔ The user should interact with the program in *What-You-See-Is-What-You-Get* fashion. In other words, a word processing document should appear on the screen exactly as it will appear when printed, with all the fonts, line spacing, and special formatting shown right on the screen. No more "blue means bold, orange means italic, and purple means bold italic." Instead, bold is displayed bold, italic is italic, and bold italic is bold italic.

- ✔ Programs should operate within *windows* on the screen, so that more than one program can operate at a time. Windows can be dragged around the screen, resized, maximized to fill the entire screen, or minimized to make them shrink down to almost nothing, completely under the user's control.

- ✔ The user works primarily with a mouse or other pointing device to interact with the program.

- ✔ Whenever a program needs to collect information from the user, it uses a special window called a *dialog box*.

There'll be more of mice and menus (as well as windows and dialog boxes) later in the chapter.

A tired analogy revisited

No chapter on graphical user interfaces would be complete without recycling the old analogy of the automobile user interface (AUI). The analogy goes like this:

If automobiles were as hard to use as computers, Ford and GM would have gone out of business long ago. Consider how standardized the user interface of a car is: Everyone knows how to start the car, steer, accelerate, brake, turn on the headlights, lock the door, back up, turn on the radio, and honk the horn. The auto industry settled on a standardized user interface for these controls long ago.

The familiar auto user interface extends beyond the driver's seat to the road: Everyone knows what a stop sign means, what the speed limit is, how to read a freeway mileage sign, what the red, green, and yellow lights mean on a traffic signal, and so on.

Why doesn't the computer industry do the same, so that computers will be as easy to use as cars and every bit as popular?

The problem with the auto user interface analogy is that it doesn't work. For one thing, the auto interface isn't as intuitive as it seems. The only reason we "instinctively" insert the ignition key in the ignition switch to start the car is that we watched our parents do it for 15 years before we got our driver's license. If you sat Leonardo DaVinci or Benjamin Franklin in the driver's seat of a Ford Taurus, gave him the key and said, "Start 'er up," you'd get a blank stare.

And the auto interface isn't as standardized as suggested, either. Every car has a slightly different arrangement of controls. Some use a button on the dashboard to turn on the headlamps, others have a knob at the end of a handle on the steering column. Some cars have a foot pedal for the parking brake, others have a handle between the driver and passenger seats. Controls for the air conditioner, heater, cruise control, windows, door locks, and mirror adjustments are different from car to car.

If the auto user interface is so easy to use, why do so many people still have trouble parallel parking?

GUI Parts

"Gooey Parts" sounds like what's left after the bubblegum-blowing contest. Yuch! I hate it when that stuff gets stuck in my beard. The following sections describe the more important parts that make up the Windows 3.1 and Windows 95 GUI. The elements of the OS/2 Warp and Macintosh GUIs are similar.

Windows

Windows (in the generic sense, not in the specific *Microsoft Windows* operating system sense) are the kingpin of graphical user interfaces. A window is the portal through which a program interacts with the user.

A window has several features that are common to all windows in the GUI. Figure 6-1 shows a window for Windows 3.1 with its various parts labeled (the window is for the program Microsoft Access, which is often used for client/server applications).

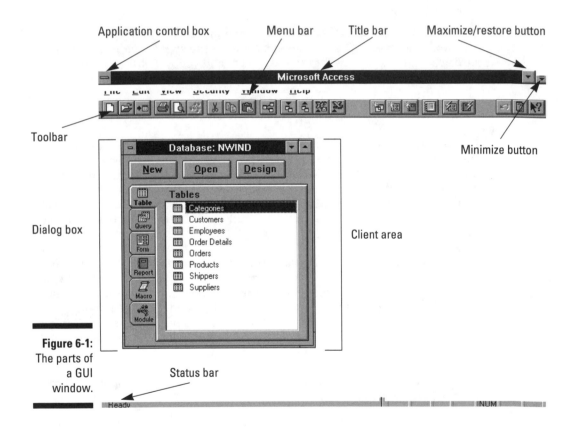

Figure 6-1: The parts of a GUI window.

Here's a brief rundown on what each of these window components does:

Title bar. The topmost portion of the window, called the *title bar*, displays the title of the application.

Menu bar. Just beneath the title bar is the *menu bar*, which contains the various commands that the user can invoke when using the program.

Status bar. At the bottom of the window, a *status bar* is optionally displayed to indicate interesting tidbits about the program's status, like which page the user is working on, or whether Caps Lock is on.

Toolbar. The *toolbar* is an optional collection of buttons the user can click to quickly perform common commands, such as opening a file or printing a document.

Salad bar. Just kidding.

Client area. The central portion of the window, where the program displays its information, is called the *client area*. Normally, this area displays the document or form the user is working on.

Application control box. Clicking on the *application control box* in the upper-left-hand corner of the window calls up a menu of things the user can do with the window. Doubleclicking it closes the application.

Minimize button. Clicking the *minimize button* shrinks the application down to an icon.

Maximize button. Clicking the *maximize button* enlarges the window so that it fills the entire screen. When the window is maximized, this button changes to the *restore button*, which returns the window to its original size.

Here are a few of the ways a user can manipulate a window:

- Windows can be resized to any desired rectangular shape by dragging one of the edges or corners of the window.

- Windows can be repositioned to any location on the screen by dragging the window's title bar — the horizontal band at the top of the window that displays the window's title.

- A window can be *maximized* so that it fills the entire screen.

- A window can be *minimized*, which reduces it to an icon, which gets the window out of the way so you can work with another program.

- A window can be *closed*, which shuts down the program running in the window and removes the window from the screen.

- Windows can overlap, as they do in Figure 6-1. Windows can also be *tiled*, which arranges them side by side so that none overlap.

- Only one window at a time can be the *active window*. The active window overlaps any other windows on the screen so that its contents are not obscured. To activate a window, the user just clicks inside it with the mouse.

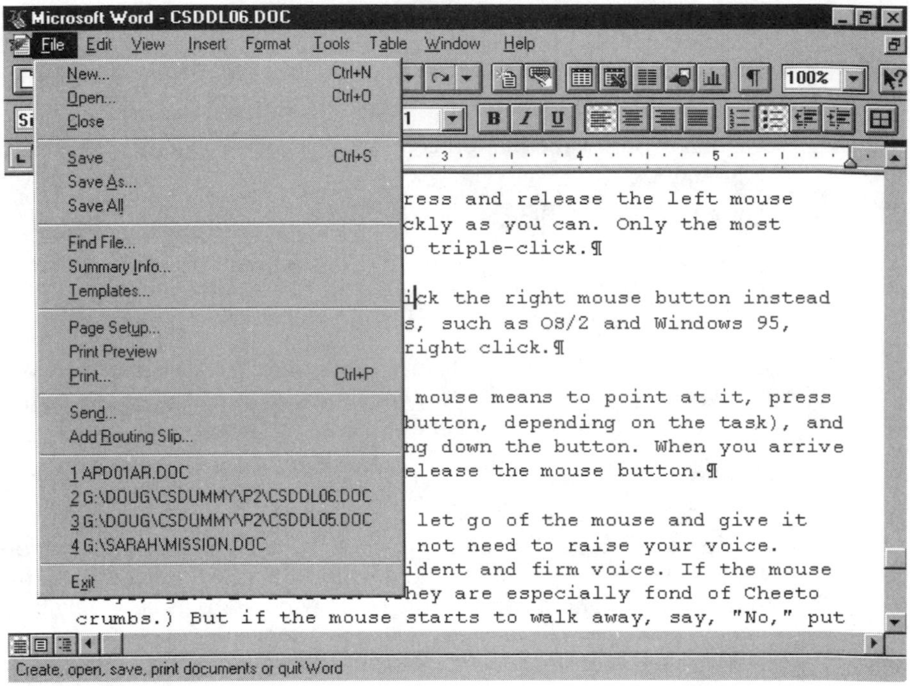

File   Edit   View   Insert   Format   Tools   Table   Window   Help

New...	Ctrl+N	
Open...	Ctrl+O	
Close		
Save	Ctrl+S	
Save As...		
Save All		
Find File...		
Summary Info...		
Templates...		
Page Setup...		
Print Preview		
Print...	Ctrl+P	
Send...		
Add Routing Slip...		
1 APD01AR.DOC		
2 G:\DOUG\CSDUMMY\P2\CSDDL06.DOC		
3 G:\DOUG\CSDUMMY\P2\CSDDL05.DOC		
4 G:\SARAH\MISSION.DOC		
Exit		

ress and release the left mouse
ckly as you can. Only the most
o triple-click.¶

ick the right mouse button instead
s, such as OS/2 and Windows 95,
right click.¶

mouse means to point at it, press
button, depending on the task), and
ng down the button. When you arrive
elease the mouse button.¶

let go of the mouse and give it
not need to raise your voice.
ident and firm voice. If the mouse
hey are especially fond of Cheeto
crumbs.) But if the mouse starts to walk away, say, "No," put

Create, open, save, print documents or quit Word

Figure 6-2:
The File
menu in
Microsoft
Word.

Menus

Most GUI programs provide *menus* that allow the user to select commands
from a list of various options. A menu bar appears at the top of the window,
just beneath the window title. For example, Figure 6-2 shows the File menu
from Microsoft Word, as displayed under Windows 95.

To select a menu command, the user clicks on the menu in the menu bar (for
example, File, Edit, or View) to reveal the menu, then clicks on the menu command (for example, New, Open, or Close).

To make menus consistent from one program to another, certain standard
menu commands are used. The exact commands vary depending on which
GUI you're using. Table 6-1 lists some of the standard menu commands for
Microsoft Windows.

Table 6-1: Standard menu commands for Windows

Menu	*Command*	*What it does*
File	New	Creates a new document.
	Open	Opens an existing document.
	Save	Saves changes to an open document.
	Save As	Saves the current document under a new name.
	Save All	Saves all open documents.
	Close	Closes an open document.
	Print	Prints a document.
	Print Preview	Displays the document exactly as it will appear when printed.
	Exit	Quits the application.
Edit	Undo	Undoes the last user action.
	Cut	Cuts selected objects to the Clipboard.
	Copy	Copies selected objects to the Clipboard.
	Paste	Pastes the contents of the Clipboard at the cursor location.
	Paste Special	Pastes the contents of the Clipboard as an embedded object or using another format.
	Find	Finds text.
	Replace	Replaces one text string with another.
Window	New Window	Creates another window for the current file.
	Tile	Arranges windows side by side.
	Cascade	Stacks windows like a deck of cards, slightly fanned so you can see the edge of each window.
	Arrange	Arranges windows so they do not overlap.
Help	Contents	Displays the Help table of contents.
	Search	Searches for help on a specific topic.
	Index	Displays an index of all help topics.
	About	Displays information about the program, including a copyright notice.

✔ If the user has a mouse phobia, he or she can access menu commands using the keyboard.

✔ The most commonly used commands can also be assigned keyboard shortcuts. Microsoft recommends certain specific keyboard shortcuts that should be common for all Windows programs. For example:

Ctrl+Z	Edit|Undo
Ctrl+X	Edit|Cut
Ctrl+C	Edit|Copy
Ctrl+V	Edit|Paste

✔ Some GUI programs let you access a quick context-sensitive menu by clicking on an object with the right mouse button. This brings up a menu that displays commands that are appropriate for the object you clicked. For example, if you right-click on a text paragraph in Microsoft Word, you get a menu that includes basic editing commands (Cut, Copy, and Paste) and basic formatting commands such as Font and Paragraph.

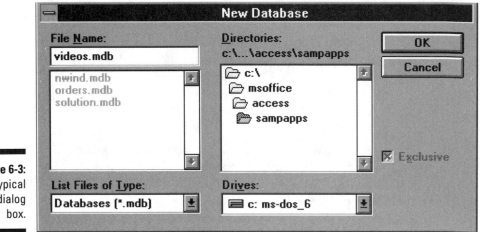

Figure 6-3:
A typical
GUI dialog
box.

Dialog boxes

Dialog boxes are how GUI programs gather information. A dialog box is a special type of window that is populated with *dialog box controls* that the user plays with to set options, enter data, or initiate actions. Figure 6-3 shows a typical dialog box.

Table 6-3 describes the most common types of controls that can appear in a dialog box.

Dialog boxes typically appear in response to user commands. For example, if the user selects the Open command from the File menu, a dialog box appears to allow the user to tell the program what file to open. The user indicates

Table 6-3: Dialog box controls

What it looks like	*What it's called*	*Description*
File Name: videos.mdb	Text box	Used to type data, such as a name, address, quantity, or any other text or numeric information.
Sample Tables: Mailing List / Contacts / Customers / Employees / Products / Orders	List box	Used to select an option from a list of possible choices.
Drives: c: ms-dos_6	Drop-down list	A space-saving list box in which the list doesn't appear until the user clicks the down arrow.
Fruit / Oranges / Apples / Bananas / Grapes / Kiwi / Lemons / Peaches / Pears	Combo box	A combination of a text box and a list box: The user can type in a value or select the value from the list.
Fruit	Check box	A box which can be checked or unchecked to select a yes/no or on/off type of option.
View: Tables / Queries / Both	Radio buttons	A set of buttons from which only one can be selected. When you click one radio button, the one that was previous selected is deselected.
OK / Cancel	Command button	A button that triggers an action. Most dialog boxes have an OK and a Cancel button, and some dialog boxes have additional buttons.

which file to open, then clicks the OK button to proceed. Alternatively, the user can back out at any time by clicking the Cancel button.

Other GUI Goodies

There's more to a full GUI than windows, menus, and dialog boxes. Here are a few other goodies that you'll find in your GUI grab-bag.

Icons

Icons are little pictures that represent objects, such as files, or actions, such as menu commands. The user can initiate an action by double-clicking on the icon. Windows 3.1 uses icons in its Program Manager to represent programs and in its File Manager to represent files. If you double-click an icon in Program Manager, the corresponding program is started. If you double-click an icon in File Manager, Windows tries to figure out which program is associated with the file, then starts the program, directing it to open the file.

Toolbars

Newer GUI programs include a toolbar. Remember that a toolbar is a collection of buttons that invoke commonly used commands. These buttons have little icons on them that are supposed to represent what each button does. For example, the Print button has a picture of a printer on it, and the Cut button pictures a pair of scissors.

Toolbars can be shown or hidden at the user's discretion, and many programs let the user customize the toolbar to include favorite commands.

Help!

All GUI programs have various forms of built-in help. Basic help is available through the Help menu, which accesses a help system supplied with the GUI operating system. The techniques for working your way through help are generally the same from one program to another.

Newer GUI programs have additional forms of help. Some programs have intelligent "Wizards" or "Assistants," which are spruced-up dialog boxes that walk you through the series of steps required to perform common tasks such as preparing a form letter or creating a new file. Other programs have "cue cards" that display step-by-step instructions on the screen while you perform common tasks.

Multiple documents

Most GUI programs allow the user to work with more than one file at a time. For example, most word processors allow you to have several documents open at a time. Each document is represented as a window within the main program window. If you maximize a document's window, it takes over the entire client area of the main program window. If you minimize the document's window, it shrinks to an icon within the client area of the main window.

In Windows, this technique of juggling several open document windows is called *MDI,* which stands for *Multiple Document Interface*. Not all Windows applications are MDI. A non-MDI application requires that you close one file before you can open another. An MDI application lets you work on several open files at once.

Compound documents: OLE!

A compound document is a document that is made up of bits and pieces that are taken from different applications. For example, a compound word processing document may include portions of spreadsheet files created by a separate spreadsheet program and graphics created by a separate graphics program.

In Windows, compound documents are created by *OLE*, which stands for *object linking and embedding*. OLE lets you embed an *object* — which is a combination of data and an identification of the program that "owns" the data — in a document. When you open the document, the object appears, either as an icon or as data within a frame. If you double-click on the object, the program that owns the data is launched so you can edit the data.

A new breed of OLE, called OLE2, allows the various programs that are responsible for working with objects to work together "seamlessly." This means that the user shouldn't be aware that a separate program has been activated. When an OLE2 object in a document is activated, that object's program takes over the main program's window, replacing the original program's menus and toolbars with its own. When the user is finished editing the embedded object, the original menus and toolbars are restored.

Compound document architecture has recently picked up a jazzy new name: *componentware*. Eventually, componentware will allow users to view their software not as "monolithic applications" but as components that may be mixed and matched at the whim of the user. The idea is to counter the recent trend of standalone programs that get bigger and bigger, instead focusing on components that become more and more specialized.

Componentware will allow you to pick and choose software like offerings at a salad bar. Two standards are duking it out for the componentware championship: Microsoft's OLE/COM (with help from Digital Equipment Corp.) and an alternative called OpenDoc, developed by Apple and embraced by an alliance of just about every computer company except Microsoft. See the sidebar, "The great componentware race," if you're interested in this stuff.

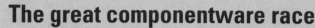

The great componentware race

Within the halls of computerdom there wages a great debate, fought fiercely by the disciples of two competing standards for component software: Microsoft's OLE vs. Apple's OpenDoc.

Object linking and embedding (OLE) has the advantage of being in place on millions of Windows-based computers, and software developers have been using OLE for years. OLE has evolved from a simple document-linking standard to a sophisticated object-based architecture.

OpenDoc, on the other hand, is new — in fact, not all of it exists yet. It doesn't have the track record that OLE has, but it also doesn't have the evolutionary burdens that OLE has.

A common line of reasoning goes like this: Sure, OpenDoc may be technically superior to OLE, but technical merit isn't enough in the competitive computer market. OLE will win the war hands down because of the broad acceptance of Windows, the clout of Microsoft, and the fact that OLE has a substantial head start.

(Of course, Microsoft rejects the notion that OpenDoc is in any way technically superior to OLE.)

Drag and drop

Drag and drop, sometimes colorfully referred to as *dragon dropping,* refers to the GUI's ability to allow the user to directly manipulate objects on the screen. The best-known example of drag and drop is the Macintosh trash can: To delete a file on a Mac, you drag the file's icon and drop it in the trash can icon. (Windows 95 uses a recycle bin — more politically correct than the Mac's trash can.) To print a file, drag its icon to the printer icon; to move a file to a network disk, drag its icon to the disk's icon.

Drag and drop has more uses than might be obvious at first. For example, you can create a compound document by dragging one document's icon into a second document. In an inventory tracking application, you could move stock from one warehouse to another by dragging and dropping icons representing inventory to icons representing warehouses. Or, in a personnel application, you could fire an employee by dragging that employee's picture to an icon representing the unemployment office.

Property inspectors

A *property inspector* is a standard way of displaying and changing the properties of an on-screen object — its color, size, name, font, alignment, and other options. In Windows 95, this is done by right-clicking the object to call up a context-sensitive menu, then selecting the Properties command to bring up the properties dialog box for the object.

Object-oriented user interface (OOUI)

Next to client/server, *object-oriented* is the hottest buzzword on the computer jargon billboard these days. The term *object-oriented* is applied to GUI operating systems that combine the notion of data files and programs to create objects. In an OOUI, the user doesn't have to know what program to launch in order to edit a document. Instead, the user just clicks on an icon that represents the document and — bam! — the program that edits the document is loaded automatically.

Windows has been able to do something like this for a long time, based on filename extensions. For example, File Manager could be told that any file that ends with .DOC is a Microsoft Word document, so if the user double clicks on a .DOC file, Microsoft Word is loaded. OOUI takes that idea several giant steps forward.

Windows 95, OS/2, and the Macintosh operating system are all OOUI systems. However, even with an OOUI, a user is still likely to think in terms of programs and data files instead of objects, and the technique of double-clicking on a document icon to open the document as nothing more than a shortcut.

Ask any Macintosh user what word processing program he or she uses and you'll probably get an answer (most likely, Microsoft Word). If OOUI were really all it's cracked up to be, Mac users wouldn't be able to tell you which word processing program they used.

How to Win a GUI Argument

Currently, four client operating systems provide graphical user interfaces:

- Microsoft Windows, including Windows 3.0, 3.1, and Windows 95.
- IBM's OS/2, including OS/2 2.0, 2.1, and OS/2 3.0 Warp.
- Apple's Macintosh, the latest incarnation of which is called System 7.5.
- X-windows, the Unix GUI that varies slightly from vendor to vendor.

Sooner or later, you're bound to end up in an argument over which GUI is better, or whether a GUI should be used at all. I don't care what side you take in these arguments. (Actually, I hope you shrug your shoulders and leave.) But in case you get drawn in, here are some facts (and pseudofacts) to throw at the enemy.

Windows 3.1

"It Works"

Pro

- Windows 3.1 has been around a long time; it's stable.
- It works.
- We already have it.
- Everyone already knows how to use it; we won't have to retrain.
- Windows 3.1 has all the basic features of other GUIs, and it's lean and mean compared with Windows 95, OS/2, or the Mac. We don't need all the new features of those other GUIs.
- Minesweeper is a great game.

Con

- Once Windows 95 takes hold, Windows 3.1 will be obsolete within a year.
- It is too program-centric.
- Two words: File Manager.
- The system resources limit cripples it, especially if you try to run several full-figured programs at once.

- ✔ OLE2 is very inefficient.
- ✔ Getting it to work on a network is a bear.

Windows 95

"It Looks Marvelous"

Pro

- ✔ It's sure to be a big success.
- ✔ Microsoft did its homework on the usability issues; it is genuinely easier to use than Windows 3.1
- ✔ It's easy to configure for network use.
- ✔ It's more of a 32-bit operating system than Windows 3.1, which means it runs more efficiently and is less likely to crash.
- ✔ I don't like IBM.
- ✔ The Freecell and Hearts games are great.

Con

- ✔ Will Microsoft ever finish it?
- ✔ It's too big. Too many disks.
- ✔ Plug & Pray.
- ✔ It doesn't run in 4MB of RAM as well as they'd like us to believe.
- ✔ They've added an application close box right where the old Maximize button used to be.
- ✔ I hate the name.
- ✔ We should wait for Windows 96.

OS/2 Warp

"Where No OS Has Gone Before!"

Pro

- ✔ It's a true 32-bit operating system.
- ✔ It runs Windows programs.

- ✔ IBM has great television commercials.
- ✔ I don't like Microsoft.
- ✔ It's even more Mac-like than the Mac.

Con

- ✔ Will it last?
- ✔ Windows 95 has better games.
- ✔ Sure it runs Windows programs, but only if you also buy Microsoft Windows.
- ✔ It doesn't run in 4MB any better than Windows 95.

The Macintosh

"Imitation Is the Sincerest Form of Flattery"

Pro

- ✔ It's the original GUI. Apple knows what they're doing.
- ✔ It's a true 32-bit operating system.
- ✔ It's a proprietary architecture, which means we don't have to deal with a million different vendors.
- ✔ It's not as expensive as it used to be.
- ✔ We can run DOS programs on Macs if we have to.
- ✔ I don't like IBM *or* Microsoft.

Con

- ✔ It's still too expensive.
- ✔ We already have PCs. Why replace them with Macs?
- ✔ It's still too proprietary. You have to deal with Apple.
- ✔ They should never have dumped Wozniak.

X-Windows

"You Don't Have to Like It: It's Unix!"

Pro

■ ✔ It's Unix.

Con

■ ✔ It's Unix.

DOS Till I Die

All right, I know this is a chapter on GUI, but if any of you DOS diehards have even made it this far, here are some pros and cons so you can jump in and argue, too.

Pro

✔ It'll run on even our oldest computers.

✔ We already have it.

✔ It works.

✔ Reaching for the mouse slows me down.

✔ GUIs are for sissies.

✔ I only run one program at a time anyway.

✔ People spend far too much time worrying about making their documents pretty.

Con

■ ✔ Wake up. Step into the 90s.

Now that you've gotten all GUI, it's time for a big helping of servers in the next chapter.

Chapter 7

Servers of All Shapes and Sizes

· ·

In This Chapter

▶ What to look for when shopping for a server

▶ The difference between file servers, database servers, and application servers

▶ Servers, processors and operating systems

▶ Fancy disk arrays

▶ Fault-tolerant servers

▶ Superservers, midrange computers, and mainframes

· ·

*W*ith few exceptions, the client computers in a client/server system are predictable: They are almost always desktop computers with Intel processors running Microsoft Windows. Sometimes they run OS/2, sometimes they're Macintoshes, and in extreme cases they're Unix workstations, but by and large they're DOS/Windows computers.

The server computers are another matter. Servers can be just about anything: souped-up desktop computers, specialized Intel-based "superservers," minicomputers, mainframe computers, or even science-fiction-class supercomputers.

This chapter is an overview of the various types of computers that can be employed as servers in a client/server system and the operating systems that run on them.

What's Important in a Server

The following sections describe some of the more important things to look for when settling on a server for your client/server environment.

Scalability

I have a coffee mug that is imprinted with various laws of computer programming. One of them reads:

Any computer program will expand to fill all available memory.

Once users discover how wonderful the new client/server system is, they'll fall in love with it and actually *use* it, which is probably the last thing anyone expected. Pretty soon *everyone* will want to use the new system. And since the new system gives your company a huge competitive advantage, business will boom and the company will go into expansion mode, creating even more demands on the system.

You can bet that any client/server system that starts with just 20 users will soon have 50. A system that starts with 500 users will soon have 1,000. And so on. You get the picture.

Scalability refers to the ability to increase the capacity of the server without unreasonable hassle. It is a major mistake to build a system around a server that is already configured at its maximum capacity. As users are added to the system, transaction volume increases, and more and more data is accumulated, the demands on the server computer will rise. Sooner or later, the demands will exceed the server's ability to serve.

Scalability can be summed up as follows: Don't paint yourself into a corner. Whatever server platform you choose, start at the bottom end of its capabilities, not the top end.

Scalability considerations include:

- ✔ Increasing memory to handle additional users
- ✔ Adding additional processors to handle increased workload
- ✔ Installing additional disk storage
- ✔ Operating system limits (number of users, total amount of disk, and so on)

Fault tolerance

Fault tolerance is what you have after 20 years of marriage (I hope). With computers, it refers to the ability of the server computer to recover from hardware failures. Some degree of fault tolerance is desirable in all client/server systems, but it is especially important in mission-critical applications.

The two most common forms of fault tolerance are backup power supplies and RAID disk subsystems. Together, these two features safeguard the server against the two most likely causes of failure: loss of power and a disk crash. To be fault tolerant enough for mission-critical applications, more is required.

For complete fault tolerance, every component of the computer system must be duplicated. The redundant components include:

✔ Processor

✔ Memory

✔ I/O bus (the slots inside the computer that I/O [input/output] devices plug into)

✔ Network interface card

✔ Disk controllers and disk subsystem

✔ Power supply

These redundant systems run in parallel, perform identical calculations, repeating the same processes. It's kind of like that annoying game of shadow kids learn in kindergarten. Want to play shadow? What to play shadow? No. No. Stop it. Stop it. I really mean it! I really mean it!

Besides running systems in parallel, the fault-tolerant computer must constantly monitor each redundant component to check for errors. If a failure occurs in one of the components, the failing component is deactivated. The remaining system can continue to operate while the failed component is repaired.

✔ Fault-tolerant computers are very expensive, and are thus used only for Mission-Critical People-Will-Die-Or-We'll-All-Go-Broke kind of applications. Examples include automated teller machines, stock market trading systems, air traffic control systems, and so on.

✔ Probably the best-known example of a fault-tolerant computer is on the Space Shuttle. In typical NASA over-engineered style, *five* redundant computers run the shuttle's navigation systems.

Service and support

Service and support are often overlooked factors when picking computers. If the server computer goes down, the entire system goes down. How long will it take to get it fixed? Don't cut corners on the maintenance contract.

If the application is critical, make sure that the contract provides for some-one to service the computer on-site within a certain time period, 24 hours or less.

Kinds of Servers

Server computers have various uses in client/server systems. The following sections describe the most common uses for server computers.

File servers

File servers provide centralized disk storage that can be conveniently shared by client computers on the network. The most common use is to store pro-grams and data files. For example, a small workgroup might use disk space on a file server to store their word processing documents.

File servers must ensure that two users do not try to update the same file at the same time. They do this by *locking* a file while a user updates the file, so that other users cannot access the file until the first user is finished. For doc-ument files (for example, word processing or spreadsheet files), the whole file is locked. For database files, the lock can be applied just to the portion of the file that contains the record or records being updated.

- ✔ Most LANs are based on a file server model: Several client computers are connected to a file server to share program and data files. The popu-lar NetWare network operating system from Novell assumes that one or more computers on a network are dedicated file servers.

- ✔ LAN vendors and consultants sometimes refer to their systems as "client/server" because they use file servers. However, a simple file-server network doesn't qualify as a client/server system because the application workload is not shared between the client computers and the file server computer. Instead, the client computer does all the work. The file server just acts like a remote disk drive. ■

- ✔ File servers often double as print servers, which are described next.

Print servers

One of the main reasons small businesses install networks is to share expen-sive laser printers. In some cases, a computer is dedicated to function as a *print server*, whose sole purpose is to collect information being sent to the printer by client computers and print it in an orderly fashion.

> ✔ A single computer may double as a file server and a print server, but performance will be improved if separate print and file server computers are used.

> ✔ With inexpensive laser printers running about $500 each, it's tempting to just give each user his or her own laser printer rather than mess around with print servers. But you get what you pay for. Instead of buying five $500 printers for five users, you might be better off buying one $2,500 laser printer and sharing it.

> ✔ Other resources besides printers can be shared with dedicated servers. Common examples include modems, fax, and CD-ROM.

Database servers

A *database server* is a server computer that runs a SQL-based database management system (DBMS). Client computers send SQL requests to the database server, which accesses the stored database to process the request and returns the results to the client computer.

SQL is the standard language for accessing relational databases. ▪

Database servers are common in client/server applications. So common, in fact, that I've devoted all of Part III to databases. Chapter 10 is an introduction to databases in general (what a database is, what a relational database is, what SQL is, and other important questions), and Chapter 11 explains what SQL is in more detail. Chapter 12 explains how programmers include SQL requests in their programs.

Application servers

An *application server* is a server computer that actually runs application programs. Application servers are sometimes used when mainframe-based applications are downsized. For example, an AS/400 minicomputer might be used to run programs that were previously run on a mainframe.

Interesting Server Gadgets

Server computers are usually equipped with some or all of the interesting hardware gadgets described in the following sections.

Disk arrays: It's a RAID!

A *RAID* disk array is a fancy type of disk storage that hardly ever fails. It works by lumping several disk drives together and treating them as if they were one humongous drive. RAID uses some fancy techniques devised by computer nerds at Berkeley that guarantee that if one of the disk drives in the RAID system fails, no data is lost. The disk drive that failed can be removed and repaired, and the data that was on it can be reconstructed from the other drives.

- ✔ RAID stands for "Redundant Array of Inexpensive Disks," but that's not on the test.

- ✔ A RAID system is usually housed in a separate cabinet that includes its own RAID disk controller. It is sometimes called a *disk subsystem*.

- ✔ In the coolest RAID systems, the disk drives themselves are *hot swappable*. That means that you can remove one of the disk drives while the RAID system continues to operate. Network users won't even know that one of the disks has been removed, since the RAID system reconstructs the data that was on the replaced disk using data from the other disks. When the failed disk has been replaced, the new disk is brought on-line without a hitch.

RAID comes in five flavors, of which only two are important. In *RAID-1*, two copies of each disk drive are maintained. One is the primary, the other is a backup in case the primary disk fails. RAID-1 is called *disk mirroring* if the two disk drives are attached to a single disk controller. If separate disk controllers are used for each drive, it is called *disk duplexing*.

RAID-5 is the most common type of RAID. It spreads data out over several drives, maintaining special Error Correction Codes (ECC) so that lost data can be reconstructed.

The other RAID flavors aren't commonly used, so they can be safely ignored.

RISC vs. CISC processors

One of the mighty debates raging in the halls of computerdom is the debate over RISC versus CISC processors. CISC stands for *Complex Instruction Set Computer*, which refers to the growing complexity of processor chips. The little elves that make computer chips keep trying to cram more and more transistors onto one chip. For example, Intel's earliest processor, the 8088, had *only* 40,000 transistors. (Keep in mind that processor chips are about as big as your thumbnail.) Intel's latest processor, the Pentium, has 1.3 million transistors, and the upcoming P6 chip is rumored to have 10 million.

Do more transistors make for a better, faster, or more powerful computer? Not necessarily. *RISC* processors are built on the premise that simplicity is best when it comes to CPU design. RISC stands for *Reduced Instruction Set Computer.*

The basic idea behind RISC is to limit the number of different instructions the CPU can process, then focus on designing the CPU so that it can execute those instructions blazingly fast, much faster than CISC processors can execute their more complex instructions.

By keeping the CPU simple, RISC designers can optimize the performance of their computers and keep the price down. A typical RISC CPU is twice as fast as an Intel CISC processor and half the price.

Why choose a CISC chip then? Because Intel's microprocessors are CISC chips, and the overwhelming majority of PC applications are designed for Intel chips.

One of the best-known RISC processors is the PowerPC, a chip designed jointly by IBM, Apple, and Motorola. The PowerPC is comparable in power to an Intel Pentium processor.

✔ RISC processors are usually used in high-powered engineering and graphics workstations, like the ones used to generate those stunning animation sequences in Disney movies.

✔ Server computers built with RISC processors usually run some variant of the Unix operating system. RISC versions of Windows NT are also available.

✔ It used to be that RISC processors had an overwhelming advantage over CISC processors for floating-point calculations, which aren't too important in most client/server applications but are very important for engineering applications.

Multiple processors

If one computer is fast, wouldn't two computers be faster? That's the idea behind *multiprocessing*, which puts two or more CPU chips in a single computer to beef up performance.

You'd think that two CPUs would be twice as fast as one, but unfortunately life isn't that simple. There's a lot of overhead involved in coordinating the work of two or more processors. Plus, multiprocessing won't work unless you use a server operating system and database server software that support multiprocessing; otherwise, the extra CPUs will sit idle.

Two forms of multiprocessing are in vogue: asymmetric and symmetric.

When *asymmetric multiprocessing* is used, processors are dedicated to specific tasks such as handling I/O requests or printing. For example, if the server computer has two CPUs, one might be responsible for handling the operating system and the database system, while the other is dedicated to handling disk input and output.

In *symmetric multiprocessing*, the CPUs are free to handle whatever work is waiting to be done, in a sort of "first come, first served" manner. In other words, the CPUs don't have to be dedicated to specific tasks such as printer or disk I/O.

- ✔ Symmetric multiprocessing is sometimes called SMP. Asymmetric multiprocessing doesn't have its own handy TLA.

- ✔ Don't confuse *multiprocessing* with *multitasking*. *Multiprocessing* refers to a computer with more than one CPU. *Multitasking* refers to the ability of a single CPU to execute more than one task at a time.

- ✔ A relatively new type of computer architecture called *parallel processing* employs dozens or even hundreds of CPUs in a single computer. For example, IBM's POWER Parallel systems can utilize up to 512 RISC processors. These systems are currently used mostly by math and engineering nerds trying to find new prime numbers or calculate *Pi* to previously unknown decimal positions, but parallel computers are starting to make their way into client/server systems.

Server Choices

Four basic choices are available for server computer platforms: LAN servers, superservers, midrange systems, and mainframes. The following sections summarize the pros and cons of each.

LAN servers

The simplest server computer choice is to use Intel-based LAN servers, which are widely available from many sources, including mail-order and discount computer stores.

The following options should be carefully considered when configuring a LAN server:

- ✔ **Processor:** Opt for a fast version of Intel's latest processor chip. Currently, a 90 or 100MHz Pentium is the chip du jour, though many 486DX2 (66MHz) systems are still being sold.

✔ **Memory:** Get as much as possible, at least 16MB and preferably 32MB or more. Make sure that the system is expandable to 128MB or more memory.

✔ **Bus:** The bus is the row of slots into which peripheral devices such as network cards and video controllers can be plugged. Most LAN servers utilize an EISA expansion bus, which provides high-speed data transfer between the CPU and peripheral devices. In addition, a high-speed local bus (PCI, VL, or VLB) is desirable.

✔ **Disk Drives:** Most desktop computers use inexpensive disk drives called *IDE* drives. These drives are adequate for individual use, but for server use, where performance is more important, another type of drive known as *SCSI* is usually used.. Make sure the server's cabinet has plenty of room to add additional disk drives. For best performance, use an EISA bus SCSI controller. RAID disk subsystems can also be used, though they are usually mounted in a separate case.

✔ **Video:** Fancy graphics aren't important for a server computer. Many are sold with modest monochrome VGA monitors. Refer back to Chapter 5 for more information about various types of video displays.

✔ **Power Supply and Case:** LAN servers usually come in oversized cases that have plenty of room for expansion. Count the empty drive bays — the spaces where disk drives can be added — to make sure you can add additional disk drives, CD-ROM drives, tape backup, and so on. Also, make sure the power supply is adequate — 300 watts is typical.

Here are a couple of additional notes about LAN servers:

✔ LAN servers are the simplest to install and operate and are ideal for small networks of 50 or fewer users.

✔ LAN servers have limited scalability. You can add additional memory up to the computer's memory limit, and you can add additional disk storage until all available disk bays are full, but you're stuck with the single-processor design. If you outgrow the raw processing horsepower of a LAN server, you must either upgrade it with a faster processor (if you don't already have the fastest one available), or add a second LAN server.

✔ The problem with LAN servers is that they're kind of like Tribles: they tend to multiply. You start with just one, then you outgrow it and add another, then another and another, and pretty soon you have a real mess on your hands. Some organizations find they have 50 or 100 or more dedicated LAN servers on their networks. You can imagine the management nightmares that must be contended with on a network with 100 servers.

Superservers

To ease the burdens of managing a gaggle of file servers, some network man-agers are turning to *superservers*, unbelievably high-powered computers that can single-handedly take on the duties of half a dozen or more mere LAN servers. Superservers employ multiple CPUs, gobs of memory, specialized I/O processors for high-speed disk I/O, and other ingenious gadgets meant to optimize the computer for use as a network server.

Superservers aren't cheap — they sell for tens of thousands of dollars, with the best ones priced at over $100,000. But they're often less expensive than an equivalent number of ordinary LAN computers, they're more efficient, and they're easier to manage.

Low-end superservers — in the $20,000 price range — typically provide two 486 or Pentium processors, 32MB of memory, and several GB of disk space. Top-of-the-line superservers can support as much as 1GB of system memory, 32 internal disk drives, and up to six Pentium processors. Whew!

✔ Superservers are more scalable than ordinary LAN servers. Unless you purchase the superserver already maxed out, you can usually upgrade it by adding additional memory, disk storage, and additional processors.

✔ One common argument against the use of superservers is the old "don't put all your eggs in one basket" line. What if the superserver breaks? The counter to this argument is that superservers are loaded with state-of-the-art fault-tolerance features that make it unlikely that they'll ever break. In contrast, if you use ten separate file servers, you actually increase the likelihood that one of them will fail, probably sooner than you'd like.

✔ If you didn't catch the "Tribles" reference, you definitely need to watch more Star Trek reruns.

Midrange systems

A decade ago, midrange systems were called *minicomputers*. Minicomputers are obsolete now, of course, so minicomputer makers now call their products *midrange computers*.

A midrange computer such as an IBM AS/400 is a suitable candidate for a server computer in a client/server system. I'll pick on the AS/400 for a moment, because it is the most widely used midrange computer. The AS/400 has many advantages as a server computer in a client/server environment:

✔ Its operating system, though proprietary, has a built-in relational data-base server called DB2/400, which IBM claims to be "The world's most widely used multiuser relational database," kind of long for a bumper sticker but a good slogan nonetheless. The AS/400 is optimized for DB2/400, so it is very fast.

✔ The AS/400 is a very scalable system. AS/400 "Advanced Servers" — designed especially for client/server environments — can be configured with as much as 1.5GB of memory, 259GB of disk storage and a wide range of processor options.

An AS/400 isn't cheap, but then again neither is an equivalent superserver or an equivalent number of simple LAN servers.

✔ A drawback of an AS/400 is that it represents one more proprietary system that must be learned. If you already have staff proficient in Unix or NetWare, and no one in the organization knows scratch about AS/400, you might want to stick with something more familiar.

Mainframes as servers

A final option for the server in a client/server environment is to use the mainframe itself as the server. If you're setting up a client/server system that will be used by 50 users, you probably can't justify purchasing a $4,000,000 mainframe when a $60,000 superserver will do. But if the company already has a mainframe, and if the data required by the application is already on the mainframe, then the mainframe may well be the best candidate for the server.

In fact, the mainframe-as-server idea is so compelling that I've devoted a whole chapter to it — Chapter 19. Feel free to skip ahead if you want.

Server Operating Systems

Several choices are available for server operating systems. The following sections outline the pros and cons of each choice.

Unix

Unix originally began as a time-sharing operating system for minicomputers, but has become one of the most popular server operating systems in client/server environments.

Unlike other server operating systems, Unix is sold in different variations by several vendors. There is no one "true" Unix. Instead, there are many different versions that look the same but aren't compatible. If you go with Unix, the best version to go with is the one that comes bundled with the server computer you use.

Table 7-1 lists the major Unix vendors and the version of Unix they sell.

Table 7-1: Unix variants

Vendor	Unix Variant
Sun	Solaris
SCO (Santa Cruz Operations)	SCO Unix System 5
IBM	AIX
Novell	UnixWare
DEC	OSF/1
Hewlett-Packard	HP/UX

✔ One of the great Unix myths is that Unix implies "Open Systems." Actually, Unix versions are as proprietary as can be, and "proprietary" operating systems such as VMS (DEC VAX) and OS/400 (IBM AS/400) have become as open as Unix.

Remember that "open systems" refers to computer systems that are designed to work with computers from different vendors. ▪

✔ Unix is the operating system of choice for database servers.

NetWare

Novell's NetWare is the most popular operating system for LAN file servers. Three versions of NetWare are in widespread use:

NetWare 2.2. NetWare 2.2 is a 16-bit operating system that was designed for 80286-based computers. It is primarily used in small networks — 10 to 15 users — for simple file and printer sharing. It isn't suitable for client/server use.

NetWare 3.12. Netware 3.12 is a 32-bit version of NetWare designed to operate on 386 or better computers. Although it is used mostly as a file and printer server, NetWare 3.12 supports add-in modules called NetWare Loadable Modules (NLMs). NLMs are what make NetWare 3.12 useful in client/server environments.

NetWare 4.1. The newest version of NetWare is a major step up from NetWare 3.12. The most significant improvement over NetWare 3.12 is a feature called *NetWare Directory Services* (*NDS*) that keeps track of resources throughout the network by name, so that users do not have to know what server owns the resources they need. (This capability is often called *global directory service*.)

Windows NT Server 3.5

Microsoft's Windows NT Server 3.5 is a part of Microsoft BackOffice, a suite of products designed for client/server computing. Here are some of the more interesting features of Windows NT Server 3.5:

- ✔ In addition to the standard Intel version, which requires a 486 or Pentium processor, versions of NT are available for several RISC systems.
- ✔ NT Server supports symmetric multiprocessing, up to 32 processors.
- ✔ It provides global directory services similar to NetWare 4.1.
- ✔ NT Server is the way to go if you want an all-Microsoft client/server solution: Windows 3.11 or Windows 95 on client computers, NT Server 3.5 as the network operating system, and Microsoft SQL Server as the database server. There's a lot to be said for obtaining all the pieces from a single vendor.

For more information on SQL servers, look ahead to Chapter 11.

OS/2 LAN Server Advanced 4.0

OS/2 LAN Server Advanced 4.0 (how's that for a catchy name?) is IBM's latest server version of OS/2. OS/2 has been much maligned in the press, but has been quietly chugging along at the heart of tens of thousands of client/server networks for years. Here are some of OS/2's more noteworthy features:

- ✔ OS/2 is available for Intel 486 and Pentium systems, plus a PowerPC RISC version is promised soon.
- ✔ Symmetric multiprocessing is supported, up to 16 processors.
- ✔ OS/2 provides global directory services similar to those of NetWare 4.1 and NT Server 3.5.
- ✔ OS/2 supports OS/2 versions of IBM's DB2 database server and CICS transaction monitor. Applications developed for DB2 or CICS can be scaled up through IBM's AS/400 servers to its mainframe servers without rewriting application code.

Now that you know what you need to know about sever computers, the next chapter will show how servers are connected to clients via local area networks.

Chapter 8

Understanding Local Area Networks

· ·

In This Chapter

▶ Ethernet

▶ Types of network cables

▶ Cable layouts and hubs

▶ Network interface cards

▶ Alternatives to Ethernet

▶ The dreaded OSI networking model

· ·

*R*emember the basic definition of client/server computing way back in Chapter 1? (This *will* be on the test.) Okay, I'll give you a hint: It divides a computer application into three basic components — a client, a server, and a (fill in the blank). Yes folks, we've finally come to the third of the basic elements, the thing that holds it all together — the network. This chapter introduces you to local area networks, with heavy emphasis on Ethernet, the most popular kind of local area network. In Chapter 9 you'll find out about wide area networks. That will about wrap up the basics, and you'll be ready to charge ahead into client/server databases and other neat stuff.

Local area networks (LANs) serve as the infrastructure for client/server applications. The LAN relays requests for services from the client computer to the server computer and carries the resulting data back to the client. There are several different ways to set up LANs, but the most common is called Ethernet.

What Is Ethernet?

Ethernet is a standardized way of connecting computers together to create a network. You can think of Ethernet as a sort of "municipal building code" for networks: It specifies what kind of cables should be used, how the cables should be connected together, how long the cables can be, how computers transmit data to one another using the cables, and more.

There are two other popular network building codes you may have heard of: token ring and ARCnet. Ethernet is more commonly used than token ring because it is less expensive. Ethernet is used more than ARCnet because ARCnet is slower. First I'll focus on Ethernet; I'll describe token ring later in this chapter. I'll conveniently ignore ARCnet, since it's not used much.

Some people treat Ethernet, token ring, and ARCnet like religions they are willing to die for. To a token ring zealot, Ethernet represents the Antichrist. Ethernet fanatics often claim you can hear satanic messages if you send data backward through a token ring network. Both treat ARCnet as if it were a Stone Age religion, possibly because of the discovery of paintings of ARCnet networking diagrams found on the walls of caves in southern France.

Do *not* engage an Ethernet, token ring, or ARCnet zealot in a discussion about the merits of his or her network beliefs over opponents' beliefs. It is futile. ∎

Without regard to the technical merits of Ethernet, token ring, or ARCnet, the fact is that the majority of local area networks use Ethernet. 'Nough said.

Ethernet is a set of standards for the infrastructure a network is built on. All the server operating systems I've discussed in this book can operate on an Ethernet network. If you build your network on a solid Ethernet base, you can easily change server operating systems later. ∎

✔ Ethernet is often referred to by network gurus as *802.3* (pronounced *eight-oh-two-dot-three*) because that's the official designation used by the IEEE (pronounced *Eye-triple-ee*), a group of electrical engineers who wear bow ties and have nothing better to do than argue about inductance all day long. It's a good thing, though, because if it weren't for them, you wouldn't be able to mix and match Ethernet components made by different companies.

✔ Ethernet transmits data at a rate of 10 million bits per second, or 10Mbps. Because there are 8 bits in a byte, that translates into roughly 1.2 million bytes per second. In practice, Ethernet can't move information that fast because data must be transmitted in packages of no more than 1,500 bytes, called *packets*. So, a 150K file would have to be split into 100 packets. ∎

This speed has nothing to do with how fast electrical signals move on the cable. The electrical signals themselves travel at about 70% the speed of light, or, as Captain Picard would say, "Warp factor point-seven-oh."

Who cares what CSMA/CD stands for?

Besides specifying the mechanical and electrical characteristics of network cables, Ethernet specifies the techniques used to control the flow of information over the network cables. The technique Ethernet uses is called CSMA/CD, which stands for "carrier sense multiple access with collision detection." This is a mouthful, but if we take it apart piece by piece, you'll get an idea of how Ethernet works (as if you want to know).

Carrier sense means that whenever a computer wants to send a message on the network cable, it first listens to the cable to see whether anyone else is already sending a message. If it doesn't hear any other messages on the cable, the computer assumes it is free to send one.

Multiple access means that there is nothing to prevent two or more computers from trying to send a message at the same time. Sure, each computer listens before sending. But suppose that two computers listen, hear nothing, and then proceed to send their messages? Picture what happens when you and someone else arrive at a four-way stop sign at the same time. You wave the other driver on, he or she waves you on, you wave, he or she waves, you all wave, and then you both end up going at the same time.

Collision detection means that after a computer sends a message on the network, it listens carefully to see whether it crashed into another message, like listening for the screeching of brakes at the four-way stop. If the computer hears the screeching of brakes, it waits for a random period of time and tries to send the message again. Because the delay is random, two messages that collide will be sent again after different delay periods, so a second collision is unlikely.

Wasn't that a waste of time?

Three Types of Ethernet Cable

Now I'm going to tell you far more about network cables than you probably need to know. This information may come in handy, though, for making small talk at client/server conventions.

An Ethernet network can be constructed using three different types of cable.

1. Thick coax (called *yellow cable* because it's usually yellow).

2. Thin coax (called *thinnet* because it's thinner than the yellow stuff, or *cheapernet* because it's cheaper than the yellow stuff, or just *coax* because it's the only kind of coax that's used much anymore).

3. Twisted pair, which looks like phone cable. Twisted pair cable is sometimes called *UTP* or *10baseT* cable, for reasons I'll try hard not to explain later.

By the way, *coax* is short for *coaxial*. I could tell you what coaxial means, but you don't need to know. Take my word for it.

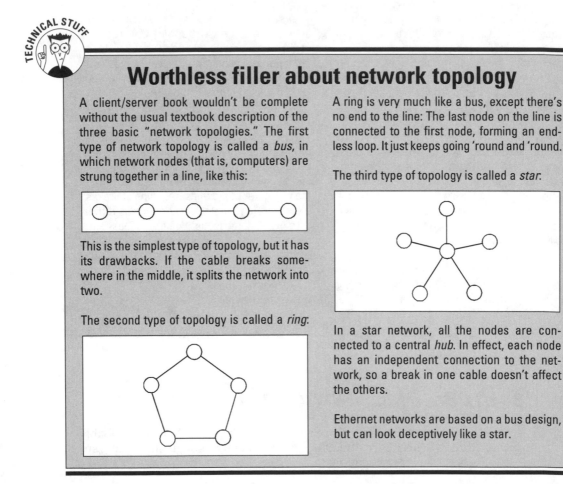

Worthless filler about network topology

A client/server book wouldn't be complete without the usual textbook description of the three basic "network topologies." The first type of network topology is called a *bus*, in which network nodes (that is, computers) are strung together in a line, like this:

This is the simplest type of topology, but it has its drawbacks. If the cable breaks somewhere in the middle, it splits the network into two.

The second type of topology is called a *ring*:

A ring is very much like a bus, except there's no end to the line: The last node on the line is connected to the first node, forming an endless loop. It just keeps going 'round and 'round.

The third type of topology is called a *star*:

In a star network, all the nodes are connected to a central *hub*. In effect, each node has an independent connection to the network, so a break in one cable doesn't affect the others.

Ethernet networks are based on a bus design, but can look deceptively like a star.

The yellow stuff

The original Ethernet networks were wired with thick, heavy cable called thick coax, or yellow cable, because of its color. Thick coax isn't used much anymore, especially for small networks, because it is expensive, heavy, and not very flexible. (I mean that literally: it's difficult to make yellow cable bend around tight corners.)

- ✔ The yellow stuff is less susceptible to interference from mongo-magnets and motors and what not, so it's still used sometimes in factories, warehouses, nuclear test sites, Frankenstein laboratories, and so on.

- ✔ Yellow cable can be strung for greater distances than other types of Ethernet cable. A single run of yellow cable (called a *segment*) can be as long as 500 meters.

- ✔ The way yellow cable is attached to individual computers is weird. Usually, a long length of yellow cable is run along a path that takes it near each computer on the network. Each computer must be connected to the yellow cable via a device called a *transceiver*. The transceiver usually includes a *vampire tap*, a clamp-like thingamabob that taps into the yellow cable without cutting and splicing it. The transceiver is connected to the network interface card (more about these soon) by means of an *AUI* cable. (*AUI* stands for *attached unit interface*, not that it matters.) ■

- ✔ I think you can see why the yellow stuff isn't used much anymore. It's really too bad, because the yellow stuff would coordinate so well with the cover of this book.

Thin coax

The most common type of cable used to wire up client computers is thin coaxial cable, usually called *thin coax* or sometimes *thinnet*. Thin coax is less expensive than yellow cable, not only because the cable itself is less expensive, but also because separate transceivers aren't required to attach computers to the cable. (Thin coax does use transceivers, but the transceiver is built into the adapter card.) Figure 8-1 shows what thin coax cable looks like.

Figure 8-1:
Thin coax
cable has a
single prong.

Thin coax is about 1/5 inch in diameter, so it's lighter and more flexible than the yellow stuff. You can easily wrap it around corners, drape it over doorways, around potted plants, and so on.

You attach thin coax to the network interface card by using a goofy twist-on connector called a *BNC connector*.

Whereas yellow cable is usually wired with a single length of cable that is tapped into using vampire taps, thin coax is run with separate lengths of cable. At each computer, a tee-connector is used to connect two cables to the network interface card. Figure 8-2 shows a typical thin coax arrangement. One length of thin coax connects the first computer to the second, another length connects the second computer to the third, and yet another length of cable connects the third computer to the fourth.

✔ A special plug called a *terminator* is required at each end of a series of thin coax cables. The terminator prevents data from spilling out the end of the cable and staining the carpet.

✔ The cables strung end to end from one terminator to the other are collectively called a *segment*. The maximum length of a thin coax segment is 185 meters, which is about 600 feet. You can connect as many as 30 computers on one segment. To span a distance greater than 185 meters, or to connect more than 30 computers, you must use two or more segments with a funky device called a *repeater* to connect each segments.

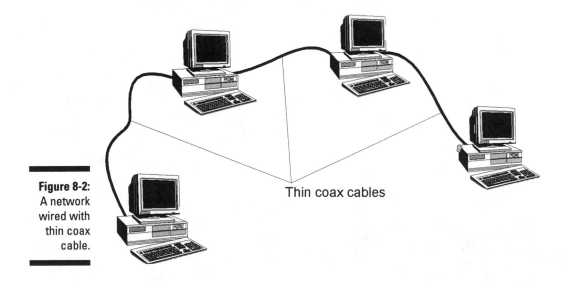

Figure 8-2:
A network wired with thin coax cable.

Thin coax cables

Unshielded twisted pair (UTP) cable

In recent years, a new type of cable has become popular with Ethernet networks: unshielded twisted pair cable, or UTP. UTP cable is even cheaper than thin coax cable, and, best of all, many modern buildings are already wired with twisted pair, because this type of wiring is often used with modern phone systems. Figure 8-3 shows a twisted pair cable.

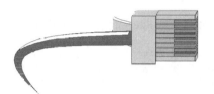

Figure 8-3: Unshielded twisted pair cable is used in phone systems as well as networks.

The biggest difference between using thin coax and UTP cable is that when you use UTP, you must also use a separate device called a *hub*. When you use UTP cable to construct an Ethernet network, you connect the computers in a star arrangement, as Figure 8-4 illustrates. In the center of this star is the hub.

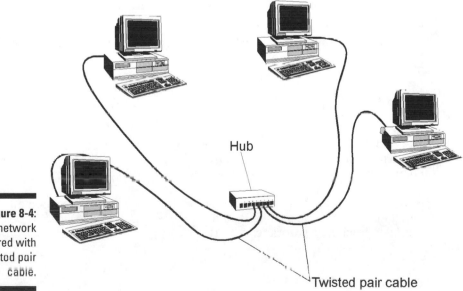

Hub

Figure 8-4:
A network
wired with
twisted pair
cable.

Twisted pair cable

Depending on the model, Ethernet hubs let you connect from 4 to 24 computers using twisted pair cable. Most hubs have connectors for 8 or 12 cables. Hubs are also sometimes called *concentrators* or *multiport repeaters*.

An advantage of this star arrangement is that if one cable goes bad, only the computer attached to that cable is affected; the rest of the network continues to chug along. With thin coax, a bad cable affects not only the computer it's connected to, but all computers unfortunate enough to lie beyond the bad cable.

UTP cable consists of pairs of thin wire twisted around each other; several such pairs are gathered up inside an outer insulating jacket. Ethernet uses two pairs of wires, or four wires all together. The number of pairs in a UTP cable varies, but is often more than two. UTP with four pairs (that is, eight wires) can be used for both a phone system and a computer network.

✔ UTP cable comes in five grades, level 1 through level 5. The higher the level number, the greater the amount of protection the cable provides from outside electrical interference. Of course, higher-level cables are also more expensive. Ethernet networks should be cabled with level 3 or better. Level 5 is preferable.

✔ UTP cable connectors look like modular phone connectors, but are slightly different. UTP connectors are officially called *RJ-45 connectors*. (Some phone systems use RJ-45 connectors.)

✔ Unlike thin coax, UTP cable is rarely sold in prefabricated lengths. You must buy bulk cable, cut it to the length you want, and attach the connectors with a special tool. However, RJ-45 connections are a lot easier to do than BNC connections.

✔ The maximum allowable cable length between the hub and the computer is 100 meters, or about 300 feet.

Hubba Hubba

As I said, the biggest difference between using thin coax and UTP cable is that when you use UTP, you also must use a hub. Hubs add an extra layer of complexity to the network, but they provide several advantages.

Hubs make it easier to add new computers to the network, move computers, find and correct cable problems, and service computers that need to be removed from the network temporarily.

Ten base what?

The IEEE, in its infinite wisdom, has decreed that the following names shall be used to designate the three types of cable used with 802.3 networks (in other words, with Ethernet):

✔ *10base5* is thick coax cable (the yellow stuff).

✔ *10base2* is thin coax cable (thinnet).

✔ *10baseT* is unshielded twisted pair cable (UTP).

In each moniker, the *10* means that the cable operates at 10Mbps and *base* means the cable is used for baseband networks as opposed to broadband networks (don't ask). The *5* in *10base5* is the maximum length of a yellow cable segment: 500 meters; the *2* in *10base2* stands for 200 meters, which is approximately the 185-meter maximum segment length for thinnet (for a group of engineers, the IEEE is odd; I didn't know the word "approximately" is in an engineer's vocabulary, except at Intel of course); and the *T* in *10baseT* stands for "twisted."

Of these three official monikers, 10baseT is the only one that's frequently used; 10base5 and 10base2 are usually just called *thick* and *thin*.

Here are the ins and outs of working with 10baseT hubs:

✔ Because you must run a cable from each computer to the hub, the hub is usually in a central location so that cables can be easily routed to it.

✔ The hub requires electrical power, so make sure there's an electrical outlet handy.

✔ You can connect hubs to one another as shown in Figure 8-5; this is called *daisy-chaining*. When you daisy-chain hubs, you connect a cable to a standard port on one of the hubs and the daisy-chain port on the other hub. Be sure to read the instructions that came with the hub to make sure that you daisy-chain them properly.

✔ You can daisy-chain no more than three hubs together. If you have more computers than can be accommodated by three hubs, don't panic. Most hubs have a BNC connection on the back so that you can connect them together via thin coax cable. The three-hub limit doesn't apply when you connect the hubs using thin coax cable.

Network Interface Cards

To connect a computer to the network, a *network interface card* (or *NIC*) is installed in the computer, and the network cable is connected to the NIC.

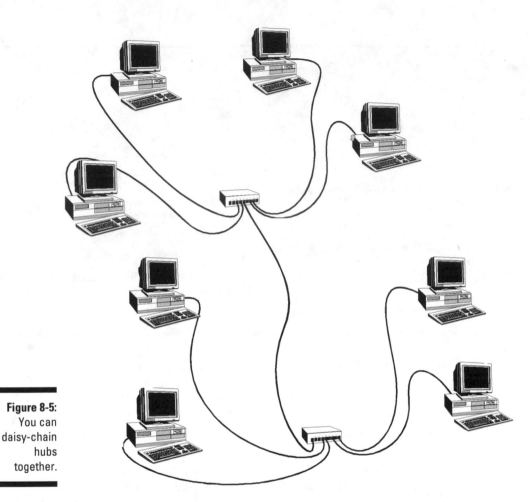

Figure 8-5:
You can
daisy-chain
hubs
together.

Naturally, the connector on the NIC must match the type of connector used on the cable. For thin coax wiring, the NIC must have a BNC connector. For twisted pair wiring, an RJ-45 connector is required.

Some network cards provide two or three connectors. I've seen them in every combination: BNC and AUI, RJ-45 and AUI, BNC and RJ-45, and all three.

It's not a bad idea to select a card that has both BNC and RJ-45 connectors. That way, you can switch from thin coax to twisted pair or vice versa without buying new network cards. ■

The standard of compatibility for network interface cards is the NE2000, which used to be manufactured by Novell but is now made by Eagle. If a card is NE2000-compatible, you can use it with just about any network.

Network cards can be a bit tricky to set up, and each one has its nuances.
You'll simplify your life a bit if you pick one card and stick with it. Try not to
mix and match network cards. ■

Token Ring: The Ethernet Alternative

Ethernet may be the most commonly used network, but it's not the only
game in town. In companies where IBM got its foot in the door long ago and
then managed to board up the door, token ring is often used for local area
networks. Token ring was originally marketed by IBM, but most networking
companies now offer token ring as well as Ethernet products.

Like Ethernet, token ring is a building code for networks. Token ring uses a
more orderly approach to sending packets through the network. (Remember
that a packet is a chunk of data of a manageable size.) Instead of sending a
message whenever it wants to, a computer on a token ring network must wait
its turn. A special packet called the *token* is constantly passed through the
network from computer to computer. A computer can send a packet of data
only when it has the token. In this way, token ring ensures that collisions
won't happen.

As its name suggests, token ring networks are wired in a ring pattern, as
shown in Figure 8-6.

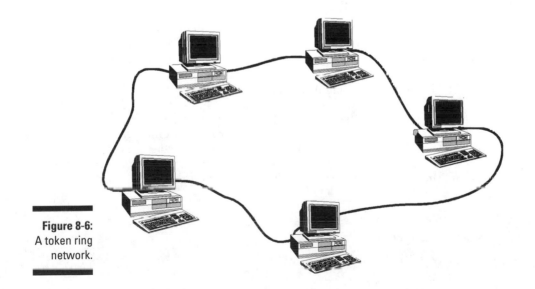

Figure 8-6:
A token ring
network.

Sometimes, a computer with a defective network interface card will accidentally swallow the token. If the token disappears for too long, the network assumes it's been swallowed, so the network generates a new token.

Two versions of token ring are in use. The older version runs at 4Mbps. The newer version runs at 16Mbps, plus it allows two tokens to exist at once, which makes the network even faster.

An ongoing warfare exists between Ethernet and token ring fanatics. Token ring fanatics love to point out that Ethernet can get bogged down if the network gets really busy and messages start colliding like crazy, whereas token ring is cool under pressure. Ethernet fanatics counter that while this may be true in theory, few networks are busy enough for this to be of concern, and Ethernet is simpler, less expensive and more flexible than token ring. ■

The OSI Networking Model

Now that you've mastered the nuts and bolts (well, actually, cables and connections) of Ethernet and token ring, let's move to a more abstract level of network design, the *OSI model*.

OSI sounds like the name of a top-secret government agency you hear about only in Tom Clancy novels. What it really stands for, as far as this book is concerned, is *open system interconnection*, as in the Open System Interconnection Reference Model, affectionately known as the OSI model.

The OSI model breaks the various aspects of a computer network into seven distinct layers. These layers are like the layers of an onion: Each successive layer envelops the layer beneath it, hiding its details from the levels above. The OSI model is also like an onion in that if you start to peel it apart to have a look inside, you're bound to shed a few tears.

The OSI model is not itself a networking standard in the same sense as Ethernet and token ring. The OSI model is a framework into which the various networking standards can fit. The OSI model specifies what aspects of a network's operation can be addressed by various network standards. So in a sense, the OSI model is sort of a standard's standard.

The seven OSI layers are:

- ✔ Layer 1: Physical layer
- ✔ Layer 2: Data link layer
- ✔ Layer 3: Network layer
- ✔ Layer 4: Transport layer

✔ Layer 5: Session layer

✔ Layer 6: Presentation layer

✔ Layer 7: Application layer

Although there are seven layers in the OSI model, the bottom two are the ones that have the most direct impact on local area networks. Networking standards like Ethernet and token ring are Layer 1 and Layer 2 standards. The higher layers of the OSI model have not resulted in widespread standards.

Layer 1: The physical layer

The bottom layer of the OSI model is the *physical layer*. It addresses the physical characteristics of the network: the types of cables that will be used to connect devices, the types of connectors that will be used, how long the cables can be, and so on. For example, the Ethernet standard for 10baseT cable specifies the electrical characteristics of the twisted pair cables, the size and shape of the connectors, the maximum length of the cables, and so on.

Don't read this if you're dyslexic

The OSI standard was developed by a group known as *International Standards Organization (ISO)*. So technically, it can be called the *ISO OSI* standard. Hold that up to a mirror and see what happens.

ISO develops standards for all sorts of stuff, like the size of sprinkler pipes and machine screws. Other candidates for ISO standards include SOI, SIO, OIS, and IOS.

Another aspect of the physical layer is the electrical characteristics of the signals used to transmit data over the cables from one network node to another. The physical layer does not define any meaning to those signals other than the basic binary values 0 and 1. It's up to higher levels of the OSI model to assign meanings to the bits that are transmitted at the physical layer.

Layer 2: The data link layer

The *data link layer* is the layer at which meaning is assigned to the bits that are transmitted over the network. A standard for the data link layer must address things such as the size of each packet of data to be sent, a means of addressing each packet so that it is delivered to the intended recipient, and a way to ensure that two or more nodes don't try to transmit data on the network at the same time.

The data link layer also provides basic error detection and correction to ensure that the data sent is the same as the data received. If an uncorrectable error occurs, the data link standard must specify how the node is to be informed of the error so that it can retransmit the data.

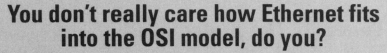

You don't really care how Ethernet fits into the OSI model, do you?

Ethernet's official name (from the IEEE) is the *802.3 standard*. It addresses both the physical layer of the OSI model and the data link layer.

You can blame the portion of the 802.3 that addresses the physical layer for the need to attach terminators to each end of a segment of thin coax, for the fact that BNC connectors are a pain in the rumpus to attach, and for the limit on the number of hubs that can be daisy-chained together when twisted pair cabling is used. The physical-layer portion of the 802.3 standard is also responsible for the colorful terms *10base5*, *10base2*, and *10baseT* (see the earlier sidebar, "Ten base what?").

The portion of 802.3 that deals with the data link layer actually deals only with one portion of the data link layer, called the Media Access Control Sublayer, or *MAC sublayer*.

The MAC portion of 802.3 spells out how the CSMA/CD operation of Ethernet works: how Ethernet listens for network traffic, sends data if the network appears to be free of traffic, and then listens for collisions and resends the information if necessary.

The other portion of the data link layer of the OSI model is called the Logical Link Control Sublayer, or (you guessed it) the *LLC sublayer*. The LLC sublayer spells out the basics of sending and receiving packets of information over the network and correcting errors. The LLC standard used by Ethernet is called 802.2.

None of this really matters unless you plan on building network interface cards in your garage.

Layer 3: The network layer

The *network layer* addresses the interconnection of networks by routing packets from one network to another. The network layer is most important when you use a router to link two different types of networks, such as an Ethernet network and a token ring network. Because the network layer is one step above the data link layer, it doesn't matter whether the two networks use different standards at the data link and physical layers.

Layer 4: The transport layer

The *transport layer* is the basic layer at which one network computer communicates with another network computer. The transport layer identifies each node on the computer with a unique address and manages connections between nodes. The transport layer also breaks large messages into smaller messages that are sent in sequence, and reassembles the messages at the receiving node.

The transport layer and the OSI layers above it are implemented differently by various network operating systems. You can thank the OSI model for the capability to run NetWare, NT Server, Unix, or just about any other network operating system on a standard Ethernet network. Ethernet addresses the lower layers of the OSI model; as long as the network operating system's transport layer is able to interface with Ethernet, you're in business.

Layer 4a: The lemon-pudding layer

The *lemon-pudding layer* is squeezed in between the rather dry and tasteless transport and session layers to add flavor and moisture. (Just kidding.)

Layer 5: The session layer

The *session layer* establishes "sessions" between network nodes. A session must be established before data can be transmitted over the network. The session layer makes sure that these sessions are properly established and maintained.

Layer 6: The presentation layer

The *presentation layer* is responsible for converting the data sent over the network from one type of representation to another. For example, the presentation layer can apply sophisticated compression techniques so that fewer bytes of data are required to represent the information when it is sent over the network. At the other end of the transmission, the transport layer then uncompresses the data.

The presentation layer also can scramble the data before it is transmitted and unscramble it at the other end, using a sophisticated encryption technique that even Sherlock Holmes would have trouble breaking.

Layer 7: The application layer

The highest layer of the OSI model, the *application layer* deals with the techniques application programs use to communicate with the network. The name of this layer is a little confusing. Application programs like Lotus 1-2-3 and WordPerfect are not a part of the application layer. Rather, it's the network operating system itself that works within the application layer.

Local area networks are designed to link computers that are relatively close to one another — in the same room, or at least in the same building. To connect computers that are far apart — in different buildings, or even in different cities or countries — a wide area network is required. That's the subject of the next chapter.

Chapter 9

Wide Area Networking: The Big Picture

- -

- -

*W*hat happens when you link up two or more LANs? You've got a *WAN*, or wide area network. A WAN usually involves linking up two or more Ethernet or token ring LANs that are too far apart to connect with coax.

Because client/server applications often involve accessing data stored in separate locations, WANs are an important part of the client/server picture. This chapter gives you an overview of the hardware and communication technologies involved in wide area networks, plus a look at two popular WAN architectures, IBM's SNA and TCP/IP, the one used for that Net of all nets, the Internet.

Gadgets for Linking Networks

Small networks — say, 50 or fewer computers — can get by without any of the gadgets described in this section. However, as a network grows or when it needs to reach out and touch other networks or host computers such as mainframes or midrange systems, gadgets like these become necessary.

Repeaters

A *repeater* is a gizmo that's designed to give your network signals a boost so that they can travel farther. It's kind of like the Gatorade stations in a marathon. As they travel past the repeater, the network signals pick up a cup of Gatorade, take a sip, splash the rest of it on their heads, toss the cup, and hop in a cab when they're sure no one is looking.

Repeaters are used when the total length of your network cable is longer than the maximum allowed for your cable type, shown in Table 9-1. (I told you more than you wanted to know about the three types of cable in Chapter 8.)

Table 9-1: Maximum length for different types of cable

Cable	Maximum Length
Thick coax (yellow stuff)	500 meters (1640 feet)
Thin coax (thinnet)	185 meters (606 feet)
10baseT (twisted sister)	100 meters (328 feet)

For coax cable (thick and thin), the cable lengths in Table 9-1 apply to cable *segments*, not individual lengths of cable. A segment is the entire run of cable from one terminator to another, and may include more than one computer. In other words, if you have 10 computers and you connect them all with 25-foot lengths of thin coax cable, the total length of the segment is 225 feet. (Made you look! Only *nine* cables are required to connect 10 computers — that's why it's not 250 feet.)

For 10baseT cable, the 100-meter length limit applies to the cable that connects a computer to the hub. In other words, each computer can be connected to the hub with no more than 100 meters of cable.

Figure 9-1 shows how a repeater might be used to connect two groups of computers that are too far apart to be strung on a single segment. When you use a repeater like this, the repeater divides the cable into two segments. The cable length limit still applies to the cable on each side of the repeater.

Repeaters are used only with Ethernet networks wired with coax cable. 10baseT networks don't use repeaters, nor do ARCnet or token ring networks.

Actually, that's not quite true; 10baseT, ARCnet, and token ring networks do use repeaters. It's just that the repeater isn't a separate device. In a 10baseT network, the hub itself is actually a multiport repeater. That's why the cable used to attach each computer to the hub is considered to be a separate segment. Likewise for ARCnet networks: The active hubs are actually

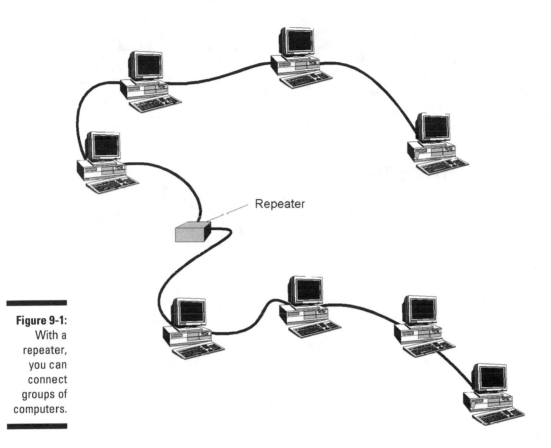

Figure 9-1:
With a repeater, you can connect groups of computers.

Repeater

repeaters. In a token ring network, each computer acts like a repeater, listening to the token and sending it to the next computer in line. ■

Most 10baseT hubs have a BNC connector on the back. This BNC connector is a thin coax repeater that enables you to attach a full 185-meter thin coax segment. The segment can attach other computers, 10baseT hubs, or a combination.

A basic rule of Ethernet life is that a signal cannot pass through more than three repeaters on its way from one node to another. That doesn't mean you can't have more than three repeaters or hubs, but if you do, you have to carefully plan the network cabling so that the three-repeater rule isn't violated. ■

Repeaters are legitimate components of a by-the-book Ethernet network. They don't extend the maximum length of a single segment; they just let you tie two segments together.

Beware of the little black boxes that claim to extend the segment limit beyond the standard 185-meter limit for thin coax or the 500-meter limit for yellow stuff. These usually work, but it's better to play by the rules. ■

Bridges

A *bridge* is a device that's used to connect two networks so that they act as if they're one network. Bridges can be used to connect two different types of networks, such as an Ethernet network and a token ring network, but they're more often used to partition one large network into two smaller networks for performance purposes.

A bridge is like a smart repeater. Repeaters listen to signals coming down one network cable, amplify them, and send them down the other cable. They do this blindly, paying no attention to the content of the messages they repeat.

In contrast, a bridge is a little smarter about the messages that come down the pike. For starters, most bridges have the capability to listen to the network and automatically figure out the address of each computer on both sides of the bridge. Then the bridge can inspect each message that comes from one side of the bridge and broadcast it on the other side of the bridge only if the message is intended for a computer that's on the other side.

This is the key feature that enables bridges to partition a large network into two smaller, more efficient networks. Bridges work best in networks that are highly segregated. For example (humor me here), suppose that the Sneetches networked all their computers and discovered that, although the Star-Bellied Sneetches' computers talked to each other frequently and the Plain-Bellied Sneetches' computers also talked to each other frequently, it was a rare occasion that a Star-Bellied Sneetch computer talked to a Plain-Bellied Sneetch computer.

A bridge could be used to partition the Sneetchnet into two networks: the Star-Bellied network and the Plain-Bellied network. The bridge would automatically learn which computers were on the Star-Bellied network and which were on the Plain-Bellied network, and forward messages from the Star-Bellied side to the Plain-Bellied side (and vice versa) only when necessary. The overall performance of both networks would improve, although the performance of any network operation that had to travel over the bridge would be slowed down a bit.

As I mentioned, some bridges also have the capability to translate the messages from one format to another. For example, if the Star-Bellied Sneetches built their network with Ethernet, and the Plain-Bellied Sneetches used token ring, a bridge could be used to tie the two together.

Routers

A *router* is similar to a super-intelligent bridge for really big networks. Bridges know the addresses of all the computers on each side of the bridge and can forward messages accordingly. But routers know even more about the network. A router not only knows the addresses of all the computers, but also about other bridges and routers on the network, and can decide the most efficient path to send each network message. In fact, the router knows everything about you and your little network. Am I scaring you?

One of the best tricks routers can do is to listen in on the entire network (no, it doesn't spy on your actual data; it can only see how busy various parts of the network are). If one part of the network is busy, the router may decide to forward a message by using a less busy route. In this respect, the router is like a traffic reporter up in a helicopter. The router knows that 101 is bumper-to-bumper through Sunnyvale, so it takes 280 instead.

The functional distinction between bridges and routers gets blurrier all the time. As bridges become more sophisticated, they're able to take on some of the chores that used to require a router, thus putting many routers out of work. (Ross Perot blames this on NAFTA.) Bridges that perform routing functions are sometimes called *brouters*. (How about having some *brouters* for *brunch*?)

Some routers are nothing more than computers with several network interface cards and special software to perform the router functions. In fact, NetWare comes with a router program that lets a NetWare server act as a router.

Routers can also be used to connect networks that are geographically distant from one another via modems. You can't do that with a bridge.

If you're confused about the distinction between bridges and routers, join the club. The technical distinction has to do with which layer of the OSI networking model the devices operate at. (Remember the OSI model from the last chapter?) Bridges operate at the MAC (media access control) sublayer of the data link layer, whereas routers operate at the next level up: the network layer. Still confused? ■

Gateways

No, not the Bill Gates way. This kind of *gateway* is a super-intelligent router, which is a super-intelligent bridge, which is a super-intelligent repeater. Notice a pattern here?

Gateways are designed to connect radically different types of networks. They do this by translating messages from one network's format to another's, much like the Universal Translator that got Kirk and Spock out of so many jams.

Gateways usually are used to connect a network to a mainframe or minicomputer. If you don't have a mainframe or minicomputer, you probably don't need a gateway.

Gateways are necessary only because of the mess computer manufacturers got us into by insisting on using their own proprietary designs for networks. If computer manufacturers had talked to each other 20 years ago, we wouldn't have to use gateways to make their networks talk to each other today.

FDDI Backbones

Many large local area networks utilize a high-speed "backbone" line that transmits data between various LAN segments at a speed of 100Mbps instead of Ethernet's normal 10Mbps or token ring's 4 or 16Mbps. Specialized routers, bridges, and hubs are used to link the 10Mbps network segments to the high-speed backbone.

These high-speed backbones are best built with fiber-optic cable using *FDDI*, which stands for *Fiber Distributed Data Interface*, an ANSI standard for creating high-speed communications (up to 100Mbps, 10 times as fast as standard Ethernet) that uses fiber-optic cable. FDDI can be used to connect computers in a local area network, but it is more commonly used as a backbone to link Ethernet or token ring LANs, as illustrated by Figure 9-2.

High-speed FDDI backbone networks are often used in *campus-wide networks* to join the various buildings of a business or university campus. The high-speed technology has the advantage not only of higher speed, but also of spanning greater distances.

FDDI uses a ring topology and a token-passing method similar to token ring. You can think of FDDI as a 100Mbps version of token ring, though FDDI incorporates several important improvements over token ring to improve speed and reliability.

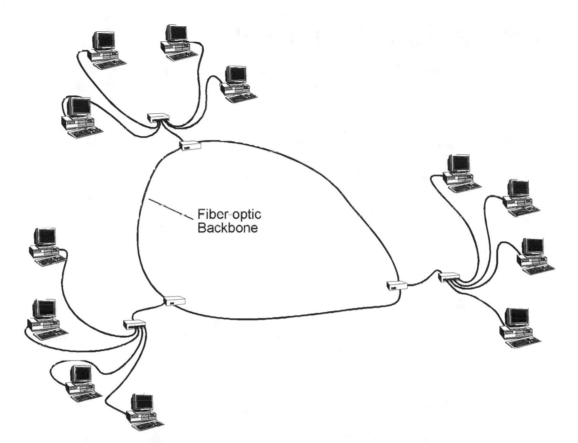

Fiber-optic Backbone

Figure 9-2: A high-speed FDDI backbone network is used to link networks at remote locations.

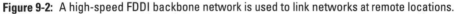

FDDI can support fiber-optic cable lengths of up to 200 kilometers (124 miles), which means the end-to-end length of an FDDI backbone can be as much as 100 kilometers (remember, FDDI uses a ring topology). As many as 1,000 devices can be connected to a single cable segment. Each device can be a computer, but is more likely to be a bridge or router that links an Ethernet or token ring segment to the FDDI backbone.

One drawback of FDDI is that fiber-optic cable is very difficult to work with. It takes a highly trained specialist to lay the cable and attach the connections. That — plus the fact that FDDI network adapters are very expensive — is why FDDI is used mostly for backbone networks rather than to link individual desktop computers.

Really Wide Area Networks

Sometimes WANs are used to link local area networks that are farther apart than allowed by even an FDDI backbone. WANs are often used to link LANs in separate cities.

There are several alternative technologies for linking networks over very wide areas. The most popular include:

- Dedicated phone lines, known as *DDS* (Digital Data Service), which can support communications up to 56Kbps.

- *T-1 lines,* high-speed dedicated digital lines. T-1 lines support bandwidth ranging from 64Kbs to 274Mbps. Special equipment called a CSU/DSU is required to connect to the T-1 line.

- ISDN, which is the all-digital phone system that integrates voice and data.

Packet-switching is often used to allow many users to share high-speed links by dividing messages into packets that can be sent over the network and routed to the proper address. Three popular packet-switching technologies are X.25, Frame Relay, and Asynchronous Transfer Mode (ATM).

SNA: IBM's Networking World View

System Networking Architecture, more commonly known as SNA, is IBM's networking world view. It got its start back in the 1970s when IBM mainframes dominated the computer world. SNA is an important part of any network that includes IBM mainframes.

In its early incarnations, SNA's basic approach to networking was that any computer that wanted to be a part of an SNA network should pretend to be a 3270 dumb terminal. SNA has since shed its mainframe-centric attitude and now allows computers to operate as peers on the network.

SNA is capable of supporting huge networks, like airline reservation systems and banking networks with tens of thousands of terminals.

SNA is built around a seven-layer structure that is similar but not identical to the OSI model described in Chapter 8. The seven SNA layers are:

- Layer 1: Physical control layer
- Layer 2: Data link control layer

✔ Layer 3: Path control layer

✔ Layer 4: Transmission control layer

✔ Layer 5: Data flow control layer

✔ Layer 6: Presentation services layer

✔ Layer 7: Transaction services layer

SNA tosses a truckload of its own acronym alphabet soup into the networking soup bowl. Following is a list of the more important SNA terms a mainframe network expert may throw at you. Nod understandingly when you hear one of these:

PU, which stands for *physical unit.* A PU is typically a terminal, a printer, or another computer. (Sometimes you hear computers talking to each other like this: "Hey, where'd you get that gorgeous PU?")

LU, which stands for *logical unit.* The LUs are what communicate with each other in an SNA unit. An LU can be associated with a physical device such as a terminal or printer, or it can be associated with a program.

APPC, which stands for *Advanced Program to Program Communication*, a communication protocol that allows programs to communicate with one another when the programs are running on separate network nodes. Each program is associated with an LU to enable the communication. APPC allows programs to carefully coordinate their processing and is commonly used for distributed transaction processing (we'll talk about that in Chapter 21) in client/server environments.

LU 6.2 is the type of logical unit that enables programs to communicate with one another over the network using APPC.

VTAM, which stands for *Virtual Telecommunications Access Method*, is the software that oversees operation of an SNA network.

SDLC, which stands for *Synchronous Data Link Control*, is the preferred data transmission protocol in SNA.

TCP/IP

TCP/IP (*Transmission Control Protocol/Internet Protocol*) is the networking world view upon which the famous Internet is founded. TCP/IP was originally developed by the U.S. government to link various agencies' computers, but is now found in universities and businesses as well. It is often used alongside Unix.

TCP/IP emphasizes the notion of *internetworking*; that is, allowing entire networks of computers to be linked together and computers on each network to communicate with one another.

Well, that's about it for the building blocks. You now know far more than you ever wanted to know about clients, servers, and networks. In the next part, I'll describe the details of one of the most important components of most client/server systems: the database.

Part III
A Database Primer

The 5th Wave   By Rich Tennant

AFTER DISCOVERING THE LAND OF LOST FILES, BILL AND IRWIN RUN INTO A TRIBE OF SQL INDIANS.

THIS IS GONNA BE TRICKY. THEY PROBABLY ALL SPEAK A DIFFERENT LANGUAGE.

In This Part...

Most client/server applications center around a database that is managed by a SQL server and accessed by client front ends. To help you better understand how these applications work, this Part introduces you to relational databases in general, and to SQL, the Structured Query Language that is the *lingua franca* of relational databases. You'll also get an overview of relational database design and distributed databases.

Some of the material in this part is a bit on the technical side, especially the stuff about SQL in Chapters 11 and 12. However, I suggest you give it your best shot and wade through these chapters even if you don't have a lot of programming background. The more you know about SQL, the more you'll be able to understand and appreciate the benefits of client/server systems.

Chapter 10

Database for $100 Please

*T*his chapter introduces you to the basic concepts of databases. Most (though not all) client/server applications are built around databases — specifically, relational databases that use SQL — so this chapter is key in your understanding of how client/server computing works.

What Is a Database?

A *database* is an organized collection of information. Here are some examples of databases from everyday life:

- ✔ Your personal address book
- ✔ The shoe box that contains your tax records for the year
- ✔ Your baseball card collection
- ✔ All those parking tickets conveniently stuffed into your car's glove compartment
- ✔ The phone book
- ✔ That pile of score cards that has been accumulating in the bottom of your golf bag for 15 years
- ✔ For you compulsive types, your Rolodex file and your Day Timer

You can think of each of these databases as a collection of records. In database lingo, a *record* consists of all the useful information you can gather about a particular thing. In your address book, each record represents one of your friends or enemies. For your tax records database, each receipt in the shoe box is a record. Each baseball card in your card collection is a record, as is each parking ticket stuffed into the glove box.

Each little snippet of information that makes up a record is called a *field*. Using the address book as an example once again, each person's record — that is, each entry in the address book — consists of several fields: name, street address, city, state, zip code, and phone number. It also may include other information, such as the person's birthday, whether you received a Christmas card from that person last year, and how much money that person owes you.

A computerized database is much like these noncomputerized databases. Like your address book or shoe box full of tax records, a computerized database is a collection of records, and each record is a collection of fields. The biggest difference is that in a computer database, information is recorded on the computer's hard disk rather than on paper. Using the hard disk yields several distinct advantages over address books and shoe boxes. For example, searching a computerized database for a particular receipt is much easier than riffling through an overstuffed shoe box.

Computer databases automatically keep records organized and enable you to search for or pull out particular records based on any field in the record. For example, if you kept your address book as a computerized database, you could quickly print a list of all your friends who live in Iowa and owe you more than $10. Try that trick with your noncomputerized address book.

> ✔ The software that lets you create and maintain databases is called a *Database Management System* or *DBMS*.
>
> ✔ In database terminology, a *file* is called a *table*. Each *record* in the file is called a *row*, and each *field* is called a *column*. These terms will make more sense when you read the next section, "What Is a Relational Database?" In a client/server environment, the DBMS is sometimes called a *database server*, which means simply that the DBMS lives on a server computer and responds to database requests from client computers. You'll find out more about database servers later in this chapter.

What Is a Relational Database?

One of the most used and abused buzzwords in the computer business (along with *client/server*) is *relational database*.

Relational databases would make a good subject for a Tim Allen routine.

"Say Al, do you think they call it a relational database because it's good at dealing with relationships?"

"I don't think so, Tim."

The term *relational database* really doesn't have anything to do with people. (Sorry if I burst your bubble. If you're really feeling bad about this, skip to the sidebar "Metaphor alert!" in this chapter, which focuses on the human side of databases.) It does have at least five common meanings in computing. A *relational database* can be:

- *A database in which data is stored in tables.* Relationships can be established between tables based on common information. For example, a customer table and an invoice table might both contain a customer number column that lets you establish a relationship between the tables.

- *A database model based upon a Conehead branch of mathematics called Set Theory.* The term *relation* in this definition refers to the way data is arranged into tables of rows and columns, not to relationships between tables.

  (It is a little-known fact that relational database theory was invented at about the same time that the Coneheads from the planet Remulak first came to Earth, back in the 1970s. I have always suspected that these two developments are — dare I say it? — *related.*)

- *A database that is accessed via Structured Query Language (SQL).* SQL provides a practical way to access data stored in relational tables. A database that meets this definition would also meet the first two, since SQL requires that data be stored in tables and SQL is based on set theory.

- *A religion whose followers believe that the world can be saved only by strict adherence to the essential tenets of the Relational Creed.* There was a time when relational database fanatics could be seen passing out tracts at airports. The Great High Priest of the relational faith, E. J. Codd, even made up a list of rules that one must follow to be considered truly relational.

- *Any database system developed since 1980, with the exception of a few recent cutting-edge, object-oriented databases.* Marketers quickly figured out that the way to sell database programs was to advertise them as relational. Just about every database program ever made has claimed to be relational.

It wasn't until recently, when the new *object-oriented* religion began to emerge, that database companies started to let go of the relational label.

We're now starting to see object-oriented databases. But that's another book. . . .

In this book, the third definition is the most important: a relational database is a database that can be accessed via SQL. SQL is such an important topic in client/server computing that I've devoted the next two chapters to it.

Skip this stuff about other kinds of databases

Relational databases are by far the most common kind of database used in client/server systems, but they're not the only kind. Here are a sampling of some of the other types of databases that you might encounter:

Flat file. A *flat file* database actually isn't a database at all. Rather, it's a file of records that do not obey any particular laws of database organization. Typically, flat files are found on existing mainframe and minicomputer applications, usually developed using the COBOL programming language.

Hierarchical database. A *hierarchical database* is a database in which carefully controlled parent-child relationships are defined for database records. For example, a hierarchical customer orders database might have a customer record at the top of the hierarchy. For each customer, there might be one or more order records at the next level of the hierarchy. For each order record, there might be one or more line item records. Each line item, in turn, has a subordinate parts record. Hierarchical databases are adept at one-to-one and one-to-many relationships, but are awkward where many-to-many relationships are concerned.

The best known hierarchical database is IBM's IMS, which is at the heart of many mainframe computer applications.

Network database. A *network database* is a database model that allows more complex relationships than can be specified with a simple hierarchical database. In particular, network databases are designed with many-to-many relationships in mind. Network databases have hierarchy, but in a more flexible manner. For example, a single child record can have more than one parent record if necessary.

Object database. An *object database* is an offshoot of the modern object craze. First we had object-oriented programming, then object-oriented operating systems, so why not object-oriented databases? Object-oriented databases have similarities with relational databases, but treat data as *objects* rather than as tables. An object consists of data, information about how the object relates to other objects in the database, and procedures for manipulating the data contained in the object. Object databases are new and still at the faddish stage, but they may become more common in the near future. (I'll talk more about object databases in Part IV, Client/Server Hot Topics.)

What Is a Join?

Joins are how tables in a relational database can be related to one another. The best way to explain how they work is to give an example, so hold on to your hat.

Metaphor alert!

The paragraphs in this box contain a sincere yet futile attempt on the part of the author to draw an analogy between the dry and lifeless database concept of *joins* and real-life human relationships. Computer book authors often lie awake at night, pondering the eternal significance of their writing and feeling guilty about the fact that, while they spend their lives hammering out meaningless computer books and actually make a decent living at it, their old college buddies who are actually far better writers are happy to sell their beautifully crafted short stories to obscure literary journals for $100.

When they finally drift off to sleep, computer book authors frequently have nightmares about meeting their college English professors and being asked to justify their life's work. This is why they so often attempt to use metaphors and other literary devices such as allusions and allegory. So here goes:

Relationships are what add spice to database life. Without relationships, databases would be empty and unsatisfied, without substance or meaning. For just as no man is an island, neither is any database an island; but rather all datakind is linked in an ever-expanding web of relationships, a vast computerized tapestry of databases joined to databases joined to databases in the circle of database life. (An Elton John song would be good here.)

And so it came to pass that the customer database knew the sales database, and the sales database knew the products database, and thus did they beget still more databases, all related, each after its kind.

Or something like that.

Suppose that you own a video rental store and you have decided to computerize your business using a client/server database system. You immediately create a database table of all your videotapes. The rows in the VIDEO table contain information about each videotape, as well as information about the customers who rent them:

- ✔ Title
- ✔ Status (IN or OUT)
- ✔ Due date

✔ Customer's last and first names

✔ Customer's street address, city, state, and zip code

✔ Customer's phone number

✔ Customer's credit card number (in case the customer skips town)

Before long, you realize that every time a customer rents a videotape, you have to type in the customer's name, address, and credit card number. To make matters worse, if the customer rents all six Star Trek movies on the same day, you have to type in this information six times. (Odds are that a customer who wants all six Star Trek movies will immediately point out how illogical such a database design is.)

Being the wise database user that you are, you decide to divide the video table into two smaller tables, one for videotapes and the other for customers. At the same time, you realize that you'll need to assign a unique number to each customer and a unique number to each videotape.

The new VIDEO table includes the following information:

✔ Video number (an otherwise meaningless number assigned to each tape so you can keep track of it)

✔ Title

✔ Status (IN or OUT)

✔ Due date

✔ Customer number

The CUSTOMER table includes:

✔ Customer number (an otherwise meaningless number that is used to identify each customer)

✔ Customer's last and first names

✔ Customer's street address, city, state, and zip code

✔ Customer's phone number

✔ Customer's credit card number

Now, whenever a customer rents a videotape, all you have to do is call up the VIDEO record for the tape and type in the customer number and due date. You have to type in the customer's name, address, and credit card information only once, in the CUSTOMER table.

That's all well and good, but what a bother to constantly have to look up information in both databases. Wouldn't it be great if you could call up both tables together to show the relationship between the customer data and the videotape data? I thought you'd never ask. That capability is exactly what joins are all about.

Join types

Just as there are different types of relationships in real life — for example, husbands and wives, parents and children, aunts and uncles and nieces and nephews, and of course, in-laws — there are different types of database relationships that you can create with joins. Three, to be exact. These three types of relationships are illustrated in textbook fashion in Figure 10-1.

One-to-one relationship

One-to-many relationship

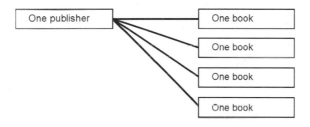

Many-to-many relationship

Figure 10-1:
Database
relation-
ships.

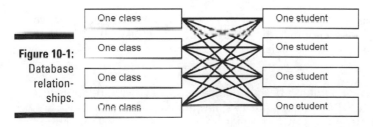

One-to-one relationships. In a one-to-one relationship, each row in one database table is related to one and only one row in another table. One-to-one joins aren't used too often because you may as well combine the two tables into a single table.

One-to-one relationships are useful in situations in which databases weren't planned very well from the start. For example, perhaps the credit department sets up a customer database to track each customer's credit history, and the marketing department sets up a customer database to track each customer's sales history. A one-to-one join would enable you to combine these databases as if they were a single database, which maybe they should have been in the first place. (The real world of client/server computing is full of such should-have's.) ■

Another good use for a one-to-one relationship is when you have a database row that contains some columns that are frequently used and some columns that are rarely used. In this case, you should consider placing the infrequently used columns in a separate table, related to the main table on a one-to-one basis. That way, you don't have to process the infrequently used columns every time you access the table.

One-to-many relationships. In a one-to-many relationship, each row in one table can be related to several rows in another table. The relationship of the CUSTOMER table to the VIDEO table is an example: Each customer can have more than one videotape rented out. The following are other examples of one-to-many relationships:

- ✔ A customer database and an invoice database: Each customer can have more than one invoice.

- ✔ An invoice database and a line item database: Each invoice can have more than one line item.

- ✔ A team database and a player database: Each team can have more than one player.

- ✔ A department database and an employee database: Each department can have more than one employee.

Notice that in a one-to-many relationship, *many* can mean zero, one, or more than one. Thus, a customer may not have any invoices. Likewise, a student may not have any classes, especially if he happens to be a basketball player at UNLV.

Also, some books on database design include a fourth type of relationship, called *many-to-one*. That just complicates matters unnecessarily, since a many-to-one relationship is a mirror image of a one-to-many relationship. Any time you have a one-to-many relationship, you also have a many-to-one relationship the other way around. For example, if departments have a one-to-many relationship with employees, employees have a many-to-one relationship with departments.

Many-to-many relationships. A many-to-many relationship exists when one or more rows in one table can be related to many rows in another table, and vice versa. For example, consider a suppliers and parts database in which each supplier can supply many different parts, and each part can be obtained from several different suppliers. The relationship between the parts database and the suppliers database is many-to-many.

Many-to-many relationships are tough. To implement this kind of relationship, you need to create a third table that contains one row for each part/supplier combination. The PARTS/SUPPLIERS table has a one-to-many relationship with the PARTS table and the SUPPLIERS table, as shown in Figure 10-2.

Parts			Parts/Suppliers			Suppliers	
Part	**Description**		**Part**	**Supplier**		**Supplier**	**Name**
1000	Framis valve		1000	100		100	Western Supply
1001	Transtator		1000	101		101	Metalworks
1002	Infindibulator		1001	100		102	Infinity Supplies
			1001	101			
			1001	102			
			1002	102			

Figure 10-2: Many-to-many relationships require an intermediate database.

In Figure 10-2, a PARTS/SUPPLIERS table links the PARTS and SUPPLIERS tables in a many-to-many relationship. You can use this table to determine which suppliers provide Framis valves (Western Supply and Metalworks) and which parts are supplied by Infinity Supplies (Transtators and Infindibulators).

Keys

Creating a join establishes a relationship between two tables. This relationship is based on a *key*, which is simply a column that the two tables have in common. In the video store example, the key is Customer Number, which appears in both the VIDEO table and the CUSTOMER table. Whenever you call up a videotape record in the VIDEO table, the correct CUSTOMER row is retrieved by using the key as a search key (assuming the tape has been checked out).

The key must have unique values in one of the tables involved in the join. In the table in which the key is unique, the key is called the *primary key*. In the other table (in which the key does not have to be unique), the key is called a *foreign key* or a *darn foreign key*.

What Is Database Integrity?

Garbage In, Garbage Out, so the old saying goes. Database integrity concerns itself with keeping garbage out of the database so that the database can be trusted.

This section describes the most common methods of upholding database integrity.

Constraints

Constraints establish acceptable values for database fields. The DBMS automatically rejects any attempt to add data to a field that falls outside of the field's acceptable values. (The techno-nerd term for "acceptable values" is *domain*.)

Here are some examples of constraints:

- Social Security numbers consist of nine digits.
- A State Code field accepts only standard uppercase, two-letter state abbreviations (AL, CA, GA, and so on).
- A Product Code field may contain only a valid product code. The DBMS may have to look up valid product codes in another table to check validity.
- Numeric quantities may be restricted to positive numbers or may be given minimum and maximum values.

Checking for proper values in a database is also called *validity checking*.

Nulls

A *null* value means that a field has no value or that the value of the field is unknown. This is different than a value of zero. To appreciate the difference, consider the difference between the terms "free" and "priceless." Something that is free has a price of zero. Something that is priceless has no known price.

The difference can be crucial in a database. For example, suppose you want to calculate the average value of a field in several records. If a particular row contains a zero in that field, the zero should be factored into the average. If the field has a null value, it should *not* be factored into the average.

Some fields can be set up so that they allow null values, others can be defined to require a non-null value. For example, if all employees must have an employee status, the Employee Status column can be defined so that it rejects null values.

Referential integrity

Referential integrity checks the relationship of data contained in one table with data referenced in another table. For example, suppose you have two tables, one containing customer information, the other containing invoice information. The customer and invoice tables are joined by a customer number field. Referential integrity addresses questions that come up in the following situations:

- ✔ What if you attempt to delete a customer row that has corresponding invoice rows?
- ✔ What if you try to add an invoice row using a customer number that does not exist in the customer table?
- ✔ What if you try to change the customer number of a customer row — should the customer number for corresponding invoice rows be changed as well?
- ✔ What if you try to change the customer number of an invoice row to a customer number that does not exist in the customer table?
- ✔ What if you delete all of the invoices for a given customer — should you also delete the customer? (In other words, does a customer have to have at least one invoice?)

There are two ways of enforcing referential integrity in relational databases: with declarative referential integrity and with triggers.

In *declarative referential integrity*, the referential constraints — such as "you can't create an invoice without a corresponding customer" — are set up when the database structure is defined via SQL. (See Chapter 11, which goes into SQL in more detail than you thought possible in a ...*For Dummies* book.)

A *trigger* is a little program that is run when table data is changed. The trigger program checks to make sure that referential integrity hasn't been violated.

Given the choice, declarative integrity is much better than triggers.

Business rules

Field validation and referential integrity may reflect *business rules* — that is, rules unique to your organization. Here are some examples of business rules:

- ✔ All orders over $500 must have a purchase order.
- ✔ A customer is considered "Inactive" if he or she has not ordered in the past 24 months.
- ✔ We do not accept orders from California.
- ✔ An invoice is considered overdue if it has not been fully paid within 90 days of the invoice date.
- ✔ Each employee can have as many as nine wage rates.
- ✔ Groundhog's Day is a paid holiday.

What Is a Database Server?

A database server is a program that runs on a server computer and allows you to set up, access, and maintain a database. In client/server, database servers are almost always SQL servers, which means simply that they use SQL databases rather than a hierarchical, network, or object databases.

The functions provided by a database server include the following:

- ✔ Client SQL access, which allows client programs and users to create and manipulate SQL databases.
- ✔ Locking, which prevents conflicts when two or more users want to access the same data at the same time.
- ✔ Deadlock detection, which watches carefully for situations in which two or more users are waiting for database resources which are held by the other. This is called a *deadlock* because both users will sit there forever, waiting for the other user to release the resources needed to complete their respective transactions. When the DBMS detects a deadlock, it kills one of the users (not literally) so that the other user can continue. This is the supreme database sacrifice, one transaction laying down its life for another. Fortunately, the dead user can usually retry his or her transaction later.
- ✔ Performance optimization, which evaluates the various ways a SQL request can be processed, then selects the most efficient one.
- ✔ Security, which prevents unauthorized access to data.
- ✔ Backup and recovery facilities, which restore database data should the system fail.

Several different SQL database servers are available. The most popular ones are:

IBM's DB2, which runs on various platforms including mainframes (MVS), midrange systems (AS/400), Unix, and OS/2. (IBM also offers a RDBMS — relational database management system — called SQL/DS, which runs on mainframes that use the VM or VSE operating systems.)

Oracle SQL Server, which runs on just about any platform imaginable including Windows NT, Novell NetWare, OS/2, Unix, VMS, VM, and MVS.

Sybase SQL Server, which runs on most servers except mainframes.

Microsoft SQL Server, which runs only on Windows NT (older versions run on OS/2 as well).

What's the Name of the Guy on First Base?

If you don't know who's on first, I'm not about to tell you.

Chapter 11

What Is SQL, and How Do You Pronounce It?

*S*QL stands for Structured Query Language. SQL is the *lingua franca* (that's not a type of pasta) of relational databases. It is a standard language for defining and accessing relational databases. All of the major database servers used in client/server applications work with SQL. You don't have to be a SQL expert to understand client/server (whew!), but a little SQL knowledge will go a long way when it comes to figuring out what client/server is all about.

This chapter will not make you a database or SQL expert. SQL is a complicated language that should be the subject of its own *...For Dummies* book (hint, hint). You'll get an overview of the basics of SQL, and for the brave, there's an excursion into creating a SQL table to extract and update information from a database. All I can hope to accomplish here is to teach you just enough SQL to make you dangerous.

This chapter begins with some general information about SQL, but ends up going pretty deep into SQL. If you don't have any programming or database experience, you may pass out if you try to read too far into this chapter. Please feel free to skip the detailed SQL information in this chapter if you have heart trouble or are easily nauseated. ■

By itself, SQL isn't of much use in client/server systems (or in any other type of system, for that matter). Instead, SQL must be used alongside a particular programming language, such as COBOL, C, or Visual Basic. This chapter focuses on how SQL works in general. Chapter 12 gets into how SQL is used in the context of particular programming languages.

Welcome to SQL

SQL is a *query language,* which means it is designed to extract, organize, and update information in relational databases. SQL was supposed to be an English-like query language that could be used by untrained end users to access and update relational database data. Of course, it is nothing like English, and it is far too complicated and esoteric for untrained end users to use.

SQL never took off as an end-user tool, but it has become the overwhelming favorite among programmers who write programs that access relational databases, especially in client/server circles.

How do you pronounce it?

Here's something you've probably been wondering ever since you first saw the letters *SQL:* "How do you pronounce it?" There are two schools of thought:

1. Spell out the letters: S-*Q-L.*
2. Pronounce it like the word *sequel.*

Either one will do, but *sequel* is more hip.

You can always tell how a writer pronounces SQL by checking to see if he or she writes, "a SQL server" or "an SQL server." ∎

You can impress even the most staunch SQL expert by pointing out that SQL was originally spelled SEQUEL by the IBM engineers who created the first version way back in the 1970s. *SEQUEL* stood for *S*tructured *E*nglish *QUE*ry *Lan*guage. Someone must have correctly pointed out that aside from borrowing a little vocabulary such as SELECT and CREATE, SEQUEL actually bore no resemblance whatsoever to English. So *English* was dropped from the name and the acronym was changed from SEQUEL to SQL. ∎

SQL dialects

Like most computer languages, there are many different dialects of SQL. In fact, every SQL server has its own unique version. These dialects are 95% the same, so a basic SQL statement is likely to work the same no matter what SQL server you use it with.

There are minor differences that can sometimes cause a SQL statement to behave differently depending on which database server is used. Unfortunately, these differences are so pervasive that it's a bit of a stretch to say that SQL is an "open" language. Each database vendor has its own peculiar SQL dialect. These dialects are similar to one another, but different enough that you client/server programmers need to pay close attention to which RDBMS is being used. ∎

The most important dialects of SQL are:

- **ANSI/ISO SQL.** ANSI is the government body that standardizes everything from computer languages to irrigation pipes to trash dumpsters. ISO is its international equivalent. ANSI/ISO SQL is also known as *SQL-89* or *SQL1*. A newer standard, called *SQL-92* or *SQL2*, has yet to be fully implemented in commercial products.

- **IBM DB2.** The *de facto* SQL standard is the SQL dialect used by DB2, IBM's mainframe relational database.

- **SQL Server, Oracle, Ingres, and others.** Each of the major SQL database servers has its own SQL dialect.

- **ODBC.** Microsoft's blueprint for client/server SQL access is called *ODBC*, which stands for *Open DataBase Connectivity*.

SQL Statements

Like other programming languages, SQL uses *statements* to get work done. Table 11-1 lists the statements you're likely to find in most SQL dialects.

You have now reached a crossroads in your SQL adventure. If you think you now know as much about SQL as you need to know or want to know, stop here. The rest of this chapter dives into the deep end of the SQL pool, exploring the details of creating a table, querying the table with a SELECT statement, and so on. Read on if you're interested in knowing the mysteries of SQL. Otherwise, skip the rest of this chapter (and the next chapter, too). ∎

Table 11-1: Common SQL statements

SQL statement	What it does
Data Manipulation	
SELECT	Retrieves data from one or more tables. This is the SQL statement that is used most.
INSERT	Inserts one or more rows into a table.
DELETE	Deletes one or more rows from a table.
UPDATE	Updates existing rows in a table.
Cursor Statements	
DECLARE	Defines a cursor, which can be used to process rows retrieved by a query. The DECLARE statement includes a SELECT statement that is used to process the query.
OPEN	Opens a cursor. Opening a cursor processes the cursor's SELECT statement and prepares the result set for processing by a program.
FETCH	Retrieves one row from the query result set.
CLOSE	Closes a cursor.
Transaction Statements	
COMMIT	Commits all changes made to this point.
ROLLBACK	Undoes all changes made to this point.
Data Definition	
CREATE	Creates tables and other database objects.
ALTER	Alters the definition of a table or other database object.
DROP	Deletes a table or other database object.
Security	
GRANT	Grants security access rights.
REVOKE	Revokes security access rights.
Dynamic SQL	
PREPARE	Prepares a SQL statement for dynamic execution.
EXECUTE	Executes a dynamic SQL statement.
DESCRIBE	Lists the columns that will be returned by a dynamic query.

Creating a SQL Table

Before you can store data in a database table, you must create the table, providing a name for the table and spelling out what columns the table will contain. In this section, I'll step you through the process of creating a set of tables for a video rental database. I'll use these tables later in the chapter to illustrate how other SQL statements (such as SELECT) work.

Although most SQL databases provide a user friendly way to create SQL tables by pointing and clicking, the "official" way to create SQL tables is by using the CREATE TABLE statement. Because CREATE TABLE is available with every SQL dialect, I'll use it here to illustrate how database tables are created.

The CREATE TABLE statement

The CREATE TABLE statement does just what it suggests: it creates a new database table. In the CREATE TABLE statement, you supply a name for the table and the following information for each column to be included in the table:

- The column name
- The data type
- A default value, if any
- Whether the column allows null values

Here is an example of a simple CREATE TABLE statement to create a table containing information about video store customers:

```
CREATE TABLE VIDCUST
   (CUSTID      INTEGER(7)   NOT NULL,
    LASTNAME    VARCHAR(20)  NOT NULL,
    FIRSTNAME   VARCHAR(20)  NOT NULL,
    ADDRESS     VARCHAR(30)  NOT NULL,
    CITY        VARCHAR(20)  NOT NULL,
    STATE       CHAR(2)      NOT NULL,
    ZIPCODE     CHAR(9),
    HOMEPHONE   CHAR(10)     NOT NULL,
    WORKPHONE   CHAR(10),
    CARDNUM     CHAR(12)     NOT NULL,
    CARDTYPE    CHAR(1)      NOT NULL,
PRIMARY KEY (CUSTID))
```

This CREATE TABLE statement creates a table named VIDCUST with eleven columns, named CUSTID, LASTNAME, FIRSTNAME, and so forth. It also specifies that the primary key for the table is the CUSTID column. This enables the CUSTID column to be referenced as a foreign key in other tables.

A *primary key* is a column (or combination of columns) that contains a unique value for each row in a table. A *foreign key* is a column in one table that contains primary key values from some other table. ■

For you programmers or would-be programmers, here are a few other interesting things to note about the CREATE TABLE statement:

✔ Notice the goofy use of parentheses (for example, the double right parentheses after the PRIMARY KEY specification). The creators of SQL probably did this just to make it hard for nonprogrammers to use SQL.

✔ NOT NULL means that the column does not allow null values; in other words, the column must contain a value for each row. If you don't specify NOT NULL, the column does not have to contain a value for each row.

✔ Don't forget the commas.

✔ Each DBMS has a maximum length for column names. For Oracle and Sybase, the limit is 30 characters. For DB2, it's 18 characters. It's best to keep the names short to stay compatible with various SQL dialects.

Table 11-2 lists the data types that are allowed for SQL table columns when using IBM's DB2 dialect. Most other SQL dialects support these data types plus others.

Referential integrity

Referential integrity ensures that relationships among database tables are kept in order. In the videos database, several referential integrity rules should be set up. For example, you shouldn't be able to delete a videotape if the tape is currently rented out.

Referential integrity rules can be set up in CREATE TABLE statements using the FOREIGN KEY clause. Here's an example:

```
CREATE TABLE VIDEOS
   (TITLE      VARCHAR(25) NOT NULL,
    RATING     CHAR(3)     NOT NULL,
    VIDEOID    INTEGER(8)  NOT NULL,
    STATUS     INTEGER,
    CUSTID     INTEGER(7),
    DATEOUT    DATE,
```

```
    DATEDUE    DATE,
PRIMARY KEY (VIDEOID),
FOREIGN KEY (CUSTID) REFERENCES VIDCUST
    ON DELETE SET NULL)
```

The CUSTID field in the VIDEOS table is a foreign key to the VIDCUST table. That way, when a videotape is checked out, it is related to a customer's row in the VIDCUST table.

Table 11-2: SQL data types (DB2)

Data type	Explanation
SMALLINT	16-bit integer, values ranging from –32768 to 32767.
INTEGER	32-bit integer, values ranging from –2,147,483,648 to 2,147,483,647.
DECIMAL(p,s)	Decimal value with an assumed decimal point. The p specifies the number of digits in the number, and s indicates how many of those digits fall to the right of the decimal point.
REAL	32-bit floating-point value.
FLOAT	64-bit floating-point value.
DOUBLE PRECISION	Same as FLOAT.
CHAR(x)	Fixed-length character string of length x.
VARCHAR(x)	Variable-length character string, up to x characters (254 bytes maximum). (Some SQL dialects allow longer VARCHAR values.)
LONG VARCHAR(x)	Long variable-length character string.
GRAPHIC(x)	Fixed-length double-byte character string, used for Japanese characters. 127 characters maximum.
VARGRAPHIC(x)	Variable-length double-byte character string. 127 characters maximum.
LONG VARGRAPHIC(x)	Long variable length double-byte character string
DATE	A 10-byte date string.
TIME	A 6-byte time string.
TIMESTAMP	A 26-byte type stamp that includes the date and time with millisecond precision.

The ON DELETE clause means that if a customer's row is deleted from the VIDCUST table while that customer has a tape checked out, any rows in the VIDEOS table for that CUSTID will have their CUSTID set to null.

As an alternative, the FOREIGN KEY clause could have been written like this:

```
FOREIGN KEY (CUSTID) REFERENCES VIDCUST
    ON DELETE RESTRICT
```

Then, SQL would not allow a customer to be deleted from the VIDCUST table if he or she has any tapes checked out in the VIDEOS table.

Querying a Database

As the name Structured *Query* Language suggests, queries are what SQL is all about. A query is an operation that is performed against one or more SQL tables that extracts data from the tables and creates a *result set* which contains the selected rows and columns.

It's crucial that you keep in mind that the result of a query is arranged into rows and columns. To get at this data in a program written in a high-level language such as C or COBOL, a special technique known as a *cursor* is required. Cursor programming is described in Chapter 12. ■

Note that after the tables have been created, they are usually loaded with initial data before they are used. In some cases, the initial data is loaded from existing databases or files. In other cases, the data must be entered from scratch. One way or another, however, data must be loaded into the tables to make the database usable.

The queries in the sections that follow all use the VIDCUST and VIDEOS tables in our video store example. The sample data for these queries is shown in Figure 11-1. By comparing the query results with the sample data, you can study the operation of each SELECT statement, if you're so inclined.

SELECT basics

The SELECT statement is used to query a SQL database. In the SELECT statement, you list the table or tables you want to retrieve data from, the specific table columns you want retrieved (you might not be interested in all of the columns in the table), and other clauses that indicate which specific rows should be retrieved, what order the rows should be presented in, and so on.

VIDCUST table data

CUSTID	LASTNAME	FIRSTNAME
5551111	Smith	John
5552222	Johnson	Mary
5553333	Wilson	Linda
5554444	Lyons	Ted

VIDEOS table data

TITLE	RATING	VIDEOID	STATUS	CUSTID	DATEOUT	DATEDUE
Star Trek: The Motion Picture	G	10002			00/00/00	00/00/00
Star Trek II: The Wrath of Kahn	PG	10003	1	5551111	04/01/95	04/03/95
Star Trek II: The Wrath of Kahn	PG	10004			00/00/00	00/00/00
Star Trek II: The Wrath of Kahn	PG	10024			00/00/00	00/00/00
Star Trek III: The Search for Spock	PG	10025			00/00/00	00/00/00
Star Trek III: The Search for Spock	PG	10005			00/00/00	00/00/00
Star Trek: The Motion Picture	G	10001			00/00/00	00/00/00
Star Trek IV: The Voyage Home	PG	10006	1	5553333	04/01/95	04/03/95
Star Trek IV: The Voyage Home	PG	10007			00/00/00	00/00/00
Star Trek V: Where No One Has Gone Before	PG	10008			00/00/00	00/00/00
Star Trek VI: The Undiscovered Country	PG	10009			00/00/00	00/00/00
Star Trek VI: The Undiscovered Country	PG	10010			00/00/00	00/00/00
Star Trek VI: The Undiscovered Country	PG	10011	1	5553333	04/01/95	04/03/95

Figure 11-1: These tables are used for the queries in this chapter.

Here is a simple example of a SELECT statement that asks for a list of all
video titles in order by VIDEOID:

```
SELECT VIDEOID, TITLE FROM VIDEOS
    ORDER BY VIDEOID
```

Let's take this statement apart piece by piece:

- ✔ SELECT VIDEOID, TITLE names the columns to be included in the query
  result.

- ✔ FROM VIDEOS names the table from which rows are to be retrieved.

- ✔ ORDER BY VIDEOID indicates that the result should be sorted into
  sequence by the VIDEOID column.

In other words, this SELECT statement retrieves the VIDEOID and TITLE for
all rows in the VIDEOS table, and sorts them into VIDEOID sequence. Here is
what the result of this query looks like:

```
videoid  title
-------- -------------------------------------------------
10001    Star Trek: The Motion Picture
10002    Star Trek: The Motion Picture
10003    Star Trek II: The Wrath of Kahn
10004    Star Trek II: The Wrath of Kahn
10005    Star Trek III: The Search for Spock
10006    Star Trek IV: The Voyage Home
10007    Star Trek IV: The Voyage Home
10008    Star Trek V: Where No One Has Gone Before
10009    Star Trek VI: The Undiscovered Country
10010    Star Trek VI: The Undiscovered Country
10011    Star Trek VI: The Undiscovered Country
```

If you want the query to retrieve all of the columns in each row, you can use
an asterisk instead of naming the individual columns:

```
SELECT * FROM VIDEOS ORDER BY VIDEOID
```

This is not a good idea, though, because the columns that make up the table
might change — a new column might be added, or an existing column
dropped. If you use an asterisk, your program won't be able to deal with such
changes to the table definition.

Both of the examples I've shown so far have included an ORDER BY clause. In
a SQL database, the rows stored in a table are not assumed to be stored in
any particular sequence. As a result, if you want the results of a query to be
displayed in sequence, you must include ORDER BY in the SELECT statement.

Narrowing down the query

Suppose you want to find information about one particular video title. To select just certain rows from a table, use the WHERE clause in a SELECT statement. For example:

```
SELECT VIDEOID, TITLE FROM VIDEOS
    WHERE TITLE='Star Trek II: The Wrath of Kahn'
    ORDER BY VIDEOID
```

This statement will select only those rows whose TITLE column equals *Star Trek II: The Wrath of Kahn*, and produce this result set, because there are two copies of that video:

```
videoid  title
-------- ------------------------------------------------
10003    Star Trek II: The Wrath of Kahn
10004    Star Trek II: The Wrath of Kahn
```

Excluding rows

It may be that you want to retrieve all rows *except* those that match certain criteria. For example, if you're not interested in *Star Trek V* (and you shouldn't be), use this query to list all videos except that one:

```
SELECT VIDEOID, TITLE FROM VIDEOS
    WHERE TITLE<>'Star Trek V: Where No One Has Gone Before'
    ORDER BY VIDEOID
```

Mathematical relations

Suppose that you want a list of all videos with VIDEOIDs greater than or equal to 10005. (I don't know why you'd want to do this, but humor me.) In order to do this, you have to use a mathematical expression in the WHERE clause to tell SQL what you want. The following symbols can be used to express mathematical comparisons in SQL:

=   Equal to

<>   Not equal to

<   Less than

>   Greater than

<=   Less than or equal to

>=   Greater than or equal to

So the following statement would retrieve all rows where the VIDEOID column is greater than or equal to 10005:

```
SELECT VIDEOID, TITLE FROM VIDEOS
    WHERE VIDEOID >= 10005
    ORDER BY VIDEOID
```

Here's the result:

```
videoid  title
-------- -------------------------------------------------
10005    Star Trek III: The Search for Spock
10006    Star Trek IV: The Voyage Home
10007    Star Trek IV: The Voyage Home
10008    Star Trek V: Where No One Has Gone Before
10009    Star Trek VI: The Undiscovered Country
10010    Star Trek VI: The Undiscovered Country
10011    Star Trek VI: The Undiscovered Country
```

Singleton SELECT

Now suppose you want to retrieve all the information about a single row of the VIDEOS table. You can use a SELECT statement such as this one to retrieve a single row:

```
SELECT VIDEOID, TITLE FROM VIDEOS
    WHERE VIDEOID = 10010
```

This type of SELECT statement is called a *singleton SELECT*, because it retrieves only one row, usually based on the primary key value. (As a primary key, the VIDEOID field prohibits duplicate values; since we've used the "equal to" expression, only one row can be selected.) Singleton SELECTs are commonly used in client/server programs to allow a user to access or update a specific database row.

Sounds like . . .

Suppose you want to retrieve information about Star Trek VI, but you can't remember the complete title. One of the more interesting variations of the WHERE clause is to use LIKE, which lets you search rows using wildcard searches. A *wildcard search* is a search that will match a search string based on a pattern rather than an exact value, and return the row containing the match. Here's an example and its result set:

```
SELECT VIDEOID, TITLE FROM VIDEOS
    WHERE TITLE LIKE 'STAR TREK VI:%'
    ORDER BY VIDEOID

videoid  title
-------- -------------------------------------------------
10009    Star Trek VI: The Undiscovered Country
10010    Star Trek VI: The Undiscovered Country
10011    Star Trek VI: The Undiscovered Country
```

UNION dues

Suppose you want to create a list of all the *good* Star Trek movies. One way to do that is with a union. A *union* is a combination of two or more result sets that are then treated as a single table. This code shows the union of three separate SELECT statements. It will produce a result set of all of the Star Trek II, IV, and VI videos in the VIDEOS table:

```
SELECT VIDEOID, TITLE FROM VIDEOS
    WHERE TITLE='Star Trek II: The Wrath of Kahn'
  UNION
SELECT VIDEOID, TITLE FROM VIDEOS
    WHERE TITLE='Star Trek IV: The Voyage Home'
  UNION
SELECT VIDEOID, TITLE FROM VIDEOS
    WHERE TITLE='Star Trek VI: The Undiscovered Country'
ORDER BY VIDEOID

videoid  title
-------- -------------------------------------------------
10003    Star Trek II: The Wrath of Kahn
10004    Star Trek II: The Wrath of Kahn
10006    Star Trek IV: The Voyage Home
10007    Star Trek IV: The Voyage Home
10009    Star Trek VI: The Undiscovered Country
10010    Star Trek VI: The Undiscovered Country
10011    Star Trek VI: The Undiscovered Country
```

If you think this example is a bit cumbersome, you're right. This same query could be accomplished without a union, by using ORs in the WHERE clause of a single SELECT:

```
SELECT VIDEOID, TITLE FROM VIDEOS
    WHERE TITLE='Star Trek II: The Wrath of Kahn'
       OR TITLE='Star Trek IV: The Voyage Home'
       OR TITLE='Star Trek VI: The Undiscovered Country'
    ORDER BY VIDEOID
```

Unions are best used when the queries combine data from several similar tables, or when the separate queries are too complicated to link with a simple OR.

Eliminating duplicates

If you want to know the titles of videos in the store, you could use a SELECT statement like this:

```
SELECT TITLE FROM VIDEOS
```

The result would look like this:

```
title
-------------------------------------------------
Star Trek: The Motion Picture
Star Trek: The Motion Picture
Star Trek II: The Wrath of Kahn
Star Trek II: The Wrath of Kahn
Star Trek III: The Search for Spock
Star Trek IV: The Voyage Home
Star Trek IV: The Voyage Home
Star Trek V: Where No One Has Gone Before
Star Trek VI: The Undiscovered Country
Star Trek VI: The Undiscovered Country
Star Trek VI: The Undiscovered Country
```

Unfortunately, each title appears once for each copy of the tape owned by the store. Wouldn't it be nice if you could eliminate the duplicates?

You can, by using the DISTINCT keyword on the SELECT statement. The following query lists all distinct titles in the VIDEOS table:

```
SELECT DISTINCT TITLE FROM VIDEOS
```

The result is as follows:

```
title
-------------------------------------------------
Star Trek: The Motion Picture
Star Trek II: The Wrath of Kahn
Star Trek III: The Search for Spock
Star Trek IV: The Voyage Home
Star Trek V: Where No One Has Gone Before
Star Trek VI: The Undiscovered Country
```

Notice that the duplicates have been eliminated; each different title appears only once in the result set.

Column Functions

What if you want a count of the total number of videos in the store? You'd need to use a special *column function*. SQL's column functions allow you to make calculations on columns. You can calculate the sum, average, largest or smallest value, or count the number of values for an entire column. These functions are summarized in Table 11-3.

Note that these functions operate on the values returned to the result set, which is not necessarily the entire table.

Table 11-3: SQL column functions

Column function	What it does
SUM(column-name)	Adds up the values in the column.
AVG(column-name)	Calculates the average value for the column. Nulls are not figured in the average.
MIN(column-name)	Determines the lowest value in the column.
MAX(column-name)	Determines the highest value in the column.
COUNT(column-name)	Counts the number of rows that have data values for the column.
COUNT(DISTINCT column-name)	Counts the number of distinct values for the column.
COUNT(*)	Counts the number of rows in the result set.

The special function COUNT(*) is used to count the number of rows in the result set.

To use one of these functions, specify it instead of a column name in a SELECT statement. The following SELECT statement calculates the number of rows in the table and the largest VIDEOID value:

```
SELECT COUNT(*), MAX(VIDEOID) FROM VIDEOS
```

Here's the result, showing that there are 11 videos and the highest-numbered VIDEOID:

```
CNT(*)  MAX(videoid)
------  -------------
    11         10011
```

If the SELECT statement includes a WHERE clause, the calculation is done only on the rows that match the WHERE condition. For example, the following query counts the number of copies of *Star Trek II* and shows the highest VIDEOID number assigned to that film:

```
SELECT COUNT(*), MAX(VIDEOID) FROM VIDEOS
    WHERE TITLE = 'Star Trek II: The Wrath of Kahn'
```

The result:

```
CNT(*)  MAX(videoid)
------  -------------
     2         10004
```

Note that the result set of a SELECT statement that uses a column function contains just one row. The advantage of this in a client/server environment is that the summary calculation is done at the server, without having to send all of the rows over the network to the client computer. In other words, the server calculates the summary information, then sends just the result to the client. ■

Groupie SELECTs

Are you still with me? Let's get a little braver and ask for a listing of the number of copies of each video title and how many of each title are rented out. The GROUP BY clause can be used in a SELECT statement to group together rows that have the same value in a specified column. The following SELECT statement calculates the number of copies of each title in the VIDEOS table and the number that are currently rented out (as indicated by a non-null CUSTID column):

```
SELECT TITLE, COUNT(TITLE), COUNT(CUSTID)
    FROM VIDEOS
    GROUP BY TITLE
    ORDER BY TITLE
```

The result:

```
title                                          CNT(title) CNT(custid)
---------------------------------------------- ---------- -----------
Star Trek II: The Wrath of Kahn                    2           1
Star Trek III: The Search for Spock                1
Star Trek IV: The Voyage Home                      2           1
Star Trek V: Where No One Has Gone Before          1
Star Trek VI: The Undiscovered Country             3           1
Star Trek: The Motion Picture                      2
```

Once again, the advantage of using GROUP BY in a client/server application is that the group summaries are calculated at the server rather than at the client computer. This can result in a big reduction in the amount of data that must be sent back and forth over the network. ■

The SELECT statement also has a HAVING clause that allows you to include only certain groups in the result set. The HAVING clause works kind of like the WHERE clause, except that it applies to rows in the result set that are grouped according to the GROUP BY clause. For example, suppose you want to list the titles of all movies you have more than one copy of. This SELECT statement will do the trick:

```
SELECT TITLE, COUNT(TITLE)
   FROM VIDEOS
   GROUP BY TITLE
   HAVING COUNT(TITLE) > 1
```

Here's the result:

```
title                                          CNT(title)
---------------------------------------------- ----------
Star Trek II: The Wrath of Kahn                    2
Star Trek IV: The Voyage Home                      2
Star Trek VI: The Undiscovered Country             3
Star Trek: The Motion Picture                      2
```

Let's All JOIN Together

In the real world, most SELECT statements retrieve data from two or more tables. In our example, let's say we want a list of all videos currently being rented, and the last names of the customers who rented them. This would involve retrieving information from both the VIDEOS table and the VIDCUSTS table. This is called a *join*, and its proper use can be one of the most difficult aspects of SQL.

A simple join

To join two tables, you simply name both tables in the FROM clause of the SELECT statement. Then, in the WHERE clause, you set up a condition that correlates rows from the two tables. For example:

```
SELECT LASTNAME, TITLE FROM VIDEOS, VIDCUST
    WHERE VIDEOS.CUSTID = VIDCUST.CUSTID
```

The result of the above query is as follows:

```
lastname            title
-----------------   ------------------------------------------
Smith               Star Trek II: The Wrath of Kahn
Wilson              Star Trek IV: The Voyage Home
Wilson              Star Trek VI: The Undiscovered Country
```

Notice that because both tables contain a column named CUSTID, I had to *qualify* the names in the WHERE clause to indicate the table: VIDEOS.CUSTID refers to the CUSTID column in the VIDEOS table, while VIDCUST.CUSTID refers to the CUSTID column in the VIDCUST table.

You can further qualify the query with other WHERE conditions, as long as you don't forget to correlate the joined tables. For example, this SELECT statement retrieves all rows for customer 5553333, and the result set shows that the customer has two videos out:

```
SELECT LASTNAME, TITLE FROM VIDEOS, VIDCUST
    WHERE VIDCUST.CUSTID=5553333
    AND VIDEOS.CUSTID = VIDCUST.CUSTID

lastname            title
-----------------   ------------------------------------------
Wilson              Star Trek IV: The Voyage Home
Wilson              Star Trek VI: The Undiscovered Country
```

Subqueries

The hardest SQL concept to understand is the notion of subqueries. If this whole section sails way over your head, don't worry about it. It's not all that important unless you want to be a SQL programmer.

Innie and outie joins

Just as there are two types of bellybuttons, innies and outies, there are two types of joins: inner joins and outer joins. An inner join is a join in which corresponding rows from two tables are combined. An outer join is a join in which any unmatched rows are added to the result of an inner join.

Come again?

This is a tough concept that is best explained with an example. Suppose you have a table of teachers called TEACHERS that includes the teacher's name and room number:

```
teacher        room
-------------  ------
Smith          13
Burns          14
Martin         15
Adams          16
```

Suppose you also have another table of students called STUDENTS, which includes among other columns, the student's room:

```
student        room
-------------  -----------
Adams, M.      13
Benny, J.      16
Benny, R.      13
Jackson, R.    15
Johnson, S.    14
Miller, B.     18
Simone, P.     16
Smith, K.      NULL
```

Notice that one of the students has not been assigned a room yet, and another is assigned a room that doesn't exist in the TEACHER table (room 18). Now suppose you join these tables using this SELECT statement:

```
SELECT STUDENT, STUDENTS.ROOM, TEACHER
   FROM TEACHERS, STUDENTS
   WHERE TEACHERS.ROOM = STUDENTS.ROOM
   ORDER BY STUDENT
```

The results are as follows:

```
student      room         teacher
-----------  -----------  -----------
Adams, M.    13           Smith
Benny, J.    16           Adams
Benny, R.    13           Smith
Jackson, R.  15           Martin
Johnson, S.  14           Burns
Simone, P.   16           Adams
```

Notice that the STUDENT rows for B. Miller and K. Smith were left out of the join because they don't have a corresponding TEACHER row.

In an outer join, any unmatched rows would be added to the result, with null values supplied for missing columns. Thus, the result of an outer join of these two tables would look like this:

```
student      room         teacher
-----------  -----------  -----------
Adams, M.    13           Smith
Benny, J.    16           Adams
Benny, R.    13           Smith
Jackson, R.  15           Martin
Johnson, S.  14           Burns
Miller, B.   18           NULL
Simone, P.   16           Adams
Smith, K.    NULL         NULL
```

The SELECT for this outer join would look like this:

```
SELECT STUDENT, STUDENTS.ROOM,
       TEACHER
   FROM TEACHERS, STUDENTS
   WHERE TEACHERS.ROOM =*
       STUDENTS.ROOM
   ORDER BY STUDENT
```

The asterisk following the equals sign in the WHERE clause indicates an outer join.

A subquery is just what its name suggests: a query within a query. A subquery is used when you need to select rows to include in a query, and a second query is necessary to evaluate each row to be included in the first query.

Huh?

An example will help. Suppose you want a list of all customers who have at least one videotape rented out. Since the VIDCUST table doesn't have a column that indicates whether or not the customer has tapes rented, one way or another this query will require you to search both the VIDCUST and the VIDEOS tables.

You could accomplish this query using a join:

```
SELECT DISTINCT LASTNAME, FIRSTNAME FROM VIDCUST, VIDEOS
    WHERE VIDCUST.CUSTID = VIDEO.CUSTID
```

The result looks like this:

```
lastname              firstname
--------------------  --------------------
Smith                 John
Wilson                Linda
```

When you use a subquery, you code a complete SELECT statement within the WHERE clause of another SELECT statement. The results of the inner SELECT statement are then used in the WHERE clause of the outer SELECT statement to determine which rows to include in the final result set.

There are four basic types of subqueries:

- ✔ Comparative
- ✔ Membership test (IN)
- ✔ Existential (EXISTS)
- ✔ Quantified (ANY and ALL)

The use of subqueries will prove that in SQL, there is always more than one way to accomplish the same query. This section is an exercise in "how many different ways can you find to do the same thing?"

TECHNICAL STUFF

A note on performance, which you can skip

One of the most important issues when creating complex queries, especially those involving subqueries, joins, unions, and compound WHERE clauses, is how efficiently the query can be processed.

The good news is that most SQL database servers include sophisticated optimizers that carefully analyze your queries to determine the most efficient way to carry them out. Unfortunately, restating a query in a different way can sometimes fool the optimizer into selecting a different method to implement the query.

One of the most valuable assets of an experienced SQL programmer is his or her knowledge of the performance trade-offs involved in picking one query technique over another. So the next time you hear a database programmer say, "You can't do that...it'll force SQL to bypass the indexes and performance will go out the window," tell 'em how much their expertise is appreciated.

A comparative subquery

Here is one way to list the customers who have movies rented out by using a subquery:

```
SELECT LASTNAME, FIRSTNAME FROM VIDCUST
    WHERE VIDCUST.CUSTID = (SELECT DISTINCT CUSTID FROM VIDEOS
                                WHERE VIDEOS.CUSTID = VIDCUST.CUSTID)
```

In this example, the outer SELECT is:

```
SELECT LASTNAME, FIRSTNAME FROM VIDCUST
    WHERE VIDCUST.CUSTID =
```

The final result set will consist of two columns — last name and first name — derived from the VIDCUST table:

```
lastname              firstname
------------------    ----------------------
Smith                 John
Wilson                Linda
```

To determine which VIDCUST rows get included in the result set, the query performs the inner SELECT statement once for each row of the VIDCUST table:

```
SELECT DISTINCT CUSTID FROM VIDEOS
     WHERE VIDEOS.CUSTID = VIDCUST.CUSTID
```

This inner SELECT statement produces a result set with just one column —
CUSTID — which will either be null or will contain one occurrence of the
CUSTID value for the VIDCUST row currently being considered.

In other words, when SQL examines the VIDCUST row for CUSTID 5551111, it
performs the subquery to determine whether there are any VIDEOS rows that
have 5551111 in the CUSTID column. If so, the subquery returns the value
5551111. If not, it returns an empty result set.

The outer query then compares the result of the inner query with the
VIDCUST.CUSTID column for the row being considered. If they are equal, the
customer has a tape rented and the row is included in the final result set. If
not, the row is skipped and the next VIDCUST row is considered.

Only the final result set is returned to the user — the intermediate result set
created by the inner query is not seen by the user.

In this description of how the subquery works, and in the descriptions of the
subqueries that follow, keep in mind that the SQL optimizer might discover a
more efficient way to process the request than is indicated by my description. It takes an experienced SQL guru to know which of several alternative
subqueries or join operations will be more efficient. ■

A membership test subquery (IN)

Another way to find out which customers have tapes rented out is to use the
IN keyword with a subquery, like this:

```
SELECT LASTNAME, FIRSTNAME FROM VIDCUST
     WHERE CUSTID IN (SELECT CUSTID FROM VIDEOS
                           WHERE VIDEOS.CUSTID = VIDCUST.CUSTID)
```

The IN keyword tests true if the column specified (CUSTID) matches one of
the rows in the result set of the subquery. In this case, the subquery creates
a result set that is either empty or consists of one or more rows, all having
the CUSTID of the VIDCUST row being examined.

The main difference between the IN subquery and the simple comparative
subquery described in the previous section is that in a comparative subquery, you must ensure that the subquery returns at most one row (you can
do that by including the primary key in the WHERE clause). In the IN subquery, more than one row can be returned. The VIDCUST row (from the outer

query) will be included in the result set if CUSTID matches any of the rows in the inner query result set.

An ANY or ALL subquery

The ANY and ALL keywords let you test each row against all of the rows that are selected for the subquery, using a relational operator such as =, <, >, and so on. If you use ANY, each row considered by the outer SELECT is included in the result set if the comparison you spell out is found to be true for at least one row in the inner SELECT's result set. If you use ALL, the condition must be true for *all* of the subquery's rows for the row to be included.

Here's how the "show me those customers who have a tape rented out" query looks using an ANY subquery:

```
SELECT LASTNAME, FIRSTNAME FROM VIDCUST
    WHERE CUSTID = ANY (SELECT CUSTID FROM VIDEOS)
```

Of all the subquery methods I've presented so far, this one is the most straightforward. For each VIDCUST row considered, the subquery returns a single-column table that consists of all the CUSTID numbers for videos that are rented out. If the VIDCUST row's CUSTID column matches any of these subquery rows, the VIDCUST row is included in the result set.

An existential subquery (EXISTS)

The EXISTS keyword lets you test to see if a subquery finds at least one row that satisfies its WHERE clause. Here's how you could use it to find customers with at least one tape checked out:

```
SELECT LASTNAME, FIRSTNAME FROM VIDCUST
WHERE EXISTS (SELECT * FROM VIDEOS
                    WHERE VIDEOS.CUSTID = VIDCUST.CUSTID)
```

For each customer in the VIDCUST table, SQL will query the VIDEOS table to find any rows that have matching CUSTID values. If at least one row is found, the customer is included in the result set.

Notice that when EXISTS is used, you don't have to indicate which column to include in the subquery. That's because the EXISTS clause tests for the existence of at least one row in the subquery result set. The data contained in the row isn't important.

Updating Table Data

Although SQL is primarily a query language, it also includes statements that let you delete, insert, and update data in SQL tables. The following sections briefly describe the use of these statements.

DELETE

The DELETE statement deletes rows from a table. In client/server systems, the DELETE statement is used in programs that allow users to delete database information.

The simplest DELETE statement deletes all of the rows from a table:

```
DELETE FROM VIDEOS
```

Obviously, a DELETE statement such as this should be used with care. It is more common to use qualified forms of the DELETE statement so that only certain table rows are deleted. ■

The DELETE statement lets you include a simple WHERE clause to specify which table rows should be deleted:

```
DELETE FROM VIDEOS WHERE VIDEOID = 10005
```

In this example, the row whose VIDEOID column equals 10005 is deleted.

You can use a subquery in a DELETE statement. This is especially useful if you want to select records for deletion based on a join with another table. For example, the following DELETE statement deletes all VIDCUST rows that do not currently have a videotape rented:

```
DELETE FROM VIDCUST
    WHERE CUSTID NOT IN (SELECT CUSTID FROM VIDEOS
                            WHERE VIDEOS.CUSTID IS NOT NULL)
```

In this example, the subquery first builds a set of CUSTID values for customers who have tapes rented out. Then, the DELETE statement deletes any rows whose CUSTID values are not in the subquery result set.

Keep in mind that not only can a single DELETE statement result in many rows being deleted from the specified table, but related rows in other tables might also be deleted or changed if referential integrity rules come into play. For example, if you delete a VIDCUST row, any VIDEOS rows that are rented out by that customer will have their CUSTID columns set to nulls.

INSERT

The INSERT statement is SQL's way of getting data into a table. It is frequently used in client/server programs to insert data entered by the user. It is also sometimes used to load starting data into a newly defined database.

Here is an INSERT statement to add a videotape to the VIDEOS table:

```
INSERT INTO VIDEOS (VIDEOID,TITLE,RATING)
    VALUES (10012, 'Star Trek: Generations','PG')
```

Notice that not all of the columns in the VIDEOS table are mentioned in this statement, just VIDEOID, TITLE, and RATING. The columns which weren't mentioned will automatically be given NULL values.

UPDATE

The UPDATE statement is used to update table data. It is frequently used in client/server programs that allow users to update database information.

For example, the following UPDATE statement might be used when a customer rents a videotape:

```
UPDATE VIDEOS
    SET CUSTID = 5551111, STATUS = 1
    WHERE VIDEOID = 10010
```

In this example, two columns in the VIDEOS row for VIDEOID 10010 are updated: the CUSTID is set to 5551111 and the STATUS column is set to 1.

UPDATE statements can also be used to update several table rows at once. For example:

```
UPDATE VIDEOS
    SET TITLE = 'Star Trek: The Longest Movie'
    WHERE TITLE = 'Star Trek: The Motion Picture'
```

This example changes the title of all copies of *Star Trek: The Motion Picture*.

Here's another example:

```
UPDATE VIDEOS
    SET CUSTID = NULL, STATUS = NULL
```

This statement sets the CUSTID and STATUS columns to NULL for all rows in the VIDEOS table. In one operation, this statement effectively "returns" all tapes.

Whew! That was a long chapter. And we're not yet done with SQL. In the next chapter, I'll explain how the SQL elements presented here are incorporated into programs written using programming languages such as C, COBOL, and Visual Basic.

Chapter 12

Programming with SQL

· ·

· ·

C hapter 11 introduced you to SQL, a standardized query language for accessing databases. SQL is not itself a programming language; it is specialized for dealing with databases. If you want to use SQL's skills for querying databases in a program written in a programming language such as C, C++, COBOL, PowerBuilder, or Visual Basic (to name a few), there are ways of invoking SQL statements from within those languages. This chapter introduces you to the most common methods of accomplishing this. I'll also touch on some of the more interesting problems that arise when SQL is used in an application program. (In this chapter, when I talk about "application programs," I'm referring to programs written in the standard programming languages, not applications such as word processing or spreadsheets.)

Don't worry if you don't know all the ins and outs of computer programming. Don't feel daunted if you don't know an assignment statement from a function call (in fact I won't even mention them). The programming examples are meant to give a basic idea of how SQL is used in programs, not to teach you the details of SQL programming, or the details of C (yuck!), C++ (double-yuck!) or even COBOL (triple-yuck!).

How Programs Use SQL

There are three basic ways that SQL statements can be incorporated into a program:

▶ *Embedded SQL*, a way of intermingling SQL statements with the statements of some other programming language, such as COBOL or C.

▶ *CLI*, which stands for *Call Level Interface*, which allows programs to issue SQL statements by calling special *interface functions* that allow communication between the application program and the DBMS. This technique is sometimes referred to as an *SQL API* (*API* stands for *Application Programming Interface*).

▶ *Visual object interfaces,* which are used in visual programming environments such as Visual Basic or PowerBuilder. Actually, an API method typically lies beneath the visual database interface. The visual interface shelters the programmer from the messy details of coding SQL calls — or at least, it tries to. Unfortunately, this sheltering also limits the SQL features that are available, so visual object interfaces aren't used much in heavy-duty client/server programming.

Most of this chapter is devoted to embedded SQL. Near the end of the chapter, I'll point out the differences that come into play when one of the other approaches is used.

Embedded SQL

Here is a portion of a program that consists of bit of C and a bit of embedded SQL. Note that C programmers tend to use lowercase for commands.

```
exec sql
    select CUSTID, LASTNAME, FIRSTNAME, ADDRESS, CITY,
            STATE, ZIPCODE
    into :CUSTID, :LASTNAME, :FIRSTNAME, :ADDRESS, :CITY,
            :STATE, :ZIPCODE
    from VIDCUST
    where CUSTID=:CUSTID;
if (sqlca.sqlcode < 0)
    goto sql_error;
```

Can you guess which part is the embedded SQL? Brilliant! Here are a few noteworthy details about embedded SQL that are apparent in this example:

✔ Everything that appears between *exec sql* and the semicolon is SQL; everything else is C. The keyword *exec sql* is an *introducer*, used to mark the beginning of an SQL statement. The *terminator*, which marks the end of the SQL statement, is the semicolon. (In COBOL, the terminator is the word END-EXEC.)

✔ *Host variables* are application program variables inserted in the embedded SQL, used to move data between the program and the database. Each host variable must be preceded by a colon. The SELECT statement in the example includes an INTO clause that lists the host variables into which the database data should be placed.

✔ After the SELECT statement, the program tests the special variable named *sqlcode*. SQL uses this variable to indicate whether any errors occurred when the SQL statement was executed. The programmer must be careful to check the *sqlcode* field with an IF statement after every embedded SQL statement.

Compiling an embedded SQL program

The following section is pretty technical, and assumes you know something about programming — at the least, what it means to compile and link a source program. If you're not a programmer, you may want to skip this part. ▪

The process for compiling an embedded SQL program is a bit more complicated than the process for compiling a normal program. Figure 12-1 shows a flowchart that diagrams the process. (The flowchart is for IBM's DB2, but other SQL servers that support embedded SQL use a similar process.)

Before the program is compiled, it is processed by a SQL *precompiler,* which looks for SQL statements embedded in the program source code. The precompiler creates two output files. The first is a translated source program, in which any embedded SQL statements have been replaced with calls to the appropriate DBMS library routines that invoke the SQL functions. The second file is a DBRM, which stands for *Database Request Module*. This file contains the SQL statements that were removed from the original source program.

Next, the translated source program is processed by the compiler, which creates an object program that can be processed by the linker to create an executable program. (These steps are identical to the steps used to compile a non-SQL program.)

Meanwhile, the DBRM is processed by a special program called *bind*. Bind examines the SQL requests, optimizes them, and creates an *application plan*, which is essentially an executable version of the embedded SQL statements that are used by the program. When the program is executed, the application plan is used to access the database.

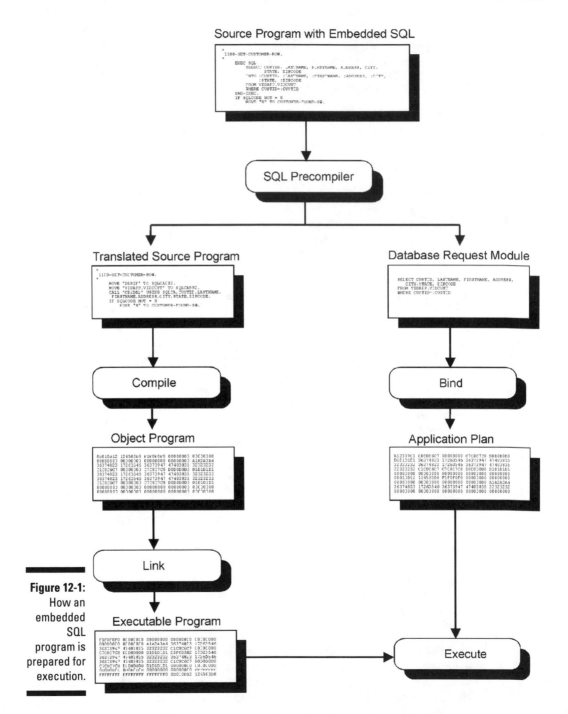

Figure 12-1:
How an
embedded
SQL
program is
prepared for
execution.

The reason for all this complexity is to perform as many of the program-preparation steps as possible *before* the program is executed. All of the steps in Figure 12-1 are performed when the programmer compiles the program.

What the heck is a cursor?

SQL is a database query language, not a procedural programming language. In SQL, a query (a SELECT statement) usually produces a result set consisting of more than one row of data. To use the result set in a COBOL or C program, some method must be provided to access the rows of the query result one at a time. In embedded SQL, that method is called a *cursor*.

A cursor is a pointer to the "current row" of a SQL result set. The cursor allows a program to issue a SQL statement that may retrieve more than one row of data, then process the data one row at a time.

Four embedded SQL statements are used when working with cursors:

✔ The DECLARE CURSOR statement supplies a SELECT statement that is used to access the database and provides a name for the cursor that will be used to access the query results one row at a time. Here's a sample DECLARE CURSOR statement to retrieve all customers from the VID-CUST table who have at least one video rented out:

```
exec sql
    declare VIDCURS cursor for
        select CUSTID,LASTNAME,FIRSTNAME,ADDRESS,HOMEPHONE
            from VIDCUST
            where exists (select * FROM VIDEOS
                            where VIDEOS.CUSTID =
                                    VIDCUST.CUSTID);
```

✔ The OPEN statement executes the SELECT statement contained in the DECLARE CURSOR statement and initiates cursor processing, positioning the cursor immediately before the first row of the result set. Here's an OPEN statement to open the VIDCURS cursor:

```
exec sql
    open VIDCURS;
```

✔ The FETCH statement retrieves the next row from the result set into host variables so the program can process it. If the last row of the result set has already been retrieved, the FETCH statement returns a NOT FOUND error via the SQLCODE variable. The NOT FOUND error is used to terminate a processing loop that fetches and processes each row until there are no rows remaining. Here's an example:

```
exec sql
    fetch VIDCURS
    into :CUSTID, :LASTNAME, :FIRSTNAME, :ADDRESS, :HOME-
    PHONE;
```

✔ The CLOSE statement ends the query processing:

```
exec sql
    close VIDCURS;
```

If we were to write down the basic logic or steps a program might use to open a cursor, fetch all of its rows, and print them in a report (or display them on the screen), it would look like this:

```
declare cursor
open cursor
do while sqlcode = 0
    fetch
    if sqlcode = 100 then exit
    process the data in the host variables
    print a line on the report
loop
close cursor
```

(Note that this example is *pseudocode*, not actual executable code.)

Some SQL dialects let you use *scrollable cursors*, which can move forward or backward through the result set at the whim of the program. These dialects support the following extended forms of the FETCH statement:

✔ FETCH FIRST, which retrieves the first row of the result set.

✔ FETCH LAST, which retrieves the last row of the result set.

✔ FETCH NEXT, which retrieves the next row, just like an ordinary FETCH statement.

✔ FETCH PRIOR, which works backward through the result set by fetching the previous result row. (This might be called FETCH PREVIOUS in some SQL dialects.)

✔ FETCH ABSOLUTE, which retrieves a specific row based on the row number. For example, FETCH ABSOLUTE 10 fetches the tenth row.

✔ FETCH RELATIVE, which fetches a row forward or backward a given number of rows from the current position. For example, FETCH RELATIVE +2 fetches two rows ahead from the current position.

Deleting and updating in a cursor

Cursors can also be used to delete or update individual rows of a query result. Special cursor-based variations of the DELETE and UPDATE statements are used for this purpose. These statements — called *positioned DELETE* and *positioned UPDATE* — are often used in programs that retrieve data from the database, then allow the user to decide whether to delete or update each row on a row-by-row basis.

To delete or update rows via a cursor, the program must first open the cursor and begin fetching rows. A row must be fetched before it can be deleted or updated. In fact, a positioned DELETE or UPDATE statement always deletes or updates the last row that was retrieved by a FETCH statement.

Here's an example of a positioned DELETE statement:

```
exec sql
    delete from VIDCUST
        where current of VIDCURS;
```

Here's a sample positioned UPDATE statement:

```
exec sql
    update VIDCUST
        set LASTNAME  = :LASTNAME,
            FIRSTNAME = :FIRSTNAME,
            ADDRESS   = :ADDRESS,
            CITY      = :CITY,
            STATE     = :STATE,
            ZIPCODE   = :ZIPCODE,
            HOMEPHONE = :HOMEPHONE,
            WORKPHONE = :WORKPHONE
    where current of VIDCURS;
```

Here's what the logic for a positioned delete/update program might look like:

```
declare cursor
open cursor
do while sqlcode = 0
    fetch
    if sqlcode = 100 exit
    process the data in the host variables
    if the row is to be deleted
        delete where current of cursor
    if the row is to be updated
        update where current of cursor
loop
close cursor
```

SQL Call Level Interfaces (CLIs)

So far, we've focused on embedded SQL. Embedded SQL can be used when coding client/server programs in C or COBOL. When working with a visual programming language such as Visual Basic, you're more likely to use one of several *Call Level Interfaces* (*CLIs*). When a CLI is used, a program requests database services by calling special SQL interface routines rather than embedding SQL statements directly in the program.

There are two distinct types of CLIs. First, each DBMS vendor provides its own unique *Application Programming Interface* (*API*) for its database. The vendor-specific API is usually the most efficient way to access the database, but each vendor's API is unique. As a result, if you decide to write programs that use a vendor API, you lock yourself into using that vendor's DBMS. However, your programs will be as efficient as possible.

The second type of CLI is a standard or open API which is supported by more than one database vendor. Several open database APIs are available:

 ✔ **SAG CLI.** The *SQL Access Group* created a standard CLI for SQL database access in 1992. The SAG CLI is also known as the X/Open CLI.

 ✔ **ODBC.** Microsoft's *Open DataBase Connectivity* (*ODBC*) is a standard CLI for accessing SQL databases from Windows. ODBC is based on the SAG CLI, but is more powerful. If you're a Microsoft follower, ODBC is where the action is.

 ✔ **IDAPI.** The *Integrated Database Application Programming Interface* (*IDAPI*) is an alternative to ODBC proposed by Borland, IBM, Novell, and WordPerfect. This is the CLI to stake your reputation on if you despise Microsoft.

One of the basic drawbacks of using a generic CLI is the "least common denominator" syndrome. In order for the generic CLI to work on all platforms, it can implement only those SQL features that are sure to be available no matter what DBMS product is used on the server. As a result, many of the bells and whistles that might make one vendor's DBMS better than another's may be unavailable if you access the DBMS through a generic CLI such as ODBC or IDAPI. ■

Any Call Level Interface must provide certain basic functions to enable a program to connect to a SQL database and access data. The following types of calls are usually provided:

 ✔ Connect to a database server
 ✔ Disconnect from a database server

     ✔ Send a SQL statement to the server

     ✔ Execute a previously sent statement

     ✔ Get the status code from a previously executed statement

     ✔ Instruct the DBMS how and where to return rows from the result set

     ✔ Fetch the next row of the result set

The techniques for programming a SQL CLI program are too complicated to even bother with an example here. (You're welcome.)

Stored Procedures

One basic difference between a CLI program and an embedded SQL program is that in an embedded SQL program, the Bind step translates and optimizes the program's SQL requests and stores them as an application plan. This makes for efficient programs, because the SQL statements don't have to be translated and optimized every time the program is run.

In a CLI program, the program sends the SQL statement to the DBMS as a text string, so the statement must be translated and optimized every time the program is run. Needless to say, this can be inefficient.

To eliminate this inefficiency, most DBMS vendors let you create *stored procedures* — collections of SQL statements that are translated, optimized, and stored in executable form at the database server. Rather than send SQL statement text to the server to be translated, optimized, and executed, a CLI program can send a request to execute a stored procedure. The result is similar to the way optimized SQL statements are stored in an application plan when embedded SQL is used.

A basic difference between embedded SQL with its efficient application plans and CLI with stored procedures is that the stored procedures can contain more than one SQL statement, and can even contain procedure code. Thus, stored procedures can be used to move much of the transaction processing in a client/server application to the server side of the equation.

Figures 12-2 and 12-3 illustrate the obvious performance advantage of using stored procedures rather than embedded SQL. In this example, a program updates five database tables: CUST, ORDERS, LINEITEM, INVENTORY, and SHIPPING. Figure 12-2 shows the embedded SQL version of this transaction. Here, each UPDATE statement requires a separate interaction between the client and the server: First the client must request the update, then the server must return the results of the update (that is, the SQLCODE status). A total of ten network transmissions are needed.

Embedded SQL

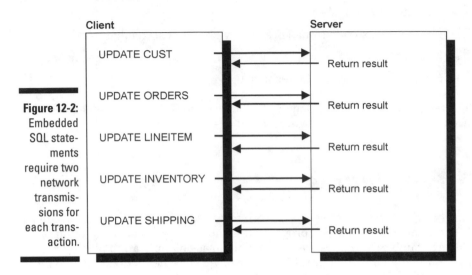

Figure 12-2:
Embedded SQL statements require two network transmissions for each transaction.

Figure 12-3 shows the stored procedure version. Notice that only two network transmissions are needed: one to initiate the stored procedure, the other to return the result. Because fewer network transmissions are involved, the client/server application is simpler and more efficient.

Stored Procedure

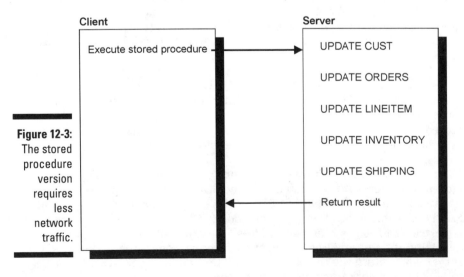

Figure 12-3:
The stored procedure version requires less network traffic.

Transaction Processing

Consider a simple application in which money is transferred from a checking account table (CHECKING) to a savings account table (SAVING). A transaction such as this will require two UPDATE statements: one to the CHECKING table, the other to the SAVING table. Both updates must be completed. If the first one succeeds and the second one fails, the customer will end up losing money: the amount will be deducted from the CHECKING table, but no corresponding amount will be credited to the account in the SAVING table.

SQL provides for this by introducing the notion of a *transaction* — a set of database updates that must be completed as a set. If SQL is unable to complete all of the updates in the transaction, then none of the updates will be made.

All of the database updates that make up a transaction are called a *unit of work*. According to SQL gurus, a unit of work must be performed *atomically*. This has nothing to do with nuclear power. It just means that the unit of work cannot be divided: either all of it must be done, or none of it. ■

Two SQL statements are used for transaction processing:

✔ The COMMIT statement marks the successful end of a transaction. It informs SQL that all of the preceding SQL updates should be considered a single unit of work. A program should issue a COMMIT statement after all of the SQL statements that make up the transaction have been successfully completed.

✔ The ROLLBACK statement marks the unsuccessful end of a transaction. It tells SQL that something went wrong with one of the SQL updates, and any changes that have been made to the database since the last COMMIT or ROLLBACK statement should be backed out.

Here is a sample of the logic a program might follow for a transaction that updates two tables (CHECKING and SAVING):

```
get data from the user

update CHECKING
if sqlcode not = 0 goto error

update SAVING
if sqlcode not = 0 goto error

commit
end program

error:
    rollback
```

If either of the two SQL statements in this program fails, a ROLLBACK statement is issued to back out all of the previous updates. Otherwise, if both statements succeed, a COMMIT statement is issued to complete the transaction.

To implement the ROLLBACK statement, the SQL DBMS must keep a copy of the original version of any table row that is updated or deleted during the transaction. These copies, called the *transaction log*, form a complete record of the transaction and allow the DBMS to roll back the transaction by restoring each updated row to its original value. When a COMMIT statement is issued, the log records for the transaction are marked as complete.

The transaction log serves another purpose as well: it lets the DBMS restore the database to a stable condition if a power outage or some other glitch should cause the database server to go down. When the database server is restored, the transaction log is examined to determine whether there were any *in-flight* transactions when the failure occurred — that is, transactions that were only partially completed. If so, the in-flight transactions are backed out.

Concurrency and Locking

One of the most challenging aspects of developing client/server SQL applications is providing for *concurrency* — that is, allowing more than one user to access the database at a time. SQL uses *locks* to ensure that multiple database users don't interfere with each other.

A lock is a hold placed on a row that prevents other users from accessing the row until the lock is released. Any user that tries to access a row that is locked must wait until the lock is released.

Locks are designed to address three common concurrency problems:

✔ **Lost updates.** Suppose two users enter an order for 50 units of part number 123 at the same time. Both users issue a singleton SELECT to retrieve the row for part 123, and both see the same value for the QTYONHAND column (let's say, 200). The first user calculates the new on-hand quantity by subtracting 50 from 200, and issues an UPDATE statement that sets the QTYONHAND column to 150. The second user subtracts 50 units from the QTYONHAND column and updates the table. The table should now show 100 units available, right? Wrong. Instead, it shows 150 units available. Why? Because the second user's update superseded the first user's update. In effect, the first user's update was lost.

✔ **Access to uncommitted data.** Now suppose that two users are entering an order for 50 units of part number 123. This time, the first user issues the singleton SELECT statement, then issues the UPDATE statement to update the row for part 123 to show 150 units on hand instead of 200, then displays a screen that allows the user to confirm or cancel the order. In the meantime, the second user begins his or her order by issuing a singleton SELECT for part 123. He or she now sees 150 units on hand because the other user already updated the table. Back to the first user, who realizes that the customer wanted part number 132, not 123, so he or she cancels the order. This causes a ROLLBACK of the transaction, which restores the row for part 123 to 200 units on hand. Then, the second user updates the table to show 100 units on hand and commits the update. 50 units of inventory have been lost because the second user was allowed to see the first user's update before it was committed.

✔ **Unrepeatable reads.** Suppose the first user runs a query program that displays a list of all rows in the inventory table. The user issues a SELECT statement and works through the result set using a cursor. When part 123 appears on the screen, showing that 200 units are available. The user moves on, displaying other rows. In the meantime, the second user receives an order for 50 units of part 123 and updates the table to show that only 150 units are now available. The first user then decides that he or she should check on part 123 again. Since the DBMS doesn't support scrollable cursors, the only way to get back to part 123 is to reissue the SELECT statement and start over from the beginning. This time, part 123 is displayed, showing 150 units on hand instead of 200. In other words, fetching a row from a table twice yielded different results because the second user was allowed to update a row which the first user was accessing via a cursor.

By default, SQL places a lock on every row that a program accesses, preventing other users from accessing the row. The lock is not released until the program issues a COMMIT statement or the program terminates. This lock prevents all three of the above concurrency problems from occurring, in each case by preventing the second user from updating the part 123 row until the first user is finished with it.

Here are some of the key aspects of SQL locking to consider:

✔ Locks usually affect more data than the row that is actually required to be locked. Most DBMS systems actually lock the entire *page* that holds the row that needs to be locked. Each page is a 4K unit of storage that may contain data from other rows. These rows will be held hostage by the lock even though they are innocent bystanders.

✔ There are two basic types of locks that can be applied: *shared* and *exclusive*. A shared lock is a read-only lock that allows other users to read the locked data but not update it. An *exclusive* lock prevents other users from reading or updating the data until the lock is released.

✔ A *deadlock* situation occurs when two users are waiting for resources that are held by each other. Figure 12-4 shows an example of how deadlock can occur. Here, User A begins by retrieving and locking Row 1 (1) and User B retrieves and locks Row 2 (2). Next, User A then attempts to read Row 2, but must wait until User B releases the lock on Row 2 (3). Finally, User B tries to read and lock Row 1 (4). At this point, a deadlock will occur. User B cannot read Row 1 until User A releases it, but User A is stuck waiting for User B to release Row 2. Both must wait forever, or until the DBMS intervenes and cancels one of the users' request. (Doesn't it sound kind of like a trick Spock would play to get an alien computer to relinquish control of the Enterprise?)

TECHNICAL STUFF

Real-world concurrency (better read this!)

SQL locks are nice, but in the real world of client/server processing, they're not enough to provide solid concurrency control and acceptable performance. The problem with SQL locks is that they must often be held while data is displayed on the screen and the user contemplates an update. This might be tolerable if users can type 200 words per minute and never get distracted, but what if a user goes to lunch while data is displayed on the screen and a lock is held? Is it acceptable to hold a lock for an hour? Or what if the user is in management and takes a two-hour lunch?

In the real world, most programs never hold a lock while data is displayed on the screen for the user to contemplate. Instead, some other mechanism is used to ensure that data is not trashed because of concurrent updates. The most common method is to place a timestamp column in the table. Any program that updates a row in the table must also update the row's timestamp column. When a program fetches a row to display on the screen, it remembers the timestamp value that was retrieved for the row, then issues a COMMIT statement to release any locks that are held. Later, when the row is updated, the row is fetched and the new timestamp value is compared with the old. If the timestamps differ, it means that someone else has updated the row, and the update must be aborted.

This timestamp method is messy, because it assumes that every program that updates the table will obey the rules by testing for a changed timestamp when updating, and setting the timestamp column before updating. It can also annoy users by informing them that their updates have been rejected because some other user beat them to the punch. But it is the way concurrency is handled in most real-world situations.

This doesn't mean that SQL locks aren't used. Locks must still be used to ensure that all of the updates made by a transaction are completed without interference from other users. But the rule of thumb is: Always relinquish locks by issuing a COMMIT or ROLLBACK statement before returning control back to the user.

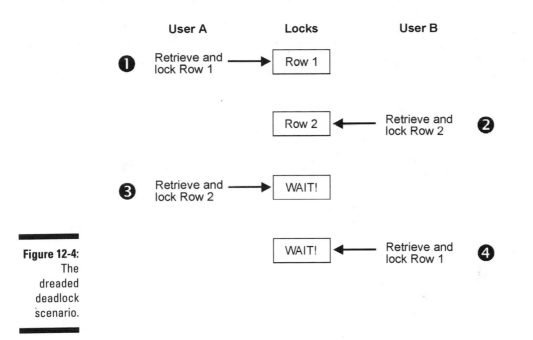

Figure 12-4:
The
dreaded
deadlock
scenario.

Enough SQL already! In the next chapter, I'll back away from the details of SQL programming a bit and explain the issues that should be considered when designing a relational database.

Chapter 13

Relational Database Design

• •

• •

*A*s a reward for slogging through the ins and outs of SQL in the last two chapters, I'm going to let you relax a little and go back to some basics: in this chapter you'll find techniques for designing good relational databases. Designing a database is sometimes referred to with the lofty term *data modeling*, which is a fancy way of saying planning your database.

Database design is a crucial part of any computer application development, client/server or not, and many books have been written about the subject. This chapter isn't a substitute for an entire book on data modeling, but it should give you enough information so that you'll know what to say when someone shoves an entity-relationship diagram in your face or asks you if you've normalized your design.

Database design is the type of process that invites authors to create step-by-step procedures, and I certainly don't want to be left out. So what follows is a list of steps you can follow to create a good database design. Keep in mind, however, that in real life most experienced analysts somehow manage to do many if not all of these steps at once.

Step 1: Create a Charter for the Database

Every database has a reason for being, and you'll be in a much better position to create a good database design if you start by considering why the database needs to exist and what will be expected of the database.

Database designers sometimes fall into one of two traps: Assuming that the data exists for its own sake, or assuming that the data exists for the sake of the Information Systems (IS) department. Of course, databases exist for users. Before designing a database, find out why the users need the database and what they expect to accomplish with it.

You can think of this purpose statement as a *mission statement* or a *charter* for the database. Here is an example of a charter for a database for a video store:

> "The purpose of the Video Rental database is to keep track of all the customers who frequent our store and the videotapes we keep in stock. The database should enable us to keep track of which tapes are rented to which customers, quickly determine if a tape is available for rental, and alert us to tapes that are more than a few days overdue. It should also help customers locate a tape when they cannot remember the exact title, or when they want to find a film starring a particular actor or actress."

For a more complicated application, the database charter might well be more detailed than this. The key point, however, is that the charter identifies the unique capabilities that the user expects from the database: in this case, the ability to highlight overdue tapes and help customers find movies. ■

An important part of this step is examining how the data is currently stored. If the data is currently stored in a Lotus 1-2-3 or Excel spreadsheet, carefully examine the spreadsheets. If paper forms are used, study the forms to see what kind of data is included on them. If the data is scribbled on the back of napkins, collect the napkins and scrutinize them.

Step 2: Make a List and Check It Twice

Once you're sure you understand the purpose of the database, sit down with a yellow pad and a box of freshly sharpened #2 pencils and start writing. Start by listing the major tables that the database includes.

When creating and fiddling with the lists of tables and data items, it is often helpful to think in terms of *entities*: tangible real-world objects that the database needs to keep track of — people and things. For the video database, you might list the following entities:

 ✔ Customers

 ✔ Tapes

 ✔ Actors

People who teach such things at universities and write books about them will probably object, but I'm just going to use the term *table* and *entity* pretty much interchangeably. Entities are abstractions of the real-world objects about which the database stores data. The various entities that make up your database design will eventually be rendered as SQL database tables, so why not think of them as tables from the start?

After you've identified the major tables (er, entities), list the data elements that fall under each one. For example:

```
Customers
    Last name
    First name
    Address
    Phone number
    Credit card number

Tapes
    Title
    Status (rented, on hold, damaged, or available)
    Customer number (if rented)
    Date out
    Date due
    Category
    Rating
    Vendor name
    Vendor address
    Vendor phone number

Actors
    Last name
    First name
    Date of Birth
    Date of Death
    Gender
```

Don't be afraid to crumple up the paper and start over. In fact, if you are doing this step right, you'll end up with lots of wads of yellow paper on your floor. You can clean up when you're done.

For example, you may realize that the vendor information stored in the TAPES table should actually be its own table. So you should break TAPES into two tables, tapes and vendors:

```
Tapes
     Title
     Status
     Customer number (if rented)
     Date out
     Date due
     Category
     Rating

Vendors
     Vendor name
     Vendor address
     Vendor phone number
```

As you design your database, creating additional tables will become a regular occurrence. You'll discover tables that should be split because they have data for two entities, or you'll discover entities that you simply forgot to include. The number of tables in a database rarely goes *down* as you refine the design.

Be sure to include tables that represent business transactions to the list. For example, when a customer rents a videotape, an invoice transaction is created. The INVOICES table might appear on your preliminary list as follows:

```
Invoices
     Customer number
     Date out
     Date due
     Date returned
     Tapes rented
     Invoice amount
```

This table has problems in its current form. For example, how do we identify which tapes have been rented? What if more than one tape is rented? What if three tapes are rented on Monday, one is returned on Tuesday, one on Wednesday, and the third tape is overdue? I'll defer these issues until we get to Step 4 in a few moments.

Step 3: Add Keys

In an SQL database, every table should have a column or combination of columns that uniquely identifies every row in the table. This column (or combination of columns) is called the *primary key*. In this step, you revisit all of the entities in your design and make sure each one has a useful primary key.

Selecting the primary key for a table is sometimes a challenge. For example, what field should be used as the primary key for the CUSTOMERS table? Several choices come to mind:

- ✔ **Last Name.** This works fine until you enroll your second customer named Smith. It can also be a problem when you enroll your first customer named Zoldoske. Every time you type in this name, you'll spell it differently: Zoldosky, Soldoskie, Zaldosky.

- ✔ **First and Last Name.** This works better than Last Name alone, but there still might be two Lucy McGillicuddy's in the neighborhood.

- ✔ **Phone Number.** Many video stores use your phone number as a customer number, but there are two problems with that. First, what happens if a customer changes his or her phone number? Changing a primary key value is possible but not desirable. Second, don't you feel a little uneasy when you walk up to the counter and the clerk says, "Phone number please?" just when you notice a suspicious looking guy in a trenchcoat hanging around? Many people would prefer not to say their phone number out loud when others can hear it.

If no field in the table jumps out as an obvious primary key, you may need to create a meaningless key for the table. For example, you could add a Customer Number data item for the CUSTOMERS table. The Customer Number would be a unique number which has no meaning other than as an identifier for a specific customer. A number of this type is often called a *counter* or a *serial number*.

A key can also be a *composite key* — a key made up of two or more columns. The column values are combined to form the complete key value.

In the Video database, I eventually decided to use a serial number as the key for all of the tables: CUSTOMERS, TAPES, VENDORS, INVOICES, and ACTORS.

Incidentally, using a meaningless serial number as the primary key for the CUSTOMERS table doesn't mean that the user has to use that number to access the database. The table can be searched on any column. So the clerk can still look up the customer by phone number or name.

As you add primary keys to your tables, you can also add those columns as foreign keys in related tables. For example, a Vendor Number column could be added to the TAPES table so that each tape is related to a particular vendor.

After the key columns have been added, the list looks like this:

```
Customers                          Vendors
    Customer number (key)              Vendor number (key)
    Last name                          Vendor name
    First name                         Vendor address
    Address                            Vendor phone number
    Phone number
    Credit card number             Actors
                                       Actor number (key)
Tapes                                  Tape number
    Tape number (key)                  Last name
    Title                              First name
    Status                             Date of Birth
    Customer number (if                Date of Death
            rented)                    Gender
    Date out
    Date due                       Invoices
    Category                           Invoice number (key)
    Rating                             Customer number
    Vendor number                      Date out
                                       Date due
                                       Date returned
                                       Tape number
                                       Invoice amount
```

Step 4: Normalize!

Normalization refers to the process of eliminating redundant information and other problems in a database design. To normalize the database, you identify problems in the design and rectify them, usually by creating additional tables. Thus, after normalizing your design, you'll almost always have more tables than you had when you started.

There are five different levels of normalization, known as the five normal forms. In case you're interested, these five normal forms are described in the sidebar, "The Five Abby-Normal Forms."

To normalize the Videos database, I made several changes to the design:

✔ I changed all the table names to singular. Before, I had used a mixture of singular and plural names.

✔ I broke the INVOICES table into two tables: INVOICE and RENTED TAPE. When a customer rents one or more tapes, one row is created in the INVOICE table and one row is created in the RENTED TAPE table for each tape rented.

✔ The Customer Number, Date Returned, and Date Due columns were removed from the TAPE table because they are contained in the new RENTED TAPE table. The Date Out column remains in the TAPE table.

✔ The Invoice Amount column was removed from the INVOICE table. The RENTED TAPE table includes a Rental Amount column, and the total amount of an invoice can be determined by summing all the Rental Amount columns for all rows for the invoice. (A more complete design might include columns such as sales tax, discount, amount paid, and balance due, but this design is already getting pretty big for a book example!)

✔ I created a separate CATEGORY table to hold the descriptions of the various categories used to shelve the movies (Horror, Drama, and so on). The TAPE table now has a Category Code column, which relates each tape to a row in the CATEGORY table.

✔ I created a new table called ACTOR/TAPE to link actors to tapes. The previous design didn't provide any way to implement this many-to-many relationship. (Each tape can have more than one actor, and each actor can appear in more than one film.)

✔ Oops...what if the same videotape is available from several vendors? I added a TAPE/VENDOR table to implement this many-to-many relationship.

The resulting design looks like this:

```
Customer
    Customer number (key)
    Last name
    First name
    Address
    Phone number
    Credit card number

Tape
    Tape number (key)
    Title
    Status
    Category code
```

```
Category
     Category code (key)
     Category description

Tape/Vendor
     Tape number (composite key)
     Vendor number (composite key)

Vendor
     Vendor number (key)
     Vendor name
     Vendor address
     Vendor phone number

Actor
     Actor number (key)
     Last name
     First name
     Date of birth
     Date of death
     Gender

Tape/Actor
     Actor number (composite key)
     Tape number (composite key)

Invoice
     Invoice number (key)
     Customer number
     Date out

Rented Tape
     Invoice number (composite key)
     Tape number (composite key)
     Date due
     Date returned
     Rental amount
```

As I mentioned, there are five degrees of normality (it's a good thing these apply to databases and not people; some of us might be off the chart), but most database designers settle for the first through third normal forms, as the requirements of the fourth and fifth normal forms are a bit picky. As a result, I won't go into the fourth and fifth normal forms here. The first three normal forms are described in the following sections.

First normal form (1NF)

A database is in 1NF when each table row is free of repeating data. For example, it would be tempting to design the INVOICE table like this:

```
Invoice
    Invoice number (key)
    Customer number
    Tape number 1
    Tape number 2
    Tape number 3
    Tape number 4
```

This design would allow the customer to rent as many as four tapes on a single invoice. But what if the customer wants to rent five tapes? That may be against store policy now, but what if the store policy changes next year? The solution to this problem is to create a separate RENTED TAPE table that is related back to the INVOICE table by using Invoice Number as a foreign key.

Second normal form (2NF)

Second normal form applies only to tables that have composite keys — that is, a primary key made up of two or more table columns. When a table has a composite key, every column in the table must depend on the entire key, not just a part of the key, for the table to be in second normal form.

Consider the following table, in which the primary key is a combination of the Tape Number and Actor Number columns:

```
Tape
    Tape number (composite key)
    Actor number (composite key)
    Title
    Actor name
```

This table breaks 2NF on two counts. The Title depends solely on the Tape Number, and the Actor Name depends solely on the Actor Number. The solution, typically, is to divide the columns into two tables and create a third table that pairs rows from the two:

```
Tape
    Tape number (key)
    Title
```

```
Actor
    Actor number (key)
    Actor name

Actor/Tape
    Tape number (composite key)
    Actor number (composite key)
```

Third normal form (3NF)

A table is in third normal form if every column in the table depends on the entire primary key, and none of the non-key columns depend on each other.

Consider this table:

```
Tape
    Tape number (key)
    Title
    Category
    Price
```

Suppose that the store prices its rentals by category: Horror, Drama, and Comedy films are $1.99, Music Videos are $2.49, and New Releases are $2.99. In this case, the Price column would depend not only on the Tape Number column, but also on the Category column. This table is not in 3NF.

The solution is to create an additional table for Prices:

```
Tape
    Tape number (key)
    Title
    Category

Price
    Category (key)
    Price
```

Step 5: Denormalize!

What! Now I'm telling you to about-face? Sometimes. There are many cases in which a database will operate much more efficiently if you bend the normalization rules a bit. In particular, it is sometimes wise to build a certain amount of redundancy into the database for performance reasons. This is

TECHNICAL STUFF

The official definitions of the five Abby-Normal forms

In case you're interested, and just to point out how esoteric these things can be, here's a list of the original definitions of the five normal forms, in the original Greek, as formulated by C.J. Date in his classic book, *An Introduction to Database Systems* (Addison-Wesley, 1974):

First Normal Form. A relation R is in *first normal form* (1NF) if and only if all underlying domains contain atomic values only.

Second Normal Form. A relation R is in *second normal form* (2NF) if and only if it is in 1NF and every nonkey attribute is fully dependent on the primary key.

Third Normal Form. A relation R is in *third normal form* (3NF) if and only if it is in 2NF and every nonkey attribute is nontransitively dependent on the primary key.

Fourth Normal Form (4NF). A relation R is in fourth normal form (4NF) if and only if, whenever there exists an MVD in R, say $A \rightarrow\rightarrow B$, then all attributes of R are also *functionally dependent* on A (i.e., $A \rightarrow X$ for all attributes X of R).

(An *MVD* is a *multivalued dependence*.)

Fifth Normal Form (5NF). A relation R is in fifth normal form (5NF) — also called projection-join normal form (PJ/NF) — if and only if every join dependency in R is implied by the candidate keys of R.

called *denormalization*, and it's perfectly acceptable as long as you do it with good reason.

Here are some examples of denormalization you might consider for the Videos database:

- ✔ Restoring the InvoiceAmount column to the INVOICE table so that the program doesn't have to retrieve all of the RENTED TAPE rows to total the invoice.

- ✔ Adding a Title field to the RENTED TAPE table so the program doesn't have to retrieve the TAPE row to display an invoice.

- ✔ Adding the customer's name and address to the INVOICE table so the program doesn't have to retrieve that information from the CUSTOMER table every time to display an invoice.

- ✔ Adding the Category Description to the TAPE table so the program doesn't have to look it up in the CATEGORY table each time.

In each case, the decision on whether the database should be denormalized depends on the performance tradeoff of updating the redundant data in several places versus the improved access speed.

Step 6: Pick Legal Names

All through the data design process, the names I've used have been descriptive enough so that I could identify exactly what each table and column represents. However, most SQL dialects won't allow tables with names like RENTED TAPE or columns with names like Date of Birth or Rental Amount. At some point in the design, you have to assign actual names that SQL will allow for tables and columns.

When picking names, it's best to use names that any SQL dialect will allow. That means adhering to these rules:

- No special characters — letters and numbers only.

- Table and column names should be 18 characters. Shorter is better, as long as the meaning is preserved. Instead of RENTED TAPE, use a name like RENTEDTAPE.

Step 7: Draw a Picture

Computer professionals love to draw pictures, possibly because it's more fun than real work, but mostly because, as they say, a picture is worth 1,024 words. A special type of diagram called an *entity-relationship diagram*, or *ERD*, is often drawn when creating a data model.

The ERD shows each of the tables that make up a database and the relationships among the tables. Usually, the tables are shown as rectangles and the relationships are shown as arrows. Sometimes the columns within each table are listed in the rectangles, sometimes not. Arrowheads are used to indicate one-to-one, one-to-many, many-to-one, and many-to-many relationships. Other notational doodads may be attached to the diagram, depending on which drawing school the database designer attended.

The ERD also uses the legal table and column names finalized in the previous step. Figure 13-1 shows a typical ERD.

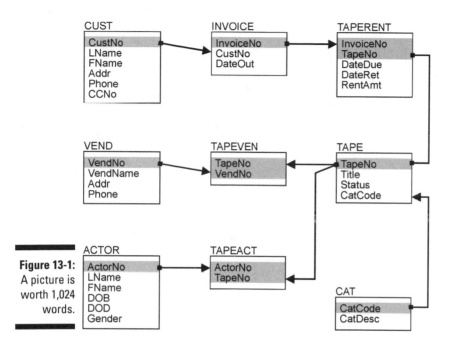

Figure 13-1:
A picture is
worth 1,024
words.

Database design gets even more interesting when portions of the database
are spread out over several locations. That's the subject of the next chapter:
distributed databases.

Chapter 14

Distributed Databases

· ·

· ·

C lient/server computing is closely tied to the development of distributed databases. In the broadest sense, *all* client/ server applications can be thought of as distributed database applications, since they deal with client computers accessing data held on remote database servers. But a true distributed database comes into play when the database is not contained on a single database server, but on several servers spread throughout an organization.

This chapter gives an overview of what a distributed database is all about, the different ways of implementing it, and the special considerations it imposes upon client/server computing.

What Is a Distributed Database?

A *distributed database* is a collection of tables that is spread out over two or more servers. For example, a customer table might be maintained on a server at the corporate office, whereas a credit history table might be kept at a server in the credit department. Together, the customer and credit history table form a complete database, but they are not stored together on the same server. Figure 14-1 depicts such a database.

Distributed database systems are not nearly as simple a matter as Figure 14-1 might lead you to believe. All sorts of things can go wrong once data has

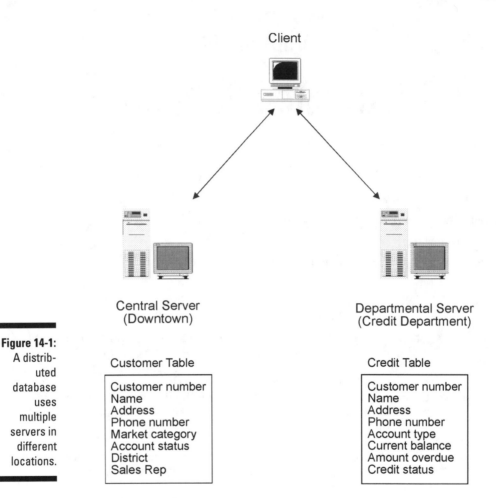

Client

Central Server
(Downtown)

Departmental Server
(Credit Department)

Figure 14-1:
A distrib-
uted
database
uses
multiple
servers in
different
locations.

Customer Table

Customer number
Name
Address
Phone number
Market category
Account status
District
Sales Rep

Credit Table

Customer number
Name
Address
Phone number
Account type
Current balance
Amount overdue
Credit status

been distributed on more than one server. The following are just some of the considerations:

✔ Notice in Figure 14-1 that certain fields are duplicated in the customer table and the credit table — in particular, the customer number, name, address, and phone number. The distributed database system must make sure that if a customer moves, the address change is reflected in both tables.

✔ What if the corporate office uses a mainframe computer running DB2, but the credit department uses a DEC minicomputer running the VAX operating system and uses Oracle as its database? Will the two database systems get along?

✔ Locking table rows while they are being updated is tougher if the tables live on different servers.

> ✔ If a customer is deleted from the customer table, should he or she also be deleted from the credit table?
>
> ✔ What happens if a transaction fails after an update has been completed to one of the tables but not the other?

Distributed Databases: Why Bother?

If a distributed database is such a big problem, why bother with it at all? Why not just store all data on one huge server (probably a mainframe), in one central location, and spare yourself the hassle of dealing with distributed data?

There are two reasons:

1. **Performance.** As a general rule, the closer you can place data to the people who use that data the most, the better the database performance will be. So, for example, the database tables that must be accessed and updated to process customer orders should be placed on a server locally accessible to the order processing department rather than on the corporate mainframe.

2. **Evolution**. Few businesses appear overnight, with ideal distributed database systems installed from the start. Client/server is often used to tie previously disconnected data together to create new applications that couldn't be implemented before. The order processing department has probably already created its own system, as have the marketing, credit, sales, research, production, and personnel departments. In short, the reason a distributed database is needed is because the data is *already* distributed.

Which Is the Greatest Commandment?

The famous database guru C.J. Date has come up with 12 rules or characteristics of "true" distributed databases. The 12 rules address the types of problems that can occur because of the mere fact that data is distributed among several systems instead of gathered in one location. In case you are interested in what the 12 rules are, they are summarized in the sidebar "Date's 12 rules" at the end of this section.

It's important to realize that none of the distributed database products available on the market today comes close to satisfying all of Date's rules. The rules define an ideal distributed database environment that doesn't yet exist. ∎

If you were to ask, "Which of the 12 distributed database rules is the greatest?" the reply would be that all of the distributed database rules can be summed up in the "Golden Rule of Distributed Database." It goes something like this:

The fact that data is distributed should make absolutely no difference to users.

In other words, distributed database should be totally transparent. It shouldn't matter to the user whether the data in question is stored on the client computer, on the LAN server down the hall, the departmental minicomputer in the basement, or the corporate mainframe halfway across the country. ■

Note that "users" in this context means both end users who work with the computers to access data and the programs themselves. In other words, the application developer shouldn't have to hard-wire information about the location of distributed data into the programs. The distributed DBMS should handle such details automatically.

Bulging at the Middleware

The term *middleware* refers to a rather nebulous category of client/server software that sits in the middle, between the client and the server. Various categories of middleware exist, but the category that concerns us here is *SQL middleware*. SQL middleware is software that is designed to eliminate the differences between various SQL servers. The middleware provides a common SQL interface that can be used in client programs to access data on any of the supported servers.

The job of the SQL middleware is to locate the data being requested, translate the SQL request into a form that can be understood by the server in question, forward the request, get the resulting data, and send it back to the client application. When it works, the program doesn't have to know or care what server is ultimately accessed.

The best-known example of SQL middleware is Enterprise Data Access/SQL (EDA/SQL), from Information Builders, Inc. EDA allows you to access data stored in dozens of different formats, including:

✔ DB2 (IBM)
✔ Oracle
✔ Ingres
✔ IMS
✔ VSAM files
✔ Lots of other database formats

C.J. Date's famous 12 rules of distributed databases

Here are C.J. Date's famous 12 rules of distributed databases:

Rule 1: Local autonomy. Each server that supports data in a distributed database should be independent of other servers and should have control over its own data. That means that each server is responsible for handling all of the gory details that go along with being a database server, such as security, locking, integrity, optimization, and so on.

Rule 2: No reliance on a central site. A distributed database system should not depend on a central site for its operation. Once again, each server provides its own security, locking, integrity, optimization, etc.

Rule 3: Continuous operation. A distributed database should not have to be shut down to perform routine maintenance tasks such as backup and recovery. These tasks should be performed while the system is operating, without substantially slowing the system down.

Rule 4: Location transparency and location independence. A program or user should never have to concern itself with the location of data it needs. If the user says "show me all the customers who are overdrawn by more than $100," the system should retrieve the information without asking the user on which server the customer information resides.

Rule 5: Fragmentation independence. If a table has been fragmented across several servers, the DBMS should reconstruct the table without bothering the user for the details.

Rule 6: Replication independence. Users and programs should not be aware that data has been replicated; replication should be an automatic function. Neither the user nor the programmer should worry about where the replicated copies are kept, or even that they exist.

Rule 7: Distributed query processing. The database server's query optimizer should be aware that data is distributed and take that into account when deciding how to best process a query.

Rule 8: Distributed transaction management. A distributed database system should be able to handle transactions that involve database updates on more than one server..

Rule 9: Hardware independence. It shouldn't matter what hardware is used for the server. You should be able to mix and match hardware throughout the system.

Rule 10: Operating system independence. It shouldn't matter what operating system is used on the server. Windows NT, OS/2, any UNIX variant, OS/400, VMS, VM, MVS, and who knows what else, should all get along.

Rule 11: Network independence. The protocols used to build the network should have no bearing on the functioning of the distributed database.

Rule 12: DBMS independence. You should be able to freely mix and match SQL servers. One server might run DB/2, another Microsoft SQL Server, and a third Oracle. Unfortunately, this isn't quite possible yet. See the section, "Bulging at the Middleware" for information about how this is being handled currently.

Three Ways to Distribute Data

There are three common ways to distribute data among various locations: downloading, replication, and fragmentation. Note that these three methods are not mutually exclusive; you can use them in combination to distribute data in whatever manner your client/server application calls for.

Downloading

The simplest and sometimes the best way to distribute data is to periodically copy a centralized database (or a portion of it) to a remote location. For example, an inventory database could be copied from a central computer location to branch offices every night. Then, the inventory database would be available locally to the branch offices.

Downloading is most appropriate in situations where data doesn't change very often, such as price lists, customer lists (for companies that don't acquire new customers in droves), employee records, and so on.

Downloading should also be limited to applications in which it is not vital that all users have access to up-to-the-minute accurate data. In the inventory example, it's possible that back orders could result because of the one-day delay in accuracy. For example, suppose 100 Framis Valves are available and two customers walk into separate branches and order 75. Both orders will be accepted, because both branches see 100 units available. One will end up being backordered.

Sometimes, downloading can be used to shield users from volatile data. For example, the marketing department may want to analyze daily, weekly, or monthly sales trends. If the sales database changes every 2.3 seconds, the marketing department won't be able to make reliable decisions. The solution is to download "snapshots" of the sales database for the marketing department to work with.

Replication

Replication means to duplicate key portions of a database in various locations, and make sure that all copies of data are simultaneously updated. Replication ensures that if a user updates his or her local copy of a table, the DBMS automatically and immediately updates all other copies of the same data, wherever it exists.

Replication is useful in situations where users at different locations must have absolutely current information, but the data should be distributed locally for performance reasons. For example, if the company policy is that customers must be informed of backorders when the order is taken, the inventory file would have to be replicated at each branch and automatically maintained rather than simply downloaded every night.

Fragmentation: Carving the table up

Fragmentation refers to splitting up portions of a table among several servers. For example, you might store all Northern California customers on a server in Sacramento, and all Southern California customers on a server in San Diego. This is called *horizontal fragmentation* because it splits a table into two or more groups of rows and stores the rows on separate servers.

Vertical fragmentation is when the table is split into two or more groups of columns. For example, an employee table might be split across two servers: one, in the payroll department, to contain the columns that are needed to issue payroll checks; the other to contain columns needed to track other employee information. (Vertical fragmentation is less common than horizontal.)

However a table is fragmented, the distributed DBMS should be able to transparently reassemble the table in its original form without the user even realizing it was fragmented.

IBM's DRDA

A true distributed database that fulfills all of Date's 12 rules remains a pipe dream. Perhaps someday we will have tools that allow databases to be distributed in a completely transparent fashion, but how do we get there from here?

Fortunately, the database gurus at IBM have laid out a fairly sensible path. It's called *Distributed Relational Database Architecture*, or *DRDA*. It lays down the groundwork for the eventual development of full-blown distributed databases.

DRDA defines four types of distributed database transactions, each progressively more advanced. (For more information about transactions, flip ahead to Chapter 18.)

Remote requests

A remote request is what happens when a client program issues independent database requests to a single DBMS running on a remote server. Each database access is considered to be a separate transaction. Thus, if a program accesses the database four times, four separate transactions are involved.

Figure 14-2 shows a client program issuing four database requests to two servers. Each request goes to one and only one server, and each database access is treated as a separate transaction. Thus, if the third database access fails, the first two are unaffected.

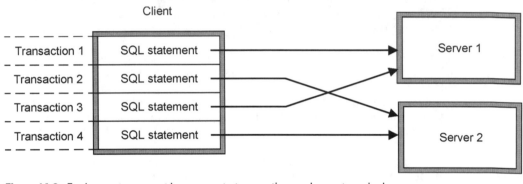

Figure 14-2: Each remote request is a separate transaction, and goes to a single server.

Remote requests are not sophisticated enough for distributed client/server transaction processing, which requires that all of the database accesses that make up a transaction be completed in all-or-nothing fashion.

Remote transactions

The next level of distributed database support is called *remote transactions*. Remote transactions allow more than one remote database access to a single database server to be treated as a single transaction, so that if the program fails at any point in the transaction, any previously completed database updates within the transaction are backed out.

Figure 14-3 shows a client program with two transactions. The first transaction consists of two database accesses to one server, and the second transaction includes two accesses to the other server.

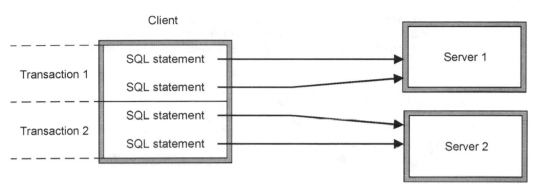

Figure 14-3: Each remote transaction can access a single server multiple times.

The limiting factor in a remote transaction is that all of the database accesses within a transaction must be to the same server. This is a definite improvement over remote requests, but is still too much of a limitation for distributed client/server transaction processing.

Distributed transactions

The third level of support, called *distributed transactions*, allows database accesses to more than one server within a single transaction. Figure 14-4 illustrates this. As you can see, the first transaction accesses data on both servers, as does the second.

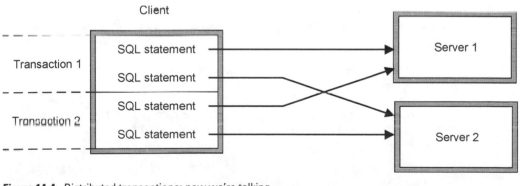

Figure 14-4: Distributed transactions: now we're talking.

Support for distributed transaction is a must if you want to update databases stored on different servers. Without distributed transaction processing, a program crash can leave distributed databases out of sync with one another.

Distributed requests

Distributed requests are the most advanced form of distributed database access. In fact, distributed requests are so advanced that it is still in the science fiction stage. Real-life SQL server products do not yet fully support distributed requests, but they're getting there.

A distributed request allows data from more than one server to be accessed in a single database request, as shown in Figure 14-5. Notice in this figure that each SQL statement issued by the client computer accesses both of the server computers.

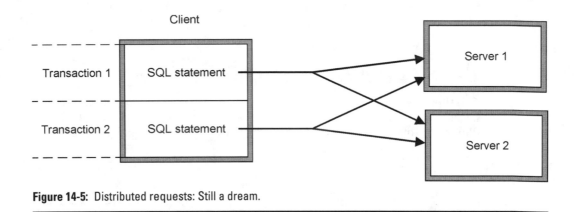

Figure 14-5: Distributed requests: Still a dream.

That's about it for client/server database processing. If you understand the basics of relational databases — what they are, how they are designed, and how they are accessed via SQL — you have a solid background for designing and working with client/server systems. In the next part, I'll turn my attention toward client/server programming issues. (Now would be a good time to take a vacation!)

Part IV
Building Client/Server Systems

The 5th Wave   By Rich Tennant

MAINFRAMEZ N the HOOD

In This Part...

Up to now, I've been describing the basic elements of client/server computing, but have managed to avoid the issue of how these systems are actually programmed. Building client/server systems involves particular program design and coding techniques, and that's what you'll see in this part.

If you're an experienced programmer but new to client/server, you'll find that some portions of these chapters present new material, while others may be a review, depending on your background.

If you're not a programmer, but just an innocent bystander who's been forced to read this book at gunpoint, you may feel you're in a bit over your head. In that case, my advice is to either skip this part and get on with some of the juicy topics in Part V, or (if you're curious about client/server programming) keep on truckin' but don't sweat the details. The point is to just get a general idea of what those programmers are doing all day when they lock themselves into their little cubicles.

Chapter 15

Client/Server Development Tools

In This Chapter

▶ CASE

▶ Visual programming

▶ Hard-core programming

▶ End-user tools

▶ Other tools

*P*rogrammers developing client/server applications, like other programmers, have a whole array of tools to assist them. Here's a quick overview
of the major tools and how they fit into client/server development.

CASE Tools

CASE stands for *computer-aided software engineering*, and refers to computer
programs that help with the task of creating computer programs. That broad
definition could include such mundane programs as text editors used to create program source files and compilers used to translate source programs
into executable programs, but the term CASE is reserved for more sophisticated programs that automate various aspects of the program-development
process.

When CASE tools were first conceived, it was hoped that they would completely automate the whole program-development process and millions of
COBOL programmers would soon be sleeping on park benches. CASE tools
aren't even close to completely automating program development, and they
probably won't ever be. At best, CASE tools increase the effectiveness of
computer programmers, enabling them to build bigger and more complicated
systems than ever before. ▪

Here is a list of some of the more popular CASE tools:

- *EasyCASE* from Evergreen CASE Tools
- *Erwin/DBF* and *Erwin/ERX* from Logic Works
- *SilverRun* from Computer Systems Advisors
- *InfoModeler* from Asymetrix
- *ORACLE*CASE* from Oracle

CASE tools focus on helping system designers with data modeling (creating the various charts and diagrams that are used to design computer systems). For example, SilverRun offers modules that create data-flow diagrams (DFD), entity-relationship diagrams (ERD), and relational database schemas. These modules are integrated by way of a *repository* — a centralized database of application design information — so they can be used together to design complex applications.

Figure 15-1 shows a data-flow diagram being developed with SilverRun DFD.

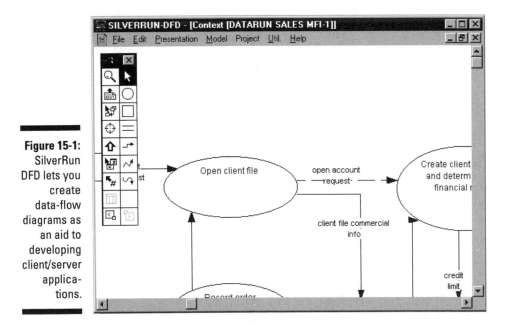

Figure 15-1: SilverRun DFD lets you create data-flow diagrams as an aid to developing client/server applications.

Some CASE tools assist in the process of data modeling by asking questions about the data model. For example, the CASE tool might examine a video rental system's data model, then ask questions such as:

> Is it necessary for a "TAPE" to be associated with a "CUSTOMER" for
> the "TAPE" to exist?

Based on the response, the CASE tool is able to establish the relationships among the tables that make up the data model. Good data modeling tools can also automatically normalize the database structure. (We talked about normalizing in Chapter 13.)

The best CASE tools have hooks to other development tools to jump-start the development process. For example, SilverRun can create SQL CREATE statements to define tables — including triggers — for most popular RDBMS (relational database management systems), including DB2, Sybase SQL Server, and Oracle7.

A *trigger* is a procedure stored with the database that is executed automatically when some condition occurs, such as when a particular table column is updated or a row is deleted. ■

Visual Programming Tools

No, this section is not about how to program your VCR (you're already way ahead of me on that, anyway). Visual programming tools are complete programming environments that enable a programmer to quickly build a GUI program by assembling various on-screen elements such as buttons, text boxes, menus, and so on (called *controls*) onto blank forms, and then filling in the processing details associated with each control.

Many visual programming products are available. All work in a similar fashion, though some provide more advanced features than others. Here are the more common ones:

- **Visual Basic (VB) and Visual Basic Professional (Microsoft).** This is probably the most widely used visual programming environment. The Professional edition is often used for client/server applications. As its name suggests, its programming language is a derivative of BASIC. VB runs only under Windows.

- **PowerBuilder Enterprise (Powersoft).** PowerBuilder is one of the most commonly used front-end tools for building client/server applications in Windows. Powersoft is currently targeting Windows NT, Macintosh, and Unix as well. The programming language used by PowerBuilder is called PowerScript and is similar in structure to BASIC. A scaled-back version called PowerBuilder Desktop is also available. It includes everything that is contained in PowerBuilt Enterprise except the drivers that allow you to connect to server databases.

✔ **SQLWindows Corporate Edition (Gupta).** SQLWindows, which runs only under Windows, is one of the most advanced visual programming tools available. Unlike other products, SQLWindows can create C++ code that can be compiled to produce more efficient programs.

✔ **VisualAge Team for OS/2 (IBM).** If you're looking for a visual programming tool for OS/2, VisualAge is the one to pick. The only disadvantage is that its programming language is based on Smalltalk, a language developed especially for object-oriented programming. This will please the object-oriented purists (both of them), but leaves the vast majority of trained programmers feeling lost at first.

✔ **Delphi (Borland).** Delphi is Borland's "Visual Basic killer." Delphi's programming language is based on Pascal and uses a true compiler rather than an interpreter. That makes Delphi programs blazingly fast. Delphi also comes in a desktop version and a client/server version.

Visual programming plays such a major role in client/server development that I've devoted all of the next chapter to illustrating how it works, using Visual Basic Professional Edition to create an example program.

Hard-Core Programming Tools

If a visual programming environment doesn't offer enough flexibility or efficiency, you can use an old-fashioned programming language to develop the client/server programs.

This route will probably result in the most efficient programs, but the development will require more expertise and will take considerably longer. Plus, the details of accessing the network and SQL will have to be worked out the hard way — by brute force, with months of brutal coding and testing.

C and C++

C and C++ are the most popular programming languages for programs intended to run on desktop computers. C was originally written as a low-level programming language used to write the Unix operating system. C++ is a newer, object-oriented version of C. C++ compilers can be used for C or C++ programs.

C++ compilers are available from Microsoft, Borland, Watcom, and Symantec.

Microsoft's Visual C++ includes a class library called *Microsoft Foundation Class*, or *MFC*, which can be used to build Windows applications. Borland C++ comes with a similar class library called *OWL* (*ObjectWindows Library*).

Don't be confused: Visual C++ is *not* a visual programming environment like Visual Basic or PowerBuilder. It's simply a Windows-based C++ compiler. ▪

COBOL

COBOL may be old, but it's not forgotten. MicroFocus markets an advanced COBOL package for PCs that lets you build Windows or OS/2 interfaces and access SQL databases. COBOL is often used for client/server systems in which IBM's CICS transaction-processing system is used as a transaction monitor.

End-User Data Access Tools

Several end-user tools for collecting and displaying data in client/server systems are available. Among these tools are:

- ✔ **Forest & Trees (Trinzic)** allows the user to set up a "dashboard" to collect and analyze data from various sources, including database servers and mainframe databases.

- ✔ **Crystal Reports Professional (Crystal Services)** is a report designer for Windows that can access SQL Server, Sybase, and Oracle data. Crystal Reports is familiar to Visual Basic programmers because a version of it is included with Visual Basic.

- ✔ **Q+E Database Editor** is an ad-hoc query tool that can generate results or queries to access data from several sources. Q+E Database Editor is familiar to Excel users because Excel version 4 included it. (Excel 5 replaces Q+E with Microsoft Query.)

- ✔ **Quest (Gupta)** provides access to SQL databases to build queries or reports.

If tools such as these are provided to end users, along with complete information about the location and structure of the underlying databases, the users might be able to build their own client/server systems so you programmers can get back to real work. (Yeah, right!)

Application Suites

The notion of software suites has become popular recently. A suite is a so-called "integrated" collection of full-function programs that usually includes a word processor, spreadsheet, database, presentation graphics, and possibly other goodies as well.

Although these suites are not themselves client/server products, they can be used to create the client side of a client/server system. For example, Microsoft Access (the database program included in Microsoft's Office suite) can be set up to access data from a SQL database server.

Currently, three suites dominate the market:

- Microsoft Office Professional (Microsoft)
- PerfectOffice (Novell)
- SmartSuite (Lotus)

Table 15-1 lists the individual applications that are included in each of these suites.

Table 15-1: What you get with the leading suites

Component	Microsoft Office Professional	Lotus SmartSuite	Novell PerfectOffice
Word processor	Word	Ami Pro	WordPerfect
Spreadsheet	Excel	1-2-3	Quattro Pro
Presentation graphics	PowerPoint	Freelance Graphics	Presentations
Database	Access	Approach	Paradox
Mail	Mail	(none)	GroupWise
Personal information manager	(none)	Organizer	InfoCentral

Each of these suites allows you to create customized applications, integrating functions by using OLE2 and the programming capabilities of the individual components. Lotus SmartSuite offers tight integration with Notes, and PerfectOffice includes a scripting language called PerfectScript that works with any application in the suite.

Testing Tools

Testing is a difficult undertaking for any software project. It is made all the more complicated for client/server systems because of the added layers of complexity. Windows itself makes testing difficult because user input is so unpredictable.

The problem with testing is that it has to be done over and over again. Every time a change is made to the system, the entire system has to be retested to ensure that the change doesn't have any unexpected side effects. This repeated testing is called *regression testing*.

Fortunately, software is available that simplifies regression testing. These products include:

- **ATF (Softbridge).** ATF stands for Automated Testing Facility.

- **SQA TeamTest (SQA).** SQA stands for Software Quality Assurance. TeamTest is specifically designed for testing client/server GUI systems. SQA also makes a version specifically designed for testing PowerBuilder applications.

- **Microsoft Test (Microsoft)**. Microsoft Test is a tool for creating automated test scripts to run under Windows. Test includes a BASIC variant that allows you to create testing programs.

Version Control

In the days of centralized mainframe computing, version control was relatively straightforward. When a new version of a program was ready to put into production, the systems programmers would come in on the weekend (they didn't have any life outside the computer room anyway) and install the new version. Then, all users throughout the company would discover on Monday morning that a new version had been installed.

The story is a little different with client/server systems because the software isn't all contained in one central location. Instead, the software is distributed all over the place. Part of it can exist on LAN servers, part on the mainframe, and part on each user's PC. Distributing a software update of a client/server system is a difficult undertaking, and tracking which computers have which versions is even more difficult.

Luckily, software tools are available to help with this problem:

- ✔ **CMVC** from IBM. CMVC stands for Configuration Management Version Control.

- ✔ **Delta** from Microsoft.

- ✔ **PVCS** from Intersolv. PVCS stands for Polytron Version Control System.

- ✔ **CCC/Manager** from Softool Corp.

- ✔ **SourceSafe** from One Tree Software.

- ✔ **Versions** from Starbase Corporation.

Well, the toolkit is full — and after a brief look at systems analysis and design, we'll plunge into some actual programming in Visual Basic.

Chapter 16

A Quick Look at Systems Analysis and Design

- -

In This Chapter

▶ The development life cycle

▶ Why computer experts like to draw pictures

▶ Data-flow diagrams

▶ Application architecture

▶ JAD, RAD, and prototyping

- -

Systems analysis and design refers to the process of planning how a computer system will be built before actually building it.

The methods for designing traditional mainframe computer systems are well established. The same methods can be applied to PC software projects. But for distributed client/server applications, many of the traditional methods seem archaic, perhaps even counterproductive.

This chapter doesn't present everything there is to know about systems analysis and design; it just summarizes some of the techniques that are useful in client/server projects.

The Development Treadmill

One of the major factors that led to the success of personal computers and, ultimately, client/server computing was the process that MIS departments used to develop new computer applications. Over the years, a bureaucratic nightmare called the *system development life cycle* evolved, mostly in a well-intentioned attempt to add order and predictability to computer system development. (See the sidebar "The proverbial computer system life cycle" for a rundown of the stages a computer project would typically go through during its life.)

The problem with the development cycle is that, more often than not, the computer system was obsolete by the time it was completed. Even modest projects could take years from conception to delivery. While the project was under development, new technology would come along, the business environment would change, or the company would go out of business altogether.

Users got tired of waiting nine months to get a simple variation of a report or an easier way to enter data, so they took matters into their own hands and started developing solutions themselves, bypassing the computer experts altogether.

Does that mean that the system development life cycle should be abandoned altogether? Not at all. On the contrary, PC users quickly discovered that although they knew how to build a Lotus spreadsheet, they knew little about building computer applications that were dependable enough to bet their jobs on. ■

In the meantime, the computer experts in the MIS department were figuring out their own ways to cut the development cycle down to size:

- The techniques of *structured systems analysis* formalize the process of analysis and design in an effort to catch major design errors early, while they are still easy to fix.
- *Computer-aided software engineering* (*CASE*) tools seek to use the computer itself to assist throughout the development cycle. (I talked about CASE tools in Chapter 15.)
- *Joint application design* (*JAD*) and similar techniques involve users in the process throughout the analysis and design phases.
- *Rapid application development* (*RAD*) and prototyping compress the entire development process by overlapping the steps, so that analysis, design, implementation, and testing are all done simultaneously, in incremental steps.

What Is an Application Design?

Glad you asked. An *application design* is a written model of a system that can be used to actually construct a working version of the system. Although the

TECHNICAL STUFF

The proverbial computer system life cycle

Over the years, computer gurus have observed that computer projects have a life of their own. The life cycle of a computer system typically goes something like this:

1. *Feasibility study.* This is the conception phase, in which the decision to undertake a new computer system is made based on the answers to questions such as: What value will the new system offer? Can it be done? What will it cost? How long will it take? The result of the feasibility study is a charter for the new project that defines the scope of the project, user requirements, budget constraints, and so on.

2. *Analysis.* Analysis is the process of deciding exactly what a computer system is to do. The traditional approach to analysis is to thoroughly document the existing system which the new system is intended to replace, even if the existing system is entirely manual and rife with inefficiency and error. Then, a specification for a new system to replace the old is created. This specification defines exactly what the new system will do, but not necessarily how it will do it.

3. *Design.* Design is the process of creating a plan for implementing the specification for a new system that results from the analysis step. It focuses on how the new system will work.

4. *Implementation.* The implementation phase is where the programs that make up the new system are coded and tested, the hardware required to support the system is purchased and installed, and the databases required for the system are defined and loaded.

5. *Acceptance testing.* In the acceptance testing phase, all of the pieces of the system are checked out to make sure that the system works the way it should.

6. *Production.* If the system works acceptably, it is put into production. In other words, the system's users actually begin using it.

7. *Maintenance.* The dreaded maintenance phase is entered the moment the computer system is put into production. Errors — hopefully minor — that weren't caught during the implementation and acceptance phases are corrected. As the users work with the system, they realize that what they really need isn't what they thought they wanted, so they request enhancements, which are gradually incorporated into the system. The biggest challenge of this phase is making sure that corrections and enhancements don't create more problems than they solve.

8. *Obsolescence.* Eventually, the new system becomes obsolete. Of course, this doesn't mean the system dies: it probably remains in production for years, perhaps even decades, after it becomes obsolete. Many obsolete COBOL systems are still in production today, and the client/server systems being built today will be in production long after client/server computing becomes passé.

Only the most obsessive project managers actually lead projects through these phases step by step. In the real world, the phases overlap to some degree. In fact — as is pointed out later in this chapter when I discuss JAD and RAD — modern development methods overlap all of the phases in a highly iterative process.

I omitted two important pieces of the computer system development puzzle because they should be integrated throughout the entire process: quality assurance and documentation. Quality needs to be built into each phase of development, and shouldn't be tacked on to the end as an afterthought. Likewise, documentation of the system should be built as the system is developed.

components of an application design can vary, a complete design usually includes the following:

- ✔ A statement of the purpose and scope of the system.
- ✔ A set of data-flow diagrams (DFDs) that completely document the system's process flow, with complete descriptions of each process.
- ✔ A data model, consisting of a set of entity-relationship diagrams (ERDs) and a detailed relational database design.
- ✔ Screen layouts for each component of the user interface.
- ✔ Report layouts for each report created by the system.

Building Models

When it comes right down to it, computer system analysis and design is nothing more than glorified model building.

Most engineering disciplines involve model building. In fact, that's what engineers do all day: sit around building fancy models of skyscrapers, bridges, freeway overpasses, culverts, storm drains, or whatever.

Not the kind of models made out of molded plastic parts held together by cement, but conceptual models drawn on paper. Architects draw floor plans, electronic engineers draw schematic circuit diagrams, structural engineers draw blueprints. These are all nothing more than models.

The reason engineers build models is that models are cheaper to build than the real thing. It's a lot easier to draw a picture of a bridge, then examine it to make sure that it won't collapse the first time the wind blows too fast or the river is too full, than it is to build an actual bridge and then find out.

The same holds true for computer application design. Building a computer system is a very expensive proposition. It's far cheaper to build a paper model of the computer system first, then test the model to make sure that it works before actually building the system.

In Chapter 13, we took a look at one kind of model that is often built when designing computer systems: a data model, which represents the structure of the database that will be used by the system. The data model is a crucial part of a computer system design, but it's not the only part. What about the programs that will process the data? They are modeled using a chart called a *data-flow diagram*, which is covered next.

Data-Flow Diagrams

A *data-flow diagram*, or *DFD*, is a chart that shows the major processes that make up a computer application and how data flows from process to process. There are various styles of drawing data-flow diagrams, but the information represented is the same regardless of the style used.

Figure 16-1 shows a simple DFD for part of a video store rental system. This chart illustrates the basic building blocks of a data-flow diagram:

- ✔ Each process is represented by a circle with a name that identifies the process within the circle. In Figure 16-1, there is one process: "rent tape."

- ✔ Entities that are external to the system are shown as rectangles. In this example, the customer is an example of an external entity: Data flows to and from the customer, but he or she is otherwise not a part of the system. External entities are sometimes called *terminators*.

- ✔ Data flows are represented by lines with arrows indicating the direction of the data flow. A data flow represents a packet of information that comes into or out of a process. Think of it as the input and output to the process.

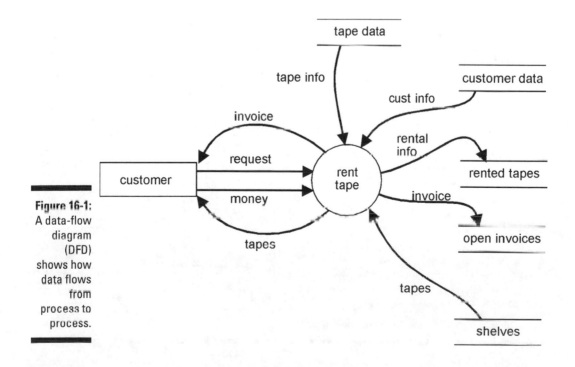

Figure 16-1:
A data-flow
diagram
(DFD)
shows how
data flows
from
process to
process.

✔ Data may flow directly from process to process, or it may wait temporarily in a *data store*, which is represented by a pair of parallel lines with an identifying name between. A data store may be a database table or a computer file, or it may be a physical storage medium. For example, notice in Figure 16-1 that a data store called "shelves" is the source of the "tapes" data flow. This data store represents the actual shelves in the video store, and the tape flow represents the actual videotapes.

Leveling with the DFD

A DFD is a great way to design the processes that make up a system and the flow of data among processes, but the amount of detail that would have to be included in a complete DFD for even a modest system is enormous. To get your mind around all that detail, DFDs can be drawn with varying levels of detail, each successive DFD "exploding" the detail of one process in the level above.

For example, the "rent tape" process that was shown in Figure 16-1 might be broken down into three smaller processes: entering rental information, retrieving the tape, and printing the invoice. A separate DFD (sometimes called a *detail DFD*) could be drawn for each of these processes. Figure 16-2 illustrates a DFD with the "rent tape" process exploded into greater detail.

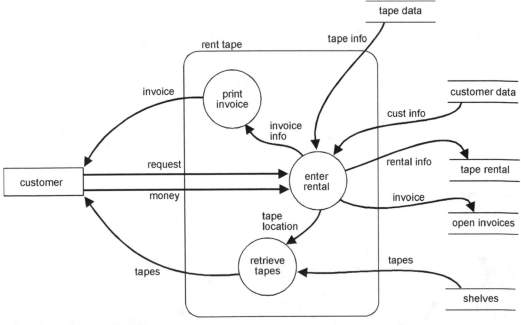

Figure 16-2: A detail DFD for the "rent tapes" process.

For the DFDs to be "leveled," the designer must make sure that the input and output data flows from the higher-level processes are preserved in the lower-level (detail) DFD. In other words, the processes that comprise the "rent tape" detail DFD must collectively have the same inputs and outputs as the "rent tape" process in the higher-level DFD.

Layered Architectures

One approach to designing client/server systems is to focus on clearly defined "layers" of the application architecture. This approach is similar to the way an architect designs a building. If you've ever seen detailed construction plans for a building, you'll know what I'm talking about. The construction plans include separate blueprints for the foundation, frame, roof, plumbing, electrical, and other "layers" of the building.

When a layered architecture is used, the layers can be designed independently, and developed by specialists, provided that the connections between layers — that is, the *interfaces* — are carefully designed.

The layers should be independent of one another. Among other things, that means:

- Each layer must have a clearly defined domain. To properly design the layers, the tasks and responsibilities of each layer should be clearly spelled out.

- Layers should mind their own business. If one layer is responsible for interacting with the user, only that layer is allowed to communicate with the user. Other layers that need to get information from the user must do so through the user interface layer.

- Clearly defined protocols must be set up for the layers to interact with one another. Interaction between the layers occurs only through these protocols.

If all this talk of layers reminds you of the 7-layer OSI networking model, that's by design. Layered networking architectures are based on the same principles. If it reminds you of a 7-layer cake, it's time to take a break.

Note that the layers are not tied directly to the specific application. For example, an architecture might work equally well for a payroll system and an on-line ordering system. As a result, layered architecture has no relationship to the data-flow diagrams that define the processes or the entity-relationship diagrams that define the data model.

A two-layer architecture

The specific layers that make up an application will vary from system to system. A typical scheme is to break the application into two layers:

- Application layer: The design of the GUI with which end users interact (the *presentation logic*) and the implementation of business rules and policies (*application logic* — the portion of the program code that decides, for example, whether a customer has exceeded his or her credit limit, or whether an order qualifies for a discount). The application layer may also handle the *transaction logic* — the code that groups database updates into transactions and ensures that all updates within a transaction are made consistently.

- Database layer: The underlying database engine that supports the application. This layer is responsible for maintaining the integrity of the database. Some or all of the transaction logic may be implemented in this layer.

In the two-layer model, the application layer is usually implemented as client programs developed with a visual programming tool such as Visual Basic or PowerBuilder. The database layer is built with an RDMBS such as Oracle7 or SQL Server.

The division between the application and database layers isn't always as clear-cut as it could be, because for performance reasons transaction logic is often shifted to the database server in the form of stored procedures, and business rules are often implemented on the server in the form of triggers. Thus, the database server is often handling some of the application logic. The solution to this messiness (if it bothers you) is to create a middle layer that handles the business rules, as described in the next section.

A three-layer architecture

In a three-layer architecture, an additional layer is added to specifically handle business rules, and the top layer becomes responsible solely for the user interface.

- User interface layer: The design of the GUI presentation logic. These programs are what the users think of as the system.

- Business rules layer: The business rules and policies that must be implemented by the system.

- Database layer: The underlying database model that supports the application. This layer is responsible for maintaining the integrity of the database.

Creating a separate layer for business rules allows you to separate the rules from the database design and the GUI presentation logic. Business rules are subject to change, but by placing them in a separate layer, changing them later is an easier task than if they were incorporated into the user interface or database design.

Designing the User Interface

Much of the success of a client/server system depends on the quality of its user interface. As far as end users are concerned, the user interface *is* the application: Users aren't interested in how normalized the data model is or whether a two-phase commit protocol is used.

In most GUI systems, the interface consists of one or more forms that contain interface objects or controls such as buttons, entry fields, drop-down lists, slider bars, and the like. Designing the user interface is simply a matter of deciding which forms are required and in what sequence, and populating them with the appropriate controls.

Then there's the matter of menu commands, toolbar buttons, keyboard shortcuts, drag-and-drop features, OLE2 implementation, and so on.

User interface design can quickly become the most complicated aspect of a client/server application. Although there are no hard and fast rules for user interface design, Microsoft does publish a design guide for developing Windows GUIs that can give some guidance. Here are some thoughts that should be kept in mind:

✔ Consider how frequently the user will use each form and how familiar he or she will be with the application. If the user must fill out the same form over and over again all day long, try to make the data entry as efficient as possible. If the form will be used only once in a while, err on the side of making the form self-explanatory so the user doesn't have to struggle to figure out how to use the form.

✔ Remember that in a GUI, the user is in control. Avoid "modal" forms that force the user into a prescribed sequence of actions.

✔ One of the trendy topics in user interface design is making new features "discoverable" by the user. The interface should invite the user to explore the program, clicking here and there to see what happens. Avoid designs that punish the user for clicking in the wrong place by discarding work in progress or displaying nasty messages like "Don't click there, stupid!"

- ✔ Some users like the mouse. Some like the keyboard. Don't force your preferences on the user: Make sure your interface works well with the mouse and the keyboard.

- ✔ Review prototypes of the user interface design with actual users. Listen to their suggestions seriously. They probably have a better idea than you of what the user interface should look like and how it should behave.

- ✔ Study programs you consider to have a good user interface.

- ✔ Don't alter any of the common interface elements of the client operating system. If the File|Open command always opens a file, use the File|Open command to open files; don't use a File|Retrieve command just because you think "retrieve" is more understandable to users than "open." ▪

Designing the Business Rules Layer

Business rules are the portion of a program that implements business policies. Here are some examples of business rules:

- ✔ Should a customer be granted a credit request?

- ✔ How much of a discount should be applied to a given order?

- ✔ How many copies of Form 10432/J need to be printed?

- ✔ How much shipping and handling should be tacked on to an invoice?

- ✔ When should an inventory item that is running low on stock be reordered?

- ✔ How much sick leave should be granted to an employee before we start to wonder if they've been skiing rather than staying home sick?

- ✔ When should an Accounts Payable be paid to take advantage of discounts while maximizing float?

The key to designing the business rules portion of an application is simply to identify the business rules that must be implemented and separate them as much as possible from the other aspects of the program. That way, if the rules change, only the modules that implement the rules need to be changed. ▪

Ideally, each business rule should be implemented only once, in a shared module that is used by any program that needs it. All too often, business policies are implemented over and over again in multiple programs, so that if the policy changes, dozens of programs have to be updated.

Isolation and reuse of business rules is best achieved using the techniques of object-oriented programming, which is briefly discussed later in this chapter, and discussed more fully in Chapter 21.

Designing the Database Layer

Much of the job of designing the database layer is designing the database itself. Database design was discussed thoroughly in Chapter 13, so I won't go into it again here. Refer back to Chapter 13 if you need a refresher on database design. Here are some pointers on designing the database layer:

- ✔ Designing the database layer also involves designing the procedures that will be used to access and update the database. For starters, you must decide what database server will be used (for example, Sybase, Oracle, or DB2) and what method will be used to access it — embedded SQL, an RDBMS-specific Call Level Interface (CLI), or a generic interface such as Microsoft's ODBC. If a middleware layer will be used to access more than one type of database, that interface must be carefully desgned as well.

- ✔ You must also decide how the application will recover from database errors, how transactions will be implemented, whether stored procedures and/or triggers will be used, and so on. These issues were discussed in Chapters 12 and 13, so I won't belabor the point again here.

- ✔ If the database will be distributed, the details of how the application will interact with the distributed database must also be designed. For more information on distributed databases, refer back to Chapter 14.

Object-Oriented Design

Object-oriented design addresses several problems inherent with the traditional data-and-process model approach to systems design:

- ✔ When the data model and the process model are designed separately, it's difficult to see the connection between the ERD (entity relationship diagram) and the DFD (data-flow diagram).

- ✔ We're constantly reinventing the wheel. Once we get a working system up and running, there's no easy way to derive a similar system from it, other than by making a copy of the original system and modifying the code.

- ✔ We're bored and we need something to get us motivated.

Because object-oriented design is relatively new and unfamiliar, I won't discuss it in detail until Chapter 21, "Distributed Objects," which explains what objects are and how they can be applied to client/server system design.

JAD

JAD, which stands for *joint application design*, is an approach to designing computer systems in which a team of designers is brought together for a workshop. During the workshop, team members work through various issues of the design and eventually settle on a complete application design that can then be implemented.

A JAD team typically consists of 10 to 12 people, with the following makeup:

- ✔ JAD workshop leader. The JAD workshop leader should be someone who is experienced with the JAD methodology. The leader prepares the materials needed for the workshop, moderates the discussions, mediates disputes, and generally keeps things moving.

- ✔ Scribe. The scribe is the official recorder of the JAD workshop. Ideally, the scribe works directly with a computer-aided design tool to document the design worked out by the JAD team — DFDs, ERDs, and so on.

- ✔ End users. End users from each of the areas affected by the application participate on the team. These users should be selected carefully. They do not need to be computer experts, but they do need a solid understanding of the business process the application will provide. They also must have the authority to make decisions that will affect their departments.

- ✔ Executive sponsor. It helps to have a high-profile "sponsor" for the new system — someone high enough on the corporate ladder to lend credibility to the entire undertaking. Ideally, the sponsor should attend all meetings and participate fully in the JAD process, but sometimes the sponsor attends only on a part-time basis.

- ✔ Technical specialists. Technical specialists should be made available to the JAD team on an as-needed basis to answer questions or evaluate unorthodox solutions.

The JAD workshop will last several days, perhaps more than a week. Make sure that all participants are able to devote full-time attention to the JAD process. One of the basic JAD rules is: telephones and pagers are not allowed!

The JAD workshop itself should be conducted in a spacious and comfortable room. It's common to provide wall charts, either dry-erase marker boards or simple butcher paper, to allow the team members to create large process (DFD) and entity diagrams.

RAD

RAD, which stands for *rapid application development*, has become popular in recent years not only because it rhymes with *JAD* but also because it shortens the overall development time by emphasizing the use of prototyping.

RAD is typically implemented using a team approach. A swat team consisting of three to five expert developers take the results of a JAD workshop and create a working prototype of the system within a few days or weeks. The prototype is then reviewed, refined, and reviewed again.

RAD becomes especially attractive when the tools used to prototype the system are also used to develop the actual production system. For example, Visual Basic can be used to create the prototype and the final product. Thus, the prototypes are actually preliminary versions of the final program.

There are a few dangers inherent in prototyping:

- Users may not realize how easy the prototype is to build compared with a production system. They may expect that if the prototype took only a few days to build, the finished system should be ready within a similar time. Prototyping is like building a house: The frames and walls go up surprisingly fast, creating the illusion of a nearly completed structure, but a lot more finishing work is required before the house is ready to be lived in.

- If money becomes tight, a nearly finished prototype may be put into production before it is ready.

- A working prototype seems more final than a plan that exists only on paper. One of the oldest and wisest of programming adages is, "Resist the urge to code." The sooner you start coding, the sooner you become fixed upon one particular solution to the exclusion of all others. Prototypes should be considered disposable.

- The cycle of reviewing and enhancing successive prototype versions can get out of hand. Every time you show a prototype to the user, the user is apt to suggest one other nice feature that could be added. At some point, you have to cut the cycle and declare the prototype to be finished.

Systems analysis and design is a huge subject. I've only given you a broad outline of the general process and some of the approaches and techniques that are out there, especially the ones used in designing client/server applications. In the next chapter we'll step through a real, live Visual Basic program to illustrate how VB works in a client front-end program for our video store example.

Chapter 17

How Visual Programming Works

● ●

In This Chapter

▶ A simple Visual Basic application

▶ How Visual Basic programs are built

▶ Creating forms and form control

▶ Writing event procedures

▶ Querying the database

▶ Adding menus

● ●

V isual programming is a common thread that runs throughout any discussion of client/server computing. Regardless of what tools are used on the back end of a client/server system, the front end — that is, the client end — is almost always created using some type of visual programming environment.

This chapter introduces you to the basics of visual programming by looking at a simple program built using Visual Basic Professional. While the example is specific to Visual Basic, the techniques are similar in other visual programming tools.

The program illustrated in this chapter is of prototype caliber. (In Chapter 16 we talked about prototypes as a stage of application design.) It isn't quite suitable for actual production use, but good enough to demonstrate the application to the users so they can evaluate the program's appearance and operation, and good enough to demonstrate the basic concepts of visual programming.

You don't have to be an expert in Visual Basic or any other programming language to benefit from this chapter, but at least some background in programming will help. We are going to get into Visual Basic programming in some detail, using actual samples of code. So if you're squeamish about such things, you might want to just read the general summaries of what we're doing and cover your eyes for the code parts. ■

The Video Search Application

Our sample program goes along with the videotape rental system that I've described in several chapters already. A videotape rental system would include programs that rent tapes to customers, record tapes that have been returned, handle late charges, print reports, and so on.

The particular program that will be shown here is a search program that lets the user locate a particular videotape in the store's inventory based on the tape's title or the last name of an actor who appears in the tape. You could use this program to find out if there are any copies of a particular movie in stock, to locate a movie if you remember just part of the movie's title, or to find out what movies starring your favorite actor or actress are available.

The program — called Video Search — also gives the user the ability to display the complete cast of any selected movie, and has an option that causes it to display only those movies that are currently in stock, omitting tapes that are currently rented out. The Video Search program would be ideal to place on the floor of a video store so that customers can search for tapes themselves, though the version that will be shown in this chapter isn't really ready for prime time in terms of user friendliness.

The Videos database

The database used by the program was described pretty thoroughly in Chapter 13, so I'll refer you back there for a detailed description of the database. The Video Search program uses just three of the tables in the complete Videos database:

- TAPE, with the following columns: TapeNo, Title, Status (0 = available, 1 = rented out), and CatCode (a category code, such as Science Fiction or Comedy; a separate CAT table contains the code and title of each category).

- ACTOR, with the following columns: ActorNo, LName (Last Name), and FName (First Name).

- TAPEACT, with just two fields: ActorNo and TapeNo. This table implements a many-to-many relationship between actors and tapes. For each row in the TAPE table, there is a row in the TAPEACT table for each actor in the tape. Likewise, for each row in the ACTOR table, there is a row in the TAPEACT table for each tape the actor appears in.

SQL queries used by the program

If you're lost in this section, you might want to go back and review Chapters 11 and 12 on the basics of SQL and programming with SQL. ■

The Video Search program will query the database using two basic SELECT statements. For a title search, a SELECT statement similar to the following will be used:

```
SELECT TapeNo, Title, Status FROM Tape
    WHERE TITLE LIKE 'search title*'
```

This query returns all of the tapes whose Title column begins with the *search title* text entered by the user. Notice that an asterisk is placed at the end of the user's search text to act as a wildcard. Thus, if the user enters "Star Trek," all of the Star Trek movies will be displayed.

Note that Visual Basic has a peculiar SQL dialect that uses an asterisk (*) as a wildcard, whereas most SQL dialects use a percent sign (%). ■

If the user checks the *Search only available titles* check box, the WHERE clause will be extended to include an additional condition:

```
SELECT TapeNo, Title, Status FROM Tape
    WHERE TITLE LIKE 'search title*'
      AND Status = 0
```

That way, only tapes whose Status column is 0, meaning that the tape is available, will be selected.

To display the complete cast of a particular tape, a SELECT statement such as this is used:

```
SELECT LName, FName FROM TapeAct, Actor
    WHERE TapeAct.TapeNo = tape number
      AND TapeAct.ActorNo = Actor.ActorNo
```

This SELECT statement is a simple join that correlates rows from the TAPEACT and ACTOR tables based on the ActorNo column and selects just the rows for the tape in question. The *tape number* value will be supplied at run time by the program.

The SELECT statement to search by an actor's last name is a little more complex.

```
SELECT DISTINCT Tape.TapeNo, Tape.Title, Tape.Status
   FROM Tape, TapeAct, Actor
   WHERE Tape.TapeNo = TapeAct.TapeNo
     AND TapeAct.ActorNo = Actor.ActorNo
     AND Actor.LName LIKE 'search name*'
```

This SELECT statement is a three-way join that returns a row for each tape that has a corresponding row in the ACTOR table that matches the *search name* entered by the user. Again, an asterisk is used after the search name as a wildcard.

As before, "AND Status = 0" will be added to the WHERE clause if the user checks the *Search only available tapes* checkbox. In this way, tapes which are rented out will not be selected.

Also, this SELECT statement includes the DISTINCT keyword so that each tape is displayed only once. This is necessary because the search name entered by the user might match two (or more) actors, both of whom appear in the same film. For example, if the user simply enters the letter *K* for an actor name search, both DeForest Kelley and Walter Koenig will match. Both actors have appeared in all six Star Trek movies, so each tape would be listed twice if the DISTINCT clause were omitted.

Understanding the operation of these SELECT statements (at least in general terms) is crucial to understanding how the Video Search program works. So if you're completely baffled by these SELECTs, consider looking back over Chapters 11 and 12 as a refresher. ■

Creating a Test Database

Before you can begin to develop a Visual Basic program that accesses a database, you must create the database or a prototype version of it that will be used for testing purposes only. If a live database already exists, you can make a copy of it on a workstation or network server, and work with the copy. This has the advantage of letting you work directly with live data rather than contrived test data. If the database is large, you can always select just portions of it to avoid contending with huge amounts of data when testing.

If the database doesn't exist yet, you'll have to create it. The easiest way to do that is by using the Visual Data sample application that comes with Visual Basic Professional. It lets you create databases and tables, plus it lets you enter and edit database data.

Figure 17-1 shows the Visual Data application in action. In this screen, I'm defining the columns for the ACTOR table.

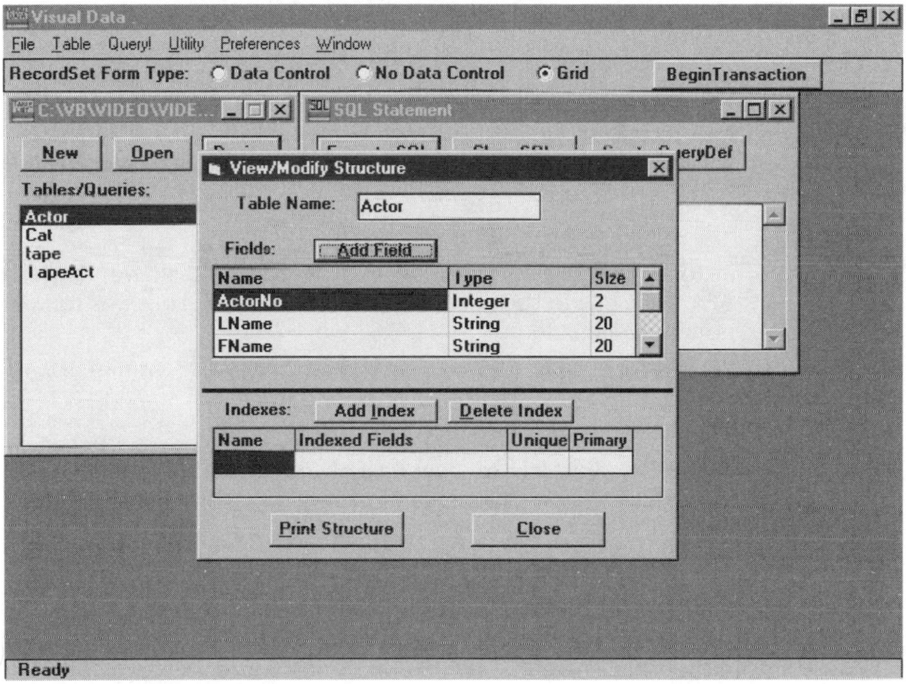

Figure 17-1:
With the
Visual Data
sample
application,
you can
create a
test
database.

After I created the tables for this database, I added sample data using Visual Data's data entry form. It's not the most efficient way to enter large quantities of data, but it's acceptable for small amounts.

Creating a Visual Basic Application

Once the database is set up, you can begin creating your Visual Basic program. Creating a Visual Basic program is an iterative process: You start with just a few elements, test them out, correct any errors, and test again. Then you add some refinements, test again, and keep going until the program is done.

Here's an overview of the general process for constructing a Visual Basic program.

1. *Start a fresh pot of coffee.* None of that decaf nonsense.

2. *Begin a new project.* In Visual Basic, a program is referred to as a *project.* A project consists of several files. Each form has its own .FRM file, plus a variety of special .VBX (Visual Basic) files are automatically included in new projects. A .MAK file coordinates the files that make up the project.

3. *Create the basic form.* You start out with a blank window, to which you add various controls like buttons, list boxes, and so on.

4. *Add code for the controls.* You write the Visual Basic statements that tell Visual Basic what to do when each control is activated by the user.

5. *Put on another pot of coffee.* If you haven't finished the first pot, you haven't been working hard enough.

6. *Add menus and related code.* Next, you add the menu commands that will be available to the user, plus the Visual Basic routines to process each menu command.

7. *Add a toolbar.* If the program will use a toolbar, you must add it as well. Usually, each toolbar button simply triggers a menu command, so little new code is required to support the toolbar.

8. *Add Help.* In this step, you design and write the help text that can be displayed if the user needs help.

9. *Make the .EXE file.* When the program is completed, it can be compiled into an executable program file and distributed to users.

10. Pat yourself on the back and go out and celebrate.

Some programs might take a different development sequence than I've listed. The Video Search program is driven mostly by button controls, so it makes sense to design and implement the buttons first. For a program that is driven mostly by menu commands, you might work on the menus first. The exact sequence depends on the program being developed, plus your own personal preferences and whims.

Here are a few general tips for working with Visual Basic:

✔ It's a good idea to keep each project in a separate directory so the files don't get mixed up.

✔ The entire development process is iterative, but that doesn't mean it should be haphazard. Visual Basic programs should have a definite structure, and you should have that structure in mind before beginning.

✔ A great way to quickly learn the ins and outs of structuring Visual Basic programs is to take a look at the sample applications that come with Visual Basic. Another way is to run out and get *Visual Basic Programming For Dummies.*

✔ Save your work often! ◼

Understanding Visual Basic Controls

Most of your time working with Visual Basic will be spent creating and refining various types of controls such as buttons, list boxes, and so on. Before I show you the specific controls used in the Video Search program, I want you to be familiar with the types of controls that Visual Basic lets you create and how they work.

In Visual Basic, controls are *objects* that interact with the outside world in three distinct ways: through *properties*, *events*, and *methods*. There are more than 30 different types of objects that can be created with Visual Basic, and each type of object has a unique combination of properties, events, and methods.

Types of control objects

In Visual Basic Professional, all of the basic Windows-type controls are available — buttons, check boxes, radio buttons, scroll bars, list boxes, and so on — plus a collection of custom controls that are available only with the Professional Edition of Visual Basic. In addition to these control types, you can obtain third-party libraries of more custom controls, or, if you're patient enough, you can create your own custom controls.

Table 17-1 lists the standard controls you can create with Visual Basic, and shows the toolbar button you use to draw each tool type.

Table 17-1: Visual Basic standard controls

Icon	Control	What it does
	Command button	A button the user can click to initiate a command.
	Image	A graphical control that displays a bitmap.
	Text box	An area in which the user can enter text.
	Label	An area that displays text that cannot be modified.
	Check box	A yes/no control that the user clicks to select or deselect.
	Option button	Part of an option group, in which only one option may be selected.

Continued

Table 17-1: Visual Basic standard controls *(Continued)*

Icon	*Control*	*What it does*
	Frame	Used to group option buttons or other controls.
	List box	Displays a scrollable list of values.
	Combo box	A combination text box and list box.
	Horizontal scroll bar	Selects a value from a range of values.
	Vertical scroll bar	Selects a value from a range of values.
	Picture box	Displays bitmaps or other graphic images.
	Timer	Generates timer events for animations. (Very useful for games!)
	Drive list box	Allows the user to select a disk drive.
	Directory list box	Allows the user to select a directory.
	File list box	Allows the user to select a file.
	Shape	Draws a rectangle, ellipse, or circle.
	Line	Draws a line.
	Data	Provides a rudimentary connection to a database.
	Grid	Displays data in spreadsheet-like cells.
	OLE	Embeds an OLE object.
	Common dialog	Creates a common dialog box for basic functions such as open, save, print, colors, and fonts.
	Menu	Creates a menu.

Visual Basic Professional Edition adds additional custom control types you can use, including animated buttons, gauges, graphs, outlines, masked edit, spin buttons, and controls styled with a chiseled 3-D effect.

Visual Basic Hungarian Notation

Windows programmers who work in the C programming language usually use a goofy method called *Hungarian Notation* to create variable names, in which a prefix is jammed onto the front of the name to indicate the variable type. For example, dwCount is a Double Word field; szMsg is a null-terminated string field; and lpszMsg is a long pointer to a null-terminated string.

Visual Basic programmers, though not quite as weird as C programmers, have fallen into the same useful habit. Left to its own devices, Visual Basic will create arbitrary names for objects you create, such as Text1, Command5, or List3. Most programmers prefer to use more meaningful names for their controls. To help keep track of what type of object each

name represents, a short prefix is used. The following table lists the prefixes for the object types used in the Video Search program along with some sample object names from the program.

Object	Prefix	Example
Form	frm	frmSearch
Command button	cmd	cmdSearchText
Check box	chk	chkAvailOnly
List box	lst	lstTitles
Label	lbl	lblTitle
Menu	mnu	mnuSearchText

Other prefixes are listed in the Programmer's Guide that comes with Visual Basic.

Properties

A *property* is an attribute of a object. Properties are used to set the appearance or behavior of an object. For example, most control objects have properties named FontName and FontSize that govern the appearance of the text that appears on the button. Other properties might enable or disable the object, hide it, or set options that are specific to the object type.

Most properties can be set either at design time — that is, while developing the program — or at run time.

A second use for properties is to set or inspect data values associated with a control. For example, a text box object has a Text property that holds the data visible in the control. The Text property can be set by the program to change the value displayed on the screen, or it can be queried by the program to determine a value entered by the user.

Visual Basic uses the following syntax to manipulate properties at run time (that is, while the program is running):

```
object.property
```

For example, to set the Text property of an object named txtMsg to "Hello World," you'd use a statement such as:

```
txtMsg.Text = "Hello World"
```

To set a program variable to the txtMsg object's Text property value, you'd code something like this:

```
TextValue$ = txtMsg.Text
```

Event procedures

Event procedures are invoked when an object is activated. The procedures consist of Visual Basic instructions that are carried out when the event is triggered.

Each type of object has a specific list of event procedures associated with it. For example, a Command Button Control object can have procedures to respond to the following events:

Click, invoked when the user clicks on the button.

DragDrop, invoked when the user completes a drag and drop operation.

DragOver, invoked when the user drags another object over the button.

GotFocus, invoked when focus is given to the button.

KeyDown, invoked when the user presses a key while this object has the focus.

KeyPress, invoked when the user presses and releases a key while this object has the focus.

KeyUp, invoked when the user releases a key while this object has the focus.

LostFocus, invoked when focus moves from the button to another object.

MouseDown, invoked when the user presses the mouse button.

MouseMove, invoked when the user moves the mouse over the button.

MouseUp, invoked when the user releases the mouse button while over this object.

As is true for all Visual Basic controls, there are far more events than you actually need to worry about. In most cases, the only event you need to provide for with a Command Button control is the Click event: it tells Visual Basic what to do when the user clicks the button.

Visual Basic event procedures are implemented as subroutines, which begin with a SUB statement and end with an END SUB statement. The name of the subroutine indicates both the object and the event the subroutine applies to, separated by an underscore character. Thus, cmdDone_Click is the subroutine for the Click event for the cmdDone object. The actual statements to be executed for the event procedure are coded between the SUB and END SUB statements.

Methods

A *method* is a function or service that is provided by an object. You can think of methods as specialized Visual Basic statements that carry out their actions on an object.

As with event procedures and properties, each type of control object has its own set of methods that apply only to that object. For example, a List Box control has the following methods:

AddItem, which inserts a new item into the list.

Clear, which removes all items from the list.

Drag, which is used to control dragging.

Move, used to move the control to a new location.

Refresh, which immediately redraws the control on the screen.

RemoveItem, which deletes a specific item from the list.

SetFocus, which gives the list box the input focus.

Zorder, which changes the order in which overlapping controls are displayed.

Visual Basic uses the same syntax for methods as it does for properties:

```
object.method
```

For example, to clear the contents of a list box control named List1, you would use this statement:

```
List1.Clear
```

Some methods require parameters (sometimes called arguments), which simply follow the method name. For example:

```
List1.AddItem "Star Trek IV"
```

This example inserts the text "Star Trek IV" as a line in the list box List1.

Now that you've got the low-down on VB control objects and their properties, events, and methods, it's time to proceed with building our application.

Building the Form

After the database has been designed, the next major step in creating a Visual Basic application is creating its main window, called a *form* in Visual Basic.

When you first start Visual Basic, you are presented with a new project named Project1. The first thing you should do is save this project using a more meaningful name, such as VIDSRCH.

Figure 17-2 shows the appearance of the Visual Basic screen after a new project has been saved. The window in the center of the screen, titled Form1, is the program's main form. The form is initially blank, which doesn't make the program useful to anyone other than perhaps Forrest Gump. To make the program useful, we'll have to make this blank form a little more interesting. (The dots on the form are a grid used to align objects placed on the form. They won't appear on the form when the program is run.)

All of the figures in this chapter were created using Visual Basic 3.0 Professional Edition running under Windows 95. That's why the standard window controls (minimize and maximize buttons, for example) look different than they do in Windows 3.1. ◼

Changing the form properties

The first step in improving the blank form is to play a bit with the form's properties. Properties for all objects are controlled through the Properties dialog box, pictured in Figure 17-3. To call up this dialog box, click on the object whose properties you want to set (in this case, the blank form), then press F4.

In this example, I've already changed several of the properties of the form. In particular, I changed the Caption property to "Video Search," and I changed

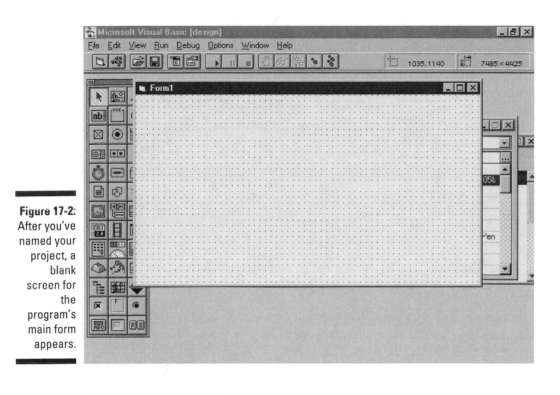

Figure 17-2:
After you've named your project, a blank screen for the program's main form appears.

Figure 17-3:
The Properties dialog box is where you change object properties.

the BackColor property to light gray. I also changed the object's Name property from the default Form1 to frmSearch.

To change a property in the Properties dialog box, you click on the property you want to change (scrolling the list if necessary), then type a new value for the property. For properties that can have only a limited set of choices (such as true/false values), double-clicking the property cycles through the choices. Clicking some properties, such as color properties, brings up a menu of available choices.

Figure 17-4 shows the frmSearch form after I've changed its background color, caption, and name. It's still blank, but it's beginning to develop some character.

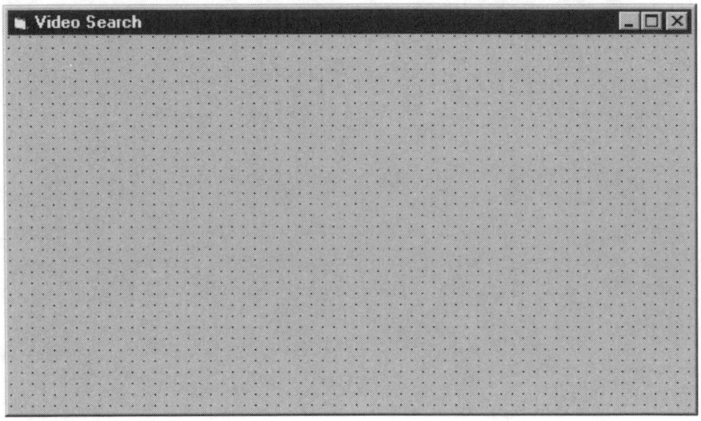

Figure 17-4:
The frmSearch form after changing the Caption, BackColor, and Name properties.

Adding a command button

Creating a form is simply a matter of drawing various control objects on the blank form and playing with their arrangement until you're satisfied with the form's appearance.

To draw a control object on the form, start by clicking the type of control you want from the palette of tools available in the Toolbox. Then, draw the control on the form by positioning the mouse at the point on the form where you want the top left corner of the control to be, pressing and holding the left mouse button, and dragging the mouse to the where you'd like the bottom right corner of the control to appear.

When you release the mouse button, the control will be placed at the location you indicated. If you've ever worked with a Windows-based drawing program, you'll have no trouble figuring out how to do this. Figure 17-5 shows a command button as it appears immediately after drawing it.

Once you've drawn a control, you can drag it around to any location on the form you wish. In addition, you can click on the control to select it, then press F4 to bring forth the Properties dialog box so you can set the control's properties. You'll certainly want to change the button's Caption property, which reflects the text displayed on the button. You may also want to change the Name property and other properties as well.

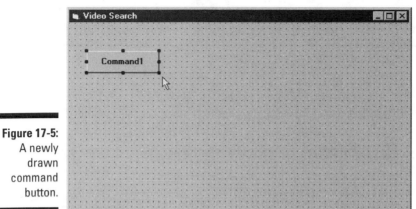

Figure 17-5:
A newly
drawn
command
button.

Completing the form

To complete the frmSearch form, I added a total of five buttons, a list box, and a check box. I played with the control layout a bit until I got things lined up satisfactorily, then I adjusted the properties of each control. Figure 17-6 shows the form with all of these controls in place, and Table 17-2 lists the properties changed from default values for each of these controls.

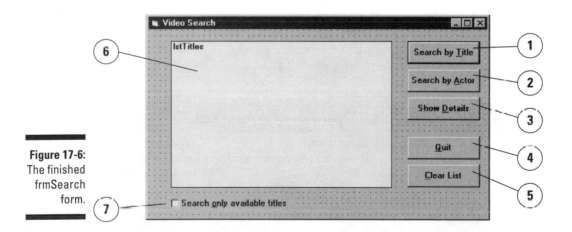

Figure 17-6:
The finished
frmSearch
form.

Notice that the Caption property for each command button includes an ampersand (&). The letter immediately following the ampersand is the button's hot key, used in combination with the Alt key. Thus, "Search by &Title" means the user can activate the Search by Title button by pressing Alt+T. Likewise, "Search by &Actor" indicates that Search by Actor can be activated by typing Alt+A.

Table 17-2: Property settings for the frmSearch controls

Object	Property	Setting
1	Name	cmdSearchTitle
	Caption	Search by &Title
2	Name	cmdSearchActor
	Caption	Search by &Actor
3	Name	cmdShowDetail
	Caption	Show &Details
4	Name	cmdQuit
	Caption	&Quit
5	Name	cmdClear
	Caption	&Clear List
6	Name	lstTitles
	Sorted	True
7	Name	chkAvailOnly
	Caption	Search &only available titles
	Value	0 - Unchecked

Adding Event Procedures

Once you have a form filled with controls, the next step in creating a Visual Basic program is writing the Visual Basic code that will be executed for the various events to which the controls should respond.

Procedures for the Video Search program

Before you begin actually writing code, it's a good idea to think through the action the program should take when each control is activated. The following paragraphs describe the action that should be taken for each of the controls in the frmSearch form:

✔ **cmdSearchTitle:** If the user clicks this button, the program should ask the user to enter the title to search for (or as much of the title as the user can remember), query the database for the selected titles, and place the titles in the lstTitles list box.

✔ **cmdSearchActor:** If the user clicks this button, the program should ask the user for the last name of the actor to search for, then query the database for all tapes that feature that actor and place the resulting titles in the lstTitles list box.

✔ **cmdShowDetail:** If the user clicks this button, the program should show in a separate dialog box all of the actors that appear in the tape that is currently selected in the lstTitles list box. If no tape is selected, this button should be ignored.

✔ **cmdQuit:** If the user clicks this button, the program should end.

✔ **cmdClear:** If the user clicks this button, the program should clear the contents of the lstTitles list box.

✔ **lstTitles:** If the user double-clicks one of the lines in this list box control, the program should display the details for the selected title as if the user had clicked the Show Details button.

✔ **chkAvailOnly:** The cmdSearchTitle and cmdSearchActor click events should check the setting of this check box to determine whether or not the query should omit tapes that are currently rented out. However, no special processing is required for any events associated with this control.

Coding the Quit button's Click procedure

We'll start coding the Video Search program's event procedures with the simplest procedure, the cmdQuit button's Click procedure. The code for this procedure simply ends the program using an End statement.

The easiest way to create the code for a control's procedure is to double-click on the control. When you do that, the Code window will appear, in which you edit the code for each procedure in the program, as shown in Figure 17-7.

As you can see in the figure, the Code window displays one procedure at a time. The Object list box lists all of the objects associated with the form, and the Proc list box lists the procedures associated with each object.

When you double-click on a control, Visual Basic takes you directly to the Click event procedure for the control. In Figure 17-7, you can see that the Object list box indicates the cmdQuit object, and the Proc list box indicates the Click procedure.

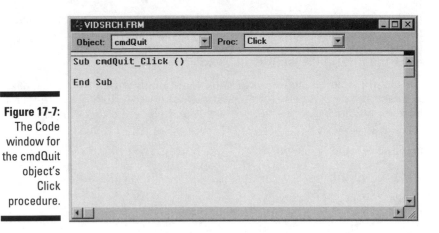

Figure 17-7:
The Code
window for
the cmdQuit
object's
Click
procedure.

When you first edit a procedure, Visual Basic creates a template of the procedure for you, consisting of nothing more than Sub and End Sub statements:

```
Sub cmdQuit_Click ()

End Sub
```

To write the code for a procedure, all you have to do is fill in the Visual Basic statements you want executed for the event between the Sub and End Sub statements. For the cmdQuit_Click procedure, the only statement necessary is End, so the procedure should look like this:

```
Sub cmdQuit_Click ()
    End
End Sub
```

Of course, other procedures will have more complicated coding requirements.

Once you've provided a mechanism for ending the program, you can test the program using Visual Basic's Run|Start command or by pressing F5. The program won't be very impressive, since all of the buttons except the Quit button will be inoperative. But the program is functional.

Understanding Database Objects

The easiest way to process a database in Visual Basic is to use Visual Basic's database and recordset objects. I'm going to throw a bunch of VB terminology at you that will be useful as we go through our example program.

✔ A *database object* represents a database. The database can be an Access database on the same computer or on a network server, an external database in one of several supported formats, including Btrieve, dBase, FoxPro, and Paradox, or ODBC databases.

✔ *Recordset objects* represent collections of database rows. Visual Basic supports three types of recordset objects:

1. *Table objects* represent individual database tables.

2. *Dynaset objects* represent the result of a database query. Rows in a Dynaset object are updateable, and any changes are automatically propagated back to the original database.

3. *Snapshot objects* are also query results, but are static. Rows in a snapshot cannot be updated, and do not reflect any changes made by other users after the snapshot is created.

Using VB's database and recordset objects is not necessarily the most efficient way to access a client/server database; it's usually more efficient to bypass Visual Basic's database objects and code function calls that access database functions directly. But for the purposes of this chapter, using VB's database objects will suffice. ■

Visual Basic snubs its nose at the standard relational database terminology of *rows* and *columns*, and uses the terms *record* and *field* instead. Recordset objects provide cursor-like methods that allow you to scroll forward or backward through the recordset data:

MoveFirst moves to the first row of the recordset.

MoveLast moves to the last row of the recordset.

MoveNext moves to the next row in sequence. If there are no more rows, the EOF (end-of-file) property is set to true.

MovePrevious moves to the previous row. If the recordset is already positioned at the first row, the EOF property is set to true.

Each recordset object contains a collection of *field objects*, which represent the individual columns in a table or query result.

To access the value of a field object in a Dynaset or snapshot object, you usually refer to the field by its ordinal number. The first column specified in the query is ordinal number 0, the second is number 1, and so on. For example, to access the value in the first column of a recordset object named dsTitles, you'd code dsTitles(0).

Visual Basic supports several other types of objects used for database processing, but since I don't use them in the Video Search program and this chapter is already getting too long, I won't present them here. You're welcome.

Opening the Database

Now to the nuts and bolts of accessing the Videos database in the Video Search program. Before the Videos database can be queried, it must be opened. Opening the database requires code in two different program modules.

First, the database needs to be defined with a Dim As Database statement in the general declarations portion of the program code. To access the general declarations, double-click on any object to bring up the Code window, then select (general) from the Object list box and (declarations) from the Proc list box. Next, add the following line of code:

```
Dim dbVideo As Database
```

This creates a database object named *dbVideo*. Because the declaration is placed in the general declarations, it can be accessed by any procedure in the main module of the Video Search program.

Having defined the database object, the next step is to open the database using the OpenDatabase function. To open the database automatically when the program starts, double-click anywhere on the background of the frm-Search form to bring up the Code window. Visual Basic will automatically position you to the Load procedure for the form, which is automatically executed when the program starts. Initially, the Load procedure will be empty:

```
Sub Form_Load ()

End Sub
```

To open the database, you use the OpenDatabase function, which returns a database object. To associate the returned database object with the database object declared with the Dim As Database statement, you have to use a Set statement, as follows:

```
Set dbVideo = OpenDatabase("VIDEOS.MDB")
```

This statement opens the database named VIDEOS.MDB, and associates the database object dbVideo with the newly opened database. The resulting Form_Load procedure looks like this:

```
Sub Form_Load ()
    Set dbVideo = OpenDatabase("VIDEOS.MDB")
End Sub
```

In an actual program, the OpenDatabase function call would probably be more complicated than this. For example, to open an ODBC database, the procedure would look something like this:

```
Sub Form_Load ()
    Set dbVideo = OpenDatabase("Videos",False,False,"ODBC")
End Sub
```

The Videos database would then have to be *registered* with ODBC to indicate the database type (SQL Server, Oracle, or whatever), the server name, the file name, and other information required to access the database.

Programming the Search by Title Button

Now that the database has been opened, we can get on with the business of querying it. We'll start with the Click procedure for the Search by Title button, cmdSearchTitle. Listing 17-1 shows the complete code for this procedure. In the sections that follow, I'll dissect the procedure piece by piece so you'll understand how it works.

```
Sub cmdSearchTitle_Click ()
    Msg = "Enter as much of the title as you can remember."
    Title = "Title Search"
    SearchTitle = InputBox$(Msg, Title, "")
    SQLtext = "SELECT TapeNo, Title "
    SQLtext = SQLtext & "FROM Tape "
    SQLtext = SQLtext & "WHERE Title LIKE '"
    SQLtext = SQLtext & SearchTitle
    SQLtext = SQLtext & "*'"
    If chkAvailOnly.Value = 1 Then
        SQLtext = SQLtext & " AND Status = 0 "
    End If
    Dim dsTitles As Dynaset
    Set dsTitles = dbVideo.CreateDynaset(SQLtext, DB_READONLY)
    lstTitles.Clear
    Do Until dsTitles.EOF
        lstTitles.AddItem dsTitles(0) & "   " & dsTitles(1)
        dsTitles.MoveNext
    Loop
End Sub
```

Listing 17-1: The Search by Title button's Click procedure.

Getting input from the user

The first three lines of the cmdSearchTitle_Click procedure ask the user to enter the title of the movie to search for:

```
Msg = "Enter as much of the title as you can remember."
Title = "Title Search"
SearchTitle = InputBox$(Msg, Title, "")
```

These lines use the InputBox$ function, a standard Visual Basic function that displays a simple dialog box to accept text from the user. The arguments to the InputBox$ function supply the message displayed in the dialog box, the title displayed in the dialog box title bar, and a default value used if the user doesn't enter anything.

InputBox$ returns a string variable, which is assigned to the variable SearchTitle to be used later in the procedure.

Figure 17-8 shows what the dialog box displayed by the InputBox$ function looks like. It's not very attractive, and further refinement of the program would almost certainly involve replacing this bare-bones dialog with something more appropriate. But we're just building a prototype here, so the InputBox$ function will have to do.

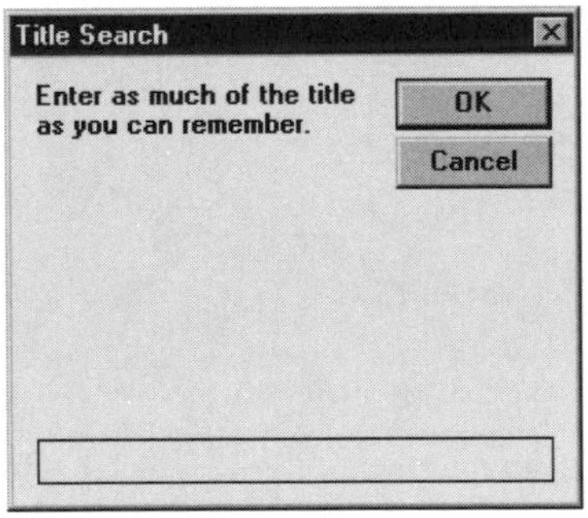

Figure 17-8:
The bare-bones
InputBox$
dialog box.

Querying the database

Having obtained the title the user wants to search for, the program must next build an SQL SELECT statement to retrieve the tape records that match the title, then query the database.

As I mentioned earlier in this chapter, the SELECT statement for the title query will look like this:

```
SELECT TapeNo, Title, Status FROM Tape
    WHERE TITLE LIKE 'search title*'
```

In Visual Basic, a SELECT statement is created in a string variable. Usually, the string variable is built up using several assignment statements, each of which adds a portion of the SELECT statement until the statement is completed. In this case the variable named SQLtext is created by the following lines:

```
SQLtext = "SELECT TapeNo, Title "
SQLtext = SQLtext & "FROM Tape "
SQLtext = SQLtext & "WHERE Title LIKE '"
SQLtext = SQLtext & SearchTitle
SQLtext = SQLtext & "*'"
If chkAvailOnly.Value = 1 Then
    SQLtext = SQLtext & " AND Status = 0 "
End If
```

The first assignment statement begins the SELECT statement, then the successive assignment statements add to it. When these statements finish, the SQLtext variable will contain the complete SELECT statement. Notice that the content of the SearchTitle variable is enclosed in quotes and followed by an asterisk wildcard. Also, " AND Status = 0" is included only if chkAvailOnly.Value is 1, meaning that the user checked the "Search only available titles" check box.

Once the SELECT statement is ready to go, a Dynaset object is defined using a Dim As Dynaset statement, then the database object's CreateDynaset method is used to create the Dynaset:

```
Dim dsTitles As Dynaset
Set dsTitles = dbVideo.CreateDynaset(SQLtext, DB_READONLY)
```

The CreateDynaset method takes a SELECT statement as an argument, processes it, and returns the result set as a Dynaset object. Specifying the constant DB_READONLY makes the Dynaset read-only, which improves performance by not enforcing a lock on the records retrieved by the query. (In a client/server environment, DB_SQLPASSTHROUGH would probably be specified as well, so that the SELECT statement is handed directly to the server for processing.)

Processing the query result

The rest of the lines in the Listing 17-1 simply move the TapeNo and Title of each selected tape to the lstTitles list box:

```
lstTitles.Clear
Do Until dsTitles.EOF
   lstTitles.AddItem dsTitles(0) & "   " & dsTitles(1)
   dsTitles.MoveNext
Loop
```

First, the lstTitles.Clear method is used to erase the results of a previous query from the list box. Then, a Do Until statement loops through the Dynaset records until the EOF property is true, indicating that the last result row has been processed.

In the loop, the lstTitles.AddItem method is used to copy the first two fields of each Dynaset record to the list box. Then, the dsTitles.MoveNext method is used to skip to the next Dynaset record.

When the loop is finished, the list box will contain one line for each tape that was selected by the database query when the Dynaset was created.

Programming the Search by Actor Button

The procedure for querying the database when the user clicks the Search by Actor button is nearly identical to the procedure for the Search by Title button, except that the SELECT statement is a bit more complex. The procedure is shown in Listing 17-2.

The only real difference between this procedure and the Search by Title procedure is that here the SELECT statement does a three-table join to query the database. If the user enters "Montalban" for the search name, the SQLtext variable will contain the following SELECT statement:

```
SELECT DISTINCT Tape.TapeNo, Tape.Title, Tape.Status
   FROM Tape, TapeAct, Actor
   WHERE Tape.TapeNo = TapeAct.TapeNo
     AND TapeAct.ActorNo = Actor.ActorNo
     AND Actor.LName LIKE 'Montalban*'
```

Other than the construction of the SELECT statement, this procedure is the same as the one that was shown in Listing 17-1.

```
Sub cmdSearchActor_Click ()
    Msg = "Enter the actor's last name."
    Title = "Actor Search"
    SearchName = InputBox$(Msg, Title, "")
    SQLtext = "SELECT DISTINCT Tape.TapeNo, Tape.Title "
    SQLtext = SQLtext & "FROM Tape, TapeAct, Actor "
    SQLtext = SQLtext & "WHERE Tape.TapeNo - TapeAct.TapeNo "
    SQLtext = SQLtext & "  AND TapeAct.ActorNo = Actor.ActorNo "
    SQLtext = SQLtext & "  AND Actor.LName LIKE '"
    SQLtext = SQLtext & SearchName
    SQLtext = SQLtext & "*'"
    If chkAvailOnly.Value - 1 Then
        SQLtext = SQLtext & " AND Status = 0 "
    End If
    Dim dsTitles As Dynaset
    Set dsTitles - dbVideo.CreateDynaset(SQLtext, DB_READONLY)
    lstTitles.Clear
    Do Until dsTitles.EOF
        lstTitles.AddItem dsTitles(0) & "   " & dsTitles(1)
        dsTitles.MoveNext
    Loop
End Sub
```

Listing 17-2: The Search by Actor button's Click procedure.

The Program So Far

The Video Search program is now complete enough that it can be tested. So far, this is how the program works:

When the program is started, it automatically displays the frmSearch form as shown in Figure 17-9. At the same time, the frmSearch_Load function is executed, which connects the program to the Videos database.

When the user clicks the Search by Title button, a dialog box appears asking the user to enter the title to search for. In Figure 17-10, the user has typed "Star Trek" before clicking OK.

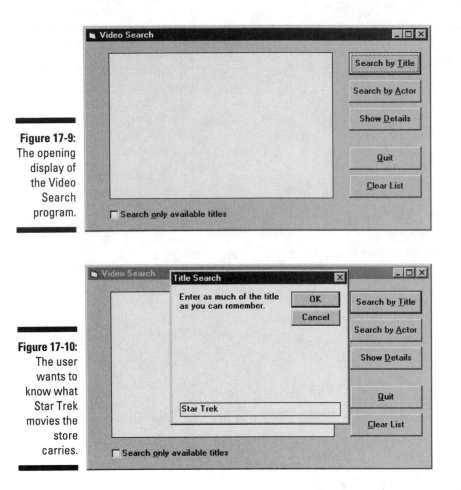

Figure 17-9:
The opening display of the Video Search program.

Figure 17-10:
The user wants to know what Star Trek movies the store carries.

When the user clicks OK, the program builds the following SELECT statement in the SQLtext variable:

```
SELECT TapeNo, Title, Status FROM Tape
    WHERE Title LIKE 'Star Trek*'
```

Next, the program creates a Dynaset, which processes the query and returns the resulting rows. Finally, the program copies data from each Dynaset row to the list box. The resulting display is shown in Figure 17-11.

Now, the user knows that Ricardo Montalban was in one of those movies, but can't remember which one. So he or she clicks the Search by Actor button, which brings up the dialog box shown in Figure 17-12.

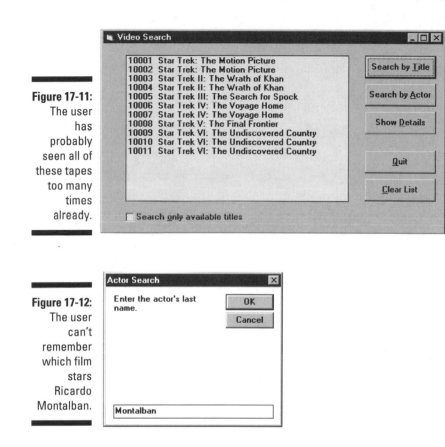

Figure 17-11:
The user
has
probably
seen all of
these tapes
too many
times
already.

Figure 17-12:
The user
can't
remember
which film
stars
Ricardo
Montalban.

When the user enters "Montalban" in the text field and clicks OK, the program queries the database for all tapes that feature actors with names matching "Montalban" and displays the result, shown in Figure 17-13. (Of course,
with a live database, other movies besides Star Trek II would probably be displayed. The test database used here has only Star Trek movies, so Montalban's other high-quality films aren't included.)

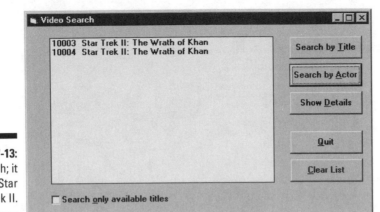

Figure 17-13:
Oh yeah; it
was Star
Trek II.

Displaying a Dialog Box

Few programs consist of just one dialog box, and the Video Search program is no exception. If the user selects a tape in the lstTitles list box, then clicks the Show Details button (cmdShowDetail), a dialog box is displayed to show the complete list of actors for the tape in question. To display this dialog box, a second form must be created, with its own controls and event procedures.

Figure 17-14 shows the Cast Details form (frmDetail) which is displayed when the user clicks the Show Details button. The form includes four controls:

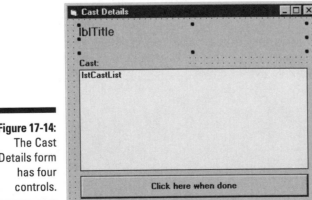

Figure 17-14:
The Cast
Details form
has four
controls.

✔ *lblTitle*, a label control used to display the title of the selected tape. The FontSize property of this control has been changed from the default (8.25) to 12 point so the title will be displayed in large type, and the BackStyle property has been changed to Transparent to allow the form background color to show through.

✔ *lblLabel1*, a label control that displays the caption "Cast:" just above the list box. The Caption property has been changed to "Cast:" and the BackStyle property has been changed to Transparent.

✔ *lstCastList*, a list box control that will be used to show the names of the selected tape's cast. The Sorted property has been set to True so the names will be shown in alphabetical order.

✔ *cmdDone*, a command button control whose Caption property has been set to "Click here when done."

Three event procedures are required to make this form operable. The first is the Click procedure for the cmdShowDetail control, shown in Listing 17-3. I won't explain every line of this procedure, but in short, it builds a SELECT statement that retrieves every actor appearing in the selected title in the lstTitles list box, creates a read-only Dynaset, copies each row from the Dynaset to the lstCast list box, then displays the frmDetail form using the form's Show method.

```
Sub cmdShowDetail_Click ()
    If lstTitles.Text = "" Then Exit Sub
    TapeNoLen = InStr(lstTitles.Text, " ")
    TapeNo = Left$(lstTitles.Text, TapeNoLen - 1)
    Title = Right$(lstTitles.Text, Len(lstTitles.Text) - TapeNoLen
            - 1)
    SQLtext = "SELECT LName, FName "
    SQLtext = SQLtext & "FROM TapeAct, Actor "
    SQLtext = SQLtext & "WHERE TapeAct.TapeNo = " & Str$(TapeNo)
    SQLtext = SQLtext & "  AND TapeAct.ActorNo = Actor.ActorNo "
Dim dsActors As Dynaset
    Set dsActors = dbVideo.CreateDynaset(SQLtext, DB_READONLY)
    frmDetail.lstCastList.Clear
    Do Until dsActors.EOF
        frmDetail.lstCastList.AddItem rtrim$(dsActors(1)) & ", " &
            rtrim$(dsActors(0))
        dsActors.MoveNext
    Loop
    frmDetail.lblTitle = Title
    frmDetail.Show 1
End Sub
```

Listing 17-3: The cmdShowDetail_Click procedure.

The second procedure created for the frmDetail form is the Click procedure for the cmdDone button, which returns to the main Search form. This procedure uses the Unload statement:

```
Sub cmdDone_Click ()
    Unload frmDetail
End Sub
```

When the user invokes this procedure by clicking on the cmdDone button, the frmDetail form will be unloaded and focus will return to the frmSearch form.

The third and final procedure is the DblClick procedure for the lstTitles list box. It is coded as follows:

```
Sub lstTitles_DblClick ()
    cmdShowDetail_Click
End Sub
```

This procedure illustrates a common Visual Basic programming technique: When the user double-clicks a line in the lstTitles list box, the cmdShowDetail_Click procedure is invoked, which in turn displays the frmDetails form. Thus, double-clicking on a title is the same as selecting the title and clicking the Show Details button. Figure 17-15 shows the Video Search program's Cast Details for a selected movie.

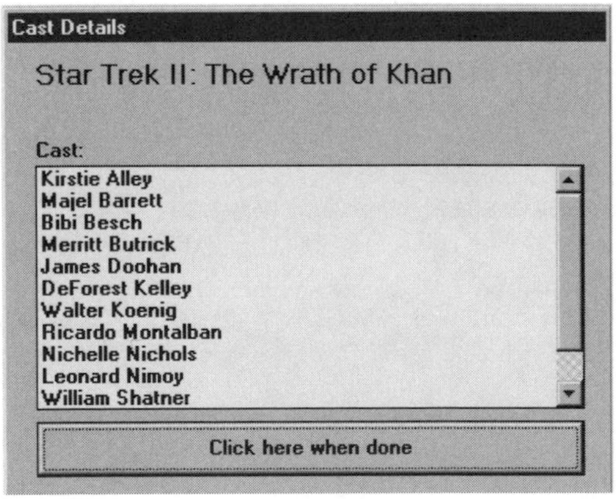

Figure 17-15:
The cast of
Star Trek II:
The Wrath
of Khan.

Adding Menus

Most client/server front-end programs have extensive menus to invoke various program functions. Although the Video Search program is fully functional without menus, I'll add a simple menu structure to it just to demonstrate how easily menus can be added using a visual programming tool. Two menus will be used: a Search menu, which will include the commmands Search by Title, Search by Actor, Show Details, Clear List, and Exit (identical in function to the command buttons on the frmSearch form), and Help, which will include an About command.

Menu design icon

To add menus to a Visual Basic program, the programmer calls up the Menu Design Window by clicking on the Menu Design icon in the top toolbar (it's not on the floating tool palette as the icons for the other controls are). The Menu Design Window represents a program's menu structure in an outline format, as shown in Figure 17-16. Each menu object has a Caption, which is the text that's displayed when the program is run, a Name, and other properties.

Notice that an ampersand (&) is used to mark each menu's hot key. Thus, the Search menu can be activated by pressing Alt+S, and the Search by Title command can be activated by pressing Alt+S, T.

Also, notice the menu item between the Clear List and Exit entries, indicated by a hyphen in the menu list. This item will be displayed as a separator line in the actual menu.

Figure 17-16: The Menu Design window is used to add menus.

```
Menu Design Window                              [X]

  Caption:  &About                          OK

  Name:     mnuHelpAbout                    Cancel

  Index:              Shortcut:  (none)        ▼

  ☐ WindowList        HelpContextID:  0

  ☐ Checked      ☑ Enabled      ☑ Visible

  [←][→][↑][↓]   Next    Insert    Delete

  &Search
  ····Search by &Title
       Search by &Actor
  ····Show &Details
  ····&Clear List
  ·····
  ····E&xit
  &Help
  ····&About
```

Figure 17-17 shows the menu as it will appear when the Video Search program is run. In the figure, the user has clicked on the Search menu to reveal its selections. Notice the chiseled appearance of the menu as provided by Windows 95. In Windows 3.1, the same menu would appear without the fancy three-dimensional look.

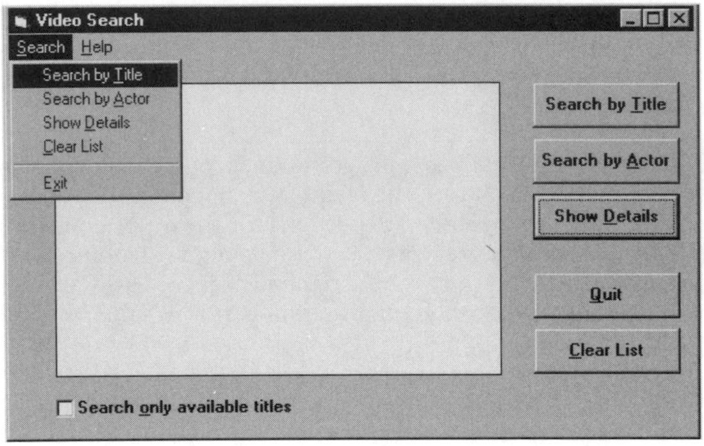

Figure 17-17:
The Video
Search
program's
Search
menu.

The only piece remaining in the menu puzzle is the coding required to implement each menu command. Listing 17-4 shows the procedures for each menu command. For all of the commands except the Help About command, the procedure simply calls the corresponding button's Click procedure. As a result, choosing the command from the menu works exactly the same as clicking on the related command button.

As for the Help About command, it simply displays a form named frmAbout by using the form's Show method. The design of this form isn't complicated, so I won't show it. Figure 17-18 shows the form as it appears when displayed in the program. (The fancy graphic was stolen from the clip art that comes with Word for Windows 6.)

Figure 17-18:
The Help
About dialog
box for the
Video
Search
program.

```
Sub mnuSearchByTitle_Click ()
    cmdSearchTitle_Click
End Sub

Sub mnuSearchByActor_Click ()
    cmdSearchActor_Click
End Sub

Sub mnuSearchShowDetails_Click ()
    cmdShowDetail_Click
End Sub

Sub mnuSearchClearList_Click ()
    cmdClear_Click
End Sub

Sub mnuSearchExit_Click ()
    cmdQuit_Click
End Sub

Sub mnuHelpAbout_Click ()
    frmAbout.Show 1
End Sub
```

Listing 17-4: The procedures for the Video Search program's menu commands.

Don't programmers ever have any fun?

Artists sign their paintings. Authors get their names on their book covers. Journalists have their bylines. What about programmers?

Not wanting to be left out, programmers started the tradition of leaving their mark on their work long ago. The earliest programmers carved their initials on the back of Neolithic counting pebbles using primitive stone tools. Today's programmers usually bury their signatures deep inside their programs, forcing the users to figure out an unlikely sequence of commands to find their hidden treasures.

These signatures are sometimes called *Easter eggs* for this reason. You can find Easter eggs in many commercial applications, including programs such as Word for Windows, Excel, and even Windows itself.

Adding an Easter egg to a program isn't too hard. I wouldn't suggest adding one to the Video Search program, of course, but if I did, it would involve adding a couple of objects to the frmAbout form and setting the Visible property for both objects to False, rendering the objects invisible to the untrained eye, then adding a procedure shown on the next page:

```
Sub Form_KeyPress (keyascii As Integer)
    Static trigger As Integer
    Select Case Chr(keyascii)
        Case "d"
            If trigger = 0 Then trigger = 1 Else trigger = 0
        Case "u"
            If trigger = 1 Then trigger = 2 Else trigger = 0
        Case "m"
            If trigger = 2 Or trigger = 3 Then
                If trigger = 3 Then trigger = 4
                If trigger = 2 Then trigger = 3
            Else
                trigger = 0
            End If
        Case "y"
            If trigger = 4 Then trigger = 5 Else trigger = 0
        Case Else
            trigger = 0
    End Select
    If trigger = 5 Then
        If InStr(frmSearch.lstTitles.Text, "Star Trek II:") > 0 Then
            picAbout.Visible = False
            picDummy.Visible = True
            lblDummy.Visible = True
            trigger = 0
        End If
    End If
End Sub
```

This procedure responds to keystrokes typed while the About dialog box is displayed. With the procedure in place, the user would simply have to follow the following sequence to activate the Easter egg:

1. Perform a search by title or author that displays any copy of the movie "Star Trek II: The Wrath of Khan."

2. Click on Star Trek II to select it.

3. Call up the About dialog box using the Help|About command.

4. Type the word "dummy."

The user will be rewarded with a modified version of the About dialog box:

We're finished! Of course, we could go on tweaking this program forever, adding feature after feature. But the program is now functional enough. I hope this little Visual Basic programming experience has enlightened you about the joys and travails of client/server programming. In the next chapter, I'll deal with a handful of client/server programming issues that didn't come up in our sample program.

Chapter 18

Other Client/Server Programming Issues

● ●

In This Chapter

▶ Database programming considerations

▶ OLE applications

▶ Mail-enabled applications

▶ Help

● ●

*T*his chapter deals with a few programming issues that often come up in client/server projects. These are the issues that keep programmers awake at night while the rest of us worry about war, the economy, or the future of baseball.

Once again, you've stumbled into a chapter that presents some pretty heavy-duty programming concepts. If programming isn't your cup of tea, feel free to skip this chapter altogether. ■

Database Programming Issues

There are a variety of issues that you'll probably come up against if you're developing a program that accesses SQL data. Here are some of the more common ones.

Using an API

The sample Visual Basic program I presented in Chapter 17 accessed its database using Visual Basic's standard database objects. Other visual programming environments have similar mechanisms for accessing database data. This form of database access spares the programmer the tedious details of interacting directly with the underlying database system by providing a high-level object-oriented database interface.

Although this is the easiest way to code database programs, it's not usually the most efficient. As an alternative, you can access the database using a low-level *Application Programming Interface*, or *API*.

If you remember from our discussion way back in Chapter 12, there are two types of APIs: product-specific APIs and generic APIs such as ODBC (Open Database Connectivity). Product-specific APIs are more efficient than generic APIs, but they aren't portable. In other words, you can't use the SQL Server API to access Oracle data, or vice versa. However, APIs have enough in common that once you've learned one, you'll have no trouble picking up another.

A generic API such as ODBC is not quite as flexible as a specific API, but is considerably more efficient and flexible than using the high-level database support of a visual programming language such as Visual Basic. In the case of Visual Basic, database objects are actually an interface between the program and ODBC. By coding ODBC function calls directly, you can bypass the middleman.

Database programming with an API invariably involves lots of coding. Instead of using programming statements built into the programming language, the programmer must code sequences of function calls, each followed by detailed error-checking instructions. The simple task of connecting to a database server, handled by a single OpenDatabase method in Visual Basic, can require dozens of lines of code when using an API.

Table 18-1 lists the core function calls that make up the ODBC API. These are the minimum function calls that an ODBC driver must support. ODBC also defines additional *extended* functions that more advanced ODBC drivers can provide. These are listed in Table 18-2.

Note: None of the function calls in Tables 18-1 or 18-2 will be on the test, so you don't have to memorize them. I'm listing them here mainly to illustrate that you pay for the additional flexibility of using an API with increased complexity.

Table 18-1: ODBC core functions

Function	What it does
Connecting to a Data Source	
SQLAllocConnect	Establishes a connection.
SQLAllocEnv	Obtains an environment handle which can be used to manage several ODBC connections.
SQLDisconnect	Closes a connection.
SQLFreeconnect	Releases a connection handle.
SQLFreeEnv	Releases an environment handle.
SQL Requests	
SQLAllocStmt	Allocates a statement handle.
SQLPrepare	Prepares an SQL statement for subsequent execution.
SQLGetCursorName	Gets a cursor name associated with a statement handle.
SQLSetCursorName	Sets a cursor name.
SQLExecute	Executes a statement that has already been prepared by SQLPrepare.
SQLExecDirect	Executes a statement.
SQLFreeStmt	Ends statement processing and closes any open cursor.
SQLCancel	Cancels an SQL statement.
SQLTransact	Transaction commit or rollback.
Retrieving results	
SQLRowCount	Returns the number of rows affected by an insert, update, or delete.
SQLNumResultCols	Returns the number of result columns.
SQLDescribeCol	Returns descriptive information about a column.
SQLColAttributes	Describes attributes of a result set column.
SQLBindCol	Associates a result set column with a program variable.
SQLFetch	Retrieves the next row of results data.
SQLError	Returns additional error information.

Table 18-2: Extended ODBC functions

Level 1	Level 2
SQLBindParameter	SQLBrowseConnect
SQLColumns	SQLColumnPrivileges
SQLDriverConnect	SQLDrivers
SQLGetConnectOption	SQLDataSources
SQLGetData	SQLDescribeParam
SQLGetFunctions	SQLExtendedFetch
SQLGetInfo	SQLForeignKeys
SQLGetStmtOption	SQLMoreResults
SQLGetTypeInfo	SQLNativeSql
SQLParamData	SQLNumParams
SQLPutData	SQLParamOptions
SQLSetConnectOption	SQLPrimaryKeys
SQLSetStmtOption	SQLProcedureColumns
SQLSpecialColumns	SQLProcedures
SQLStatistics	SQLSetPos
SQLTables	SQLSetScrollOptions
	SQLTablePrivileges

Efficiency techniques

For any database query, there are probably half a dozen ways to accomplish the desired result. For the programmer to select the best alternative, he or she must be aware of the alternatives and have a good understanding of the strengths and weaknesses of each.

There are usually several processing choices even when working with the high-level database support of a language such as Visual Basic. For example, here are some of the options for performing database queries in Visual Basic (if some of this terminology is new, go back and review Chapter 17 on the basics of VB):

✔ Use a table object. This allows you to efficiently access rows from a single table, but does not permit joins or other complicated queries.

✔ Use a Dynaset object. This allows complicated queries including joins, but places locks on each page accessed. Data for a Dynaset object is sent to the client one row at a time, as each row is fetched.

✔ Use a read-only Dynaset object. This relaxes the locks placed on the affected rows.

✔ Use a Dynaset object with optimistic locking. This does not hold locks against updated pages.

✔ Use a Snapshot object. Snapshots are not updateable. All of the data for a Snapshot object is sent to the client when the Snapshot is created. Thus, the Snapshot presents a "static" picture of the database. If the number of rows retrieved by the query is small, a Snapshot may be the best choice. For a large amount of data, a Snapshot may not be a good idea.

✔ Use a QueryDef, in which the query is stored in the database rather than built on-the-fly by the program.

✔ Use the SQL PassThrough option with a Dynaset, Snapshot, or QueryDef object, which causes the SQL text to be passed directly to the database server rather than processed by Visual Basic.

Is that enough choices for you? If not, remember that in addition to these choices, there are usually many choices in the way you construct the actual SQL SELECT statement for the query.

Error handling

Any database request can fail for a variety of reasons. Client/server database programs must be written in a way that makes sure that no errors go unnoticed.

Different APIs use different error-handling techniques. ODBC returns status information with every API function call. The program must check the status information, never assuming that a function call has completed successfully. If an ODBC call results in an error, additional error information may be obtained by calling the SQLError function.

On the other hand, the SQL Server API for Visual Basic (VBSQL) sets up a message handler object that responds to error events. The programmer must code procedures to handle these events.

Database names and locations

TIP If it can be avoided, you should not hard-code database names and locations into your programs. Instead, you should provide a flexible way to supply the database name and location at run time. One way to do that is by creating a private .INI file to contain the database names and locations. An alternative is to display a dialog box that allows the user to select the database. ◼

For direct access to an Access database, you specify the network path and filename for the database. For example, \\SERVER1\DB\VIDEOS.MDB. This information should be stored in a private .INI file rather than hard-coded into the program.

ODBC requires that databases be *registered* before they can be used. You can register the database from within a program by using the Visual Basic RegisterDatabase statement or its equivalent, or you can do it by accessing ODBC from the Control Panel.

When you register a database with ODBC, a *data source* name is associated with the database. The program can access the database using the data source name, without worrying about the database name or location. ODBC uses the registration information to locate the database on the correct server.

OLE2

OLE, which stands for *object linking and embedding*, is the Windows method for creating compound documents, in which data from one application can be embedded into a document from another application. The latest version of OLE, OLE 2.0, is a major improvement over the older OLE 1.0.

In OLE 2.0, an *object* is a discrete unit of data that is made available, or *exposed*, by an OLE application. Various types of objects can be exposed. For example, a spreadsheet program might expose worksheets, charts, cells, cell ranges, or macros. A word processing program might expose documents, paragraphs, sentences, or its spelling checker.

An application that can contain embedded objects is called a *container* application. For example, when you embed a chart object in a Word for Windows document, Word for Windows serves as the container application for the chart object.

OLE 2.0 supports several important features for client/server programs:

> ✔ *In-place activation*, which means that you can edit an object from within the container application, without launching into a separate window. When in-place activation is used, the container program's menus and toolbars are replaced by the menus and toolbars from the program that is associated with the object.
>
> ✔ *Drag and drop*, which activates OLE when the user drags an OLE object and drops it on a container.
>
> ✔ *OLE automation*, which means that the object includes not only data but methods that can be invoked by the container application. In short, this means that you can program the objects of another application.

If you are developing a client/server application that is intended to be used alongside another program, OLE2 might be the way to create the interaction between the programs. For example, a client/server marketing application might be built using a combination of custom Visual Basic programs, Microsoft Word's mail merge objects, and Excel's charting objects.

Microsoft sells an Office Developers Kit that documents the OLE2 objects that are exposed by Excel, Word for Windows, and Project. To appreciate the complexity of these interfaces, consider that Excel exposes 77 different types of OLE automation objects representing various Excel functions. Word for Windows takes a different approach: it exposes only one object type. But that object has more than 900 methods, which allow a Visual Basic program to invoke just about any Word function.

Creating Mail-Enabled Applications

Groupware is one of the hottest rages these days, so you may find yourself involved with a client/server application that must be *mail-enabled* — that is, ready to use in conjunction with an electronic mail system.

The two most common standards for building mail-enabled applications are MAPI (*Messaging Application Program Interface*), promoted by Microsoft, and VIM (*Vendor Independent Messaging*) by Lotus, Borland, and other companies with an anything-but-Microsoft attitude. MAPI usually means Microsoft Mail, and VIM usually means Lotus's cc:Mail.

Visual Basic Professional includes objects that let you incorporate common e-mail functions into your programs, such as:

> ✔ Retrieving messages currently in the Mail Inbox
>
> ✔ Composing a new message and addressing it to one or more users
>
> ✔ Attaching objects to messages

- ✔ Sending messages
- ✔ Saving, copying, or deleting messages
- ✔ Accessing the user's Address Book
- ✔ Replying to messages
- ✔ Forwarding messages to other users

Note that Microsoft Exchange, due about the time Windows 95 becomes available, will significantly enhance the capabilities of MAPI.

Keep in mind that if electronic messaging is at the heart of your client/server application, Lotus Notes may be the best development tool for the application. ■

Help

Users have come to expect top-quality help to accompany GUI programs. It's very frustrating to get knee-deep in the middle of a custom Windows program, press F1 to look at the help, and discover that the only help is an About box.

Windows uses a built-in help engine to display help files for all Windows programs, which is a real plus to users because it provides a consistent interface for displaying help. To add help to a program, you must first create one or more help files that are stored in a special word-processing format called *RTF (Rich Text Format)* using a word processor that supports the RTF format, such as Microsoft Word. Then, you compile the file using Microsoft's Help Compiler to create the .HLP files that can be displayed by Windows Help.

Unfortunately, creating good help for a Windows program is a tedious, time-consuming job. The text must be carefully marked up to create topics, adding graphics, coding keywords that can be searched for, and so on. Microsoft's Help compiler comes with a 175-page manual that explains the details of setting up help files.

Figure 18-1 shows a sample of a help file displayed in Word for Windows.

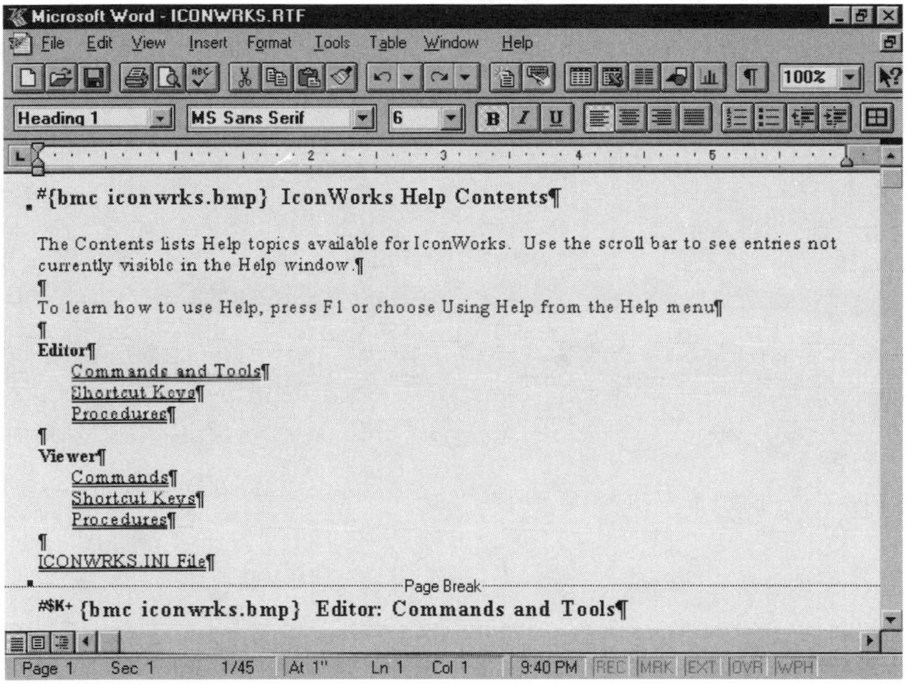

Figure 18-1:
You can
create help
files in
Microsoft
Word and
save them
in RTF
format.

```
Microsoft Word - ICONWRKS.RTF

File  Edit  View  Insert  Format  Tools  Table  Window  Help

Heading 1        MS Sans Serif        6      B  I  U

#{bmc iconwrks.bmp}  IconWorks Help Contents¶

The Contents lists Help topics available for IconWorks.  Use the scroll bar to see entries not
currently visible in the Help window.¶
¶
To learn how to use Help, press F1 or choose Using Help from the Help menu¶
¶
Editor¶
     Commands and Tools¶
     Shortcut Keys¶
     Procedures¶
¶
Viewer¶
     Commands¶
     Shortcut Keys¶
     Procedures¶
¶
ICONWRKS.INI File¶
···························Page Break···························
#$K+ {bmc iconwrks.bmp}  Editor: Commands and Tools¶

Page 1     Sec 1      1/45    At 1"    Ln 1    Col 1      9:40 PM  REC  MRK  EXT  OVR  WPH
```

Third-party tools are available to simplify the task of preparing help files, but
it is still a time-consuming proposition. If you're going to include adequate
help in a client/server application, be sure to allow plenty of time to develop
a thorough set of help files. ■

Part V
Client/Server Hot Topics

The 5th Wave   By Rich Tennant

THE OVERLOOKED VERSATILITY OF THE MAINFRAME TERMINAL

PAPERWEIGHT   SNACK TABLE

HAT & GLOVE DRYER   NIGHT LIGHT

In This Part...

Several issues in client/server are often the subject of heated debate in the halls of IS departments, where computer nerds love to argue passionately about things that normal people have never even heard of.

Most of these arguments center around operating systems: Windows, Windows 95, Windows NT, OS/2, Unix, and so on down the line. I've already covered these arguments elsewhere in this book, but there are a few hot topics that I've only hinted at so far. Such as: Should mainframes be sold for scrap? What's the buzz about data warehouses? Are objects the future of client/server? And what about managing client/server systems?

That's what the chapters in this Part are about.

Chapter 19

The Mainframe Is (Not!) Dead

Many people equate client/server computing with mainframeless computing. Although the role of the mainframe has changed dramatically from the almighty position it held a few years ago, mainframe computers are not vanishing from the face of the earth in great numbers, and for good reason: Most larger companies have too much invested in mainframes to simply toss them out the window. Plus, there are still many applications for which the mainframe is the best technology.

A basic understanding of what mainframes are all about is important to understanding and appreciating client/server computing. This chapter is a whirlwind tour of mainframe computing, emphasizing those aspects of mainframes that play an important role in client/server applications.

You'll probably notice that this chapter focuses exclusively on IBM mainframe computing. Although it's true that there are other brands, IBM almost totally dominates the mainframe computer market.

IBM Mainframes

The IBM mainframes of today are direct descendants of IBM's original System/360 computers, introduced around the time the Beatles invaded the United States (mid '60s). The original System/360 computers were about as powerful as a Nintendo, but the engineers at IBM who designed the System/360 were the first to popularize the idea of a computer *architecture* —

a set of blueprints for the way a computer operates that can be used to build an entire family of compatible computers — small, medium, and large.

The architecture of the System/360, combined with IBM's great marketing force, led the System/360 to be the most successful computer ever. The System/360 architecture has gone through three major improvements over the years:

- ✔ Around 1970, the System/360 architecture was enhanced to support virtual storage, a memory management technique that allows the computer to pretend it has more memory than it actually does. The new architecture was called *System/370*.

- ✔ In the 1980s, the System/370 architecture was enhanced to increase the amount of addressable memory from 16MB to 2GB. The new architecture was called *eXtended Architecture*, or *XA*.

- ✔ In the 1990s, the XA architecture was enhanced to support several new features, including a new fiber-optic I/O subsystem. The new architecture was called *Enterprise Systems Architecture* (*ESA*).

Just to keep life interesting, IBM periodically introduces new processor families with different model designations. As a result, you might hear the mainframe referred to as a 3090 or an ES/9000. These are just different models of mainframe processors. The ES/9000 is the newest generation of mainframe processors. The 3090 is a bit older but still in widespread use. You might come across other models, too, such as 43xx or 308x.

Just How Big Are Mainframes, Anyway?

Everyone knows that mainframe computers are bigger than PCs, but you frequently read or hear about how today's PCs are more powerful than the mainframes of just a few years ago. Is this true? Not really.

If you use only one measure of a computer's size, such as the number of instructions the CPU can execute in one second, PCs may seem nearly as fast as mainframe computers. Mainframes still hold the lead in this department, but not by much.

Mainframe computers typically have more memory than their PC counterparts. Computers sold at supermarkets have 4MB or 8MB these days. Well-equipped server computers have 32MB or so. A typical mainframe computer has several hundred megabytes of RAM. PCs are catching up in this area, too.

Where mainframes still beat the pants off of PCs is in disk storage. In terms of raw disk capacity, most PC-based LAN servers top out at a few dozen GB. Disk storage capacity for mainframes can be measured in TB — *terabytes*, or *billions* and *billions* of bytes, as Carl Sagan would say.

It's not just raw disk capacity, it's the mainframe's ability to efficiently move tons of data around that sets them apart from PC LAN servers. Mainframe computers rely on an array of smaller computers to handle the details of moving data. The major players in this computer array are:

- ✔ *Channels*, which are specialized I/O computers that manage the flow of information between the processor and I/O devices. IBM mainframes use two basic types of channels: old-style parallel channels and newer, high-speed ESCON channels. (See the next sidebar on types of channels.)

- ✔ *Disk controllers,* which handle the I/O processing for a group of disk drives. IBM mainframes use a two-tiered hierarchy of disk controllers. Disk drives are connected to *string controllers*, which are connected to *storage controls*, which are connected to channels. Each string controller handles a group of disk drives called a *string*; a string typically has 32 drives. A storage control manages two strings, or 64 drives total. The storage control contains up to 1GB of high-speed cache memory. Plus, the storage control can support more than one channel connection, which allows more than one I/O operation to be performed simultaneously.

- ✔ *Communication controllers*, which are dedicated computers whose sole task in life is handling network traffic. The software that runs in an IBM communication controller is called *Network Control Program*, or *NCP*, an important part of IBM's *System Network Architecture*, or *SNA*.

Because of these powerful subsystems, mainframe computers are able to support hundreds, thousands, or even tens of thousands of users. Although PC LAN servers are getting more powerful all the time, they still don't have near the I/O capacity that mainframes do. ▪

MVS Is Not a Roman Numeral

MVS is the main operating system for IBM mainframe computers. MVS is a descendant of the OS operating system, which was originally created shortly after the System/360 was released in 1965.

MVS stands for *Multiple Virtual Storage*, which doesn't really matter except that it does relate to the way MVS manages memory. In MVS, each job is assigned its own virtual storage address space. (A *job* is a time-sharing user or a batch program.) Each address space is protected from other address spaces, so that jobs cannot interfere with one another's memory.

Skip this stuff about the two types of mainframe channels

A *channel* is a specialized computer that handles the flow of data to and from the central processing unit in a mainframe computer. Each channel is capable of supporting several control units such as disk storage controls, which in turn can support many individual devices.

There are two basic types of channels used in IBM mainframes. The basic channel design uses heavy copper cables and transmits data at the rate of 4.5MB per second. These cables can be no longer than 400 feet, which means that all disk controllers must be located within 400 feet of the processor. That might seem like more than enough, but in larger computer systems, 400 feet is a major limitation.

The newer channel technology is called *ESCON* (*ESCON* stands for *Enterprise System Connection*, in case you were afraid to ask). ESCON uses lightweight fiber-optic cable which is 80 times lighter than the copper cable used for standard channels. ESCON is nearly four times faster than standard channels (17MB per second rather than 4.5MB/second), plus ESCON cables can be run 26 miles. This allows disk devices to be located on another floor or even in another building.

The notion of jobs running in separate address spaces is similar to the famous protected mode on 386 and better PCs. Unfortunately, PC operating systems have not taken advantage of protected mode in the same way as MVS. ■

There are three versions of MVS:

- ✔ MVS/370, which is no longer supported by IBM but still found in occasional use, has a 16MB limit to each address space.

- ✔ MVS/XA, which extends the address space limit to 2GB. To remain compatible with older MVS programs, MVS/XA still recognizes the 16MB line, referring to the first 16MB of each address space as "below the line" and memory from 16MB up as "above the line."

- ✔ MVS/ESA, which supports the new Enterprise architecture along with ESCON channels, and allows each job to have more than one 2GB address space.

IBM does offer two alternatives to MVS for its mainframes. *VSE* is a smaller, less-expensive operating system designed for smaller, less-expensive mainframes. *VM* is an operating system's operating system. It is used to create two or more *virtual machines* on the mainframe, each of which can run another operating system such as MVS or VSE to function or a special single-user operating system known as CMS, which is supplied with VM.

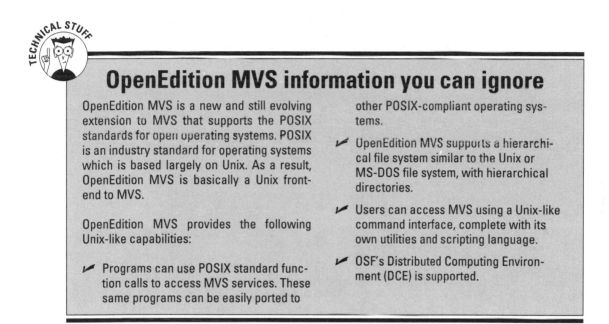

OpenEdition MVS information you can ignore

OpenEdition MVS is a new and still evolving extension to MVS that supports the POSIX standards for open operating systems. POSIX is an industry standard for operating systems which is based largely on Unix. As a result, OpenEdition MVS is basically a Unix front-end to MVS.

OpenEdition MVS provides the following Unix-like capabilities:

✔ Programs can use POSIX standard function calls to access MVS services. These same programs can be easily ported to

other POSIX-compliant operating systems.

✔ OpenEdition MVS supports a hierarchical file system similar to the Unix or MS-DOS file system, with hierarchical directories.

✔ Users can access MVS using a Unix-like command interface, complete with its own utilities and scripting language.

✔ OSF's Distributed Computing Environment (DCE) is supported.

What Is JCL, and Why Bother?

JCL stands for *job control language*. It is a programming language (sort of) that is used in MVS (and other mainframe operating systems, too) to control the execution of jobs.

Get a job

In mainframe parlance, a *job* is collection of programs that are run as a set. Jobs are the essence of traditional mainframe batch processing, in which programs run without direct interaction with users.

A payroll job might run three programs: one to update employee records, one to print an employee report, and one to print payroll checks. The job would run these three programs in sequence (as a batch), one after the other.

The following list describes the life cycle of a job, from the time it enters the system to the time its last line of output is printed:

1. The job is submitted for execution by a computer operator. In the old days, the operator submitted a job by placing a stack of cards called the *job deck* in the card reader and pressing the Start button. Nowadays, of course, the "job deck" is stored on disk.

2. The job waits in the job queue along with other jobs submitted by other users. How long it waits depends on how busy the system is and what the job's priority is.

3. Eventually, the job is selected for execution.

4. As the job is processed, each program that makes up the job is executed in sequence.

5. When the job is completed, any printed output produced by the job is sent to the print queue.

6. The print output waits in the queue until a printer becomes available.

7. After the print output is printed, the job is purged from the system.

JCL statements

Jobs are defined by a set of control statements written in JCL. JCL consists of a dozen or so statements, the most important of which are JOB, EXEC, and DD:

- ✔ The JOB statement appears at the beginning of the job and provides information that pertains to the entire job, such as the job name and the job's priority.

- ✔ The EXEC statement executes a program. One EXEC statement is required for each program to be executed by the job.

- ✔ A DD statement is required for each data set (that's the mainframe word for file) processed by a program. The DD statements must follow the EXEC statements they pertain to.

Just to give you an idea for the flavor of JCL, Listing 19-1 lists the JCL for a simple job that runs three programs, named EXTR1, SORT, and EXTR2. You don't have to remember any of the details in this example. I just wanted to give you an idea of what JCL looks like, since it is so pervasive in the main-frame world.

VSAM

VSAM is the name of the MVS software that is responsible for creating and maintaining most data files on MVS systems.

```
//SYDOEA    JOB   USER=SYDOE,PASSWORD=XXXXXXXX
//EXTR1     EXEC  PGM=EXTR1
//SYSOUT    DD    SYSOUT=*
//EXMSTR    DD    DSN=SYDOE.EXMSTR,DISP=SHR
//EXTR01    DD    DSN=SYDOE.EXTR01,DISP=(NEW,KEEP),
//                UNIT=SYSDA,VOL=SER=MVS100,
//                SPACE=(CYL,(30,10)),
//                DCB=(DSORG=PS,RECFM=FB,LRECL=400,BLKSIZE=3200)
//SORT1     EXEC  PGM=SORT
//SYSOUT    DD    SYSOUT=*
//SORTIN    DD    DSN=SYDOE.EXTR01,DISP=(OLD,DELETE),
//                UNIT=SYSDA,VOL=SER=MVS100
//SORTOUT   DD    DSN=SYDOE.EXTR02,DISP=(NEW,CATLG),
//                UNIT=SYSDA,VOL=SER=MVS100,
//                SPACE=(CYL,(30,10)),
//                DCB=(DSORG=PS,RECFM=FB,LRECL=400,BLKSIZE=3200)
//SORTWK01  DD    UNIT=SYSDA,VOL=SER=MVS100,
//                SPACE=(CYL,(10,1))
//SYSIN     DD    *
 SORT   FIELDS=(16,5,CH,A,1,5,CH,A)
/*
//REPORT    EXEC  PGM=EXTR2
//EXROTIN   DD    DSN=SYDOE.EXTR02,DISP=SHR
//REPORT    DD    SYSOUT=*
```

Listing 19-1: You should be thankful you don't need to know JCL.

Catalogs and data set names

VSAM maintains information about all of the files on the system in a series of catalogs. Every MVS system has a *master catalog* and one or more *user catalogs*. The master catalog keeps track of important MVS system files and all the user catalogs. Actual user data sets are cataloged in the user catalogs.

The use of catalogs means that users don't have to know what disk volume contains the files they use. That's important, since mainframe systems often have hundreds of disk volumes.

Files — or *data sets* as they are called in mainframe circles — are named a bit differently on mainframes than on PCs. On an IBM compatible PC, a filename consists of an eight-character name and a three-character extension. On a mainframe, a data set name can be up to 44 characters long, but must be broken up into groups of eight or fewer characters separated by periods. For example, here are some valid mainframe data set names:

```
RSYS.ACCOUNT.FILE
SYDOE.MASTER.DATA
AR.TRANS.Y95
PAY.TRANS.JUN.Y95
```

Each group of characters is called a *qualifier*. The first qualifier in each data set name, called the *high-level qualifier*, indicates the user catalog that contains the file. Thus, RSYS, SYDOE, AR, and PAY refer to user catalogs in the above examples.

MVS's naming structure appears to be similar to the use of directory paths in MS-DOS filenames, but with periods instead of backward slashes, but it's not the same thing at all. For example, consider the MS-DOS file \AR\TRANS\Y95. Here, the file Y95 is contained in the subdirectory TRANS, which in turn is contained in the directory AR on the current drive. For the MVS filename AR.TRANS.Y95, however, the complete filename is AR.TRANS.Y95. AR identifies the user catalog that contains the file. ■

VSAM file organizations

VSAM lets you create several different types of files. Much of the so-called legacy data of mainframe systems is stored in VSAM files, so it helps to have a general understanding of how these files work. The following paragraphs describe the various types of VSAM file organizations:

- ✔ **Entry Sequenced Data Set (ESDS).** An ESDS is a *sequential file*. It consists of data records that can be any length up to 32K, stored one after the other in consecutive sequence. Records are usually accessed in sequential order, one after the other.

- ✔ **Relative Record Data Set (RRDS).** An RRDS is like a sequential file, except that each record can be accessed directly by specifying its record number. RRDS is the least-used VSAM file organization.

- ✔ **Key-Sequenced Data Set (KSDS).** A key-sequenced data set is an *indexed file*. It allows you to directly access any record in the file by using a primary key value — a field that contains a unique value for each record, such as a customer number for a customer file. A KSDS actually consists of two separate parts: a *data component*, which contains the actual data records of the file, and an *index component*, which contains the index that allows records to be retrieved by key value.

> ✔ **Alternate Index (AIX).** An alternate index is a file that lets you access a KSDS by a key field other than the primary key. For example, an alternate index could be used to access a customer file by salesrep. Unlike a primary key, an alternate key does not have to be unique. Although less common, an alternate index can also be used to access an ESDS.
>
> ✔ **Linear Data Set (LDS).** A linear data set is a file that has no organization. Linear data sets are processed as a stream of bytes grouped into 4K blocks.

How do VSAM files compare with DOS files? There's really no basis for comparison. DOS has no equivalent to the file organizations provided by VSAM. As far as DOS is concerned, all files are treated as a stream of individual bytes grouped into 512-byte sectors. In this respect, DOS files are like VSAM linear (LDS) files.

Of the various file organizations, KSDS is the most widely used. It's likely that much of the legacy data pent up in your organization's mainframes is stored in KSDS files.

IMS

Here's some more mainframe alphabet soup for you. IMS, which stands for *Information Management System*, is a hierarchical database management system that is older than DB2, IBM's relational database manager, and is still in widespread use. IMS forces you to organize data records into a hierarchy with clearly defined parent-child relationships among record types. For example, customer records might be parent to invoice records, which are parents to line item records.

IMS is very efficient for transaction-processing systems, which is why it is still widely used. IMS data is not easy to get to from client/server applications, but gateway products are available that allow you to access IMS data using SQL.

TSO/ISPF

TSO, which stands for *Time Sharing Option*, is the main way that terminal users can access an MVS system. TSO treats each terminal user as a job, so that each user is assigned his or her own address space. This is not particularly efficient, so large terminal-oriented systems are usually implemented with CICS rather than TSO. TSO is mostly used by the support staff responsible for keeping MVS up and running, and by programmers who develop software that runs under MVS.

TSO includes a command processor that vaguely resembles a DOS command prompt. It has its own set of commands that are similar to DOS commands, and its own batch-file capability known as *CLIST*.

Because the TSO command prompt is hard to use, most MVS systems also include *ISPF*, which stands for *Interactive System Productivity Feature*. ISPF is a full-screen interface to TSO that includes a sophisticated text editor and other utilities. If you have used EDLIN, the old MS-DOS command-line text editor and the new EDIT command that was introduced with MS-DOS 5.0, you already have a feel for the difference between TSO and ISPF.

CICS

I've been dropping this name for 18 chapters now, and as a reward for hanging in there I'm going to tell you what it is. *CICS*, which stands for *Customer Information Control System*, is a transaction-processing monitor that is the foundation of most mainframe-based data processing systems. CICS is capable of handling large terminal networks with thousands or even tens of thousands of terminals, efficiently processing transactions and updating VSAM files and IMS or DB2 databases.

CICS allows multiple users to access an MVS system without creating a separate address space for each user. Instead, CICS occupies a single address space and provides its own form of multitasking within that address space. (For you techno-types out there, this arrangement is very similar to the way in which Windows 95 supports older 16-bit Windows applications. Think about it until you get a brain freeze.) ■

CICS is the de facto industry-standard transaction monitor. Nearly all of the Fortune 500 companies support their mission-critical transaction-processing systems on CICS. IBM offers CICS not only for mainframes running MVS, VM, or VSE, but also on AS/400, AIX systems, HP/UX systems, and OS/2.

Of course, CICS was originally designed for centralized systems that used dumb 3270 terminals. However, CICS has since evolved into a sophisticated transaction monitor that can support not only dumb 3270 terminals but also operate as a transaction server for client/server systems.

CICS transactions

A key concept in CICS is the notion of the *transaction*. A transaction is a unit of work that can be initiated by a terminal user. Each transaction has a unique four-character name called a *trans-id* which is used to start the transaction and an associated program name. (And you thought the DOS limit of eight characters for a filename was bad.)

When a transaction is started, CICS looks up the trans-id to find the program associated with the transaction. It then initiates a task on behalf of the user who started the transaction, establishes a connection between the task and the user's terminal, and loads and executes the program. That program may, in turn, load and execute other programs. The task continues until the last program finishes executing. Then the task is terminated.

CICS coined the term *transaction* decades ago, before database systems even existed and the modern database meaning of a transaction — a series of database updates that must be completed all-or-nothing — was formulated. Don't get the two mixed up. (In typical IBM fashion, CICS uses a new term — *logical unit of work,* or *LUW*, to refer to a database transaction.) ∎

CICS programming

CICS application programs are usually written in COBOL, although newer versions of CICS support C. CICS uses a preprocessor just like embedded SQL does. In fact, CICS programs look a lot like embedded SQL programs. CICS commands are intermixed with regular COBOL statements, separated by EXEC CICS and END-EXEC markers, as in this example:

```
EXEC CICS
    RECEIVE MAP('EXMAP1')
            MAPSET('EXSET1')
            INTO(EXMAP1I)
END-EXEC.
IF CUSTNOL = ZERO OR CUSTNOI = SPACE
    MOVE 'N' TO VALID-DATA-SW
    MOVE 'You must enter a customer number.' TO MESSAGEO
ELSE
    EXEC CICS
        READ DATASET('CUST')
            INTO(CUSTOMER-RECORD)
            RIDFLD(CUSTNOI)
            RESP(RESPONSE-CODE)
    END-EXEC.
```

In this example, two CICS commands — RECEIVE MAP and READ — are processed. Between them is an ordinary COBOL IF statement. The CICS preprocessor converts the CICS commands to COBOL CALL statements that invoke the correct CICS functions when the program is executed.

Notice the MAP and MAPSET parameters in the RECEIVE MAP command. These parameters relate to another important CICS facility called *Basic Mapping Support*, or *BMS*. BMS lets a programmer create a *map* that outlines the format of a 3270 data display, placing text fields on the screen in specific locations. Once the 3270 is formatted to display the map, the program just sends the data to be displayed; the terminal takes care of positioning the information on the screen in the proper locations.

Pseudo-conversational processing

Don't you like that phrase? It sounds like what my wife accuses me of when I'm not really paying attention. Actually, it *is* something like that — it's a special way that the mainframe can pretend that it's talking to you while it's actually doing something else.

The key to CICS' success is the efficiency of its multitasking kernel. CICS does not create and maintain a task for every terminal user on the system. That would require managing thousands of tasks, something that could not be done efficiently. Instead, CICS creates a task for each user only when the user sends input from his or her terminal. CICS creates a task for the terminal, invokes a program to process the terminal input, update files or databases if necessary, and send output back to the user. Then the task ends.

This mode of processing is called *pseudo-conversational* because it appears that the program is maintaining an ongoing conversation with the user, when in fact it is not. When pseudo-conversational processing is used, a CICS system can juggle several thousand users with only a few dozen tasks active at any given moment.

A basic rule of pseudo-conversational CICS programming is that whenever any data is sent to a terminal, the very next CICS command should be RETURN with TRANSID, which terminates the task and indicates which transaction should be started next, when the user enters more data. ■

The alternative to pseudo-conversational processing is *conversational processing* (which my wife would prefer), in which a task does not end when it sends data to the user. Instead, the task waits patiently while the user reads the data on the screen, thinks about what to do next, answers the phone, grabs a quick lunch, or maybe leaves for the weekend. During this time, any memory allocated to the task must be retained, plus the overhead required simply to maintain an active task must be maintained.

The ratio between the time that most conversational programs actually spend doing useful work and the time they spend waiting for the user to do something is staggering. Conversational programming is so inefficient that no self-respecting CICS programmer would employ it. Though much more complicated, pseudo-conversational programming is the norm.

As luck would have it, pseudo-conversational programming actually plays right into client/server. (Were you wondering when we were going to get back to client/server?) Most pseudo-conversational CICS systems consist of programs that are written to handle "messages" initiated by users at 3270 terminals. If only we could replace the 3270 terminals with PCs and a pretty graphical user interface which would send messages back to the CICS system that looked as if they were coming from 3270 terminals, we'd have the makings of a client/server system. The old, boring 3270 screens would be replaced by vibrant, colorful GUI displays, but the back-end processing would be done by unmodified CICS programs. This is how so-called *screen scrapers* work, by fooling the mainframe into thinking that a PC with a GUI interface is a 3270 terminal. (I talked about screen scrapers in Chapter 4.)

CICS and Distributed Processing

CICS has several features for distributed processing, several of which are important in client/server systems. These distributed processing features let two or more CICS systems work together. Keep in mind that CICS runs not only on IBM mainframes, but also on AS/400 midrange systems, Hewlett-Packard RISC systems, and on PCs running OS/2. Thus, the distributed processing features of CICS can be used in client/server environments that include these smaller computer systems.

The distributed processing features used for client/server computing are called *InterSystem Communication*, or *ISC*. ISC includes the following distributed processing techniques:

- ✔ Transaction routing
- ✔ Function shipping
- ✔ Distributed program link
- ✔ Asynchronous processing
- ✔ Distributed transaction processing

The following sections describe each of these techniques.

Transaction routing

In *transaction routing*, a user running on a terminal connected to one CICS system may start a transaction that is actually processed by another

CICS system. The user is not aware that the transaction is running on a remote CICS system.

Function shipping

Function shipping allows a CICS program running on one CICS system to access a resource that is owned by another CICS system. Function shipping works on a command-by-command basis. For example, the following CICS READ command uses a SYSID parameter to indicate that the file to be read is not located on the local CICS system, but can be found on the CICS system named BOSTON:

```
EXEC CICS
    READ DATASET('EMPMAST')
         INTO(EMPLOYEE-RECORD)
         RIDFLD(EMP-NO)
         SYSID('BOSTON')
         LENGTH(EMPMAST-LENGTH)
         KEYLENGTH(6)
         RESP(REPONSE-CODE)
END-EXEC.
```

Ordinarily, the name of the remote system would not be hard-coded into the program. Instead, the local CICS system would know which data sets and other resources are remote, and would automatically route requests to the appropriate system.

CICS automatically handles locking and commit/rollback processing for file updates that use function shipping.

Distributed program link

Distributed program link, or *DPL*, lets a CICS program running on one CICS system directly invoke a program running on another CICS system. The calling program is suspended until the called program finishes executing on the remote system. It is possible to pass data to the called program, and for the called program to pass data back to the calling program. DPL is designed specifically for client/server processing.

Asynchronous processing

Asynchronous processing is similar to distributed program link, except that the calling program is not suspended until the called program finishes. Instead, the calling program and the called program run simultaneously.

When asynchronous processing is used, CICS does not automatically roll back updates in one system if an asynchronous process on another system fails. Thus, asynchronous processing is not a very good idea for programs that update files and databases.

Distributed transaction processing

Distributed transaction processing, or *DTP*, is the CICS implementation of the APPC (Advanced Peer-to-Peer Communications) protocol that allows two programs running on separate computers to communicate with one another and coordinate their work. When DTP is used, one program — called the *front-end* program — initiates the *back-end* program and directs its work.

The task of establishing the communication between the front-end and back-end programs and coordinating their work is tedious at best. Fortunately, most client/server applications can be more easily implemented using distributed program link, which simplifies the communication between programs.

In many companies, "client/server" means "mainframeless." I hope this chapter has helped you see that mainframe systems, particularly those that utilize DB2 and CICS, can play an important role in client/server systems. DB2 can be used as a SQL server database just as Sybase or Oracle can, and CICS has features designed specifically to promote the development of client/server systems that incorporate mainframes.

Chapter 20

Data Warehouses

● ●

In This Chapter

▶ Operational vs. analytical data

▶ What is a data warehouse?

▶ DSS and EIS

▶ Getting data to the warehouse

● ●

*W*henever I hear the term *data warehouse*, I think of that scene at the end of *Raiders of the Lost Ark*, where the Lost Ark of the Covenant is crated away to a government warehouse that contains hundreds of similar crates, each of which apparently contains some mysterious artifact. (I'm not sure, but I think that same warehouse may have shown up several times on *The X-Files*.)

The information resources of most companies are kind of like that. Who knows what treasures lie crated up somewhere, if only you could get into the warehouse and had time to open all the crates?

This chapter is a brief introduction to a relatively new concept called the *data warehouse*, which is simply a method of making the accumulated data of an enterprise more accessible to folks who like to snoop around to see what they can see. Data warehouses are often what constitute the back-end (server) databases in client/server applications.

The terms *information warehouse* and *data warehouse* are used interchangeably. *Information warehouse* is the term used by IBM; *data warehouse* is a term coined by industry guru Bill Inmon. ▬

The Great Data Dichotomy

In any business organization, there are two kinds of data. There is *operational data*, which consists of the information necessary to conduct day-to-day business, such as outstanding invoices, account balances, and so on. Then there is *analytical data*, which helps management study the business to decide how things are going, to pinpoint problem areas or to exploit opportunities, and so on.

These two different types of data are like the left and right sides of the human brain. The left side of the brain is the rational, logical side. It's the accountant in all of us. The left side is like a good Presbyterian: everything is done decently and in order. In contrast, the right side of the brain is the creative side. It sparks new ideas, challenges old assumptions, makes connections between unlikely ideas that the left side would never dream of, because the left side generally doesn't dream.

Operational data is on the left side of the business. It counts the beans, keeps the company ducks in a row, and — am I running out of metaphors yet? Naw! — keeps the hatches battened down.

Analytical data is on the right side. It looks for trends it hasn't seen before. It paints upside down. It wants to see the forest for the trees.

Operational data goes by several names: *production data*, *OLTP data*, *primitive data*, *raw data,* and *on-line data* are a few. Analytical data also has a few a.k.a.'s: *informational data*, *decision support data*, *derived data*, *extracted data*, and *summary data,* for example.

Why Operational and Analytical Data Shouldn't Intermarry

There is a clear distinction in the purpose and use of operational and analytical data.

✔ Operational data must always be up-to-the-moment and accurate. When a customer pays a bill, the accounts receivable file must be immediately updated to show the current account balance. When inventory is sold, the inventory records must be immediately updated to show the new on-hand quantity. Operational data must never be allowed to go stale.

✔ Analytical data, on the other hand, must be sheltered from the variations of the moment-to-moment nature of operational data. It must be static. Otherwise, an analysis that you run at 9:00 in the morning will no longer be repeatable at 9:05. You'd never be able to make meaningful comparisons, because the data would be a moving target. Analytical data is not accurate to the moment, but accurate to a specific time period: the end of business yesterday, last week, last month, last year.

✔ Operational data must focus on the trees rather than the forest. A customer doesn't care that 13% of all your customers ordered the same product last week, he just wants to make sure *his* order gets shipped correctly.

✔ Analytical data, on the other hand, must allow users to focus on the forest rather than the trees. 10,000 order records aren't very helpful unless some meaningful summaries can be drawn from them.

✔ Operational data is updated repeatedly by a known, controllable set of transactions such as orders, payments, returns, adjustments, and so on. Operational data is *predictable*.

✔ Access to analytical data, on the other hand (how many hands do I have, you want to know), is unpredictable. You never know when a user is going to query the entire 10 million record marketing history database to find how many customers ordered Widgets more than three times within a two-year period.

The long and the short of this comparison is that operational and analytical data are too different to be kept together. A good analytical database makes a lousy operational database, and a good operational database makes a lousy analytical database. The solution is surprisingly simple: don't mix operational and analytical data. Instead, maintain separate operational and analytical databases. ■

Table 20-1 highlights some of the more important differences between operational and analytical data.

Table 20-1: A comparison of operational and analytical data

Operational data	*Analytical data*
Shows a dynamic view of the business.	Shows a static view of the business.
Must be kept current at all times, up to the moment.	Must be sheltered from moment-to-moment changes.
Updated by transactions entered by data-entry operators or specially trained end users.	End-user access is usually read-only.
Obsessed with detail. Every *i* must be dotted and every *t* must be crossed.	More concerned with summary information.
Utilization is predictable. Systems can be optimized for projected workloads.	Use is unpredictable. You never know what the users will do next.
Lots of transactions, each of which affects a small portion of the data.	A small number of queries, each of which may access large amounts of data.
Users don't need to understand the database; they just enter the data.	Users need to understand the database to draw meaningful conclusions from the data.

Extract Programs Run Amok

Because of the conflicting characteristics of operational and analytical data, computer professionals realized long ago that the two types of data should not be mixed. In other words, separate operational and analytical databases should be set up. Special programs, called *extract programs*, would periodically update the analytical database based on data in the operational database.

For example, a sales-extract program might be run once a week to extract the week's sales data from the operational database, storing the information in a weekly sales file. Then the user could access that file all week to analyze the previous week's sales, knowing that the data would be the same on Tuesday as it was on Monday.

By running the extract program once a week and keeping each week's file, the company would soon have a huge collection of weekly sales data. This information could be used to detect trends in weekly sales performance and, hopefully, project future performance.

Unfortunately, extract programs are surprisingly easy to write. Any second-semester COBOL student can write a program that reads through an invoice file, extracts sales information, and writes records to a weekly sales summary file. Here's a scenario of what can happen:

✔ Some young whipper-snapper newbie in the marketing department decides he could make a big impression with his boss if he only had a weekly report listing how many black widgets were sold to each region each week. So he orders up a special Black-Widget-By-Region extract program (BLAKWIDR). This program is put into production and now runs every week. The young whipper-snapper newbie is fired shortly thereafter, but no one remembers that he was the only one interested in the BLAKWIDR program, so it continues to run once a week, building up a huge extract file of weekly sales figures for black widgets.

✔ The replacement marketing kid, also eager to impress, wants a weekly report of who ordered the most blue bonkers every other week. He orders up a Maximum-Blue-Bonkers program (BLUEMAX), which is put into production. He too is fired, but his legacy program continues to run every week.

✔ This cycle continues over the years. Pretty soon there are dozens of extract programs running weekly, monthly, semi-monthly, biweekly, every third Tuesday, and so on, extracting sales data for Red Hair Rings, White Porcelain Elephants, and who knows what else.

This company, like most companies, has lost control over its analytical data. It is extracted and stored all over the place: in mainframe files as well as on local file servers in the form of dBase databases and Lotus 1-2-3 spreadsheets.

These folks desperately need to get a grip on all this analytical data. The Data Warehouse is the solution.

What Is a Data Warehouse?

A data warehouse, or an *information warehouse* to use IBM's terminology, is an integrated database of analytical information culled from an organization's operational database.

I know I just said this, but it's important to remember that a data warehouse organizes and stores a company's *analytical* information — the data that management studies and uses to analyze the business, produce reports, make forecasts, and so on. This analytical information is periodically extracted from the *operational* database, the day-to-day record of business transactions. Figure 20-1 shows how this works. ■

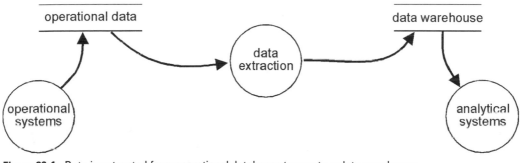

Figure 20-1: Data is extracted from operational databases to create a data warehouse.

A data warehouse usually includes detailed transaction data for the most recent period (typically one month), plus archived transaction data for previous periods. As the size of the warehouse expands, the oldest detail information may need to be archived to off-line storage (tape).

In addition, the data warehouse should contain well-thought-out summary data. For example, weekly sales might be summarized along product lines, regions, or whatever other criteria are deemed important.

A good data warehouse has the following characteristics:

✔ It is separate from the operational databases. Typically, the data warehouse is built using a relational DBMS such as DB2, whereas operational data is more often stored in ordinary VSAM files or in IMS databases. (VSAM is a non-database file system used on IBM mainframes, and IMS is a nonrelational database used on mainframes.)

✔ It is based on an integrated and comprehensive data model of an entire organization's information resources.

✔ Its data is derived from multiple operational databases.

✔ It is automatically maintained. Users do not have to concern themselves with the details of how the data warehouse is kept up to date.

✔ It is periodical, meaning that it is updated at regular intervals, and past versions of data are kept in the warehouse. The data warehouse could be compared to time-lapse photography, with one frame taken every week, month, year, or whatever interval is appropriate.

✔ It is consistent, meaning that data items that record similar information are stored in a similar format. In operational databases, similar information is often stored in incompatible formats. A classic example is units of measurement. One database might measure an item in feet, another in meters, and some really old legacy systems might use cubits. In the data warehouse, all of these measurements would be converted to a standard unit of measure. (It doesn't matter what the standard is, as long as it is applied consistently.) Another example is coded fields. In too many cases, different applications use different codes to stand for the same thing. In the warehouse, the codes should be consistent.

✔ It can be accessed by a host of query tools using standard SQL dialects such as ODBC.

✔ It is read-only. The data warehouse contains historical information, and you are not allowed to rewrite history unless you have been elected to Congress or the White House.

✔ It may be replicated. The data warehouse does not have to be kept in a single, central location. For performance reasons, it may be replicated and distributed to locations where users can efficiently access it. Replicated copies are automatically kept synchronized.

✔ It is self-defining, meaning that information about the structure of the data warehouse is kept in the data warehouse. This helps users discover what information lies buried in the warehouse.

Uses for Data Warehouses

Data warehouses are used primarily for ad-hoc information gathering. Two main types of systems that do this are decision support systems and executive information systems.

Decision support systems

A *decision support system* (*DSS*) is software that provides managers with information they need to make decisions. Originally, decision support systems were customized extract-and-report programs that printed specific reports a manager would need to make a decision. For example, a credit manager might use a program that prints a specific customer's complete credit history to make credit authorization decisions.

Soon, ad-hoc reporting tools became available which allowed users to create their own customized reports. DSS users could then print whatever reports they needed, assuming they knew enough about the underlying database structure to create a meaningful report.

For many users, PC spreadsheet programs like Lotus 1-2-3 and Excel became the greatest decision support tools. Once users figured out how to get corporate data off the mainframe and onto a PC in the form of a spreadsheet (no small task), they could use the spreadsheet to manipulate and analyze the data in just about any way imaginable.

Decision support tools are playing with only half a deck without a data warehouse, however. While the decision support tool might have powerful analytical capabilities, its analysis isn't completely trustworthy unless the data it is analyzing is solid. It's like that story from the Good Book about the fellow who built his house on the sand. Big mistake. The house looked pretty solid until the sand started shifting under it. The whole purpose of a data warehouse is to provide solid ground for decision support.

Executive information systems (EIS)

A good *executive information system* (*EIS*) is the dream of the modern-day executive, second in importance only to stock options on the list of things-I-gotta-have.

An EIS is a concise (one screen, if possible) snapshot of how the company is doing today. Think of it as an electronic executive briefing.

EIS can be built with many different types of tools, from specialized EIS tools to generic office applications. In fact, the Microsoft Office Developer's Kit comes with a neat little example of an EIS for a make-believe company called Northwind Traders. Figure 20-2 shows its main screen.

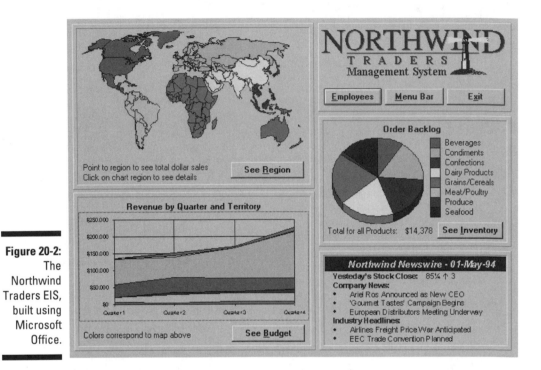

Figure 20-2:
The Northwind Traders EIS, built using Microsoft Office.

Many executive information systems use a *home screen* such as the one in Figure 20-2 to present key summary data. The Northwind traders system shows four boxes of information on its home screen:

- A color-coded map of the world that shows sales for each region. All the user has to do is move the mouse over a region, and the sales for that region will appear at the bottom of the box.

- An area chart that plots sales by quarter and territory, based on up-to-date sales information obtained via an ODBC link to a corporate database.

- A pie chart showing the order backlog by product category.

- A news window that lists several newsworthy items, starting with the company's closing stock price from the day before.

An EIS should allow the user to explore areas of interest or concern by displaying additional layers of detail. This is called *drill down*. For example, if the user wants to see additional sales information, he or she can click the See <u>R</u>egion button. Then, the spreadsheet shown in Figure 20-3 will be displayed.

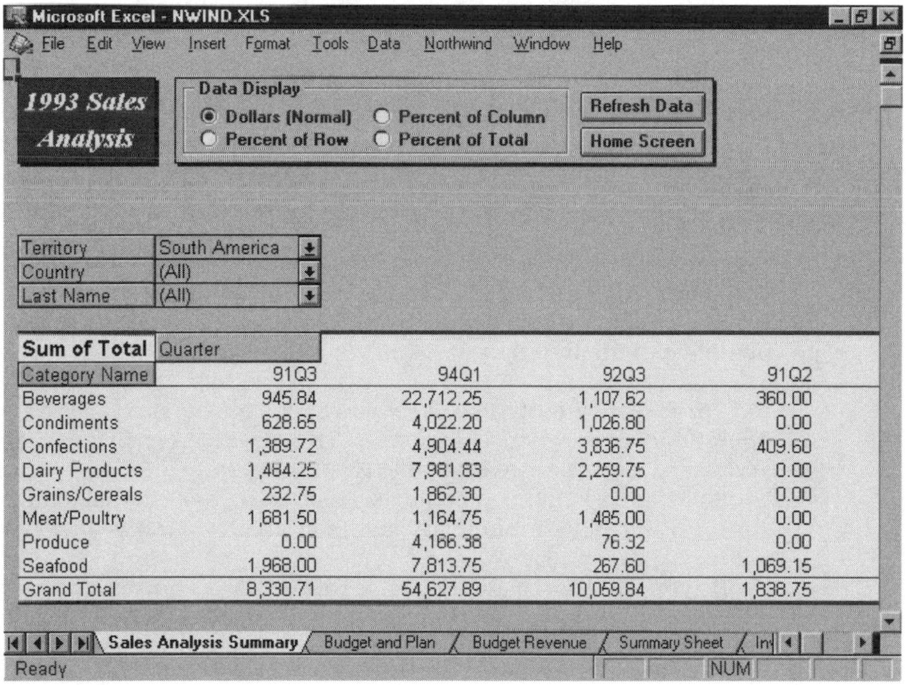

Figure 20-3:
An EIS
allows the
user to
display
additional
levels of
detail.

How It Gets There from Here

A critical aspect of any data warehouse project is planning the route that data will take on its way from operational data to warehouse data. The journey involves more than simply copying files from the production system to the warehouse system. Information must usually be extracted and converted from nonrelational databases and files, and data formats must often be changed along the way. The entire journey must be carefully planned so that it will work automatically once the warehouse is in place.

The first step in moving data from operational databases to a data warehouse is extracting the data to be warehoused. The data is usually moved in one of two ways:

✔ By a *refresh*, in which the entire contents of the warehouse database (or a portion of it) is replaced by fresh data from the operational database

✔ By an *update*, in which only changes since the last update or refresh are copied from the operational database to the warehouse

Naturally, an update can be processed more quickly than a refresh if large amounts of data are involved.

Although COBOL programs could be written to perform the extraction, it's better to use software designed specifically for this purpose. For example, IBM has a program called DataPropagator that fits the bill. It comes in two versions: a relational version that copies operational DB2 data, and a nonrelational version that works with IMS.

It's common to create a time delay between updates to operational data and updates to the warehouse database. To do this, updates from the operational databases are *staged* in a temporary database, which places the updates in a holding pattern until they are applied to the warehouse in a batch.

Data propagation tools also allow you to change the data as it travels from operational to warehouse databases. This is where consistency issues can be addressed, such as converting measurements to a common form or changing coded fields to a common coding scheme. Also, operational data can be summarized, and only the summary information moved to the warehouse.

I hope you can appreciate the major role data warehouses can play in client/server systems. A well-designed and managed data warehouse can form the backbone for many client/server systems that require access to corporate data.

Chapter 21

Distributed Objects

● ●

● ●

According to most computer industry pundits and soothsayers, objects are the future. Object-oriented programming has been around for better than a decade now, and most programmers know that if they haven't learned C++ yet, they'd better start boning up. OLE 2.0 is finally beginning to mature into a useful and usable Windows feature. And object-oriented database systems are starting to make their mark.

I've touched on objects elsewhere in this book, but in this chapter, I pull all the discussion about objects together, explain just what objects are and how they are used, let you in on the latest object jargon, and show you why objects may well be the future of client/server computing.

If I Had a Hammer...

The people who earn big bucks explaining what objects are love to use metaphors. One of the most common compares objects with hammers and nails. This metaphor is useful for understanding a basic distinction between object-oriented systems and traditional systems.

Traditional systems focus on *tools* — hammers, screwdrivers, staple guns, and so on. In computer terms, the tools are programs. Windows 3.1 is tool-oriented. Before you can edit a word processing document, you first get the tool ready — you start the word processing program. (Actually, the word processing program is more like a toolbox than a tool. It contains many subtools: an editor, a spell checker, formatting commands, a printing module, and so on.)

The object approach focuses on the *objects* the tools are used on rather than the tools themselves. An object-oriented carpenter would reach for a nail first, not a hammer. The nail is what the user wants to manipulate; the hammer is merely the tool used to strike the nail. Hammers are tools; nails are objects.

The nail-as-object metaphor illustrates several of the more important points of object thinking:

- In a truly object-oriented carpentry shop, the hammer would be selected *automatically* when the user picks up a nail. In fact, the hammer wouldn't actually be a separate tool. Instead, the nail would be self-driving. The user would simply position the nail at the right spot and say something like, "Bang!" and the nail would drive itself into the wood. The user wouldn't even have to be concerned with how the nail drives itself in. This is called *encapsulation*.

- "Bang" would be considered a *method* of the nail object. Another method the nail object might include is "Oops," which uses the claw-end of the hammer to pry out the nail.

- Because the hammer is built into the nail, you don't have to worry about smashing your thumb when banging it.

- Aren't you sick of the hammer analogy yet?

- A nail is actually a subclass of a more generic class called *Fastener*. An object-oriented carpentry shop would have many different types of Fastener objects: Nails, Screws, Staples, Nuts and Bolts, Rivets, and so on. The normal way to "Bang" a fastener is to hit it with a hammer. If the "Bang" method were built into the Fastener class, subclasses such as Nails, Screws, and Staples would inherit the "Bang" method. That's what *inheritance* is all about. Not all Fasteners "Bang" by being hit with a hammer. Thus, some of the Fastener subclasses override the "Bang" method, providing their own implementation. For example, say "Bang" to a Screw object and it will use a screwdriver to screw itself into the wood. This ability to implement the same method in different ways depending on the object's class is called *polymorphism*.

TECHNICAL STUFF

Objectspeak: The jargon of objects

Objects are a religion, and every religion has its own vocabulary. Don't attempt to discuss Object religion with a zealot until you have a basic understanding of the following terms:

Object. An *object* is an amalgamation of code and data. It contains a specific type of data, plus whatever procedural code is needed to create, sustain, and nourish that data.

Attribute or **property.** Objects have *attributes* or *properties*. That's just a fancy word for the data that the object contains.

Collection. A *collection* is a type of attribute that contains more than one value.

Method. A *method* is a procedure that is a part of an object. A method is similar to a subroutine that can be called, except that in an object, the method is coupled with the data it manipulates.

Exposed. The properties and methods which are made public for all to see are said to be

exposed. Not all of an object's properties and methods need to be exposed. The ones that aren't are said to be *private*.

Class. A *class* is a logical definition of a particular type of object. The class indicates which properties and methods a particular type of object provides.

Instance. A specific object is an *instance* of the object's class.

Subclass. A *subclass* is a further refinement of a higher-level class.

Inheritance. When a new class is created as a subclass of an existing class, the new class *inherits* the properties and methods of the parent class.

Polymorphism. A $64 word that means simply that a method may behave differently depending on the class of the object in question.

Four Kinds of Object Technology

With everyone talking so much about objects these days, it's hard to sort out what's what. One cause of confusion is that there are at least four different arenas in which object orientation is important, but object discussions often don't identify which arena they're talking about.

The four arenas of object technology are:

✔ **Object-oriented programming languages**. Objects made their first big splash with object-oriented programming languages such as C++ and Smalltalk, which allow programmers to code programs using an object model rather than the more traditional programming model, in which code and data are separate entities.

> ✔ **Object-oriented system software.** Object-oriented system software provides the building blocks to manage objects at the operating system level. Object systems allow objects created by different companies, perhaps using different programming languages, to work together. Examples of object systems are OLE, OpenDoc, and SOM/DSOM.
>
> ✔ **Distributed objects.** Eventually, object-oriented system software will let objects on different systems across the network work together. This is what *distributed objects* are: objects that can communicate with one another even though they are not located on the same computer.
>
> ✔ **Object-oriented databases.** These are database management systems that replace the relational database model with an object-oriented model. Object-oriented databases are still a bit futuristic, and the jury is still out on whether or not they will eventually replace relational databases in client/server systems.

What's So Great About Objects?

What's the big deal about objects? Why all the hype?

The simple answer is the promise of *reusable software*. Reusability has long been the Holy Grail of software development. Ever since the first programmer strung together a bunch of patch cords to program the ENIAC computer to calculate artillery trajectories back in the 1940s, programming has largely been a matter of reinventing the wheel. And the quest of good programmers has been to *stop* reinventing the wheel.

Subroutines were invented as a way to stop reinventing the wheel. The idea was that you could build up a library of reusable subroutines that would have to be coded and tested only once, but could be reused in any program that needed the same function. This works great for utility-type functions, such as figuring the difference between two dates or displaying a graph. But beyond trivial functions, subroutines don't go very far toward creating reusable software.

Objects provide the first real opportunity to realize the potential of software reusability. Instead of focusing on sharing and reusing small, almost trivial bits of code like date calculations or graphs, reusable objects can be built on a much grander scale. Reusable objects with names such as Inventory, Customers, Orders, and Shipments have a much bigger potential for payback than objects with names like CalculateDate or ShowGraph.

In other words, object technology lets you encapsulate large chunks of a computer application, hiding the details of their code and data from the rest of the system, but exposing critical properties and methods so that the object can be used in a controlled way. ∎

Consider as an example a Credit Authorization object. This object would encapsulate the details that go into granting or refusing a credit request. The Credit Authorization object would expose several methods, the most important one being a request for a credit authorization.

Here are just some of the benefits of implementing the Credit Authorization process as an object:

- The team responsible for developing the Credit Authorization object can use whatever programming language and other development tools they decide are best for the project.

- If credit requirements change, the Credit Authorization object can be updated without reinstalling or upgrading any other part of the system, provided the update still exposes the same methods and properties as the previous version.

- If some other object in the application changes, the Credit Authorization object is not affected and does not have to be reinstalled or upgraded.

- The Credit Authorization object can be deployed at its most optimal location. If performance is best with the Credit Authorization object replicated on each client machine, so be it. If it's best to place the object on a server machine, so be it. The physical location of the object is transparent to the other system objects that use it. (Or at least, that's the goal of distributed objects.)

- If one department wants to alter the credit requirements somewhat, that department doesn't change the Credit Authorization object. Instead, they subclass it by creating a new object type, using the Credit Authorization object class as the parent class. The new subclass inherits the methods and properties of the parent class, so only those methods which differ from the parent class methods have to be changed.

- Suppose that the company realizes that they have developed the world's best Credit Authorization object, and they decide to sell it. Once again, subclassing and inheritance can be used to customize the object without fiddling with the basic Credit Authorization object.

Distributed Objects

Objects have become reality now in the form of OLE 2.0, but the real potential of objects as a solution for client/server systems won't be realized until distributed objects become the norm. *Distributed objects* are objects that can be located anywhere on the network and interact with one another as if they were on the same machine.

Another extended metaphor would be good here

Another commonly used metaphor that helps explain the benefit of object technology is to compare objects with integrated circuits, those little thumbnail-sized wafers of silicon that contain thousands if not millions of little microscopic transistors.

By the late 1950s, the electronics industry had a serious problem on its hands. Small transistors had almost completely replaced bulky vacuum tubes, but as electronic circuits became more complex, the problem of connecting individual transistor circuits with wires became almost insurmountable. Then along came the integrated circuit (IC), first invented in 1959.

At first, integrated circuits were seen as simply a further development in miniaturization: first bulky vacuum tubes, then small transistors, then tiny ICs. From the beginning, IC makers have managed to double the number of transistors on a single chip every year or so. The first IC had four transistors. Today's ICs have a million times that many.

But the real beauty of ICs is not their size. Instead, it's the simple fact that they can be manufactured in quantity, so that complete circuits become commodities. Transistor circuits had to be assembled piece by piece. Each circuit had to be designed from the ground up. Today, circuit designers rely on catalogs of standardized integrated circuits to design their systems.

The current state of software engineering is kind of like the transistor circuit stage of electrical engineering. Programmers are still designing systems from the ground up, assembling them by hand. Objects are like integrated circuits in that they promise to eventually arm each programmer with a huge catalog of prefabricated components from which to choose. When object technology really starts to take off, we may see an exponential growth in software development like we've seen in hardware.

For distributed objects to work, there must be some mechanism in place to keep track of where the objects are and to route requests to the correct objects. At present there are three major standards or technologies for dealing with objects: CORBA, Microsoft's OLE/COM, and OpenDoc. The most important proposal for how this mechanism should operate is CORBA.

CORBA

CORBA stands for *Common Object Request Broker Architecture*. It is a detailed framework for interoperable objects developed by OMG, the Object Management Group. OMG is a consortium of about 100 computer vendors that strives to promote all things object-oriented, and to develop open standards for object-oriented systems.

CORBA is not itself a product, just a standard. Several vendors offer products that are *CORBA-compliant*. CORBA includes four major components:

- ✔ **The Object Request Broker (ORB),** which handles the details of establishing a connection between objects, whether the objects are located on the same machine or on separate machines on the network. ORB is a type of middleware that facilitates the connection between client objects and server objects. ORB maintains a repository of known objects with unique names for every object on the network. Plus, it provides a standardized way to invoke object methods. The ORB also handles the details of network communication, so that the objects themselves don't have to concern themselves with such details.

- ✔ **Object services,** which provide services such as a naming service that translates between human-readable object names and object references, which are not meaningful to ordinary humans but are unique across the network.

- ✔ **Common facilities,** which provide end-user oriented services for building compound documents à la OLE2 or OpenDoc.

- ✔ **Application objects,** which are the actual objects themselves.

With a CORBA-compliant ORB in place, objects can be distributed throughout a network. Whenever a client invokes an object method, the ORB steps in, locates the object, passes the request to the object, waits for the method to finish, and returns the result to the client.

The original version of CORBA provided a framework that allowed objects to work together over a network. Unfortunately, it did not require that different vendors' implementations of CORBA would be interchangeable with one another. The new CORBA 2.0 specification does require that ORBs from different vendors work together.

Microsoft's OLE and COM

OLE 2.0 is Microsoft's object technology for use with Windows (Macintosh and Unix versions are rumored, but not yet available). The technical foundation for OLE2 is called *COM,* which stands for *Component Object Model.* Think of COM as Micr0soft's answer to CORBA.

The current version of OLE/COM does not support distributed objects. However, Microsoft is moving OLE/COM toward support for distributed objects, in which the location of an object is completely transparent to the application that uses the object.

One of the criticisms often leveled at OLE/COM by object zealots is that OLE/COM does not support one of the fundamentals of objects: inheritance. In OLE/COM, the easiest way to create an object that "inherits" methods from an existing object is to completely contain the existing object within the new object. Then, the new object acts as a front end to the existing object, filtering methods and providing its own implementation for new methods or methods that should behave differently than in the original object. Microsoft is busily trying to figure out how to incorporate true inheritance into OLE/COM.

OpenDoc

The major competitor to OLE/COM is *OpenDoc*, an object standard put together by a group called the Components Integration Labs, or CIL. CIL is a consortium of several computer vendors, the most important being IBM, Apple, and Novell. The main purpose of CIL, it would seem, is to prevent Microsoft from dominating the object game just like they dominate everything else.

OpenDoc zealots can cite the following benefits of OpenDoc over OLE/COM:

✔ OpenDoc, as its name suggests, is open: it is not tied to Windows as OLE/COM is.

✔ OpenDoc is not anti-CORBA. It utilizes IBM's *System Object Model* (*SOM*) to provide CORBA-compliant object management services.

✔ IBM's *Distributed System Object Model* is a CORBA-compliant ORB, allowing objects to be distributed throughout a network.

✔ OpenDoc supports true inheritance. OLE/COM does not.

It remains to be seen whether OpenDoc or OLE/COM will get to the top of the Object Mountain first. Considering the success of Microsoft Windows, OLE/COM is the safe bet. OpenDoc may be technically superior, but both IBM and Apple have proven that technical superiority is not always enough to win. ■

Chapter 22

Managing Client/Server Systems

● ●

● ●

Centralized mainframe systems are relatively easy to manage. Sure, the computers are complicated, and the technical staff has to know their stuff, but the technical staff has complete control over the computers. There's not much the users can do to mess things up.

PCs are easy to manage too, because the burden of management is dropped in the laps of the users. If users lose a file, that's their fault: they should have backed it up. If they get a virus, too bad: they should know better. If someone steals their files, it's no skin off your nose: they should have locked their office doors.

Client/server networks throw a huge monkey wrench into the whole system management game. Now, vital corporate data is housed not just on the central computer where it is out of harm's way, but on servers all over the organization. Users aren't confined to dumb 3270 terminals that can access corporate data only in prescribed ways; now they have Windows, general-purpose query tools, and — shudder at the thought — *File Manager*.

Without a doubt, one of the biggest obstacles to client/server computing is that we haven't quite figured out how to manage it yet. This chapter introduces some of the key client/server management issues, in the hopes that you'll understand what the problems are and know what kinds of solutions to look for.

A common thread that runs throughout this chapter is the need for *distributed systems management*. Client/server systems are by nature distributed: the parts of the system that need to be managed are spread out across the entire enterprise. Management would be next to impossible if every computer system — server and client alike — had to be managed separately. The best distributed management tools allow the entire network to be viewed as a single entity and managed from a single location.

Client/Server Security

If you're not worried about security in a client/server system, you should be. Providing adequate security in a client/server system (or any computer system, for that matter) is a difficult proposition because effective security requires that you balance two contradictory goals:

> ✔ No one should be allowed to use any part of the system unless they have a legitimate reason to use the system, they have been authorized to do so, and they can prove that they are who they say they are.

> ✔ Those who do have a legitimate need to use a system should not be hassled.

A security administrator must decide how much security is enough to prevent unauthorized access without unnecessarily annoying legitimate users. Usually, this cannot be done: users will periodically have to memorize passwords, and they'll occasionally be denied access to something they'd like to see. The security administrator is not usually someone to whom users are endeared.

Most people think of network security in terms of keeping bad guys — hackers, embezzlers, disgruntled postal workers, and the like — out of the computer system. But bad guys are only a part of the threat. Security not only keeps bad guys out, it also keeps legitimate users from accidentally deleting someone's files, unwittingly admitting a virus into the network, or impolitely reading somebody else's e-mail. ■

Physical security: Lock your doors!

The first level of security in any computer system is physical security. It amazes me whenever I walk into the reception area of an accounting firm and see an unattended computer sitting on the receptionist's desk. As often as not, the receptionist has logged into the system, then walked away from the desk and left the computer unattended.

Physical security is especially important for server computers. Any hacker worth his or her salt can quickly get around all but the most paranoid security measures if he or she can gain physical access to the server. To protect the server:

TIP

✔ Keep it in a locked room.

✔ Give the key only to people who are trusted, and keep track of who has the keys.

✔ Use the computer's key to lock the keyboard.

✔ Consider disabling the floppy drives in the server.

✔ Keep a trained guard dog in the computer room, and feed it only enough to keep it hungry and mad. (Well, maybe that's a little paranoid, but you get the point.) ▪

Client computers should be physically secure as well. Users should be instructed not to leave their computers logged-in and unattended. In high-traffic areas, users should secure their computers with the keylock. And doors should be locked when possible.

Authentication: Who are you?

The next level of computer security is *authentication*: telling the computer who you are so that the system will grant you access to the resources you are entitled to use. Authentication usually requires both a user ID and a password. The user ID identifies each user's identity, and the password verifies that the user really is who he or she claims to be.

At least, that's the theory. Unfortunately, too many users don't take passwords as seriously as they should. For LAN users, passwords are a nuisance. In a client/server system, however, they are a must. The password grants access not only to shared files and printers on a LAN server, but to vital corporate data on servers throughout the company. Passwords must be taken seriously.

Here are some tips for managing passwords:

TIP

✔ Don't let users pick their own passwords. No matter what you tell them, they'll pick obvious passwords like their phone number, their kid's birthdates, or the make and model of their car.

✔ Use long passwords. The difficulty of guessing a password increases exponentially with the length of the password. Eight or ten characters is a good minimum.

✔ If the network has a feature that allows only a limited number of incorrect password entries — such as 10 or 20 — enable it. When the limit is reached, the user's account will be temporarily disabled. This will prevent brute-force password guessing.

✔ Require all users to change their passwords periodically. They'll hate you for it, but the security administrator doesn't get paid for being nice.

✔ Do not allow passwords to be kept in batch files. Make the user enter it at the keyboard each time he or she logs in.

✔ Make sure that all default passwords — such as for the SUPERVISOR account — are changed.

✔ Any user found with his or her password written on a Post-it™ note that's stuck on his or her computer monitor should be forced to listen to the sound of fingernails dragging across a chalk board for 30 minutes.

✔ Whenever an employee leaves the company, change the passwords for every one of that employee's co-workers. ■

Encryption: Etsla eakspa ina ecretsa odeca

Encryption is the process of taking an original, uncoded message (called *plaintext*) and scrambling it up with a special algorithm that uses a *key* to produce unintelligible *ciphertext*. *Decryption* is the reverse: it takes ciphertext, runs it through an algorithm with the key, and recreates the original plaintext message.

In a secure client/server network, information is encrypted before it is transmitted from one computer to another over network cable. The receiving computer decrypts the data before processing it.

Why is encryption important? Because it's surprisingly easy to steal information from a network cable. Network analyzers — invaluable tools for network managers — can be used to monitor all data that travels over a network. In the hands of a hacker, a network analyzer can be used to bypass other security controls.

At the minimum, passwords should always be encrypted before being sent over the network. Otherwise, a network analyzer can be used to capture passwords as they are sent over the network.

The federal government created a standard for data encryption in 1977, called *DES*, for *Data Encryption Standard*. It uses a 56-bit key for encrypting data, which makes the code next to impossible to crack except perhaps by the NSA, the CIA, and U.N.C.L.E.

Client/Server Backup

Backup is one of those chores that PC users hate to do (and most don't do at all), and mainframers take great pride in. Large mainframe data centers usually have a staff of people who sit around loading tapes all day. Regular backup is a fact of life in mainframe computing, managed by sophisticated software and carefully followed procedures.

When data is distributed across several servers in a client/server system, backup becomes a bit more complicated because the data to be backed up is distributed across several sites. Consider just two of the backup problems that can occur in a system in which some data is stored on a host mainframe, and other data is stored on a departmental LAN server:

✔ Data stored on the mainframe is fully backed up to tape every day, with several generations of archived data retained. Data stored on a departmental file server, on the other hand, is backed up fully once per week and incrementally every day (an *incremental backup* is a backup of just those files that have changed since the last backup was done). This difference in backup schedules and cycles between data stored on the mainframe and on the departmental server can complicate matters if data is lost and needs to be restored. You must take extra care when distributed data is restored from backups to ensure that data at distributed sites remains consistent.

✔ What if a user restores data to the LAN server without also restoring the mainframe data? This would cause the mainframe and LAN data to become unsynchronized.

Backup procedures and tools in a client/server system must ensure that backup of distributed data is done in a consistent manner, and the data integrity is not compromised by a partial restore.

Here are some tips for backing up client/server systems:

✔ Make sure all of the data is backed up every day. If the data is distributed across several servers, make sure all servers are backed up.

✔ If possible, use a centralized backup tool that will automatically back up data on all servers involved in the system.

✔ Periodically check your backups to make sure they are working. If the backup software has a "verify after backup" feature, use it. ∎

Keep several generations of backup data on hand. If data is distributed, make sure that the generation cycle is the same for all data sites. *Disaster recovery* is also important in client/server systems. What happens if an errant Scud missile falls on your data center? In a typical mainframe environment, disaster recovery can be planned for by providing a backup site for the data center, ensuring that backup data is stored off-site, and establishing a procedure to be followed should a disaster occur, so that the backup site can be up and running without significant delay.

In client/server, the critical system components that must be accounted for in a disaster recovery plan are not all centrally located. Thus, multiple backup sites and plans must be devised. The idea is the same, but disaster recovery for client/server systems is more complicated because of the more distributed nature of the systems.

Network Management

Like any network, the network that supports a client/server system must be managed. Network management includes:

- Keeping tabs on the network's performance
- Isolating and correcting problems that prevent the network from operating properly
- Keeping track of what computers, printers, bridges, gateways, and other devices are on the network

Until recently, network managers had to invest in good diagnostic equipment, clipboards, and walking shoes. Managing the network was akin to an Australian Walkabout: the network manager had to go to each computer to gather information, solve problems, update software, and so on.

Now, such basic tasks are handled over the network itself. It is usually necessary to actually visit a computer only if the computer is suffering from a hardware problem such as a bad cable or adapter card.

The most popular network management protocol standard is *SNMP*, for *Simple Network Management Protocol*. Other protocol standards are emerging, but SNMP is still the most widely used.

SNMP relies on *managers,* the software that does the actual network management, *agents*, little bits of software that run on each network component that can be managed (computers, routers, bridges, and so on), and *protocols* that standardize the communication between managers and agents. The agents collect information about the status of the network and store it in a *Management Information Base* (*MIB*) which can be examined and analyzed by the management software.

The best SNMP management software can search out SNMP network devices and automatically construct a map of your entire network. Then you can examine performance and troubleshooting data for the network. Corrective actions can even be automated, so that the management software can automatically correct network problems as they develop. (This is, of course, the ideal. In the real world, the network manager must still have a good pair of walking shoes.)

Accounting

With mainframe computer applications, it is common to use a chargeback mechanism to account for the cost of running computer applications. The IS department maintains detailed records of who uses the computer and how much, and bills each department accordingly. The MVS operating system includes facilities specifically for this purpose.

Client/server systems that replace traditional mainframe systems must also use a chargeback system to pay for themselves. The chargeback mechanism is more complicated in a client/server system, especially when more than one server is involved. Statistics must be gathered at each server and chargebacks made accordingly.

Client/server is still the new kid on the block, and most companies are still in the process of figuring out how to manage it. The main point to take home from this chapter is that client/server systems need to be managed as carefully as their mainframe predecessors. ■

Part VI
The Part of Tens

The 5th Wave — By Rich Tennant

WHAT DO YOU MEAN THERE'S A UNIX OPERATING SYSTEM IN THE LOBBY?

In This Part...

If you keep this book in the bathroom, this is the section that will get read the most. Each of these chapters consists of ten things (more or less — I do my addition on a Pentium) that are worth knowing about.

So without further ado, here they are, direct from the home office in Fresno, California.

Chapter 23

Ten Client/Server Commandments

"The wise developer builds his system upon industry standards, but the foolish developer regardeth the standards not, but goes his own way."

— Developers 1:1

And so it came to pass that these client/server commandments were handed down from generation unto generation, to be worn as frontlets taped to the computer nerd's glasses. Obey these commandments and it shall go well with you, your server, and your middleware.

I. Thou shalt not neglect the management of thy network

Networks do not and will not take care of themselves. If your background is with mainframe computers, you know all about systems management and how important it is. Select good management tools for the client/server network, learn how to use them, and put them to work.

If your background is with LANs, you know about network management but you're probably not used to dealing with the type of mission-critical data that is maintained by client/server systems. Client/server raises the network management bar. Be prepared to spend more time managing the network than ever before.

II. Thou shalt not cripple thy users with underpowered clients

One surefire way to ruin a client/server project is to deploy the system on underpowered client computers. It won't matter how slick the application is if the users twiddle their thumbs and curse at you under their breath because every mouse click holds them up for 15 seconds.

The minimum client computer changes almost daily. As I write this, the bottom line is a 486 computer with at least 8MB of RAM and 200MB of hard disk. Anything less will practically doom the client/server system to failure.

III. Thou shalt train up thine IS staff in the way which they should go

When it comes to client/server, just about everyone in your IS organization has something to learn. The mainframers have to learn Windows programming. The C programmers have to learn SQL. The LAN specialists have to learn SNA. The MVS folks have to learn Unix. And on and on.

Make sure the technical staff who will be responsible for developing and maintaining the client/server system have the opportunity to learn the technical skills that will be necessary to pull the project through. Training takes time; you can't drop a stack of books on a COBOL programmer's desk on

Friday and expect him or her to be a proficient PowerBuilder programmer by Monday.

IV. Thou shalt backeth up thy data

Prayer is a wonderful thing, but when it comes to protecting vital corporate data, nothing beats a well-thought-out, religiously followed schedule of backups.

V. Thou shalt adopt standards for thyself, and liveth according unto them

One of the problems with client/server computing compared with mainframe computing is the diversity that comes with using hardware and software from a plethora of vendors. In the mainframe days, just about everything came from IBM: the computer, the terminals, the network, the operating system, the DBMS, the compiler, the network management tools, and everything else.

With client/server, there are choices to be made at every turn. Before you get too far into client/server, it's important that you settle on some choices. Pick a network operating system, a DBMS, a front-end development tool, and whatever other tools you need. Then, stick to your guns. If you've decided to go with PowerBuilder, resist the urge to do just this one little application in Visual Basic. If your database is Oracle, make it Oracle all the way.

Of course, rigid standardization isn't always possible. As often as not, client/server systems inherit a hodge-podge of existing systems. Indeed, one of the main benefits of client/server is its ability to tie together dissimilar systems. But whenever possible, pick a standard and stick to it.

VI. Thou shalt not unplug thy mainframe

Client/server doesn't mean that the mainframe is history. Be objective when evaluating the various server alternatives for the application. In many cases, the mainframe is still the best choice.

VII. Thou shalt not promise the moon

It's all too easy to become evangelistic about client/server computing and make all sorts of unreasonable promises. Client/server will probably not reduce costs or improve programmer productivity. It won't save a failing business. It won't cure the common cold. It probably won't even get you out of taking the dog to the vet.

VIII. Remember thy data, to keep it pure

If there's one thing to watch out for in a client/server system, it's weaknesses in the integrity of your data. Pick a DBMS that includes adequate data integrity controls, and carefully study your data model looking for integrity problems. Make sure that transactions are designed and implemented properly so that data integrity isn't compromised by transactions that fail in-flight.

Developers coming from a mainframe background need to make sure they take nothing for granted. Mainframe software such as CICS often provides transaction recovery features that are transparent to application programmers. Client/server systems generally do not. Client/server programs must not assume that if their program crashes, any in-flight transactions will be rolled back.

IX. Thou shalt not skimp when selecting development tools

Buy only the best. The cost of the development tools is but a small part of the total cost of a client/server project.

X. Thou shalt protect thine users from themselves

With mainframe applications, users don't have many options about what they can do with the system. That may seem inflexible, but it's also safe: It's pretty hard for a mainframe computer user to accidentally format a hard disk or delete an important file. Not so with client/server systems that use Windows. With Windows, users can get themselves into all sorts of trouble.

You should at least consider disabling Windows features that can get unsophisticated users into trouble — such as File Manager, the ability to create and delete Program Manager groups, and so on.

Chapter 24

Ten Client/Server Acronyms Decoded

● ●

In This Chapter

▶ A handful of important acronyms

▶ Plus some that aren't important, but that you should know anyway

● ●

My, but there are a lot of acronyms to deal with! This chapter decodes the ten most important ones for client/server computing.

RPC

What it stands for: Remote Procedure Call.

What it's good for: RPC is a way for programs running on client computers to invoke the services of a program running on a server computer. All programmers are familiar with procedure calls; they're the building blocks of large programs. RPC allows a program to call a procedure that doesn't exist on the local computer; instead, the RPC mechanism locates the procedure on a network server and sends a message to the server to invoke the function. The server receives the message, invokes the function, and sends the results back to the client. When the client receives the results, it relays them back to the client program.

The key to RPC is that the client program isn't aware that the procedure wasn't a local procedure. RPC hides the details of locating the procedure on a network server, communicating with the server, and so on. About the only evidence the client program would have to indicate that the procedure was remote is the slowness of the request: RPC is naturally slower than a local procedure call, since information must be sent over the network.

MOM

What it stands for: Message Oriented Middleware.

What it's good for: MOM is an alternative to RPC for invoking server functions. RPC attempts to hide the fact that a procedure on a remote server is being invoked. MOM does not. MOM is a messaging system, in which clients communicate with servers by sending and receiving messages.

MOM allows asynchronous communication between client and server. That means that once the client has sent a message to a server, the client can continue processing. Eventually, the server will get the message, perform whatever service is requested of it, and send a message containing results back to the client. When the client notices that a message has been sent from the server, it can receive it and process the results.

OLTP

What it stands for: On-Line Transaction Processing.

What it's good for: OLTP forms the backbone of most American business. OLTP applications are the so-called mission-critical applications that handle day-to-day transactions such as order processing, receivables, collections, shipping, payables, and so on.

OLTP applications have traditionally been implemented using mainframe computers with hard-core transaction monitors such as IBM's CICS and dumb terminals such as 3270s. More and more companies are beginning to create client/server OLTP applications that use Windows or other graphical user interfaces.

ACID

What it stands for: Atomicity, Consistency, Isolation, and Durability.

What it's good for: ACID is a standard way of making sure that transactions are handled properly. The four qualities of a "good" transaction are:

- ✔ *Atomicity*, which means that the transaction cannot be broken apart. Either all of it is completed, or none of it is.

- ✔ *Consistency*, which means that a transaction must leave the system in a consistent condition. A transaction must complete every update necessary to leave the system in consistent state, or it must cancel itself.

- ✔ *Isolation*, which means that a transaction must be protected from the effects of other transactions that operate simultaneously. This is accomplished by placing locks on the resources that the transaction will update.

- ✔ *Durability*, which means that once the transaction finishes, the updates it makes become permanent.

DBMS

What it stands for: Database Management System.

What it's good for: Most client/server systems use a DBMS running on a server computer to provide database services. The DBMS usually creates and maintains relational databases using the SQL language to access and update the database.

A DBMS can be a PC-based SQL server such as Microsoft or Sybase SQL Server, Oracle, or Gupta's SQLBase; or a mainframe database such as IBM's DB2. A database gateway such as Information Builder's EDA/SQL or Microsoft's ODBC might be used to allow common access to different vendors' DBMS products.

NOS

What it stands for: Network Operating System.

What it's good for: A NOS is required to operate server computers in a client/server system. The most common NOS choices are:

- ✔ Novell's NetWare
- ✔ Unix
- ✔ Windows NT
- ✔ OS/2 LAN Server

GUI

What it stands for: Graphical User Interface.

What it's good for: A GUI provides an attractive and flexible way for users to work with computers. One of the main reasons for many client/server developments is to replace aging mainframe-based applications using dumb-terminal interfaces with modern GUI interfaces.

OOP

What it stands for: Object-Oriented Programming.

What it's good for: OOP is a programming technique or mindset in which code and data are melded to create reusable *objects*. Object orientation manifests itself in OOP programming languages such as C++ and Smalltalk as well as object-oriented programming interfaces such as OLE2 and OpenDoc.

APPC

What it stands for: Advanced Program to Program Communication.

What it's good for: If you're a loyal "Blue Till The Day I Die" IBM camper, APPC is the way you do client/server computing. It is a communication protocol that allows programs running under various IBM systems, such as CICS on a mainframe, AS/400, Unix, or OS/2, to communicate.

MYL

What it stands for: Made You Look.

What it's good for: I could only think of nine acronyms that were really worth knowing, and I needed a tenth one to round out the chapter.

Chapter 25

A Baker's Dozen Client/Server Networking Standards

● ●

In This Chapter

▶ Networking standards

▶ SQL standards

▶ Open systems standards

▶ Object standards

● ●

This chapter reviews some of the more important standards that provide the framework for client/server computing. (Yes, I know there are more than ten standards covered here. No charge for the extras.)

Networking

The following standards relate to network architectures and protocols.

OSI reference model

The OSI (Open System Interconnection) reference model provides a framework for networking. It breaks network architecture into the following seven layers:

1. The physical layer, which includes cables, connectors, and the like.

2. The data link layer, which governs how data flows through the physical layer.

3. The network layer, which addresses the routing of packets among networks.

4. The transport layer, which identifies individual nodes on the network.

5. The session layer, which establishes "sessions" between nodes.

6. The presentation layer, which converts data to various forms that can be recognized by nodes.

7. The application layer, which allows applications to access the network.

Ethernet

Ethernet is the most common networking standard for local area networks. Ethernet implements a collision-detection method of handling network traffic, in which each network node first listens to the network to see if any other nodes are talking, sends its message, and then listens to see if the message got through or if it collided with another message sent at the same time by another node.

Ethernet provides for three basic types of cabling:

- 10base5, which uses thick coax cable.
- 10base2, which uses thin coax cable.
- 10baseT, which uses unshielded twisted-pair cable.

The official Ethernet standard is published by the IEEE (Institute of Electrical and Electronics Engineers) and is known as "802.3," pronounced *eight-oh-two-dot-three*.

TCP/IP

TCP/IP stands for *Transmission Control Protocol/Internet Protocol* and is, as the name suggests, the official network protocol of the Internet. It is widely used with Unix systems. TCP/IP is a *de facto* standard, which means it just sort of grew as the Internet grew.

Token ring

Token ring is IBM's standard for local area networks. It requires that network nodes be wired in a ring arrangement, and passes a special packet called a *token* around the ring from node to node. If a node wants to send a message, it must wait for the token. When the token arrives, the node staples its message to the token, then passes it around. When the node to whom the message is addressed receives the token, it removes the message and forwards the token. Like Ethernet, token ring was standardized by IEEE. It's official designation is 802.5.

SQL

SQL — *Structured Query Language* — was invented at IBM and was originally the language of IBM's relational database products. It has since become an industry standard, though several flavors exist.

SQL-89

SQL-89 is the basic international standard for SQL, adopted by both the American National Standards Institute (ANSI), the International Standards Organization (ISO), and as a Federal Information Processing Standard (FIPS). SQL-89 is essentially the DB2 version of SQL with a few minor variations.

SQL-92

SQL-92 is a major update to SQL-89 that includes support for embedded SQL, dynamic SQL, collating sequences, standard system tables, standard error codes, and more.

SAG and ODBC

The SQL Access Group developed a call-level interface (CLI) for SQL, known as the SAG CLI, in 1992. Microsoft enhanced it with Windows-specific features in the form of ODBC, for *Open DataBase Connectivity*. SAG CLI/ODBC allows a program to access SQL data using a common subset of SQL, without knowing which specific vendor's SQL DBMS will service the request.

Open Systems

There are several important standards for creating open computing environments.

DCE

DCE, for *Distributed Computing Environment*, is an all-encompassing standard for distributed computing from the Open Software Foundation (OSF). It includes the following components:

- DCE RPC, a Remote Procedure Call standard to allow clients to invoke server procedures.
- Distributed directory services, which provide a unified naming model for distributed networks.
- Threads service, which allows multiple execution threads.
- Time service, which allows nodes to synchronize their clocks.
- Security, which uses a separate security server to verify user access.
- Distributed File System, which provides a single system-image of the file system which may actually be distributed over multiple file servers.

OSF/1

OSF/1 is a standardized version of Unix from the Open Software Foundation.

POSIX

POSIX stands for *Portable Operating System Interface*. It is an IEEE standard that provides a common interface to operating system functions, based on Unix. Although POSIX is usually associated with Unix, IBM has recently announced POSIX support for MVS.

Objects

Several standards for object technology are floating about. The most important are CORBA, OLE2/COM, and OpenDoc.

CORBA

CORBA, for *Common Object Request Broker Architecture*, is the distributed object standard from the Object Management Group (OMG). CORBA defines a standard *Object Request Broker*, which allows applications to communicate with objects that may be on remote machines in much the same way that RPC allows programs to call remote procedures. (In fact, some ORB implementations are based on DCE RPC.)

OLE2/COM

OLE2, for *Object Linking and Embedding 2.0* and COM, for *Component Object Model*, is Microsoft's answer to CORBA. Because of the dominance of Windows, OLE2 is the most widely used object standard. Time will tell if Microsoft will be as successful with distributed objects.

OpenDoc

OpenDoc is a non-Microsoft alternative for object-based compound documents from Apple, IBM, Novell, and others. Its proponents claim it is technically superior to OLE2, but even if it is, it doesn't have the clout of Windows driving it.

Chapter 26

Ten-Point Summary of Client/Server Computing (For Lazy Readers)

In This Chapter

▶ A concise summary of the key points of client/server computing

▶ Nothing else

*T*his chapter is for those who don't want to read the rest of the book, but still want to be able to discuss client/server computing at the water cooler. Or, it's for those who have just finished the preceding 25 chapters, but still aren't sure they understand what client/server computing is really all about.

Client/Server Distributes Processing Among Computers on the Network

The essence of the client/server model is that the actual work of a computer application is split up among several computers that request services from one another. The computer doing the requesting is called the *client;* the computer servicing the request is called the *server.*

Most Clients Provide a GUI

In most client/server systems, the role of the client computer is to provide a graphical user interface (GUI) so that the user can easily access the system.

The GUI is usually Windows, but can be OS/2, Unix Motif, or even a Macintosh.

Note that a GUI is *not* a requirement for the client/server model. It just happens that the client/server model lends itself to this type of application.

Most Servers Provide SQL Processing

A typical client/server application has the client computer providing the GUI and the server computer providing database access via a SQL server. The advantage of this model is obvious when you consider how a database application must work when client/server is not used. Without client/server, a computer must retrieve every record just to select records based on a search criteria. Each record would have to be sent over the network. With client/server, the client computer sends the SQL request to the server computer, which processes the request and returns just those records that match the search criteria.

Business Rules Can Go on the Client or the Server

In most client/server systems, the client handles the details of the user interface and the server handles the details of the database access. The other major portion of the application is the business rules — the logic that implements business policies, such as whether or not to approve credit, determining whether a customer qualifies for a discount, and so on. Such policies can be implemented in the client portion of a client/server system, or in the server.

If located on the server, business rules can be implemented via programs that are invoked using a Remote Procedure Call (RPC) mechanism or as stored procedure in a DBMS.

Clients Are Typically Programmed with a Visual Programming Tool

The programs that run on the client computers are usually developed using one of the new breed of visual programming tools, such as Powersoft's PowerBuilder, Microsoft's Visual Basic, or Borland's Delphi.

Visual programming lets you create a GUI interface by dragging various controls onto a blank form, then coding procedures that are invoked when the controls are activated or when other events occur. Visual programming may seem foreign to experienced mainframe developers, but the concepts are straightforward and they should catch on fast.

Transaction Processing Is One of the Biggest Challenges of Client/Server

Transaction processing is the Achilles' heel of client/server. Mainframe computers have a 30-year history of providing reliable transaction processing for mission-critical applications. Client/server tools are just beginning to catch up to the sophistication offered by mainframe transaction processing.

Mission-critical client/server applications must be able to support transactions that are distributed across several servers, so that if a failure occurs at any point during the transaction, all updates on all servers affected by the transaction are rolled back.

Middleware Is Software That Sits Between Clients and Servers

Middleware is software that operates between the clients and servers. Middleware's main purpose in life is to facilitate successful communication between clients and servers. Network operating systems and protocols can be thought of as middleware, but most people think of middleware as software that reconciles differences between clients and servers, such as different SQL dialects for various DBMS servers.

Client/Server Standards Are Starting to Take Hold

Client/server standards breed like rabbits. It seems as if a new standard emerges every few months. Fortunately, however, the industry is starting to gather around a relatively small group of standards that are begining to dominate. These standards were listed in Chapter 25.

Objects May Be the Future of Client/Server

Objects have been around for several years now, but the notion of distributed objects is just now emerging. Distributed objects are software components that have well-defined interfaces and can be distributed transparently throughout a network. Special middleware called an *object request broker* (ORB) locates objects as they are needed and manages the interactions among objects.

Client/Server Costs More than Most People Think

If there's one common misconception about client/server computing, it's that it is cheaper than traditional mainframe computing. Studies have shown this to be false. While the purchase price of the hardware itself — PCs vs. mainframes — may be less, the total cost of developing and maintaining a client/server system is usually more than the cost of an equivalent mainframe system, primarily because client/server systems require more maintenance and training than their mainframe counterparts.

A Client/Server Trade Show for Dummies (Without the Travel!)

. . . .

*O*ne of the best ways to learn about any computer subject is to take a week off from work and go to a conference that focuses on the subject. Client/server is no exception, and there are several conferences devoted to it.

Unfortunately, few of us have the clout to get an all-expenses-paid trip to Palm Springs to learn about client/server computing, which is probably why you bought this book instead of packing your golf clubs. That's okay, because this book so far has covered most of the material that you would find in the seminars of a typical client/server convention. I've covered all the basics of client/server technology, given you my opinions, some practical real-world tips, and included a few bad jokes here and there to spice things up.

The seminars are only one part of a convention. There's also the Exhibit Hall, where vendors gather to show their wares. I've found in most of the conventions I've attended that I learn as much in the Exhibit Hall as I do in the seminars. In the Exhibit Hall, you find out which companies offer what products, and how the companies and products differentiate themselves. You get to walk around half the day carrying an ever-growing plastic bag filled with product brochures, pamphlets, and business cards, not to mention letter openers, ballpoint pens, and other giveaways.

Of course, you have to keep in mind that much of what you learn in the Exhibit Hall is nothing more than hype. Still, it is a great way to quickly learn who's who and what's what.

Think of this part of the book as the Exhibit Hall at a Client/Server Trade Show for Dummies. Be sure to put on a good pair of walking shoes before you read on.

Note that this is not intended to be a comprehensive directory of client/server vendors, so please don't be offended if I left out your favorite company or product. Nor is it intended to be an in-depth review, comparing features and recommending specific products. I simply selected the companies and products I thought everyone interested in client/server should know about.

Within this section, I've used five new icons to identify certain types of products:

Computers suitable for use as servers, including RISC systems and even mainframes

Operating systems suitable for network use and related products

Relational database management systems suitable for use as SQL servers, and SQL middleware products

Programming tools, such as visual development environments or compilers

End-user applications such as word processors or spreadsheet programs that can be used to create the client side of a client/server application

Booth 1
Borland

Borland International, Inc.
P.O. Box 660005
Scotts Valley, CA 95067
800-331-0877
Faxback: 800-408-0001

Borland is well known for its programming development tools and application software.

Delphi

Delphi is Borland's new entry into the visual programming race. Delphi works in a visual environment similar to Visual Basic or PowerBuilder, but its procedures are based on Pascal rather than BASIC, and are compiled for improved performance. Borland claims Delphi is 10 to 20 times faster than Visual Basic.

Borland C++

Borland's C++ compiler includes a Windows-based development environment and a code generator called AppExpert that creates source code that provides a framework for complex applications. Borland's OWL (ObjectWindows Library) is a complete class library that provides an object interface to the Windows API.

Borland also supplies database tools that include the Paradox database engine and allow Borland C++ programs to access ODBC databases.

Paradox

Paradox is a relational database system designed for individual desktop or multiuser network use. It also includes SQL tools that allow it to access data on a SQL server.

Paradox includes a programming language called Object PAL that allows you to create scripts. You can also create custom forms and attach scripts to form controls. In this way, you can use Paradox as a front-end tool for client/server applications.

Booth 2
Computer Associates

Computer Associates International, Inc.
One Computer Associates Plaza
Islandia, NY 11788
800-225-5224
Faxback: 800-225-5224

Computer Associates is one of the largest software companies in the world. CA sells accounting software, plus development tools and utilities. A few of their products are listed here.

CA-Visual Objects

CA-Visual Objects is an object-oriented visual programming environment for Windows, similar to PowerBuilder or Visual Basic. Visual Objects is designed specifically for client/server development, with database connectivity, access to the entire Windows API, and a powerful programming language that is compiled rather than interpreted.

CA-Visual Express

CA-Visual Express is a Windows-based database access, query, and reporting tool that uses ODBC to access different vendors' SQL data.

CA-Visual Realia

CA-Visual Realia is a visual programming environment for COBOL — yes, I said COBOL. It allows you to create COBOL programs that take full advantage of the Windows GUI.

CA-Realizer

CA-Realizer is a visual programming language based on BASIC, similar to Visual Basic or PowerBuilder.

AccPac

AccPac is the world's most popular accounting system. In fact, one recent study indicated that AccPac accounts for nearly one-fourth of all accounting packages sold in the United States, more than twice as many as the nearest competitor.

Booth 3
Digital

Digital Equipment Corp. (DEC)
P.O. Box CS2008
Nashua, NH 03061
800-344-4825
Faxback: 800-344-4825

Digital Equipment Corp. — DEC — is one of the largest computer companies in the world, with thousands of products. DEC is best known for its midrange VAX and Alpha AXP computers.

AlphaServers (AXP)

The AlphaServer family contains Digital's high-performance RISC (Reduced Instruction Set Computer) servers. These computers are based on Digital's own 64-bit Alpha RISC chip. Digital offers six basic groups of AlphaServer systems:

- **AlphaServer 1000 4/200**, which sports a single Alpha CPU chip that operates at 200MHz, up to 512MB of memory, and 168GB of disk storage.

- **AlphaServer 2000 4/200**, with one or two Alpha CPU chips running at 190MHz, up to 640MB of memory, and 200GB of disk storage.

- **AlphaServer 2100 4/200**, with up to four Alpha CPUs running at 190MHz, up to 2GB of memory, and 300GB of disk.

- **AlphaServer 2100 4/275,** with the same specs as the 2100 4/200, except the CPU runs at a clock speed of 275MHz.

- **DEC 7000 Model 700**, a mainframe-class system that supports up to six Alpha CPUs running at 275MHz, up to 14GB of memory, and more than 10TB of disk storage. (TB stands for *terabyte*, one trillion bytes.)

All of the AlphaServers except the DEC 7000 can run one of three operating systems: DEC OSF/1, OpenVMS, or Windows NT Server. The DEC 7000 can run OSF/1 or OpenVMS.

For what it's worth, the *AXP* is not an acronym; the letters don't stand for anything. They're just random letters that the marketing geniuses at Digital thought sounded good.

VAX midrange systems

Although Digital gets more attention these days for its Alpha RISC systems, DEC continues to sell plenty of its popular VAX midrange computers. The VAX product line is similar in size and speed to the AlphaServers but uses the older VAX CISC architecture rather than the Alpha APX RISC architecture.

OpenVMS

VMS was originally the operating system for the DEC VAX minicomputer system that was Digital's bread and butter in the 1980s. VMS was a proprietary operating system that had few links to the non-DEC world. The official name of the operating system was VAX/VMS.

Rather than develop an entirely new operating system for the Alpha AXP line of computers, Digital renamed VAX/VMS to OpenVMS, partly because VMS was now supported on two distinct hardware platforms, but also to emphasize the open systems features that had been built into the new version of VMS.

OpenVMS is the first non-Unix operating system to have passed the difficult open-systems tests administered by X/Open, the official keepers of the Unix Holy Grail. In every respect, OpenVMS is as open as any operating system, Unix or not.

Ultrix

Ultrix is DEC's version of the Unix operating system for use with VAX systems.

DEC OSF/1

For those who aren't convinced that OpenVMS really is as open as Unix, Digital offers DEC OSF/1, based on the Open Software Foundation's version of Unix.

DEC Rdb

DEC Rdb is Digital's relational database management subsystem for OpenVMS VAX systems. DEC Rdb was recently purchased by Oracle, who will market it under the name Oracle Rdb.

Booth 4
Easel

Easel Corp.
25 Corporate Dr.
Burlington, MA 01803
800-525-1411

Easel offers several products for client/server development, the most important being Enfin.

Enfin

Enfin is an object-oriented client/server development tool based on Smalltalk, the father of object-oriented programming languages. Enfin is available in Windows and OS/2 versions.

Synchronicity

Synchronicity is an object-oriented analysis and design tool that is designed to be used with Enfin. It allows you to create entity-relationship diagrams (ERDs) and model business objects. Once the business model is completed, Synchronicity can generate Smalltalk code that can be brought into Enfin.

Object Studio

Object Studio is a package that includes Enfin and Synchronicity, plus Team-Builder, a collection of development tools designed to facilitate development teams.

Booth 5
Gupta

Gupta Corp.
1060 Marsh Rd.
Menlo Park, CA 94025
800-876-3267
Faxback: 415-617-4600

Gupta is best known for its PC-based database server, SQLBase, and its client/server development tool, SQLWindows.

SQLBase Server

SQLBase Server was the first PC-based SQL database server on the market. Here are some highlights.

- ✔ Supports ANSI/ISO SQL-89 Level 2.
- ✔ Embedded SQL is supported for COBOL.
- ✔ Stored procedures and triggers are supported.
- ✔ Backward cursor scrolling is supported.
- ✔ Declarative referential integrity is supported.
- ✔ Runs under Windows, OS/2, Unix, or NetWare.

SQLWindows

SQLWindows is an object-oriented, visual development tool for creating client/server applications à la Visual Basic and PowerBuilder. SQLWindows has an excellent reputation, and is the client/server tool of choice for many developers.

Like most other visual development tools, SQLWindows procedures are interpreted rather than compiled, which does not yield the best possible performance. However, SQLWindows allows some portions of a program to be exported as C++ source code that can be compiled using a Microsoft Visual C++ to produce very efficient applications.

Booth 6
Hewlett-Packard

Hewlett-Packard Co.
3000 Hanover St.
Palo Alto, CA 94304
800-752-0900
Faxback: 800-231-9300

A few years ago, Hewlett-Packard was best known for those scientific calculators that only the rich nerds at my high school could afford.

Now Hewlett-Packard is one of the biggest computer companies around, with more than $20 billion in annual sales.

I should have bought HP stock in 1986.

Hewlett-Packard refers to its overall client/server strategy and products as *Open Client/Server Computing Solutions*. Their main product is the HP 9000 series of RISC servers and the HP-UX version of Unix it runs, but they also offer educational and consulting services as well.

HP 9000 server computers

The HP 9000 server computers are designed to be used as servers in client/server systems. These computers use a flexible 64-bit RISC architecture known as PA-RISC. (*PA* stands for *Precision Architecture*, an obvious selling point when comparing HP 9000 computers with servers that that use Pentium processors.)

HP servers are available in many sizes, from the small E-series servers to the powerful T500 multiprocessor model. Here are some examples of the range of capabilities available from the smallest HP 9000 (the E25) to the largest (the T500, which sounds like something out of a Schwarzenegger movie):

- The E25 has one PA-RISC processor running at a clock speed of 48MHz. The T500 can have up to 12 PA-RISC processors running at 90MHz.

- The E25 comes with 16MB memory standard, expandable up to 512MB. The T500 comes with 256MB standard and can be expanded up to 2GB.

- The E25 can support up to 144GB of external disk storage. The T500 can accommodate 1900GB of disk storage.

> ✔ The E25 can accommodate up to 4 I/O cards. The T500 can accommodate 112.
>
> ✔ All HP 9000 computers run the same HP-UX Unix operating system.

The point is that the smallest of the HP 9000 servers is comparable in speed and capacity to an Intel-based LAN server, whereas the largest HP 9000 is comparable to a small mainframe. Of course, there are many models in between, too.

HP-UX Unix operating system

HP 9000 computers run Hewlett-Packard's own version of Unix, called HP-UX. HP-UX, currently at version 10, runs on all of HP's PA-RISC processors, including the HP 9000 server computers used as servers in client/server systems, as well as desktop workstations that are typically used in engineering applications.

HP-UX has some exotic features that set it apart from the competition:

> ✔ Scalability across the entire HP 9000 product line. IBM can't do that: try running OS/2 on an AS/400 or a 3090, or running MVS on a PC.
>
> ✔ A feature called *Logical Volume Manager/9000* that lets you set up virtual disk volumes that span more than one physical disk drive.
>
> ✔ SAM: System Administration Manager, a set of sophisticated tools for maintaining an HP-UX system.
>
> ✔ HP Software Distributor/UX, used to control the distribution of applications in client/server environments.
>
> ✔ Support for distributed transaction processing via DCE (DCE/9000), Encina (Encina/9000), or IBM's CICS (CICS/9000).

HP OpenView

HP OpenView is a collection of products for integrating and managing those multivendor computer networks that are commonplace in most client/server environments. HP OpenView products include:

> ✔ **Network Node Manager (NNM)**, the main HP OpenView product, which lets you manage a sprawling network from a single location. NNM draws maps of your network and graphs of network activity. Products are also available to bring NetWare and SNA into the OpenView fold.
>
> ✔ **HP NetMatrix** adds advanced monitoring and troubleshooting capabilities.

- ✔ **HP OpenView Operations Center** lets a computer system operator control Unix systems from HP, Sub, IBN, and NCR from a single console.

- ✔ **HP PerfView** is a performance monitor for multivendor networks.

- ✔ **HP OpenView Software Distributor** handles the details of distributing software throughout a multivendor network.

- ✔ **HP OpenView OmniStorage** is a disk storage management system that automatically moves seldom-used files to slower and less expensive storage devices, and vice versa.

- ✔ **HP OpenView OmniBack II**, an automatic multivendor backup system.

- ✔ **HP OpenView OpenSpool**, a multivendor print management system that lets you control printing on servers throughout the network.

Booth 7
IBM

IBM Corporation
Old Orchard Road
Armonk, NY 10504
800-426-3333
Faxback: 800-426-4329

IBM is the largest computer company in the world, and offers so many client/server products that it could probably fill up the entire exhibit hall of most convention centers all by itself.

IBM's products fit best into the IBM client/server world view, in which the dominant networking architecture is SNA, the database is DB2, and the operating systems are MVS, OS/400, and OS/2.

IBM is seen by many as the opposite of Open Systems. This may have been true 10 or 15 years ago, but IBM systems today are as open as any other vendors systems, probably more so.

Mainframe servers: ES/9000

IBM is perhaps best known for its mainframe computers, and it still manages to sell and support plenty of them in spite of rumors of the mainframe's death. Mainframes are the Rolls-Royce of computers, offering top-of-the-line processor performance, memory, disk storage capacity, I/O speed, and networking support.

IBM has recently begun to promote its mainframe computers in the role of gigantic server computers for large client/server systems. Existing mainframes are often used as servers to begin the transition to the client/server model. Plus, a mainframe server is sometimes actually cheaper than smaller servers when all costs are factored in.

The current versions of IBM mainframes are known as ES/9000 systems, though sometimes the family name System/390 is used. These computers usually use the MVS/ESA operating system, a huge behemoth that comes with enough technical manuals to fill a 16-wheeler and requires a staff of systems programmers to tune, troubleshoot, and offer occasional live sacrifices.

In addition to MVS/ESA, most IBM mainframes are equipped with a virtual alphabet soup of IBM software: TSO, ISPF, CICS, VTAM, DB2, and IMS are the most popular.

For smaller mainframes, the VSE/ESA operating system is sometimes used. VM is also sometimes used in conjunction with VSE/ESA or MVS/ESA.

Midrange servers: AS/400

IBM's AS/400 system is one of the most popular minicomputers in the world. It is a direct descendant of IBM's System/38, which was very popular in the 1970s and 1980s. Like IBM's mainframes, the AS/400 is being redressed in the role of server computer for client/server systems, and it is well suited to the task.

The AS/400 uses a 48-bit processor, but IBM is moving toward a 64-bit RISC design. Its operating system is called OS/400.

The AS/400 is the only computer system available that actually has a relational database system — a special version of DB2 — built into its operating system. The tight integration of DB2/400 with the AS/400 hardware and operating system results in what IBM claims is the most widely used multiuser database system in the world.

Traditional host-based AS/400 systems use dumb terminals called 5250 terminals. PCs can be connected to AS/400 systems by imitating 5250 terminals, but a feature called Client Access/400 allows DOS, OS/2, Windows, and Macintosh computers to access AS/400 systems as clients.

The newest versions of the AS/400 series, and the ones best suited for client/server use, are the AS/400 Advanced Series computers. Just for the sake of comparison, here are the specs for the top-of-the-line AS/400 Advanced System 9406 Model 320:

- ✔ 48-bit processor
- ✔ 128MB RAM standard, up to 1536MB
- ✔ Up to 151 feature cards
- ✔ Disk capacity: 259GB
- ✔ Up to 2,160 terminals

This is a blow-your-socks off minicomputer system.

RISC servers: RS 6000

IBM's RS 6000 series computers are suitable for use as servers in client/server environments. Many different RS 6000 models are available. Here are the specifications of the RS 6000 POWERServer 990, one of the more powerful models:

- ✔ Power2 RISC processor (64-bit)
- ✔ 128MB RAM, expandable to 2GB
- ✔ Up to 150 users
- ✔ Runs IBM's AIX version of Unix

PowerParallel servers

IBM's most interesting and innovative computers are the new PowerParallel systems. The PowerParallel system uses dozens or even hundreds of RISC processors all working in tandem under the AIX operating system to achieve processing power that boggles the mind.

The idea behind the PowerParallel systems is that you can expand the system at any time by adding additional processors. This characteristic makes the PowerParallel one of the most scalable computers ever. IBM has even coined a cute slogan for the PowerParallel: "Palmtops to teraFLOPS," which is supposed to mean that the same system architecture can be scaled from hand-held computers all the way up to world-class supercomputers used to calculate previously unknown prime numbers.

PowerParallel systems are still pretty exotic. As I wrote this, only a few hundred systems had actually been sold, mostly at universities or government research agencies. These systems are cost-effective as high-performance servers in commercial client/server environments, so we'll probably see more of them in commercial applications over the next few years.

PS/2 servers

IBM also sells Intel-based server computers in the form of its PS/2 Server series. These computers use IBM's proprietary MicroChannel bus architecture, which limits you a bit on expansion options but helps ensure blistering-fast performance. Here are the specs for the top-of-the-line PS/2 Server 95 Array 566:

- Pentium processor (66MHz)
- 16MB RAM, expandable to 256MB
- 4GB disk standard, room for nine additional drives
- Eight MicroChannel expansion slots
- Supports RAID 5 disk arrays, with hot-swappable drives

DB2

DB2 is IBM's relational database product. It is one of the oldest and most mature relational database products on the market, and is often used as the standard against which other relational databases are judged.

DB2 is undoubtedly the most ubiquitous relational database system. There are versions of DB2 for just about every conceivable computer system, with the possible exceptions of Macintosh and Super Nintendo. Here's a list of the more popular versions:

- **DB2 for MVS.** This is the granddaddy of them all.
- **DB2 for VM and VSE.** The DB2 version that runs under the VM and VSE operating systems is also known as SQL/DS.
- **DB2 for OS/400.** This is the AS/400 version.
- **DB2 for AIX.** This is for IBM systems that run AIX, most notably the RISC 6000 systems.
- **DB2 Parallel Edition for AIX.** This is a special version designed for the PowerParallel systems.
- **DB2 for OS/2.** Runs on OS/2 servers to provide database services for LANs.

CICS

CICS is the transaction processing engine that is at the heart of most mainframe-based application systems. Like DB2, it has become ubiquitous. Here are some of its incarnations:

- ✔ **CICS/ESA.** This is the powerhouse version, capable of supporting tens of thousands of terminal users on mainframes running MVS/ESA or VSE/ESA.

- ✔ **CICS for OS/400.** This version is sometimes used to downsize mainframe-based CICS applications to AS/400 systems.

- ✔ **CICS for AIX.** The AIX version of CICS allows transaction processing systems to be used with RISC 6000 systems in a Unix environment.

- ✔ **CICS for OS/2.** There are two flavors of CICS for OS/2. CICS for OS/2 Single User is meant to be used as a development environment for developing CICS applications which will eventually be run on mainframe CICS, though it can also be used in a client/server arrangement. CICS for OS/2 Multi-User is a CICS-based transaction server intended for LAN use. It includes a new feature that allows you to build GUI front-end programs that invoke CICS transactions.

The various versions of CICS can be used together to build complete CICS-based client/server applications, with GUI front ends running on OS/2 clients and hard-core CICS transactions running on LAN, midrange, or mainframe-class servers.

IMS Client/Server

Most client/server systems are built with relational SQL databases. However, for all the talk about DB2, there are still many users of IMS, IBM's older, non-relational database system. IMS Client/Server allows you to build client/server front ends for existing IMS systems without forcing you to convert the IBM data to a relational database.

IMS Client/Server is available for OS/2 or DOS/Windows clients.

VisualAge

VisualAge is IBM's front-end visual programming tool, comparable with Microsoft's Visual Basic or Powersoft's PowerBuilder. It is available in OS/2 and Windows versions.

VisualAge is based on Smalltalk, an object-oriented language that has a small but loyal following. It includes a large library of prefabricated user-interface, database, and other objects that can be incorporated into applications.

VisualGen

Most visual programming environments — including IBM's VisualAge — are designed to let you create client-side front-end programs that access server-based relational databases. VisualGen takes this model one step further by providing a fourth-generation language (4GL) which lets you create server-based applications that can be invoked from client front ends.

VisualGen supports OS/2 and Windows clients and CICS/ESA or CICS OS/2 servers.

Booth 8
Information Builders

Information Builders, Inc.
1250 Broadway
New York, NY 10001
800-969-INFO

Information Builders, Inc. (IBI) has long been known for its mainframe application development tool, FOCUS. IBI's main claim to client/server fame is its EDA/SQL relational database middleware.

FOCUS for Windows

FOCUS is one of the original fourth-generation development tools which were supposed to eliminate mainframe programming problems 20 years ago. FOCUS for Windows is the latest incarnation of the venerable FOCUS. It has evolved into a full-featured object-oriented development environment which should be considered, especially if your organization already uses FOCUS.

EDA/SQL

EDA/SQL (*EDA* stands for Enterprise Data Access) is a SQL middleware product that allows client/server applications to access data from various RDBMS servers using a single, common SQL dialect. EDA can access more than 50 different database and file formats, including all of the major RDBMS systems, plus traditional mainframe databases and files such as IMS and VSAM.

EDA/SQL is ideal for client/server systems that must access data that is scattered throughout the company in different database formats. For example, if a client/server problem-management system must access DB2 customer data, IMS inventory data, and shipping data stored in VSAM files, EDA may be able to drastically simplify the project by allowing the system's developers to access the data using a common SQL dialect.

Booth 9 Informix

Informix Software Inc.
4100 Bohannon Dr.
Menlo Park, CA 94025
800-331-1763

Informix is best known for its relational database server, but they also have a pretty good visual programming environment and other client/server tools.

Informix Online

Informix Online is a popular relational database server that runs under Unix. Here are some of its highlights:

- ✔ ANSI SQL Level 2 is supported.
- ✔ Includes a Call Level Interface (CLI), ODBC support, and embedded SQL in C.
- ✔ Stored procedures and triggers are supported.
- ✔ Declarative referential integrity is supported.
- ✔ Supports row-level locking.
- ✔ Support for distributed databases, including optimized distributed queries, recovery, and detection of deadlocks.

Informix NewEra

NewEra is a visual client/server programming tool for creating client/server applications. Like Visual Basic, PowerBuilder, and the rest, it lets you visually create a program's user interface and write code using a special object-oriented programming language. For improved performance, New Era programs are compiled rather than interpreted.

Booth 10
Lotus

Lotus Development Corp.
55 Cambridge Pkwy.
Cambridge, MA 02142
800-343-5414
Faxback: 800-346-3508

Lotus's main claim to fame in the client/server world is Notes, the industry-leading groupware environment.

Lotus Notes

Lotus Notes is the premier client/server development tool for groupware applications — applications that are designed specifically with group collaboration via a network in mind. In fact, Lotus Notes is practically the accepted definition of "groupware."

Unlike visual programming environments such as Visual Basic or Power-Builder, Notes applications do not revolve around SQL and a relational database server. Instead, Notes applications use a special Notes database, which is an object-oriented database that holds documents of various types.

SmartSuite

SmartSuite is a bundle of the following popular end-user applications:

- Ami Pro (word processor)
- Freelance Graphics (presentation graphics)
- Approach (database)

✔ Lotus 1-2-3 (spreadsheet, in case you've been on Mars for the past 10 years)

✔ Organizer (personal information manager)

Although SmartSuite is not itself a client/server product, the individual applications can be used to create the client side of a client/server system. SmartSuite also offers tight integration with Notes.

Booth 11
Microsoft

Microsoft Corporation
One Microsoft Way
Redmond, WA 98052
800-426-9400
Faxback: 800-426-9400

As you stroll through our Client/Server Trade Show for Dummies, when you enter the huge Microsoft Pavilion, a gangly young man introduces himself as "the world's wealthiest computer nerd" and begins to describe Microsoft's vision of the computing future, known as "Information at Your Fingertips," a vision in which every man, woman, and child on the planet has a Pentium computer that runs Windows 95, the Banana Slug is declared the National Mollusk, and the state of Washington is renamed "Gatesland."

Microsoft is one of the largest software companies in the world, and it has a wide selection of client/server products. In fact, it is possible to build complete client/server systems using only Microsoft software.

Microsoft BackOffice

In September 1994, Microsoft introduced a suite of products designed to provide a complete package of server software for client/server applications, known as *Microsoft BackOffice*. BackOffice is not itself a product, but a package of server products, some new, some old. BackOffice includes the following:

✔ Microsoft Windows NT Server 3.5, a 32-bit network server operating system based on Windows NT

✔ Microsoft SQL Server 4.21, a relational DBMS

- ✔ Microsoft SNA Server 2.1, which allows client/server applications to access IBM mainframe computers that communicate using SNA

- ✔ Microsoft Systems Management Server 1.0, a new product which lets you manage all the PCs on a LAN

- ✔ Microsoft Mail Server 3.2, the server software for the Microsoft Mail electronic mail system

- ✔ Microsoft Exchange Server, a new product (which doesn't actually exist yet), that serves as the back end to Microsoft's groupware product, Microsoft Exchange

Microsoft NT Server

Windows NT Server 3.5 is the latest incarnation of Microsoft's 32-bit server operating system based on Windows NT. The new version is considerably faster than the previous version, and requires 4 to 8MB less memory. Here are some of the noteworthy features of NT Server 3.5:

- ✔ Requires 16MB of RAM; supports up to 4GB

- ✔ Supports more than 400TB (terabytes) of disk storage

- ✔ Supports symmetric multiprocessing configurations with up to 32 processors

- ✔ Unlimited number of user connections

- ✔ Runs on Intel, Alpha, or MIPS processors

- ✔ Automatically tracks names for TCP/IP addresses

- ✔ Supports all the popular protocols, including NetWare IPX/SPX, NetBIOS, TCP/IP, and AppleTalk

Microsoft SQL Server

Microsoft's SQL Server, version 4.21a, is a DBMS server designed for use with Microsoft NT Server 3.5. For years, Microsoft developed its SQL server in cooperation with Sybase, but the two companies recently decided to go their separate ways.

Unlike most other SQL servers, Microsoft SQL Server is available for only one OS platform (Windows NT Server, naturally). (Previous versions also ran under OS/2.)

Here are some other product highlights:

- ✔ Supports ANSI/ISO SQL-89 Level 1, plus SAG, CLI, ODBC, and MAPI. Embedded SQL is supported for C and COBOL.

- ✔ SQL Server provides its own Call Level Interface known as DBLIB, which is compatible with Sybase SQL Server.

- ✔ Stored procedures and triggers are supported.

- ✔ Backward cursor scrolling is supported.

- ✔ Declarative referential integrity is *not* supported.

Microsoft SNA Server

Microsoft SNA Server runs on Windows NT Server 3.5 and allows a PC LAN to connect to an SNA network. The current version of SNA Server is 2.1. It supports up to 2,000 PCs on the LAN and a total of 10,000 sessions with an SNA host. (Each PC can have more than one concurrent host session.)

SNA Server allows LANs to connect to the following types of IBM systems:

- ✔ Mainframes (System/390, 3090, and so on) that run VTAM 3.2 and NCP 5.2.1 or later

- ✔ AS/400 systems running OS/400 2.2 or later

SNA Server is most often used with terminal emulation software that allows LAN computers to emulate IBM 3270 or 5250 terminals. This allows users to run host applications on their desktop PCs.

Microsoft Systems Management Server

Microsoft Systems Management Server is designed to simplify the management of networked PCs. Systems Management Server is a new product, currently in version 1.0. It provides four basic functions:

- ✔ **Hardware and software inventory**. Information about the hardware and software for every computer attached to the network can automatically be collected and stored.

- ✔ **Software distribution and installation**. Software can be automatically distributed and installed to computers on the network.

- ✔ **Performance monitoring and analysis**. Network bottlenecks can be identified.

- ✔ **Troubleshooting.** Remote troubleshooting features allow problems with one network computer to be diagnosed from another computer. Help desk managers love this feature.

Systems Manager Server supports the DMI (Desktop Management Interface) standard, and a software development kit is available that allows you to customize or extend System Management Server's basic features.

Microsoft Mail

Microsoft Mail is Microsoft's electronic mail system, which consists of client support for Windows, MS-DOS, Macintosh, and OS/2. Any MS-DOS-compatible network server can be used as a Mail server.

Microsoft Mail is actually a family of products, including:

- ✔ Microsoft Mail Clients for MS-DOS, Windows, Macintosh, and OS/2
- ✔ Microsoft Mail Server
- ✔ Microsoft Schedule+, a workgroup scheduling tool that lets you keep an appointment book and schedule meetings with other Mail users
- ✔ Microsoft Electronic Forms Designer (EFD), a client-side programming tool that works alongside Visual Basic for building groupware applications based on Microsoft Mail
- ✔ Microsoft Workgroup Template, which is a small collection of ready-to-go forms for specific business applications

Microsoft Exchange

Microsoft Exchange is a forthcoming product that integrates e-mail and groupware into a single product. At the time I wrote this, not much was known about the final form of Exchange or exactly when it would ship.

Microsoft Visual Basic Professional

Visual Basic is one of the most popular front-end development tools for client/server applications. It allows you to create Windows programs using a visual development environment, coding event scripts in a dialect of the Basic programming language. (The example program in Chapter 17 is done in Visual Basic.)

The current version, 3.0, includes several features that are useful for client/server development:

- ✔ The Microsoft Access relational database engine, which provides access to local databases or, in a client/server environment, to SQL Server, Oracle, or any ODBC database

- ✔ Special data object types that allow the programmer to incorporate SQL into a Visual Basic program

- ✔ Data-aware controls that can automatically retrieve data from the database

- ✔ A report writer based on the popular Crystal Reports

- ✔ Full OLE2 support

Microsoft Access

Microsoft Access is a relational database system that is designed for individual desktop use but can be used to develop sophisticated multiuser applications that access shared databases stored on a file server. Applications of this sort aren't really client/server applications, in that all of the application processing is done by Access on each client computer; the server computer acts only as a file server on which the shared database is stored.

Access can be used to build client/server applications by attaching to ODBC tables or by using special "pass-through" queries that pass SQL statements to an ODBC-compliant SQL server.

Access has its own visual programming language called Access Basic, which is similar to but not identical to Visual Basic.

Microsoft Office Professional

Microsoft Office Professional is a suite of end-user applications that can be used to build the front end for a client/server system. The suite includes:

- ✔ Microsoft Word 6.0
- ✔ Excel 5.0
- ✔ PowerPoint 4.0
- ✔ Access 2.0
- ✔ Mail (client license only)
- ✔ MOM (Microsoft Office Manager)

Booth 12
Novell

Novell, Inc.
122 East 1700 South
Provo, UT 84606
800-453-1267
Faxback: 800-638-9273

Novell is best known for its network operating system, NetWare.

NetWare

NetWare is Novell's flagship network operating system. The current version (4.1) includes *NetWare Directory Services* (*NDS*), which keeps track of resources throughout the network by name so that users do not have to know what server owns the resources they need.

Here are the vital statistics for NetWare 4:

- ✔ Requires 8MB of RAM; supports up to 4GB.
- ✔ Supports up to 32TB (terabytes) of disk storage.
- ✔ Does not support symmetric multiprocessing configurations.
- ✔ Up to 1,000 users.
- ✔ Runs only on Intel processors.
- ✔ Supports all the popular protocols, including IPX/SPX, NetBIOS, TCP/IP, and AppleTalk.

Novell Visual AppBuilder

Visual AppBuilder is Novell's visual development tool for client/server applications. Visual AppBuilder lets you combine prebuilt application modules called AppWare Loadable Modules (ALMs) to form complete applications. Visual AppBuilder comes with a library of ALMs, and you can create your own ALMs to provide additional object types.

One thing that sets Visual AppBuilder apart from other visual programming tools is that Visual AppBuilder bypasses programming altogether. Instead of writing event procedures using a programming language, you simply drag and drop ALM components to build a complete application, connecting ALMs with lines and arrows that represent events.

Tuxedo

Tuxedo is a Unix-based transaction monitor, used to build client/server transaction processing systems. Tuxedo provides a common API which client programs running on Unix, Windows NT, OS/2, or Macintosh clients can use. Here are some of Tuxedo's highlights:

- Two-phase commit is provided for distributed transactions.
- Location transparency is provided via a naming service.
- Works with all major Unix DBMS servers.

UnixWare

UnixWare is Novell's version of Unix, designed to operate with NetWare servers. In fact, the ability to painlessly connect to NetWare is the chief reason to use UnixWare over other Unix versions.

PerfectOffice Professional

PerfectOffice Professional is a suite of application software from Novell, WordPerfect, and Borland. The suite is integrated by AppWare and can be used to build the front end for client/server systems. PerfectOffice includes:

- WordPerfect for Windows 6.1
- Borland Quattro Pro 6.0
- Borland Paradox 5.0
- WordPerfect Presentations 3.0
- Envoy 1.0
- GroupWise 4.1
- InfoCentral 1.1
- AppWare 1.1

Booth 13
Oracle

Oracle Corp.
500 Oracle Parkway
Redwood Shores, CA 94065
415-506-7000
Faxback: 415-506-6985

When you enter the Oracle booth, you'll be greeted by two or more identical-looking sales representatives, who simultaneously say, "Hello (fill in name), have you heard about Oracle's new parallel processing architecture, Parallel Everything?"

Most people think of Oracle as the manufacturer of one of the most successful SQL database servers, and rightfully so. According to most reports, Oracle generates more revenue from database server sales than any other software company, owning 35% to 40% of the market. With its new parallel processing features, Oracle will probably continue to be the RDBMS to beat for the foreseeable future.

Oracle is not a one-product company, however. In addition to database servers, Oracle sells client/server development tools and a complete line of client/server application packages.

Oracle 7

Oracle's state-of-the-art RDBMS server, Oracle7 (now at release 7.1) is the Cadillac of database servers. It is available on just about any platform imaginable, including Unix, NetWare, Windows NT, OS/2, MVS, VM, and VMS. Special versions are even available which take advantage of IBM's PowerParallel architecture.

Here are some of the more useful features of Oracle7 that deserve to be highlighted:

- ✔ Oracle7 uses a fancy concurrency technique called *multiversioning*, which means that rows do not have to be locked to provide cursor stability.
- ✔ Stored procedures and triggers are supported.
- ✔ Declarative referential integrity and cascaded deletes are supported.

✔ Row-level locking is used rather than the more common page-level locking used by most other RDBMS servers.

✔ There is support for distributed databases, including optimized distributed queries and automatic replication.

Cooperative Development Environment (CDE)

CDE is a collection of products that can be used to develop client/server applications. CDE includes CASE tools, application generators, testing tools, and so on.

CDE actually consists of 18 products, which can be grouped as follows:

✔ **Repository:** Oracle Exchange, which maintains a repository of information that is used by all of the CDE components.

✔ **Analysis and design tools:** Oracle Strategy, Oracle Designer and Oracle Dictionary, Oracle Forms Generator, Oracle Reports Generator. These are the CASE tools that allow the developer to model a system and automatically generate prototypes.

✔ **Development tools:** Oracle Forms, Oracle Reports, Oracle Graphics, Oracle Card, Oracle Precompilers. These are the tools the developer uses to implement an application.

✔ **Production:** Oracle Book, Oracle Browser, Oracle Glue.

Cooperative Applications

Oracle sells a complete set of applications known as the Oracle Cooperative Applications suite. The applications fall into these categories:

✔ Financial management

✔ Manufacturing

✔ Distribution

✔ Human resource management

✔ Government financials

✔ Project control

Naturally, Oracle's applications all utilize the Oracle7 RDBMS. In addition, the applications themselves are built with the CDE tools, and Oracle provides an API to the applications so they can be customized.

Booth 14
PeopleSoft

PeopleSoft, Inc.
1331 North California Blvd.
Walnut Creek, CA 94596
800-947-7753

PeopleSoft is a supplier of customizable client/server applications, primarily in the financial and human resource areas.

PeopleSoft applications

PeopleSoft offers a full line of financial and human resources applications, including general ledger, payables, receivables, asset management, payroll, and others.

PeopleSoft is not tied to a particular RDBMS. You can use any of six different RDBMS products for the database server.

PeopleSoft is based on a three-tier client/server model, where application logic is implemented separately from the GUI logic and the database access. Customers have the option of deploying the application layer on a separate application server or on the same client computer as the GUI layer.

Booth 15
Powersoft

Powersoft Corp.
561 Virginia Rd.
Concord, MA 01742
800-273-2841
Faxback: 508-287-1600

Powersoft is the maker of PowerBuilder, one of the most popular visual tools for developing client/server applications.

PowerBuilder

PowerBuilder is one of the best-known and most widely used visual programming environments. It is similar to Microsoft's Visual Basic or Borland's Delphi. PowerBuilder lets you visually design forms by dragging control objects onto the form. Then, you write procedural code to handle events for each control object.

PowerBuilder includes a powerful Database Painter that lets you create and maintain databases on remote servers, including Sybase, Oracle, Informix, XDB, and any database that can be accessed via ODBC.

PowerBuilder's scripting language, called PowerScript, is similar to BASIC.

PowerBuilder runs under Windows, but Macintosh and Unix versions are underway.

Booth 16
Sybase

Sybase Inc.
6475 Christie Ave.
Emeryville, CA 94608
800-879-2273

Sybase is best known for its RDBMS, SQL Server. However, Sybase also sells a visual client/server development environment known as Gain Momentum, as well as other client/server tools designed to complement a SQL Server.

Sybase refers to its client/server SQL products as the "System 10" family.

SQL Server

Sybase SQL Server is an RDBMS, currently at version 10.1, and is the product Sybase is best known for. SQL Server runs on most LAN platforms: NetWare, Windows NT Server, OS/2, and Unix, as well as on DECVMS. Among the more notable features of SQL Server:

✔ Sybase uses its own SQL dialect for transaction processing, called Transact-SQL.

✔ Stored procedures (Sybase invented them) and triggers are supported.

✔ Declarative referential integrity is supported.

✔ Distributed database features allow access to multiple servers within a transaction.

✔ Gateways for DB2, IMS, and other mainframe databases are available.

✔ SQL Server includes Backup Server, which automatically makes backup copies of SQL data.

✔ A coordinated set of administration, connectivity, and replication tools is available.

OmniSQL Gateway

OmniSQL is a SQL middleware product that provides SQL-based access to many different types of data. OmniSQL accesses DB2, IMS, VSAM, ISAM, RMS, Oracle, and other data sources.

Replication Server

Replication Server is a distributed database product that automatically handles data that is replicated at multiple sites. Replication Server works by duplicating transactions that have been committed at a primary site to secondary sites where the affected data is replicated.

Gain Momentum

Gain Momentum is a client/server development environment that focuses on multimedia applications. Gain Momentum is intended for developing information kiosks, on-line catalogs, training and performance support systems, decision support systems, and so on.

Here are some of the key features of Gain Momentum:

✔ A visual programming environment is used to design the objects that make up an application. Objects can be the usual GUI elements (buttons, check boxes, sliders, and so on), or multimedia objects like video and sound.

✔ A high-level language called GEL is used to craft the behavior of the objects used by an application.

✔ Sybase SQL Server is used for database access. (Other data sources can be accessed as well.)

Glossary

● ●

10base2 The type of coax cable most often used for Ethernet networks.

10base5 The original Ethernet coax cable, now used mostly used as the backbone for larger networks.

10baseT Twisted pair cable, commonly used for Ethernet networks.

802.3 The IEEE standard known in the vernacular as *Ethernet*.

8088 processor The microprocessor chip around which IBM's original PC was designed, marking the transition from the Bronze age to the Iron age. The original 8088 design was found painted on the walls of caves in southern France.

80286 processor *Computo-habilis*, an ancient ancestor of Intel's 386 and 486 processors, used in IBM-compatible PCs; still used by far too many people but ill-suited for client/server.

80386 processor The first 32-bit micro-processor chip used in personal comput-ers, now replaced by the 486 chip. 386 computers are slower than their 486 counterparts, but they get the job done.

80486 processor The most popular CPU chip for personal computers today. The Pentium is newer and better, but still too expensive.

access method Software used to manage access to I/O devices on mainframes. See *VSAM* and *VTAM*.

acronym An abbreviation made up of the first letters of a series of words. See *TLA*.

active window In a GUI, the window that has the focus — that is, the window that will process user input events.

adapter card An electronic card that can be plugged into one of your computer's adapter slots to give it some new and fab-ulous capability, like displaying 16 million colors, talking to other computers over the phone, or accessing a network.

Advanced Peer-to-Peer Networking (APPN) An IBM networking standard that enables APPC sessions between networks.

Advanced Program-to-Program Commu-nication (APPC) A communication proto-col that allows programs to communicate with one another when the programs are running on separate network nodes.

AIX IBM's version of Unix for its AS/400 systems.

American National Standards Institute (ANSI) A group that meets in a smoke-filled room to dole out standards of all sorts, from the electrical characteristics of high-speed network circuits to the size of trash dumpsters.

ANSI See *American National Standards Institute*.

ANSI/ISO SQL The international standard for SQL. The older 1989 standard is called SQL-89 or SQL1. The newer 1992 version is called SQL-92 or SQL2. A new version, called SQL3, is currently under consideration.

API See *Application Programming Interface.*

APPC See *Advanced Program to Program Communication.*

AppleTalk Apple's networking system for Macintoshes.

application layer The highest layer of the OSI reference model, which governs how software communicates with the network.

application logic The portion of an application that governs how the application responds to various inputs — for example, what should the application do when a user enters an order? Same as *business logic.*

application plan The executable form of the SQL statements contained in an embedded SQL program.

Application Programming Interface (API) A documented set of instructions by which a program can invoke the functions of a system, such as a DBMS or a transaction processing monitor.

application server A network server that runs applications on behalf of client computers.

APPN See *Advanced Peer-to-Peer Networking.*

AS/400 IBM's popular midrange computer system.

asymmetric multiprocessing A multiprocessing system in which CPUs are devoted to specific tasks such as handling I/O requests or printing.

back end A program that runs on a server to provide services requested by a front-end program.

backbone A trunk cable used to tie sections of a network together. The backbone is often 10base5 or fiber-optic cable.

backup A copy of your important files made for safekeeping, in case something happens to the original files; something you'd better do every day. PC users all too often don't.

benchmark A repeatable test used to judge the performance of computer hardware or software. The best benchmarks are the ones that closely duplicate the type of work done in the real world.

Binary Large Object (BLOB) A relatively new database data type that is most often used to represent a graphic image.

bind A process by which the SQL statements in a DBRM are compiled, optimized, and stored in an application plan so they can be executed.

BLOB See *Binary Large Object.*

bottleneck The slowest link in your network, which causes work to get jammed up. The first step in improving network performance is identifying the bottlenecks.

BPR See *business process reengineering.*

bridge Not the popular card game, but a device that lets you link two networks together. Bridges are smart enough to know which computers are on which side of the bridge, so they only allow those messages that need to get to the other side to cross the bridge. This improves performance on both sides of the bridge.

buffer An area of memory that's used to hold data en route to somewhere else. For example, a disk buffer holds data as it travels between your computer and the disk drive.

bus A type of network topology in which network nodes are strung out along a single run of cable called a *segment*. 10base2 and LocalTalk networks use a bus topology. *Bus* also refers to the row of expansion slots within your computer.

business logic See *application logic*.

business process reengineering (BPR) Reinventing a business by redesigning its fundamental processes, often without regard to how things were done in the past.

cache A sophisticated form of buffering in which a large amount of memory is set aside to hold data so that it can be accessed quickly.

Call Level Interface (CLI) A method of programming with SQL in which a program calls special SQL interface routines to execute SQL statements.

cc:Mail A popular electronic mail program.

CGA A crude type of graphics display used on early IBM computers. CGA stands for *Crayon Graphics Adapter*.

check box In a GUI, a control that can be checked or unchecked to select a yes/no or on/off type of option.

Chicago Microsoft's internal codename for Windows 95.

CICS *Customer Information and Control System*, a transaction-processing system originally used on IBM mainframes, but now available on midrange and personal computers too. Often pronounced *kicks*.

CISC *Complex Instruction Set Computer*, a normal Intel-style computer CPU, which knows how to execute many different types of instructions. See *RISC*.

CLI See *Call Level Interface*.

click What you do in Windows to get things done.

client A computer or program that requests services from another computer or program. See *server*.

client area In a GUI, the central portion of the window, where the program displays its information.

client/server computing What this book is all about: a form of computing in which work is shared in a balanced fashion between client and server computers connected by a network.

CMS *Conversational Monitor System*, an IBM operating system that works in conjunction with VM to provide terminal access to a mainframe computer.

coaxial cable A type of cable used to connect computers in a network. Usually refered to as *coax*.

Codd, E. F. One of the original relational database gurus. See *Date, C. J.*

column In relational database terminology, a *field* — a snippet of information such as a customer's name, address, phone number, or Zip code.

combo box In a GUI, a dialog box control made up of a combination of a text box and a list box.

command button In a GUI, a button that triggers an action.

COMMIT A SQL function that completes a transaction, ensuring that all of the database updates made by the transaction will become permanent.

componentware A trendy term used to describe a possible future form of application software, in which each program manages just one type of software, and complex documents are held together by compound document architectures such as OLE. Componentware is the opposite of the current trend of applications to get bigger and bigger.

compound document A document that is made up of bits and pieces taken from other programs, such as text from a word processor, a table from a spreadsheet program, and a graph from a charting program.

concentrator In Ethernet, a multiport hub used mostly with 10baseT cabling. The hub typically has 8 or more ports, plus a BNC connector for 10base2 and an AUI port for a 10base5 transceiver.

concurrency Allowing more than one user to access a database simultaneously while ensuring that the database is not corrupted.

constraint A restriction placed on the values that may be entered into a column in a relational database.

container an application that can support an embedded OLE object.

conventional memory The first 640K of memory on a DOS-based computer.

CPU The *central processing unit*, or brains, of the computer.

CSMA/CD An acronym for *Carrier Sense Multiple Access with Collision Detection*. The traffic management technique used by Ethernet.

CSU/DSU The equipment required to connect to a T1 line.

cursor A SQL programming technique that allows a program to process the rows in a query result one at a time.

cursor stability A guarantee that the data obtained through a cursor will remain consistent until the cursor is closed.

daisy chain A way of connecting computer components in which the first component is connected to the second, which is connected to the third, and so on. In 10baseT Ethernet, hubs can be daisy-chained together.

Data Flow Control Layer The second layer of the SNA networking model.

data flow diagram (DFD) A diagram that depicts the processes that make up an application, emphasizing the flow of information between processes.

Data Link Control Layer The second layer of the SNA networking model.

Data Link Layer The second layer of the OSI model, responsible for transmitting bits of data over the network cable.

database An organized collection of information.

database management system (DBMS) A computer program designed to manage databases.

Database Request Module (DBRM) A special file that contains the SQL statements that are included in an embedded SQL program. The DBRM is automatically created by the precompiler.

database server A computer dedicated to the task of handling database requests.

Date, C. J. The other original relational database guru. See *Codd, E. F.*

DB2 *DataBase 2*, IBM's premier relational database product.

DBMS See *database management system.*

DBRM See *Database Request Module.*

DDS See *Digital Data Service.*

deadlock A situation in which two or more users are stuck indefinitely waiting for resources held by one another.

DFD See *data flow diagram.*

dialog box In a GUI, a window containing one or more controls that the user manipulates to select options or enter values.

Digital Data Service (DDS) Leased phone lines that can be used to transmit data at up to 56Kbps.

dinosaur Giant creatures that once roamed the earth. Some say they were wiped out by a huge meteor, but others hold that the dinosaurs are not really extinct, but have evolved into modern day birds.

distributed database A database made up of tables stored at multiple locations.

Distributed Relational Database Architecture (DRDA) IBM's blueprint for distributed database management. See *remote request, remote transaction, distributed transaction,* and *distributed request.*

distributed request In IBM's DRDA, the most advanced form of distributed database in which a single SQL statement may access data at multiple locations.

distributed transaction In IBM's DRDA, a form of distributed database in which a transaction may consist of SQL statements, each of which accesses data at a different location. See *Distributed Relational Database Architecture.*

domain The set of values that are acceptable for a particular column in a relational database table.

DOS *Disk Operating System*, the most popular operating system for IBM and IBM-compatible computers.

downsizing Replacing larger computers with smaller ones that do the same work.

DRDA See *Distributed Relational Database Architecture.*

drop-down list box In a GUI, a type of list box in which the list doesn't appear until the user clicks the down-arrow.

dumb terminal Back in the heyday of mainframe computers, a monitor and keyboard attached to the central mainframe. All of the computing work occurred at the mainframe; the terminal only displayed the results and sent input typed at the keyboard back to the mainframe.

dynaset The results of a query in Visual Basic.

e-mail An application that lets you exchange electronic messages with other network users.

EGA The color monitor that was standard with IBM AT computers, based on 80286 processors. Now obsolete, but plenty of them are still in use.

embedded SQL A method of programming with SQL in which SQL statements are freely intermixed with the statements of some other programming language, such as COBOL, C, or C++.

enterprise computing A trendy term that refers to a view of an organization's complete computing needs, rather than just a single department's or group's needs.

entity-relationship diagram (ERD) A diagram that depicts the relationships among tables in a relational database design.

Entry-Sequenced Data Set (ESDS) A VSAM file organization commonly found on mainframe computers.

ERD See *entity-relationship diagram.*

ESA *Enterprise Systems Architecture*, the current version of the MVS operating system for IBM mainframes.

eschatology The study of the End Times.

ESDS See *Entry-Sequenced Data Set.*

Ethernet The world's most popular network standard.

EtherTalk What you call Ethernet when you use it on a Macintosh.

ETLA *Extended Three Letter Acronym*. An acronym with four letters. See *TLA.*

event handler A program module that provides the program's response to a user-initiated event.

event-driven programming A program-

ming style in which the program consists of *event handlers* that respond to user-initiated events, such as clicking a button or dragging a slider.

exclusive lock A database lock that prevents other users from accessing data. See *shared lock.*

expanded memory An ancient technique for blasting past the 640K DOS memory limit. Unlike extended memory, expanded memory can be used with 8088 computers.

extended memory Memory beyond the first 640K. Available only on 80286 or better computers. Most computers today have extended memory.

fault tolerance The ability of a computer system to recover from failure without losing data.

FDDI *Fiber Distributed Data Inferface*, a 100-Mbps network standard used with fiber-optic backbones. When FDDI is used, FDDI/Ethernet bridges are used to connect Ethernet segments to the backbone.

fiber-optic cable A blazingly fast network cable that transmits data using light rather than electricity. Fiber-optic cable is often used as the backbone in large networks, especially where great distances are involved.

field See *column.*

file server A network computer containing disk drives that are available to network users.

firkin A small cask that used to hold beer or butter. See *noggin* and *piggin.*

flat file A standard file of records not managed by a DBMS.

foreign key A column that corresponds to the primary key column (or columns) of another table.

form In Visual Basic and other similar programming tools, a window that can contain controls and other objects the user interacts with.

fragmentation A method of distributing database data in which tables are split across two or more locations. (This term also refers to an undesirable condition that sometimes develops on disk drives when free space becomes scattered about the drive rather than consolidated into one contiguous range of free space.)

front end A program that runs on a client computer and requests services from a back-end program running on a server computer.

gateway A device that connects dissimilar networks. Gateways are often used to connect Ethernet networks to mainframe computers.

GB Gigabyte, roughly a billion bytes of disk storage (1024MB to be precise). See *K*, *MB*, and *TB*.

glass house The room where the main-frame computer is kept. Symbolic of the mainframe mentality, which stresses bureaucracy, inflexibility, and heavy iron.

graphical user interface (GUI) The type of user interface used by Windows, OS/2, Macintosh, and X-window computers. A GUI interacts with the user via pictures and what-you-see-is-what-you-get displays and uses a mouse in addition to the keyboard for input.

groupware A relatively new category of client/server software that's designed to allow and even promote collaborative work.

GUI See *graphical user interface*.

guru Anyone who knows more about computers than you do.

heritage systems See *legacy systems*.

hierarchical database A database in which records are organized according to a parent-child hierarchical structure.

host processing A computing model in which all of an application's processing occurs on a central host computer; the terminal serves only as a rudimentary I/O device for displaying information and cap-turing user input.

host variable A variable in a program-ming language such as COBOL, C, or C++ which is used to transfer data values between the program and a SQL database server.

hub See *concentrator*.

icon In a GUI, a picture that represents an object or an action.

IDAPI See *Integrated Database Application Programming Interface*.

IEEE See *Institute of Electrical and Elec-tronic Engineers*.

IMS *Information Management System*, IBM's older nonrelational database system.

inheritance In object-oriented program-ming, the ability to create new objects that inherit properties and methods from existing objects.

inner join In SQL, a join in which corresponding rows from two tables are combined. See *outer join*.

Integrated Database Application Programming Interface (IDAPI) A SQL Call Level Interface proposed by Borland, IBM, Novell, and WordPerfect as an alternative to ODBC.

Institute of Electrical and Electronic Engineers (IEEE) Where they send computer geeks who've had a few too many parity errors. (Actually, just another standards organization.)

International Standards Organization (ISO) The organization whom we can thank for the OSI standard.

Internet A humongous network of networks that spans the globe and gives you access to just about anything you could ever hope for, provided you can figure out how to work it.

interoperability Providing a level playing field for incompatible networks to work together, kind of like NAFTA.

IPX The transport protocol used by NetWare.

ISDN An all-digital phone system that integrates voice and data.

ISO See *International Standards Organization*.

ISPF *Interactive System Productivity Feature*, a use- friendly interface to TSO for IBM mainframe computers.

join A database operation in which related rows from two or more tables are combined to form a single result table.

K Kilobytes, roughly one thousand bytes (1024 to be precise). See *GB*, *MB*, and *TB*.

key A column or combination of columns that uniquely identifies each row in a table. Also known as a *primary key*.

Key-Sequenced Data Set (KSDS) A VSAM indexed file organization commonly found on mainframe computers.

KSDS See *Key-Sequenced Data Set*.

LAN See *local area network*.

LAN Manager A network operating system from Microsoft, superseded by Windows NT Server.

LAN Server IBM's version of LAN Manager.

LANtastic A popular peer-to-peer network operating system.

legacy systems All of those computer systems that have been inherited from past generations of computer programmers.

list box In a GUI, a control used to select an option from a list of possible choices.

LLC sublayer The *logical link sublayer* of Layer 2 of the OSI model. The LLC is addressed by the IEEE 802.2 standard.

local area network A network of computers located close to one another, usually in the same building.

lock A hold placed on database data so that other users cannot access or modify the data until a transaction has been completed.

logical unit (LU) A node in an SNA network. An LU can be associated with a physical device such as a terminal or printer, or it can be associated with a program.

Lotus Notes The most popular groupware program, from Lotus Corp.

LU See *logical unit.*

LU 6.2 The logical unit type used for APPC communications.

MAC sublayer The *media access control* sublayer of layer 2 of the OSI model. The MAC is addressed by the IEEE 802.3 standard.

Macintosh A cute little computer that draws great pictures and comes with built-in networking.

mail server The server computer on which e-mail messages are stored. This same computer also may be used as a file and print server, or it may be dedicated as a mail server.

mainframe A huge computer housed in a glass house on raised floors. The cable that connects the disk drives to the CPU weighs more than most PCs (unless the mainframe uses fiber-optic cables).

MAPI *Messaging Application Programming Interface*, used to create mail-enabled applications in the Microsoft environment.

maximize button In a GUI, a button the user can click to enlarge a window so it fills the entire screen.

MB Megabytes, or roughly one million bytes (1024K to be precise). See *GB, K,* and *TB.*

MDI See *Multiple Document Interface.*

menu bar In a GUI, a row of menu commands that the user can invoke when using the program.

metaphor A literary construction suitable for Shakespeare and Steinbeck but a bit overused by computer writers.

method In object-oriented programming, executable code associated with an object.

Microsoft Mail A popular e-mail program from that big company in Redmond, WA.

middleware Software that floats around between clients and servers, whose purpose in life is to facilitate the client/server connection by smoothing over the differences and irregularities inherent in an open systems environment. See *SQL middleware.*

midrange system A multiuser computer system that is smaller than a mainframe.

minicomputer What they used to call a midrange system.

minimize button In a GUI, a button the user can click to shrink a window down to an icon.

mission-critical application A computer application without which a business cannot function.

Motif A popular window manager for Unix systems.

mouse The obligatory way to use Windows. When you grab it and move it around, the cursor moves on the screen. After you get the hand-eye coordination down, using it is a snap. *Hint:* Don't pick it up and talk into it like Scotty did in Star Trek 4. Very embarrassing, especially if you've travelled millions of miles to get here.

Multiple Document Interface (MDI) A standard Windows technique for creating programs that can access more than one document at a time.

multiprocessing A computer system that has two or more CPUs. See *asymmetric multiprocessing* and *symmetric multiprocessing*.

multitasking The ability of a computer and operating system to run more than one program at a time.

MVS *Multiple Virtual Storage*, IBM's biggest and most powerful operating system for mainframe computers.

n-tuple The official relational database term for a row. See *relation*.

NETBIOS *Network basic input output system*, a high-level networking standard developed by IBM and used by most peer-to-peer networks. It can be used with NetWare as well.

NetWare The chief priest of network operating systems, the proud child of Novell, Inc.

NetWare 2.2 NetWare's "Good" version, designed for 80286-based processors and that is still widely used on smaller networks.

NetWare 3.11 NetWare's "Better" version, designed with 80386 processors in mind.

NetWare 4.1 NetWare's latest and "Best" version, filled with all sorts of bells and whistles for larger networks.

NetWare Directory Services The cool new feature of NetWare 4 whereby the resources of the servers are pooled together to form a single entity.

NetWare Loadable Module (NLM) A program that's loaded at the file server.

NLMs extend the functionality of NetWare by providing additional services. Btrieve runs as an NLM, as do various backup, antivirus, and other utilities.

network Two or more computers connected together to share information and resources such as printers and disk drives.

network database A database model that promotes many-to-many relationships.

network interface card (NIC) An adapter card that lets the computer attach to a network cable.

network layer One of the layers somewhere near the middle of the OSI reference model. It addresses the interconnection of networks.

Network Operating System (NOS) An operating system for networks, such as NetWare or Windows NT Server.

NIC See *network interface card*.

NLM See *NetWare Loadable Module*.

node A device on the network, typically a computer or printer.

noggin A small mug. See *piggin* and *firkin*.

non-preemptive multitasking The form of multitasking used by Windows and by CICS, in which each program must voluntarily reliniquish control of the computer so that other programs can have a turn.

normalization The process of reducing a relational database design to a simpler form by eliminating redundancies and undesirable dependencies.

NOS See *Network Operating System*.

Novell The folks you can thank or blame for NetWare, depending on your mood.

null In a SQL database, an unknown value. Zero is not the same as null: the value zero is a known value.

object A package that combines data and procedural code and is the basis of all the hoopla about object-oriented computing.

object database A database in which data and procedure are bound together to create objects.

Object Linking and Embedding (OLE) Microsoft's standard for creating compound documents in Windows.

object-oriented programming (OOP) A new style of programming in which programmers deal with objects rather than separate data and code.

object-oriented user interface (OOUI) A style of user interface in which the user deals with objects rather than merely documents and programs.

ODBC See *Open DataBase Connectivity.*

office automation A well intentioned idea of the 1970s and 1980s in which computers were supposed to totally automate the office and white-collar worker productivity was supposed to skyrocket. It didn't happen.

OLE See *object linking and embedding.*

OLTP See *On-Line Transaction Processing.*

On-Line Transaction Processing (OLTP) A transaction processing system in which terminal users enter transaction data that is immediately processed.

OOP See *object-oriented programming.*

OOUI See *object-oriented user interface.*

Open DataBase Connectivity (ODBC) Microsoft's standard interface accessing SQL databases from Windows applications.

Open Software Foundation A nonprofit group that promotes open systems.

open systems Computers and computer equipment that doesn't lock you in to a single vendor's products.

optimizer The portion of a SQL server that selects the most efficient method to process a query.

Oracle The company that makes *Oracle Server.*

Oracle Server A popular relational database server.

OS/2 *Operating System/2*, IBM's operating system for personal computers.

OS/2 LAN Server A network server version of OS/2.

OS/2 Warp IBM's internal codename for OS/2 version 3, which IBM decided to retain in the final, official name of the product. Some say the codename was inspired by the mindset IBM must have adopted when believing that OS/2 could actually compete with Windows.

OS/400 *Operating System/400*, IBM's operating system for its AS/400 midrange computer system.

OSI The agency Lee Majors worked for in *The Six Million Dollar Man.* Also, the *Open System Interconnection* reference model, a seven-layer framework upon which networking standards are hung.

outer join In SQL, a join in which corresponding rows from two tables are combined, then added to any unmatched rows. See *inner join*.

packets Data is sent over the network in manageable chunks called *packets*, or *frames*. The size and makeup of a packet is determined by the protocol being used.

page A 4K portion of a database table, which usually contains more than one row of data.

page-level locking A database locking technique that locks entire pages. A page may contain more than one table row. See *row-level locking*.

parallel processing A computing technique in which large numbers of CPUs are used in a coordinated fashion.

Path Control Layer The second layer of the SNA networking model.

peer-to-peer network A network in which any computer can be a server if it wants to be. LANtastic, NetWare Lite, and Windows for Workgroups are examples of peer-to-peer networks.

Physical Control Layer The first layer of the SNA networking model.

physical layer The lowest layer of the OSI reference model.

physical unit (PU) A device connected to an SNA network.

piggin A wooden milk pail. See *noggin* and *firkin*.

pixel A single dot of color on a computer monitor. Hundreds of thousands of pixels

are required to form a complete image on the monitor.

plug 'n play A new feature of Windows 95 that automatically detects and configures hardware devices.

pocket protector A status symbol among computer geeks.

positioned DELETE A method of deleting database rows while fetching result rows via a cursor.

positioned UPDATE A method of updating database rows while fetching result rows via a cursor.

precompiler A program that processes a source program that contains embedded SQL statements before the program is compiled.

preemptive multitasking A form of multitasking in which the operating system itself decides when to suspend one program to allow another program to execute. See *non-preemptive multitasking*.

presentation layer The sixth layer of the OSI reference model, which handles data conversions, compression, decompression, and other menial tasks.

presentation management The thankless job of providing a user interface for an application.

Presentation Services Layer The second layer of the SNA networking model.

primary key See *key*.

print server A computer that handles network printing.

process Something that a business does to create value for customers.

property An attribute or data value associated with an object.

property inspector In a GUI, a method of displaying and modifying all of the attributes of an object.

protocol The rules of the network game. Protocols define standardized formats for data packets, techniques for detecting and correcting errors, and so on.

PU See *physical unit*.

query An operation performed against a relational database table to select specific information from the table. The result of a query is a *result set*.

queue A list of items waiting to be processed. The term usually refers to the list of print jobs waiting to be printed, but networks have lots of other types of queues as well.

radio buttons In a GUI, a set of buttons from which only one can be selected. When you click one radio button, the one that was previous selected is deselected.

RAID *Redundant Array of Inexpensive Disks*, a bunch of disk drives strung together and treated as if they were one drive. The data is spread out over several drives, and one of the drives keeps checksum information so that if any one of the drives fails, the data can be reconstructed.

RAM *Random access memory*, your computer's memory chips.

record See *row*.

reengineering See *business process reengineering*.

referential integrity A feature of SQL

databases that ensures that relationships among tables are properly cared for.

relation The official relational database term for a table. The formal definition of *relation* is: "An unordered set of n-tuples." See *n-tuple*.

relational database A type of database in which information is organized into tables.

Relative-Record Data Set (RRDS) A VSAM file organization commonly found on mainframe computers.

remote request According to IBM's DRDA, the most primitive form of distributed database in which a program may issue an isolated SQL request for a remote database. See *Distributed Relational Database Architecture*.

remote transaction In IBM's DRDA, a form of distributed database in which a program may request a complete transaction consisting of several SQL statements to be executed on a remote database. See *Distributed Relational Database Architecture*.

repeater A device that strengthens a signal so that it can travel on. Repeaters are used to lengthen the cable distance between two nodes. A *multiport repeater* is the same as a *hub* or *concentrator*.

replication A method of distributing database information by maintaining duplicate copies of database data. Ideally, the software used to provide the replication automatically keeps the data up to date and consistent at all locations.

resource heaps Special areas of Windows memory used to keep track of windows, dialog boxes, buttons, fonts, and other aspects of the user interface. When Windows runs out of space in the resource heaps, bad things start to happen.

result set The result of a query against a relational database.

rightsizing Moving a computer application to a system appropriately sized for the task. Often a euphemism for *downsizing*.

ring A type of network topology in which computers are connected to one another in a way that forms a complete circle. Imagine the Waltons standing around the Thanksgiving table holding hands and you have the idea of a ring topology.

RISC *Reduced Instruction Set Computer*, a type of computer design in which the CPU is optimized by reducing the number of different types of instructions the computer can understand. See *CISC*.

RJ-45 The kind of plug used by 10baseT networks. It looks kind of like a modular phone plug, but it's bigger.

ROLLBACK A SQL function that cancels a transaction and reverses any database updates that were made by the transaction.

router A device that works like a bridge, but can handle different protocols. For example, a router can link Ethernet to LocalTalk or a mainframe.

row A single record of information; all of the columns for a specific thing, such as a particular customer.

row-level locking A database locking technique that locks table rows individually. See *page-level locking*.

RRDS See *Relative-Record Data Set*.

SAG See *SQL Access Group*.

SAG CLI A standard Call Level Interface for SQL database access proposed by SAG. See *SQL Access Group*.

scalability The ability of a computer system to grow by increasing the speed and/or capacity of the system. The bigger the range from the smallest to the largest member of a computer family, the more scalability the family has.

scheduling software Software that schedules meetings of network users. Works only if all network users keep their calendars up to date.

scrollable cursor An advanced type of SQL cursor that allows result rows to be fetched forward or backward.

SCSI *Small computer systems interface*, a connection used mostly for disk drives but also suitable for CD-ROM, tape drives, and just about anything else. Also winner of the Acronym Computer Geeks Love to Pronounce Most award.

SDLC See *Synchronous Data Link Control*.

segment A single-run cable, which may connect more than two computers, with a terminator on each end.

SELECT The main statement of SQL. A SELECT statement processes a query.

server A computer that is on the network and shares resources with other network users. The server may be dedicated, which means that it's sole purpose in life is to provide service for network users, or it may be used as a client as well. See *client*.

session layer A layer somewhere near the

middle of the beloved OSI reference model that deals with sessions between network nodes.

SFT See *system fault tolerance.*

shared lock A database lock that allows other users to read but not update data. See *exclusive lock.*

shielded twisted pair (STP) cable Twisted pair cable with shielding, used mostly for token ring networks. See *twisted pair.*

Silver Bullet What the Lone Ranger used to kill bad guys. The computer industry has long been looking for a Silver Bullet that would guarantee success.

SNA *Systems Network Architecture*, a networking standard developed by IBM that dates from the mid-Mainframerasic era, approximately 65 million years ago. Used by fine IBM mainframe and AS/400 minicomputers everywhere.

SNMP *Simple Network Management Protocol*, a standard for exchanging network management information between network devices that is anything but simple.

SPECmark A standard benchmark test used to rate the performance of high-speed computers.

SQL An industry-standard database access language for relational databases. Pronounced *sequel.*

SQL Access Group (SAG) A consortium of database vendors whose purpose is to promote peace, harmony, and database interoperability.

SQL middleware Software that provides a common interface to diverse database products.

SQL1 The original, 1989-vintage ANSI/ISO SQL standard.

SQL2 The revised, 1992 version of the ANSI/ISO SQL standard, that adds advanced join operations and other interesting features.

SQL3 The not-yet-finalized future enhancement to the ANSI/ISO SQL standard.

star A type of network topology in which each node is connected to a central wiring hub. This gives the network a star-like appearance.

status bar In a GUI, an optional display of various aspects of a program's status.

stored procedures A mixture of SQL statements and procedural statements that can be stored on certain SQL servers and executed as a transaction.

subquery A query within a query, used to handle complex queries.

super VGA A VGA-compatible monitor with resolutions higher than standard VGA. See *VGA.*

superserver A server computer that seems more like a mainframe than a PC.

symmetric multiprocessing A multiprocessing system in which each CPU can handle any task assigned to it by the operating system.

Synchronous Data Link Control (SDLC) The preferred data transmission protocol in SNA.

system fault tolerance (SFT) A set of networking features designed to protect the network from faults, such as stepping on the line (known as a "foot fault").

System 7 The latest and greatest operating system for Macintoshes.

system fault tolerance See *SFT*.

System/360 The grandfather of modern mainframe computers.

T1 Line A high-speed phone line that can transmit data at up to 274Mbps.

table A collection of information in a relational database organized into rows and columns.

task For a technically accurate description, enroll in a computer science graduate course. For a layperson's understanding of what a task is, picture the guy who used to spin plates on the Ed Sullivan show. Each plate is a task. The poor guy had to frantically move from plate to plate to keep them all spinning. Computers work the same way. Each program task is like one of those spinning plates; the computer must service each one periodically to keep it going.

TB Terrazzo bytes, imported from Italy. (Actually, it stands for *terabytes*.) A terabyte is approximately one trillion bytes (1024GB to be precise). See *GB*, *K*, and *MB*.

TCP/IP *Transmission Control Protocol/Internet Protocol*, the protocol used by Internet.

terminator The little plug you have to use at each end of a segment of thin coax cable (10baseT) or PhoneNET cable.

text box In a GUI, a control used to type data, such as a name, address, quantity, or any other text or numeric information.

three-letter acronym (TLA) A three-letter abbreviation such as FAT (File Allocation Table), DUM (Dirty Upper Memory), and HPY (High Priority Yodel).

time sharing A technique for allowing more than one user to access a computer by doling out short portions of computer time to each user.

title bar In a GUI, the topmost portion of the window, in which an application's title is displayed.

TLA See *three-letter acronym*.

token The thing that gets passed around the network in a token ring topology. See *token ring*.

token ring A network that is cabled in a ring topology in which a special packet called a *token* is passed from computer to computer. A computer must wait until it receives the token before sending data over the network.

toolbar In a GUI, a collection of buttons that the user can click to quickly perform common commands.

topology The shape of the network; how its computers and cables are arranged. See *bus*, *star*, and *ring*.

transaction A set of two or more database updates that must be completed in all-or-nothing fashion.

transaction log A record of database updates made by a transaction, used by the DBMS to roll back the transaction if necessary.

transaction monitor Software that handles the details of transaction processing. The most popular transaction monitor is IBM's CICS.

Transaction Services Layer The second layer of the SNA networking model.

Transmission Control Layer The second layer of the SNA networking model.

transport layer One of those layers somewhere near the middle of the OSI reference model that addresses the way data is escorted around the network.

triage A screening process which categorizes incoming transactions according to the amount of attention they require.

trigger In certain SQL servers, a procedure that is automatically executed when certain conditions are met, such as when a table row is updated or deleted.

TSO *Time Sharing Option*, a feature of the MVS operating system that provides terminal access to mainframe computers by using time sharing techniques.

twisted pair A type of cable that consists of one or more pairs of wires that are twisted in a certain way to improve the cable's electrical characteristics. See *unshielded twisted pair* and *shielded twisted pair*.

two-phase commit A commit protocol used to support distributed transactions.

union A relational database operation in which the results of two or more queries are combined into a single result set.

unit of work All of the database updates that make up a single transaction.

Unix A nerdy operating system often used on network servers in client/server systems.

unshielded twisted pair (UTP) Twisted

pair cable that doesn't have a heavy metal shield around it. Used for 10baseT networks. See *twisted pair*.

upper memory The portion of memory jammed in between 640K and 1MB. It's set apart for use by device adapters like disk controllers and video cards. Because much of it is unused in most computers, DOS 5 and 6 can reclaim it for other uses.

upsizing Moving a computer application from a small computer such as a PC LAN to a midrange or mainframe computer.

user interface How a program interacts with its user. See *graphical user interface*.

UTP See *unshielded twisted pair*.

VGA *Video Graphics Array*, the current standard in video monitors. Most VGA adapters these days are actually *super VGA* adapters, which are compatible with VGA adapters but have extra bells and whistles.

VIM *Vendor Independent Messaging*, an alternative to MAPI.

Vines A network operating system made by Banyan, comparable to *NetWare* or *LAN Manager*.

Visual Basic Microsoft's visual programming tool for Windows.

visual programming A relatively new style of programming in which the programmer works with on-screen objects such as forms and controls, writing actual code only as a last resort.

VisualAge IBM's visual programming tool for client/server systems, based on the Smalltalk programming language.

VisualGen An IBM visual programming

tool designed for creating both ends of a client/server application.

VM *Virtual Machine*, an IBM operating system for mainframe computers that allows the computer to simulate two or more separate systems.

VSAM *Virtual Storage Access Method*, a common way of accessing flat files on IBM mainframes.

VSE *Virtual Storage Extended*, an IBM operating system for smaller mainframe computers.

VTAM *Virtual Telecommunications Access Method*, the software that implements SNA for mainframe computer networks.

Warp See *OS/2 Warp*.

window In a GUI, a rectangular portion of the screen through which a program and user interact.

Windows 3.1 An "operating environment" that makes DOS computers easier to use, courtesy of Microsoft.

Windows 95 The long-anticipated successor to Windows 3.1, which will be able to run 32-bit Windows programs.

Windows for Workgroups The peer-to-peer network version of Windows.

Windows NT A 32-bit version of Windows.

Windows NT Server A network server version of Windows NT.

Wonka, Willie "Little surprises around every corner but nothing dangerous."

workstation An extra-high-powered desktop computer, usually based on a RISC processor and running Unix.

WYSIWYG *What You See Is What You Get*, a user-interface technique in which a document is displayed on the screen just as it will appear when printed.

X-Windows A windowing system for Unix.

X/Open A watchdog group dedicated to the development and preservation of standards that promote interoperability between otherwise incompatible systems.

Index

DUMMIES PRESS™

IDG BOOKS WORLDWIDE

BOOK SERIES FROM IDG

10/31/95

The Fun & Easy Way™ to learn about computers and more!

Windows® 3.11 For Dummies® 3rd Edition
by Andy Rathbone
ISBN: 1-56884-370-4
$16.95 USA/$22.95 Canada
SUPER STAR

Mutual Funds For Dummies™
by Eric Tyson
ISBN: 1-56884-226-0
$16.99 USA/$22.99 Canada
SUPER STAR

DOS For Dummies® 2nd Edition
by Dan Gookin
ISBN: 1-878058-75-4
$16.95 USA/$22.95 Canada
SUPER STAR

The Internet For Dummies® 2nd Edition
by John Levine & Carol Baroudi
ISBN: 1-56884-222-8
$19.99 USA/$26.99 Canada

Personal Finance For Dummies™
by Eric Tyson
ISBN: 1-56884-150-7
$16.95 USA/$22.95 Canada
SUPER STAR

PCs For Dummies® 3rd Edition
by Dan Gookin & Andy Rathbone
ISBN: 1-56884-904-4
$16.99 USA/$22.99 Canada

Macs® For Dummies® 3rd Edition
by David Pogue
ISBN: 1-56884-239-2
$19.99 USA/$26.99 Canada
SUPER STAR

The SAT® I For Dummies™
by Suzee Vlk
ISBN: 1-56884-213-9
$14.99 USA/$20.99 Canada
SUPER STAR

Here's a complete listing of IDG Books' ...For Dummies® titles

Title	Author	ISBN	Price
DATABASE			
Access 2 For Dummies®	by Scott Palmer	ISBN: 1-56884-090-X	$19.95 USA/$26.95 Canada
Access Programming For Dummies®	by Rob Krumm	ISBN: 1-56884-091-8	$19.95 USA/$26.95 Canada
Approach 3 For Windows® For Dummies®	by Doug Lowe	ISBN: 1-56884-233-3	$19.99 USA/$26.99 Canada
dBASE For DOS For Dummies®	by Scott Palmer & Michael Stabler	ISBN: 1-56884-188-1	$19.95 USA/$26.95 Canada
dBASE For Windows® For Dummies®	by Scott Palmer	ISBN: 1-56884-179-5	$19.95 USA/$26.95 Canada
dBASE 5 For Windows® Programming For Dummies®	by Ted Coombs & Jason Coombs	ISBN: 1-56884-215-5	$19.99 USA/$26.99 Canada
FoxPro 2.6 For Windows® For Dummies®	by John Kaufeld	ISBN: 1-56884-187-6	$19.95 USA/$26.95 Canada
Paradox 5 For Windows® For Dummies®	by John Kaufeld	ISBN: 1-56884-185-X	$19.95 USA/$26.95 Canada
DESKTOP PUBLISHING/ILLUSTRATION/GRAPHICS			
CorelDRAW! 5 For Dummies®	by Deke McClelland	ISBN: 1-56884-157-4	$19.95 USA/$26.95 Canada
CorelDRAW! For Dummies®	by Deke McClelland	ISBN: 1-56884-042-X	$19.95 USA/$26.95 Canada
Desktop Publishing & Design For Dummies®	by Roger C. Parker	ISBN: 1-56884-234-1	$19.99 USA/$26.99 Canada
Harvard Graphics 2 For Windows® For Dummies®	by Roger C. Parker	ISBN: 1-56884-092-6	$19.95 USA/$26.95 Canada
PageMaker 5 For Macs® For Dummies®	by Galen Gruman & Deke McClelland	ISBN: 1-56884-178-7	$19.95 USA/$26.95 Canada
PageMaker 5 For Windows® For Dummies®	by Deke McClelland & Galen Gruman	ISBN: 1-56884-160-4	$19.95 USA/$26.95 Canada
Photoshop 3 For Macs® For Dummies®	by Deke McClelland	ISBN: 1-56884-208-2	$19.99 USA/$26.99 Canada
QuarkXPress 3.3 For Dummies®	by Galen Gruman & Barbara Assadi	ISBN: 1-56884-217-1	$19.99 USA/$26.99 Canada
FINANCE/PERSONAL FINANCE/TEST TAKING REFERENCE			
Everyday Math For Dummies™	by Charles Seiter	ISBN: 1-56884-248-1	$14.99 USA/$22.99 Canada
Personal Finance For Dummies™ For Canadians	by Eric Tyson & Tony Martin	ISBN: 1-56884-378-X	$18.99 USA/$24.99 Canada
QuickBooks 3 For Dummies®	by Stephen L. Nelson	ISBN: 1-56884-227-9	$19.99 USA/$26.99 Canada
Quicken 8 For DOS For Dummies® 2nd Edition	by Stephen L. Nelson	ISBN: 1-56884-210-4	$19.95 USA/$26.95 Canada
Quicken 5 For Macs® For Dummies®	by Stephen L. Nelson	ISBN: 1-56884-211-2	$19.95 USA/$26.95 Canada
Quicken 4 For Windows® For Dummies® 2nd Edition	by Stephen L. Nelson	ISBN: 1-56884-209-0	$19.95 USA/$26.95 Canada
Taxes For Dummies™ 1995 Edition	by Eric Tyson & David J. Silverman	ISBN: 1-56884-220-1	$14.99 USA/$20.99 Canada
The GMAT® For Dummies®	by Suzee Vlk, Series Editor	ISBN: 1-56884-376-3	$14.99 USA/$20.99 Canada
The GRE® For Dummies™	by Suzee Vlk, Series Editor	ISBN: 1-56884-375-5	$14.99 USA/$20.99 Canada
Time Management For Dummies™	by Jeffrey J. Mayer	ISBN: 1-56884-360-7	$16.99 USA/$22.99 Canada
TurboTax For Windows® For Dummies®	by Gail A. Helsel, CPA	ISBN: 1-56884-228-7	$19.99 USA/$26.99 Canada
GROUPWARE/INTEGRATED			
ClarisWorks For Macs® For Dummies®	by Frank Higgins	ISBN: 1-56884-363-1	$19.99 USA/$26.99 Canada
Lotus Notes For Dummies®	by Pat Freeland & Stephen Londergan	ISBN: 1-56884-212-0	$19.95 USA/$26.95 Canada
Microsoft® Office 4 For Windows® For Dummies®	by Roger C. Parker	ISBN: 1-56884-183-3	$19.95 USA/$26.95 Canada
Microsoft® Works 3 For Windows® For Dummies®	by David C. Kay	ISBN: 1-56884-214-7	$19.99 USA/$26.99 Canada
SmartSuite 3 For Dummies®	by Jan Weingarten & John Weingarten	ISBN: 1-56884-367-4	$19.99 USA/$26.99 Canada
INTERNET/COMMUNICATIONS/NETWORKING			
America Online® For Dummies® 2nd Edition	by John Kaufeld	ISBN: 1-56884-933-8	$19.99 USA/$26.99 Canada
CompuServe For Dummies® 2nd Edition	by Wallace Wang	ISBN: 1-56884-937-0	$19.99 USA/$26.99 Canada
Modems For Dummies® 2nd Edition	by Tina Rathbone	ISBN: 1-56884-223-6	$19.99 USA/$26.99 Canada
MORE Internet For Dummies®	by John R. Levine & Margaret Levine Young	ISBN: 1-56884-164-7	$19.95 USA/$26.95 Canada
MORE Modems & On-line Services For Dummies®	by Tina Rathbone	ISBN: 1-56884-365-8	$19.99 USA/$26.99 Canada
Mosaic For Dummies® Windows Edition	by David Angell & Brent Heslop	ISBN: 1-56884-242-2	$19.99 USA/$26.99 Canada
NetWare For Dummies® 2nd Edition	by Ed Tittel, Deni Connor & Earl Follis	ISBN: 1-56884-369-0	$19.99 USA/$26.99 Canada
Networking For Dummies®	by Doug Lowe	ISBN: 1-56884-079-9	$19.95 USA/$26.95 Canada
PROCOMM PLUS 2 For Windows® For Dummies®	by Wallace Wang	ISBN: 1-56884-219-8	$19.99 USA/$26.99 Canada
TCP/IP For Dummies®	by Marshall Wilensky & Candace Leiden	ISBN: 1-56884-241-4	$19.99 USA/$26.99 Canada

Microsoft and Windows are registered trademarks of Microsoft Corporation. Mac is a registered trademark of Apple Computer. SAT is a registered trademark of the College Entrance Examination Board. GMAT is a registered trademark of the Graduate Management Admission Council. GRE is a registered trademark of the Educational Testing Service. America Online is a registered trademark of America Online, Inc. The "...For Dummies Book Series" logo, the IDG Books Worldwide logos, Dummies Press, and The Fun & Easy Way are trademarks, and ---- For Dummies and ... For Dummies are registered trademarks under exclusive license to IDG Books Worldwide, Inc., from International Data Group, Inc.

For scholastic requests & educational orders please call Educational Sales at 1. 800. 434. 2086

FOR MORE INFO OR TO ORDER, PLEASE CALL ► 800. 762. 2974

For volume discounts & special orders please call Tony Real, Special Sales, at 415. 655. 3048

Title	Author	ISBN	Price
The Internet For Macs® For Dummies® 2nd Edition	by Charles Seiter	ISBN: 1-56884-371-2	$19.99 USA/$26.99 Canada
The Internet For Macs® For Dummies® Starter Kit	by Charles Seiter	ISBN: 1-56884-244-9	$29.99 USA/$39.99 Canada
The Internet For Macs® For Dummies® Starter Kit Bestseller Edition	by Charles Seiter	ISBN: 1-56884-245-7	$39.99 USA/$54.99 Canada
The Internet For Windows® For Dummies® Starter Kit	by John R. Levine & Margaret Levine Young	ISBN: 1-56884-237-6	$34.99 USA/$44.99 Canada
The Internet For Windows® For Dummies® Starter Kit, Bestseller Edition	by John R. Levine & Margaret Levine Young	ISBN: 1-56884-246-5	$39.99 USA/$54.99 Canada

MACINTOSH

Title	Author	ISBN	Price
Mac® Programming For Dummies®	by Dan Parks Sydow	ISBN: 1-56884-173-6	$19.95 USA/$26.95 Canada
Macintosh® System 7.5 For Dummies®	by Bob LeVitus	ISBN: 1-56884-197-3	$19.95 USA/$26.95 Canada
MORE Macs® For Dummies®	by David Pogue	ISBN: 1-56884-087-X	$19.95 USA/$26.95 Canada
PageMaker 5 For Macs® For Dummies®	by Galen Gruman & Deke McClelland	ISBN: 1-56884-178-7	$19.95 USA/$26.95 Canada
QuarkXPress 3.3 For Dummies®	by Galen Gruman & Barbara Assadi	ISBN: 1-56884-217-1	$19.99 USA/$26.99 Canada
Upgrading and Fixing Macs® For Dummies®	by Kearney Rietmann & Frank Higgins	ISBN: 1-56884-189-2	$19.95 USA/$26.95 Canada

MULTIMEDIA

Title	Author	ISBN	Price
Multimedia & CD-ROMs For Dummies® 2nd Edition	by Andy Rathbone	ISBN: 1-56884-907-9	$19.99 USA/$26.99 Canada
Multimedia & CD-ROMs For Dummies® Interactive Multimedia Value Pack, 2nd Edition	by Andy Rathbone	ISBN: 1-56884-909-5	$29.99 USA/$39.99 Canada

OPERATING SYSTEMS:

DOS

Title	Author	ISBN	Price
MORE DOS For Dummies®	by Dan Gookin	ISBN: 1-56884-046-2	$19.95 USA/$26.95 Canada
OS/2® Warp For Dummies® 2nd Edition	by Andy Rathbone	ISBN: 1-56884-205-8	$19.99 USA/$26.99 Canada

UNIX

Title	Author	ISBN	Price
MORE UNIX® For Dummies®	by John R. Levine & Margaret Levine Young	ISBN: 1-56884-361-5	$19.99 USA/$26.99 Canada
UNIX® For Dummies®	by John R. Levine & Margaret Levine Young	ISBN: 1-878058-58-4	$19.95 USA/$26.95 Canada

WINDOWS

Title	Author	ISBN	Price
MORE Windows® For Dummies® 2nd Edition	by Andy Rathbone	ISBN: 1-56884-048-9	$19.95 USA/$26.95 Canada
Windows® 95 For Dummies®	by Andy Rathbone	ISBN: 1-56884-240-6	$19.99 USA/$26.99 Canada

PCS/HARDWARE

Title	Author	ISBN	Price
Illustrated Computer Dictionary For Dummies® 2nd Edition	by Dan Gookin & Wallace Wang	ISBN: 1-56884-218-X	$12.95 USA/$16.95 Canada
Upgrading and Fixing PCs For Dummies® 2nd Edition	by Andy Rathbone	ISBN: 1-56884-903-6	$19.99 USA/$26.99 Canada

PRESENTATION/AUTOCAD

Title	Author	ISBN	Price
AutoCAD For Dummies®	by Bud Smith	ISBN: 1-56884-191-4	$19.95 USA/$26.95 Canada
PowerPoint 4 For Windows® For Dummies®	by Doug Lowe	ISBN: 1-56884-161-2	$16.99 USA/$22.99 Canada

PROGRAMMING

Title	Author	ISBN	Price
Borland C++ For Dummies®	by Michael Hyman	ISBN: 1-56884-162-0	$19.95 USA/$26.95 Canada
C For Dummies® Volume 1	by Dan Gookin	ISBN: 1-878058-78-9	$19.95 USA/$26.95 Canada
C++ For Dummies®	by Stephen R. Davis	ISBN: 1-56884-163-9	$19.95 USA/$26.95 Canada
Delphi Programming For Dummies®	by Neil Rubenking	ISBN: 1-56884-200-7	$19.99 USA/$26.99 Canada
Mac® Programming For Dummies®	by Dan Parks Sydow	ISBN: 1-56884-173-6	$19.95 USA/$26.95 Canada
PowerBuilder 4 Programming For Dummies®	by Ted Coombs & Jason Coombs	ISBN: 1-56884-325-9	$19.99 USA/$26.99 Canada
QBasic Programming For Dummies®	by Douglas Hergert	ISBN: 1-56884-093-4	$19.95 USA/$26.95 Canada
Visual Basic 3 For Dummies®	by Wallace Wang	ISBN: 1-56884-076-4	$19.95 USA/$26.95 Canada
Visual Basic "X" For Dummies®	by Wallace Wang	ISBN: 1-56884-230-9	$19.99 USA/$26.99 Canada
Visual C++ 2 For Dummies®	by Michael Hyman & Bob Arnson	ISBN: 1-56884-328-3	$19.99 USA/$26.99 Canada
Windows® 95 Programming For Dummies®	by S. Randy Davis	ISBN: 1-56884-327-5	$19.99 USA/$26.99 Canada

SPREADSHEET

Title	Author	ISBN	Price
1-2-3 For Dummies®	by Greg Harvey	ISBN: 1-878058-60-6	$16.95 USA/$22.95 Canada
1-2-3 For Windows® 5 For Dummies® 2nd Edition	by John Walkenbach	ISBN: 1-56884-216-3	$16.95 USA/$22.95 Canada
Excel 5 For Macs® For Dummies®	by Greg Harvey	ISBN: 1-56884-186-8	$19.95 USA/$26.95 Canada
Excel For Dummies® 2nd Edition	by Greg Harvey	ISBN: 1-56884-050-0	$16.95 USA/$22.95 Canada
MORE 1-2-3 For DOS For Dummies®	by John Weingarten	ISBN: 1-56884-224-4	$19.99 USA/$26.99 Canada
MORE Excel 5 For Windows® For Dummies®	by Greg Harvey	ISBN: 1-56884-207-4	$19.95 USA/$26.95 Canada
Quattro Pro 6 For Windows® For Dummies®	by John Walkenbach	ISBN: 1-56884-174-4	$19.95 USA/$26.95 Canada
Quattro Pro For DOS For Dummies®	by John Walkenbach	ISBN: 1-56884-023-3	$16.95 USA/$22.95 Canada

UTILITIES

Title	Author	ISBN	Price
Norton Utilities 8 For Dummies®	by Beth Slick	ISBN: 1-56884-166-3	$19.95 USA/$26.95 Canada

VCRS/CAMCORDERS

Title	Author	ISBN	Price
VCRs & Camcorders For Dummies™	by Gordon McComb & Andy Rathbone	ISBN: 1-56884-229-5	$14.99 USA/$20.99 Canada

WORD PROCESSING

Title	Author	ISBN	Price
Ami Pro For Dummies®	by Jim Meade	ISBN: 1-56884-049-7	$19.95 USA/$26.95 Canada
MORE Word For Windows® 6 For Dummies®	by Doug Lowe	ISBN: 1-56884-165-5	$19.95 USA/$26.95 Canada
MORE WordPerfect® 6 For Windows® For Dummies®	by Margaret Levine Young & David C. Kay	ISBN: 1-56884-206-6	$19.95 USA/$26.95 Canada
MORE WordPerfect® 6 For DOS For Dummies®	by Wallace Wang, edited by Dan Gookin	ISBN: 1-56884-047-0	$19.95 USA/$26.95 Canada
Word 6 For Macs® For Dummies®	by Dan Gookin	ISBN: 1-56884-190-6	$19.95 USA/$26.95 Canada
Word For Windows® 6 For Dummies®	by Dan Gookin	ISBN: 1-56884-075-6	$16.95 USA/$22.95 Canada
Word For Windows® For Dummies®	by Dan Gookin & Ray Werner	ISBN: 1-878058-86-X	$16.95 USA/$22.95 Canada
WordPerfect® 6 For DOS For Dummies®	by Dan Gookin	ISBN: 1-878058-77-0	$16.95 USA/$22.95 Canada
WordPerfect® 6.1 For Windows® For Dummies® 2nd Edition	by Margaret Levine Young & David Kay	ISBN: 1-56884-243-0	$16.95 USA/$22.95 Canada
WordPerfect® For Dummies®	by Dan Gookin	ISBN: 1-878058-52-5	$16.95 USA/$22.95 Canada

Windows is a registered trademark of Microsoft Corporation. Mac is a registered trademark of Apple Computer. OS/2 is a registered trademark of IBM. UNIX is a registered trademark of AT&T. WordPerfect is a registered trademark of Novell. The "...For Dummies Book Series" logo, the IDG Books Worldwide logos, Dummies Press, and The Fun & Easy Way are trademarks, and ---- For Dummies and ... For Dummies are registered trademarks under exclusive license to IDG Books Worldwide, Inc., from International Data Group, Inc.

DUMMIES PRESS™ PROGRAMMING BOOKS

IDG BOOKS WORLDWIDE

10/31/95

COMPUTER BOOK SERIES FROM IDG

For Dummies who want to program...

Delphi Programming For Dummies®
by Neil Rubenking

ISBN: 1-56884-200-7
$19.99 USA/$26.99 Canada

Access Programming For Dummies®
by Rob Krumm

ISBN: 1-56884-091-8
$19.95 USA/$26.95 Canada

TCP/IP For Dummies®
by Marshall Wilensky & Candace Leiden

ISBN: 1-56884-241-4
$19.99 USA/$26.99 Canada

HTML For Dummies®
by Ed Tittel & Carl de Cordova

ISBN: 1-56884-330-5
$29.99 USA/$39.99 Canada

Windows® 95 Programming For Dummies®
by S. Randy Davis

ISBN: 1-56884-327-5
$19.99 USA/$26.99 Canada

Mac® Programming For Dummies®
by Dan Parks Sydow

ISBN: 1-56884-173-6
$19.95 USA/$26.95 Canada

PowerBuilder 4 Programming For Dummies®
by Ted Coombs & Jason Coombs

ISBN: 1-56884-325-9
$19.99 USA/$26.99 Canada

Visual Basic 3 For Dummies®
by Wallace Wang

ISBN: 1-56884-076-4
$19.95 USA/$26.95 Canada

Covers version 3.

ISDN For Dummies®
by David Angell

ISBN: 1-56884-331-3
$19.99 USA/$26.99 Canada

Visual C++ "2" For Dummies®
by Michael Hyman & Bob Arnson

ISBN: 1-56884-328-3
$19.99 USA/$26.99 Canada

Borland C++ For Dummies®
by Michael Hyman

ISBN: 1-56884-162-0
$19.95 USA/$26.95 Canada

C For Dummies® Volume I
by Dan Gookin

ISBN: 1-878058-78-9
$19.95 USA/$26.95 Canada

C++ For Dummies®
by Stephen R. Davis

ISBN: 1-56884-163-9
$19.95 USA/$26.95 Canada

QBasic Programming For Dummies®
by Douglas Hergert

ISBN: 1-56884-093-4
$19.95 USA/$26.95 Canada

dBase 5 For Windows® Programming For Dummies®
by Ted Coombs & Jason Coombs

ISBN: 1-56884-215-5
$19.99 USA/$26.99 Canada

Windows is a registered trademark of Microsoft Corporation. Mac is a registered trademark of Apple Computer. Dummies Press, the "...For Dummies Book Series" logo, and the IDG Books Worldwide logos are trademarks, and ----For Dummies, ... For Dummies and the "...For Dummies Computer Book Series" logo are registered trademarks under exclusive license to IDG Books Worldwide, Inc., from International Data Group, Inc.

For scholastic requests & educational orders please call Educational Sales, at 1. 800. 434. 2086

FOR MORE INFO OR TO ORDER, PLEASE CALL ▶ 800. 762. 2974

For volume discounts & special orders please call Tony Real, Special Sales, at 415. 655. 3048

IDG BOOKS WORLDWIDE™

Order Center: **(800) 762-2974** *(8 a.m.–6 p.m., EST, weekdays)*

9/19

Quantity	ISBN	Title	Price	Total

Shipping & Handling Charges

	Description	First book	Each additional book	Total
Domestic	Normal	$4.50	$1.50	$
	Two Day Air	$8.50	$2.50	$
	Overnight	$18.00	$3.00	$
International	Surface	$8.00	$8.00	$
	Airmail	$16.00	$16.00	$
	DHL Air	$17.00	$17.00	$

*For large quantities call for shipping & handling charges.
**Prices are subject to change without notice.

Ship to:

Name _____

Company _____

Address _____

City/State/Zip _____

Daytime Phone _____

Payment: ☐ Check to IDG Books Worldwide (US Funds Only)

☐ VISA   ☐ MasterCard   ☐ American Express

Card # _____ Expires _____

Signature _____

Subtotal _____

CA residents add
applicable sales tax _____

IN, MA, and MD
residents add
5% sales tax _____

IL residents add
6.25% sales tax _____

RI residents add
7% sales tax _____

TX residents add
8.25% sales tax _____

Shipping _____

Total _____

Please send this order form to:

IDG Books Worldwide, Inc.
7260 Shadeland Station, Suite 100
Indianapolis, IN 46256

Allow up to 3 weeks for delivery.
Thank you!